# Patterns of Dominance

*by the same author*

An Essay on Racial Tension
*Oxford University Press for Chatham House*

Christianity and Race
*Lutterworth Press*

Birth of a Dilemma: The Conquest and Settlement of Rhodesia
*Oxford University Press for Institute of Race Relations*

Year of Decision: Rhodesia and Nyasaland in 1960
*Oxford University Press for Institute of Race Relations*

Common Sense about Race
*Gollancz*

Prospero's Magic: Some Thoughts on Class and Race
*Oxford University Press*

India and Ceylon: Unity and Diversity (Ed.)
*Oxford University Press for Institute of Race Relations*

as 'Philip Woodruff'
(*Published by Jonathan Cape*)

The Men Who Ruled India

The Founders ⎫
The Guardians ⎭ *history*

Colonel of Dragoons: an historical chronicle

Call the Next Witness ⎫
The Wild Sweet Witch ⎬ *novels*
The Islands of Chamba ⎭

Whatever Dies: stories

The Sword of Northumbria ⎫
Hernshaw Castle ⎭ *adventure*

# PHILIP MASON

# Patterns of Dominance

*Published for the*
*Institute of Race Relations, London*
OXFORD UNIVERSITY PRESS
LONDON   NEW YORK   TORONTO

*Oxford University Press, Ely House, London W. 1*

GLASGOW NEW YORK TORONTO MELBOURNE WELLINGTON
CAPE TOWN SALISBURY IBADAN NAIROBI DAR ES SALAAM LUSAKA ADDIS ABABA
BOMBAY CALCUTTA MADRAS KARACHI LAHORE DACCA
KUALA LUMPUR SINGAPORE HONG KONG TOKYO

ISBN 0 19 218186 6

© Institute of Race Relations, 1970

*First published* 1970
*Reprinted (with corrections)* 1971

*Printed in Great Britain*

# Contents

*XII   The Caribbean*

*XIII   Brazil*

## PART IV

*XIV   Conclusions*

O! When degree is shak'd,
Which is the ladder to all high designs,
The enterprise is sick. How could communities,
Degrees in schools, and brotherhoods in cities,
Peaceful commerce from dividable shores,
The primogenitive and due of birth
Prerogative of age, crowns, sceptres, laurels,
But by degree, stand in authentic place?
Take but degree away, untune that string,
And hark! what discord follows. . . .

*Troilus and Cressida*, Act I, sc. 3.

There is no man born of God marked above
another, for none comes born in to the
world with a saddle on his back, neither any
booted and spurred to ride him.

Richard Rumbold, the Leveller, speech on the
gallows in 1685, *State Trials*, Vol. XI.

# Foreword

This book began many years ago with one simple thought. Why was the situation as between black and white in South Africa so different from that in Brazil or the Caribbean? Was it in fact so different as it seemed to be on the surface? It seemed worth trying to analyse, in various parts of the world, situations in which different ethnic groups were living together in harmony or tension, and to enumerate and assess the changing factors present in each case, trying to reach some conclusions as to why one situation was tense and another relaxed. I wrote a preliminary essay on this, published by the Oxford University Press in 1954 as *An Essay on Racial Tension*. It was little more than a series of hypotheses and suggestions, many of which are discussed at greater length in this book. It was followed by some years' study of Africa and particularly of what was then the Federation of Rhodesia and Nyasaland. Three books were published on this subject, one by Richard Gray and two by myself. These were completed in 1960 and I turned back to the idea of a much wider comparison. A lack of sufficient width seemed to me a weakness in many studies of race relations; again and again one found writers putting forward explanations for some phenomenon which did not hold good as soon as the terms of reference were broadened. But without help it would be presumptuous to attempt so wide a comparison as I thought desirable.

After much discussion, the Ford Foundation made funds available for a series of studies, of which I was to summarize the conclusions. The studies would deal with the development of relationships between ethnic groups in the Spanish-speaking parts of America, in the Caribbean, Brazil, India, Africa, and South-East Asia. It was not an easy matter to find scholars prepared to undertake the kind of study which was proposed over such wide areas. But eventually the team was made up. Julian Pitt-Rivers agreed to write on Mexico, Central America, and the Andean countries of the Inca civilization; David Lowenthal on the Caribbean; David Maybury-Lewis on Brazil; and Guy Wint on India, Pakistan, and South-East Asia.

Shortly after he had been asked to write, Guy Wint suffered a severe stroke at an early age. His physicians were of the opinion that he would make a quick recovery, and we continued to hope that he would be able to complete his books; at one time he contemplated three, one on each of the three areas. He did recover sufficiently to visit India and

Pakistan but found travel far more tiring than he had expected. He completed a first and second draft of his book on India but, in spite of valiant efforts, could not produce a manuscript which he regarded as satisfactory. A second stroke ended his life in January 1969; he was a great loss, not only to those who knew him, but to all interested in the affairs of India and the Far East. But, long before his death, he had realized that he could not cover the whole area, and Guy Hunter agreed to write on South-East Asia. Hunter's book, *South-East Asia: Race, Culture, and Nation*, was the last to be commissioned and the first to be published of the whole series. Wint's drafts on India and Pakistan contained brilliant insights but it was clear that even if he was able to revise the second to his own satisfaction, the result would be highly personal and far more impressionistic than had been intended. It seemed essential to complement it by other views and we accordingly assembled a collection of essays on Indian society which was published as *India and Ceylon: Unity and Diversity*.

Donald Wood's *Trinidad in Transition*, a historical study on a much smaller scale, is also a by-product of this enterprise. Very closely linked by its subject-matter (although financed by UNESCO) is Guy Hunter's *Industrialisation and Race Relations*, to which my debt is considerable. As this book goes to print, the three remaining studies—on the Caribbean, on Brazil, and on Meso-America and the Andes—are not yet complete; drafts are in process of final improvement. But I could not have attempted to cover so wide an area without the help of the three writers—Pitt-Rivers, Lowenthal, and Maybury-Lewis—on whose preliminary drafts I have drawn freely, and who have checked the specialized sections in Part III for gross error. They are not, of course, responsible for all my views.

The human mind proceeds by analysing, dissecting, separating, and then reconstructing the elements into a whole that is more clearly understood than before. It seeks to construct patterns and discern regularities between phenomena which in spite of their resemblances are unique. Something of the reality is necessarily lost in each process, analysis, and reconstruction. In reaction against some nineteenth-century writers, who generalized about human society with insufficient detailed knowledge, it has been a more recent tendency to specialize on more manageable sections, limited in time and space. This has been invaluable. But, as I have said, it has sometimes led to the construction of theories which do not apply outside the limited field. This book in its turn is an attempt to make use of the patient detailed work of specialists to construct a synthesis. No one can be more sensible than I of its weaknesses and of the extent to which it is open to criticism.

It is inevitable that specialists on particular areas should feel treatment on this scale inadequate; I cannot hope to write on three

continents with their detail, their precision, or their authority. But this
is a difficulty inherent in the plan and I must accept it. From the point
of view of this enterprise itself, it is a more valid criticism that it does
not include *enough* case histories. Hawaii ought to be contrasted with
New Zealand; there should be some consideration of Mauritius and
Fiji. More seriously, there is no detailed discussion of the United States
or Britain or Australia. These have not been absent from my thoughts
as I wrote, but Britain is the subject of the Institute's Survey of Race
Relations, published by the O.U.P. in the summer of 1969, and the
literature on the United States is so vast that I do not feel competent
to add to it usefully. This book is already quite long enough and to
condense further might well make for harder reading. It has certainly
touched more controversies than it can claim to have settled; my chief
hope is that it will challenge others to venture on wider comparisons
than before and induce anyone who frames theories about race relations
to ask whether his ideas fit all the situations of which he has knowledge.

An example is the controversy, on which many books have been
written, as to why in the United States anyone with any element of
Negro blood is reckoned a Negro, while in another former slave
society, Brazil, this is emphatically not so. I have suggested several
possible factors which I believe have contributed to the difference, and
discounted others. But the only points on which I can be dogmatic
are that no single *simple* explanation is satisfactory and that it is not
sensible to discuss the question without reference also at least to
Jamaica and South Africa. Each of these societies is unique; each has
some factors in common with one or two of the others; every simple
explanation based on one factor breaks down when applied to all the
others.

The arrangement of the book embodies an attempt to preserve some
balance between the two principles, that a picture of the whole must
not be lost sight of, and that analysis of each situation into factors may
throw light not only on that situation but on others. Part I is a consideration of the present confrontation of white and non-white seen as
a stage in human development, part of the collapse not only of
colonialism but of the hierarchical principle which was for long a
condition of progress. Part II is analysis, an attempt to break down into
component factors a number of situations in which one group has
established dominance over another, to compare them, and to see what
factors appear to contribute to what results. Part III is a return to the
holistic, studies on the growth of systems of inequality in five areas.
Part IV draws some tentative conclusions.

A book of this scope draws on reading over sixteen years and owes
much to many people. I cannot possibly repay or even acknowledge
most of the debts. Two seminars, each lasting three days, were held as
part of the enterprise; one was at Ditchley Park and one at Burley

Manor in the New Forest. I am grateful to all who took part; the book that has resulted bears little direct relation to our discussions but they had a liberating and fructifying effect. I acknowledge their contribution by name in the notes. There have been special difficulties also about attribution to sources. In the end, it seemed best to give special references in footnotes only to quotations, and to provide at the end of the book notes of the sources I have leaned on most heavily, followed by a Reading List which I believe includes everything on which I have drawn. I hope that this exclusion of specific reference of each point to an authority liberates the argument and clarifies the thought. I must also admit that there is some repetition of thoughts, and illustrations of thoughts, which I have used before. But when a point still seems of importance, and to be most aptly illustrated in a particular way, it would be silly to be inhibited by having made it ten years ago in another context.

Most writers know the miasma of irritated depression that assails one while attempting to formulate the actual shape of a task long contemplated. I must thank all my colleagues in the Institute of Race Relations who so forbearingly put up with this, and in particular Simon Abbott, on whom fell a good deal of extra work while I was writing it, and Janet Evanson, of whom the same is true, but who also constantly encouraged me to persevere with the idea, from its beginning in 1960. I also owe a quite unpayable debt to Ambalavaner Sivanandan, the Librarian of the Institute, not only for getting me books and tracing references but for help in the selected bibliography. Finally, I must thank Joseph Slater, then of the Ford Foundation, who believed this enterprise was worth undertaking and helped me to frame the application for funds which made it possible.

May 1969                                        PHILIP MASON

# PART I

## INEQUALITY AND OBLIVION

### CHAPTER I

# The Growth of Inequality

### *1 Myth and Oblivion*

There is a story in *The Memoirs of William Hickey* of the King of Oudh in
the late eighteenth century entertaining a British officer to whom he
was boasting of the accuracy and long range of a new sporting gun he
had received from London. To illustrate his point, he fired it from the
veranda where they were sitting. As he fired, a man fell, and the officer
exclaimed: ' "Good God, what have you done? I fear Your Highness
has shot an unfortunate man." "A man!" exclaimed the King with the
utmost coolness, "it is only a washerman." ' Clearly, Hickey did not
approve of such an attitude to a fellow human being. But only forty
years earlier the East India Company held a lease of Calcutta and its
neighbourhood which authorized the punishment of criminal offences
which English law would have punished with hanging, and in such
cases it was the custom that 'the lash should be inflicted until death'.

It would be easy to multiply examples of behaviour like this, which
could hardly take place if the person in power thought of the other
party as being a person in whose place he might himself have stood. It
ranges from active cruelty to humiliating disregard. Nor is it confined
to one continent, one period, or one form of relationship. In the mid-
nineteenth century, Lewanika, King of the Barotse (or Lozi), a
primitive empire in what is now Zambia, justified himself to the
missionary Coillard for raiding a neighbouring tribe with a threefold
excuse. They had ill-treated a missionary whom he had ordered them
to protect; 'besides, they are not human beings, they are quite naked',
and, finally, 'we must have more cattle'. Here are the classic reasons
for war, in the classic order—political occasion, psychological justification, economic advantage. But the important point here is the second:
'they are not human'. It is not necessary to tell once more the horrors
of the slave-trade, which have been told often enough. But whether it
was carried on by Europeans on the West Coast or by Arabs on the
East, the branding-iron, the slave-stick, the whip, the crammed shelves
below deck, tell the same story; these are slaves, not people.

And in England in the early nineteenth century, the poor were not always people. Men could be hanged for a trifling theft or transported to Australia if caught out of doors after dark with a net; until 1827, it was legal to set mantraps and spring guns; they were intended to kill or maim poachers, and that a poacher might lie undiscovered in agony till morning clearly cannot have weighed much with the gentlemen who preserved game and who made and administered the laws. A mantrap might also destroy the limb of someone gathering fallen wood—but this would be a poor person and if life was to be tolerable the hearts of the rich had to be closed against the poor. In 1834, the new Poor Law proclaimed that there should be no relief for any poor person except in a work house; the work house must be less attractive than work in field or factory, and what the law really meant was that if a man was out of work, he and his family must either starve or be imprisoned separately in harsh conditions. The men who made such laws did not try to imagine what it would be like to change places with the poor. England was in fact the two nations described by Dickens and Disraeli.

To-day, American Negroes are engaged in a protest against a society which, they would say, tore them from their motherland, enslaved them, treated them as cattle, and then, when at last slavery ended, behaved as though they did not exist, denied them any identity but that of a menial, at best comic and faithful, at worst degraded and criminal. For generations, every decision had been made for them; they had been told what work to do, where to sleep. They had at one time been forbidden to marry but later were allowed to form some kind of union, which could be as permanent as the parties wished, and which might be ratified by the ignoble ceremony of jumping over a broomstick in the presence of the man who owned them. This was a ceremony intended, surely, as a jocular, contemptuous comment on their capacity for permanent affection or a true place in human society.

When the slaves were suddenly freed, there was no longer an owner to feed, clothe, and employ them; they no longer represented capital. Few of them indeed could be called well equipped to earn their living in a competitive world; little was done to remove their handicaps. Society as a whole ignored, forgot them; to-day, most of their descendants are still trapped in a morass of poverty and despair. Of those who have escaped, a handful of writers proclaim their desperate need for an intellectual heritage which is not derived from those responsible for their humiliation. Among the masses, many have given up hope of co-operation with whites; they can assert their identity only by refusing what they believe to be white, whether by joining extravagant sects or by crying: 'Burn, baby, burn!'

It is one thesis of this book that there is something in common between the concern of the Negro intellectual for a cultural pedigree and the urge of the Negro unemployed to smash and burn; between the impatience of the coloured workers' groups in Britain with white liberals and the anger of African leaders at British and American complicity in the social system of South Africa. These people remember the same wrongs and share the same emotions. They understand the anger and frustration in Cuba, in Bolivia, in Vietnam, and indeed all over the world—anger that is expressed in a variety of forms, as nationalism, as communism, as resentment of white racialism. It is expressed as anger or resentment, but at root it is a quest for social justice, for self-respect, and for the respect of others.

But it is another thesis of this book, and one just as important, that this reaction is not only a matter of colour. Colour gives it a special sharpness, just as it gave an added, more active, cruelty to the dominance which went before. But Russian serfs were not much better off than Negro slaves and the reaction of the oppressed against the dominant is surely part of a world-wide phenomenon, a stage in the development of human populations from simple food-gathering groups to far more complex and highly organized societies. This development has now reached a stage which we do not yet understand. At an earlier stage, it everywhere involved a growing specialization of function and stratification in layers—slave and free, noble and simple, twice-born and untouchable—and these could only be tolerable if supported by a variety of myths.

There were several reasons for this first change in structure from simple and undifferentiated to complex and stratified. The most obvious is economic; it was an advantage if the best spearmaker made the spears for everyone. There was next a similar need for political specialization; someone was needed to distribute the surplus goods produced by economic specialization. Thus the leaders came to have power, which as a rule they used to make life more comfortable for themselves than for their subordinates. It next became a psychological necessity for both parties to believe that this kind of organization was due to inherent differences between the rulers and the ruled and that these differences were divinely ordained or at least quite unalterable by men. The rulers must relegate the ruled to a psychological limbo, regard them as barely human, insensitive to the pain, cold, hunger, and love felt by their betters. A compulsive oblivion must shut them out from the sympathy that would be extended to a fellow clansman, a kinsman, another gentleman, a fellow slave-owner.

Another psychological need also arose, for rulers and ruled alike. The first groups had been small; everyone knew everyone else. Now, in the great cities, the need arose for some limitation on the size of the groups within which people knew each other and thought of each other as 'we'.

By a bitter irony, the myths that were used to justify this compulsive oblivion were everywhere linked in some degree to something which in one form or another is universal to the earliest groups of men, a sense of awe in the face of eternity, in the face of birth and death and life and the forces of nature. The developing societies of man arranged a marriage of convenience between that sense of the numinous and the rules for governing conduct which each society seemed to need. Included in the marriage settlement—together with rules that were hygienic or genetic or merely convenient in that time and place—was often a set of rules governing the dominance of rulers over ruled. But—and here lies the irony—that same sense of awe was one of the parents of the contrary idea, that men ought to have an equal chance of developing the best that was in them. In the revolt against inequality and against ritual tabus that have become irrelevant to modern life, both partners to the marriage of convenience are attacked and expelled; the sense of eternity goes out of the window with the tabu on pork. The result is a psychological as well as a social vacuum and an agonizing attempt to find a new framework for human life. It is not simply a matter of the underprivileged moving up into the places left vacant by their former superiors. There is nothing left to move into.

But although the growth of systems of inequality and the revolt against them are alike world-wide and seem to be an inevitable part of man's development, there are many variations. Some forms of dominance are such that they can only be ended by complete destruction. Revolution of this kind means heavy loss of life in a double sense; many people are killed, others are torn apart from their friends or imprisoned; often poverty and privation are worse even than before. There is a period of desolation, a long cold hiatus—in the visual arts, in music and literature, in the amenities of ordinary life—before a new framework for life can be built. But other situations seem at first sight as though they might answer to more gradual treatment. Is it possible to make effective changes without radical revolution?

It is a main purpose of this book to look at the general development of human society towards patterns of dominance and subordination and then to consider the revolt against them. Against this background, in the second part of the book, are described in more detail, but in relation to this main framework, some of these patterns—the systems and myths that have been used to make inequality permanent in different parts of the world. We shall try to find out why they are different and what is the special element that a difference in race adds to such relationships.

Why is Brazil so different from South Africa? Are we, in fact, quite sure that it is so different as it seems? Is one merely at another stage of development in a pattern common to both, or are there factors present in one situation which make them different in kind? How are they likely to develop? How do they differ from India, where one great meeting of races took place three thousand years ago or more? We shall contrast the dominance of Brahmans in South India with that of Afrikaners in South Africa and of Spaniards in Mexico and Peru; we shall look at the Caribbean as well as Brazil. We shall look also at the differences between North and South India and at differences between the British presence in India and in different parts of Africa. All these situations have a racial element, in the sense that there is some physical difference between the dominant and the subordinate groups: we shall try to pick out this element of physical visibility and see how far it affects the situation, in contrast with feudal societies in Europe and modern class structures, where the visible difference lay in clothes and not in skin colour.

There is an element of myth in all these systems of dominance. As Michael Banton has pointed out, it seems to be a rule, at least at one stage of development, that societies are organized more easily if people think they are more different than in fact they are.[1] So the myths are built up, to make oblivion possible, to help men to shut out other men from ranking as their fellow creatures. And it is hard to be neutral; oblivion often leads quickly to hatred and contempt. But, whether a difference is real or imagined or exaggerated, conflict, for whatever goods are in short supply, tends to crystallize along the lines of difference that people *believe* to exist. These are the kind of regularities —resemblances between differing situations—that we shall expect to find emerging as the story unfolds.

## 2 From Simple to Stratified

The simplest kinds of human society which still survive are to be found in the deserts of Australia and the southern part of Africa. The Bushmen of the Kalahari when they first met Europeans were Stone-Age people, organized in small groups; they were food-gatherers and hunters—and hunters of course need leadership, but it is a leadership based on age, experience, skill, and ability; there is no class of slaves or serfs. The Bushmen in this sense formed an undifferentiated society. All African societies are now in flux, but within human memory there were present in Africa a variety of different kinds of organization which between them represented the succession of stages in man's development. Food-gathering groups, pastoral nomadic tribes, agricultural tribes practising shifting cultivation, primitive states making war upon their neighbours, primitive empires exacting tribute from vassals—all these were to be found before the coming of Europeans. There was regression as well as movement forward; empires, like the Monomotapa's south of the Zambezi, might decline and break up, but there was also movement towards a greater complexity. Just as the Aztecs established themselves

[1] See Michael Banton, *Race Relations*. Throughout the text, short references are used. For full bibliographical references, see select Reading List, p. 345.

in Mexico, and the Incas in Peru, by a series of conquests over other groups, so in Africa a small group like the Zulus established their rule over the eastern Nguni and became a primitive empire.

One can arrange these societies in a mental perspective, an orderly progress from the simple to the complex, but it does not follow that there is a similar progress in time and that each society moves in succession from one stage to the next. The different stages will co-exist, even within the same political system, and stages which resemble each other will be reached in different continents at different moments of sidereal time. There are primitive food-gathering groups in the reed-beds of Lake Titicaca when the gigantic stones of Sacsahuaman at Cuzco are being fitted into place with exact precision; the highest glory of Inca civilization was reached more than four thousand years later than the First Dynasty in Egypt. Progress in complexity and progress in time, then, form a highly syncopated counterpoint with each other, but there are certain regularities about the progress in complexity. As society becomes more complex, it seems to be a general rule that there is a movement towards inequality between classes of people, towards a status that is permanent, that is, derived from the fact of having been born in a certain group.

There is a famous saying of Sir Henry Maine that 'the movement of the progressive societies has hitherto been a movement from Status to Contract'[1] and this is true of the period of which he was thinking; but at an earlier stage of man's development, surely something very different was happening. Indeed, in an earlier lecture, Maine refers to the stage I am thinking of when he speaks of 'the dominion of aristocracies' who 'laid claim to a quasi-sacred character'.[2] Progress at this earlier stage was far more often *away* from the extended family group, in which classes were undifferentiated, and *towards* stratification in groups with very unequal rights, power, and privileges. The great empires of the Middle East and of Middle America—Egypt, Babylon, Mexico, Peru—represent one stage in development, although they were four thousand years apart in time.

They were founded on inequality. The men who dragged the stones to the pyramid of Cheops or to the temple of the Sun at Cuzco were hewers of wood and drawers of water for life. The civilizations of Mohenjo-Daro and Harappa in the Indus valley belong to the same stage; at Mohenjo-Daro, says A. L. Basham, 'the urban lay-out bespeaks authority', and 'centralised and effective control of an autocratic or bureaucratic kind'.[3] It is known that some elements of the religion of the Indus civilization were adopted by the Aryan invaders

---

[1] Henry Maine, *Ancient Law: Notes on the History of Ancient Institutions*.

[2] Ibid.

[3] V. A. Smith, *The Oxford History of India*, Part I, revised by Sir Mortimer Wheeler and A. L. Basham.

and became incorporated in what developed into Hinduism; it is a reasonable inference that the germs of caste also came from the Indus cities and that the invaders superimposed their own system of dominance by conquest upon a stratified and diversified system which they found already there.

These imperial capitals arose from the specialization of function which enabled one man to produce more than he needed; the surplus had to be distributed and so produced the need for organization and the opportunity for exploitation. A specialized society is likely to defeat a simpler society and provide a lower tier still of enslaved and conquered peoples. The rulers and organizers sought security for themselves and their children; to perpetuate the power, the esteem, and the comfort they had achieved, it was necessary not only that the artisans and labourers should work contentedly but that the rulers should sleep without bad dreams. No one can say with certainty how the myths originated, but it is surely relevant that when one of the founders of Western thought set himself to frame an ideal state that would embody social justice, he—like the earliest city dwellers—not only devised a society stratified in tiers but believed it would be necessary to persuade the traders and work-people that, by divine decree, they were made from brass and iron, while the warriors were made of silver and the rulers of gold. There is—as one might expect—another side to Plato's picture. His is a typical upper-class myth; sometimes the subordinates console themselves with other beliefs. American Indians in one township of Chiapas think that God created men, that is Indians, from honest earth, but the Spanish-speakers who despise them they believe He made from horse-droppings.[1]

Sharply differentiated societies, split into layers with unequal rights, were then a condition without which the first steps in progress—in the arts, in mastery of the environment and amelioration of human life—have nowhere been taken. Everywhere, the top classes made some kind of alliance with the belief that the world was divinely ordained and persuaded their subjects that it was by divine intention that they must work so hard for so little. The results have been widespread and far-reaching; for centuries and over almost the whole of the globe, it has been a basic assumption in societies of any size or complexity that some men are born to power and luxury, others to toil and poverty.

But, from early times, there began to develop a contrary tendency, a movement, as Sir Henry Maine noted, from stratification by status to stratification on a more temporary basis, by contract and competition. In these 'progressive' societies, tightly-knit clans and large family groups have tended to be replaced by much smaller family groups and a much more individualist outlook. It was in these far more individualist societies that there developed on the one hand the views of causation

[1] Julian Pitt-Rivers, *After the Empire: Race and Society in Middle America and the Andes.*

that have resulted in modern science and, on the other, the demand for social justice, which has spread, inevitably, from its homelands to the peoples who were once colonial.

It is a minor hypothesis of this book that the ease with which small numbers of people from Western Europe established dominion over the greater part of the world was due not merely to technical superiority, but to a different kind of society and a different view of the universe. Technical superiority was of course important in the nineteenth century, but by itself it will not account for the conquests of Mexico, Peru, and India by such tiny handfuls; the superiority was at that stage not really very marked, particularly in India, where Europeans had no monopoly of gun-powder or cannon, and sword-blades were as fine as any in Europe. It is a second hypothesis, more central to the argument, that the development in social structure was linked with the development of science and was due to very complex factors, foremost among which were the two ideas, closely linked, though reached by very different routes, of equality before the law and the fatherhood of God, which implies the brotherhood of man. These are radical ideas, destructive of the social framework which was the first condition of progress.

Equality before the law is a Greek idea spread by the Romans. But it is a commonplace that in the minds of neither was it of universal application. Athenian democracy was highly egalitarian so far as it went; lots were drawn for public office, generals took turns to command troops, and rich citizens were expected to provide the state with warships. Women and slaves, however, were excluded and, in attempting to justify the exclusion of slaves, Aristotle suggested that some men were slaves by nature. He was probably right in supposing that some people prefer to be dependent—but of course it does not follow that all such people were slaves or that all slaves were such people. Again, Roman law not only recognized slaves but distinguished between Roman citizens and others. The idea of equality needed fructifying sperm to become lively; when that arrived, the result was at once recognized as not only active but dangerous. Those who preached it were crucified and persecuted. These ideas operated like a serum which sets up its own antibodies as soon as it is introduced into a living organism.

This is clearly not the place to discuss in any detail the fusion of the Graeco-Roman idea of equality before the law and the Judaeo-Christian idea of the brotherhood of man. But it is necessary to the argument to point out that when Christianity became the official religion of the Empire, a compromise was made with the basically egalitarian doctrines which were an essential part of its teaching. The radical and destructive elements were not suppressed; they were blandly built into the hierarchical structure. But they had been proclaimed; indeed they were read daily in the gospels. They were in conflict with unstated social assumptions and they were largely ignored, or a distinction was made and it was held that although men might be equal in the sight of God, rank in this world was a very different matter. But the religious ideal of brotherhood and equality never wholly died; from time to time it was proclaimed again, and not only in a purely religious dimension by saints and friars, but also by peasants' revolts and by religious movements of protest in which there were political and economic undertones, such as those of the Lollards or the Hussites.

The Middle Ages came to an end in that great flowering of the human spirit, the Renaissance, which was in part an assertion of the individual in art against the anonymous. Feudal systems began to give way to national societies; the Age of Reason gave birth to the American and French Revolutions and now the revolt against inequality had been formally declared. However imperfectly they applied it, two nation states proclaimed that they were founded on the contrary principle of equality. But until this stage, the general assumption had almost everywhere been that men were unequal; society had once been stratified mainly by birth, but in the West, other factors, such as wealth, education, ability, were coming increasingly into the account.

This phenomenon, of increasing individualism, of the decay of inequality prescribed by birth, was hardly apparent in the nineteenth century outside Europe, North America, and the British Dominions. Of the great world systems of thought, Islam—a strong stem thrown out from Judaism and Christianity—similarly proclaimed equality but in fact established despotisms in which men were manifestly unequal; from the sixteenth century onward, Islam was in regression, both in a military sense, being driven out of Spain and back from Hungary, and in thought, having fallen back from the days when Avicenna and Averroes were the leading scientists of Islam, outstripping any rivals in Christendom. Hinduism enthroned inequality and justified it by the doctrine of reincarnation. Buddhism in neither of its principal forms produced markedly egalitarian societies; nor could this be expected, because it regarded the material world as illusion. Even where the principle of equality was proclaimed as an ideal, it still had many enemies and its progress in Europe in the nineteenth century was chequered with battles, many of which were lost. This was not only because the contrary principle worked to the advantage of the rulers, but because most of their subjects for most of the time acquiesced.

## 3 The Psychological Advantages of Dependence

A social system based on inequality has to provide some degree of psychological satisfaction. Such systems could not otherwise have been so widespread nor have lasted so long. The hypothesis here suggested is that the processes of evolution have encouraged a tendency to distrust those outside a given group and to find some satisfaction in loyalty within the group. The tendency may have been thrown up by natural selection in the harshest physical sense; it is surely to be expected among the simple food-gathering groups. It is to be seen among animals, among both deer and wolves in a rudimentary form as well as among the higher primates. If this is accepted, the most essential of all social problems is the definition of the group; whom do we regard as 'we'? The clan, the village, the Trade Union, the nation?

In the kind of progress we have been imagining, there would be no need for Bushmen to define the group to which they belonged; everyone must have known everyone else. But by the time the organization has grown complex enough to be called an empire—at the stage of the great metropolitan capitals—the need is pressing and the more the social structure is split into defined groups the easier it will be for people to feel comfortable. For the rulers, as we have already suggested, it is clearly useful to separate themselves from the ruled. It is also to their interest that the ruled should be sub-divided. But it is not only a question of the rulers' interest; the subjects themselves will be too many to feel secure unless they are grouped together in clans or castes or guilds, within which they have a recognized part to play, a known position in the hierarchy and known obligations to fulfil. It will also be satisfying to primitive urges to look outward from the group of which one is a part, to regard other groups with fear, distrust, or aversion and to attribute to them the qualities most feared and disliked in oneself. Those who look from below towards a superior group will project on to that the dislike of social compulsion which they have themselves most disliked in elders or parents. And this will reinforce the resentment they feel against the social system in general.

It is not hard, then, to see the reasons for segmentation. But this explanation immediately presents two further problems. We are picturing a group of rulers at the top of the picture and below them a number of segmented groups, clans, guilds, or castes; the rulers have to devise some means of keeping themselves in power and perpetuating this state of affairs for their children. At the same time they have to bind the whole mass together so that it can withstand external attack and remain in being as a whole. They have to persuade their subjects to acquiesce in a situation that is to their disadvantage. It is to the rulers' interest that the subjects should think of the rulers as so different from themselves that they can never hope to supplant them, but also as 'their' rulers whom they must defend against outsiders. At the same time, the rulers would like their subjects to be segmented and regard each other with suspicion—but with only just enough suspicion to prevent their combining against the rulers and not enough to prevent their supporting the rulers against other enemies and being conscious of belonging to a whole. At this stage, this is the essential social and political problem. Let us first consider what makes the subordinate groups at least outwardly quiescent.

The fear of reprisals is not the only force that keeps the slaves, the serfs, the peasants, the workers, subservient. Fear is there, and with good reason; when Crassus crushed a revolt of slaves he lined the Appian Way with six thousand crucified captives and the treatment of slaves recaptured in the Americas was often as sickening and obscene. But fear operates only intermittently; force cannot be everywhere and force itself depends on obedience. Soldiers are needed to enforce the system— but they are part of it and they too have to be kept in obedience. Not all men are leaders or rebels and for much of the time men will put up with hard work, discomfort, and the lack of freedom, provided only that two conditions are fulfilled. They must somehow be led to believe that the system is part of the order of nature and that things will always be like this—that is to say, the very idea of revolution must seem remote or impossible; secondly, they must feel themselves so different from the superior group that they do not compare their own lot with that of their masters. If these conditions are met, it may well be that resentment at the social system and at social compulsion will be successfully repressed and that both parties for most of the time will forget that it exists.

There is plenty of evidence supporting this point. It is a historical commonplace that revolutions do not occur where misery is at its deepest but when the burden begins to lift. It was not in Eastern Europe that the Bastille was stormed nor when the King would yield nothing; in Russia, the serfs were freed two generations before the October revolution, and this again took place at the moment when a liberal sovereign was making concessions. The same principle is to be seen on a much less dramatic scale in experiments conducted by American scholars,[1] who found that in a section of the United States army in which there was very little chance of promotion, there was far more contentment than in another corps where chances of promotion were good. In the first, no one expected anything better than he had and did not compare himself adversely with his companions; in the second, those not promoted felt they had failed or been slighted and even those who had gone up one step compared themselves with those who had gone up two. Again, a British scholar found that even in 1961[2] manual labourers in Britain compare themselves not with the very rich, whom they feel to be totally irrelevant to their own situation, but with those who are slightly better off than themselves.

[1] Quoted in W. G. Runciman, *Relative Deprivation and Social Justice.*
[2] Quoted ibid.

There is also the familiar case, constantly repeated, of the American Negro from the South who is disillusioned when he reaches the North, because although at first he seems more free, in fact he no longer 'knows where he is'. The same has been said of a move from Barbados to Jamaica.[1] In Barbados, there used to be a colour bar of a rather special kind unknown elsewhere in the Caribbean; the social scene is much more fluid in Jamaica. It has been said too of a move from the United States to Britain; the situation in Britain is much less easy to understand because there are no rules and the signals by which the English indicate acceptance and disapproval are less obvious.

'Dependence' has been described in Madagascar by O. Mannoni.[2] He regards it as a typical element in the personality of those belonging to a society in which a man plays a known part in a position fixed without any act of his own. He is thinking of the Malagasy's position in traditional society, set on a ladder between the ancestors he worships and the unborn who will worship himself when he is dead. Mannoni describes how this secure dependence is destroyed when the Malagasy leaves his traditional society to work for cash in a society dominated by individualist European ideas; here the Malagasy will frequently try—like a plant or animal moved from its native habitat—to reconstruct the old conditions and make a new security, a new dependence, sometimes by attaching himself to a European, to whom he is prepared to give total obedience in return for total protection. But the European, who is accustomed to enter into contracts for specified services for specified rewards, expects neither the obedience nor the protection to be so complete. He wants service of a particular kind during office hours, for which he pays; he does not expect his clerk, let us say, to attend his private house in order to welcome his guests at a dinner-party, nor does he think it his duty to back the clerk in his lawsuit with a village neighbour. The Malagasy in such circumstances feels defrauded and disappointed. Almost exactly the same reactions to employment by Europeans are recorded by Jacques Maquet[3] of the people of Ruanda. But Maquet attributes the difference in their behaviour not so much to their position between the dead and the unborn as to the highly stratified structure of society in Ruanda, which is based, he suggests, on 'the premise of inequality'. Society in Ruanda illustrates so exactly one aspect of the introductory thesis of this book that I shall describe it briefly in the final section of this chapter.

There is a point to be emphasized here. Aristotle thought some people were slaves by nature; no doubt in his day many slaves counterfeited a dependence on their masters which they would secretly have liked to repudiate. No doubt also many were affected by the role they had

---

[1] Verbally to author.

[2] O. Mannoni, *Prospero and Caliban*.

[3] J. J. Maquet, *The Premise of Inequality in Ruanda*.

to play, becoming servile in spirit because they simulated servility. In the same way, a colonial society, like the Madagascan described by Mannoni, will produce conformists who are rebels at heart. Not all Malagasies were dependants by nature, nor is this psychological tendency unknown among Europeans. All one can suggest is that pre-industrial societies like the Malagasy produced a higher *proportion* of people content to be dependent, while a modern industrialized society produced a higher *proportion* of people anxious to dispel their own sense of inferiority by pushing themselves to the front.

That so many people for so much of history have accepted treatment manifestly unfair must always be puzzling to an observer from an individualist society, particularly in an age of revolt against privilege and inequality. I have touched on some factors which throw some light on this—the habit of taking for granted the assumptions behind the whole society in which one lives; the habit of comparing one's lot with the nearest class and not with the most remote; the habit of making the best of circumstances which seem unlikely to change. These are brittle elements in a social situation and they can quickly be shattered by a rumour of change or by a demagogue with a gift for rhetoric. More profound is the lifelong habit of dependence which has made so many of mankind unfit for freedom, truly slaves by nature. But it is a corollary to this general point that the habit of dependence usually conceals a repressed resentment which is liable to flare out with a special fury once the relationship is disturbed or even threatened.

## 4 A Sketch of Ruanda

The mountainous kingdom of Ruanda, south of Uganda and east of what used to be the Belgian Congo, was isolated for many centuries. There was virtually no Arab influence and the first European reached the country only in 1894; it has therefore been possible to reconstruct from the memories of people then alive a picture of society as it existed in Ruanda before it was disturbed by Europeans. The kingdom had apparently been stable since the sixteenth century; the reigning King in 1960 was said to be the fortieth of his dynasty. It was a kingdom with a number of features which admirably illustrate some of the main themes of this book, as does the revolution which has brought the system to an end.

In the first place, the population was divided into three ethnic groups, who were as a rule physically distinguishable. The Tutsi, the ruling group, were generally expected to be tall, slender, and fair in comparison with the Hutu, who were expected to be shorter, stouter, and darker. In fact, physical measurements to-day confirm that there are differences, though they are somewhat exaggerated in the popular mind. Average height for the Tutsi was reported to be 1·75m. or 5' 10";

for the Hutu 1·66m. or 5' 6"; and for the Twa, a pygmoid group, only
1·55m. or 5' 2". The Hutu are Negroid Bantu-speakers who practise
agriculture; no one knows how long they have been in this territory
but the Tutsi, pastoral nomads, established their rule in the sixteenth
century. In the census of 1956, the Tutsi were 13 per cent of the
population, while the Hutu were 86 per cent and the Twa only 1 per
cent.

The Twa can be dealt with quickly; they were forest food-gatherers
and are looked on with disdain by the other two groups, both of whom
say the Twa are more like monkeys than men and both of whom
repudiate the idea of intermarriage with them. But since they are too
few to be regarded as a danger, they are treated with some indulgence
and some of them hold the kind of posts under the Tutsi lords that
dwarfs, foreigners, and eunuchs have held in the courts of Europe and
Asia; they are described as 'hunters, potters, jesters, torturers, execu-
tioners, pimps, dancers, and musicians' and were direct vassals of the
Mwami or King. The relationship between the Tutsi and the Hutu is
more interesting.

It was one of almost complete domination. The Tutsi regarded
manual labour as beneath their dignity, and in fact did none except
milking and cattle-herding. They were essentially an aristocratic
people, and Tutsi young men spent some time at the King's court,
where they received systematic instruction, designed to make them conform to the ideal of a noble warrior. They were trained in sports and
dances, in poetry, and in eloquent and witty conversation; they must
strive to attain three virtues, the first being physical courage and the
second the quality of being a man and a leader, which included liberality
to the poor and the moral courage to accept responsibilities and fulfil
promises. The third was self-mastery; it was essential for a Tutsi to be
always self-controlled and polite; only vulgar people like the Hutu lost
their temper or showed emotion. The whole social system revolved on
the superiority of the Tutsi, who were regarded by the Hutu as different
from themselves not only physically but morally. They were believed
by both Hutu and Tutsi (writes Maquet) to be 'intelligent, capable of
command, refined, courageous, and cruel', while the Hutu were
thought by both groups to be 'hardworking, not very clever, extrovert,
irascible, unmannerly, obedient, physically strong'—the universal
stereotype of the peasant.

Asked if a Hutu boy could be changed if he were brought up by the
Tutsi as though he were one of themselves, Maquet's informants from
both groups replied that only very limited changes could be made; the
differences were inherent and a matter of nature. It is surely significant
that the Tutsi not only consumed a different diet from the Hutu but
observed rules that made it seem more different than it was. Until
evening, a Tutsi noble would subsist entirely on curdled milk and mead

or banana beer; the only solid food of the day was taken in the evening, in the presence of his wife and children, Hutu servants being rigidly excluded. If on a journey, he was not supposed to touch solid food at all; some older Tutsi boasted of never eating solid food at any time. The Hutu were represented as greedy and the Twa as more gluttonous still; the kinds of food which were the staple foods of the Hutu, and indeed of Bantu-speakers from all over Africa—porridge of maize or millet and sweet potatoes—were regarded with contempt by the Tutsi. Beer made from millet—again the staple drink of Africa—the Tutsi looked on as fit only for Hutu.

An elaborate social, military, and economic system supported this pattern of psychological dominance. The people are divided into lineage groups of varying depths, from the extended family or large household to the clan; the country is divided into districts, which are subdivided into 'hills'. On this framework was superimposed a fourfold network of allegiance and subordination, of which the most significant will be described last. In the first place, cattle and grazing formed one channel for the exercise of power, while land and agriculture formed another. In each district, there was a cattle chief and a land chief; these important officials settled disputes, each in his own sphere, about cattle and grazing rights, about land, cultivation, and grain. They also collected taxes in their respective spheres, of labour, grain, and bananas from the Hutu, of milk and cows from the Tutsi. The dues were equivalent to about one-third of one man's work from each household, which would usually consist of several adults; over the whole country it was perhaps rather more than one-tenth of the produce. But it might weigh far more heavily on one household than on another—partly because of the numbers in the household but even more because of the favour of the collector. This would be influenced by the conduct and record of the head of the household and sometimes by pressure brought to bear on the collector, through other Tutsi lords to whom the householder also owed allegiance. There was a hierarchy of lesser chiefs below the land chief and the cattle chief of the district.

Another channel of allegiance by which goods were conveyed to the centre was military. Every person, Tutsi, Hutu, or Twa, was affiliated, with his whole lineage group, to a military formation which Maquet calls an 'army', though perhaps 'regiment' would convey the meaning more exactly. Only a certain number of young Tutsi constituted the warriors of this regiment; from time to time a new company of young Tutsi would be formed, and periodically there would be a new regiment. Other Tutsi made up the herdsmen's section of the regiment, and the Hutu were the labourers, servants, and porters. The regiment was not only a means of defending the Mwami's territory, or, much more often, attacking and looting neighbours; it was also an alternative channel for tribute of cattle, milk, and labour to the King; a means of increasing his power by patronage, and a chain of power and favour that constituted a rival to those of the district cattle chief and the district land chief. Perhaps not least, it was a training-ground, particularly for the Tutsi, and a unifying factor because it cut across other allegiances.

In addition to the two administrative channels and the military, there was a fourth channel, which may be loosely called feudal, though it was not the same as the European feudal system and in some ways was nearer the relationship of patron and client which is common in Northern India and South America. This too centred on the exchange of cattle, milk, and services, but it had the unusual feature of being, in appearance at least, voluntary. A man would approach a superior with a present and some such phrase as 'be my father' or 'I ask for milk' or 'make me rich' or 'I will be your child'. If the offer was accepted, a relationship arose in which there seem to have been certain areas of specified commitment on either side but also considerable areas of unspecified but generally accepted obligation, for which occasions might never or only occasionally arise. The patron or lord would give his client or vassal a cow or several cows, depending on his status; the vassal would have the right to the milk, to male calves, and to the meat and skin if the cow died or had to be slaughtered. The cow itself, and any female calves, remained the property of the lord, while the vassal was in a sense its tenant. The vassal must periodically pay his respects to the lord, bringing as a rule presents, and, if he was a Hutu, he would also have to perform menial services. An important lord with many vassals would allot different services to different vassals and the number of cows allotted would vary with the services. But there was general agreement that the value of the services was (at least in the case of Hutu vassals) a good deal more than the value provided by the tenancy of cows.

This difference is really explained by the nature of the obligations which were not normally specified but which operated on both sides. The vassal might have to go with his lord on a journey, or go with him to court or on a hunt; he might be sent with messages or summoned to his lord's help in almost any crisis. But on the other hand he too could call on his lord for protection against any other lord or high official; he could expect backing in a lawsuit against a neighbour or a petition to the King, help if he was faced with unexpected expense, even vengeance if one of his family was murdered. The lord might have to pay the vassal's fine if he committed an offence or he might look after his widow or children if he died and had no close relations in the male line. In short, behind the foreground of carefully drawn obligations lies a much more shadowy background which can be summed up as total allegiance in return for total protection.

The allegiance was supposed to be voluntary, and indeed, since the vassal chose his lord, it was to that extent voluntary, and so differed from the feudal system in Europe. But if a small man decided not to have a lord, life would be very difficult for him. 'To live without a lord was to invite trouble.' In theory he could transfer his allegiance, but again he would be a bold man who made a proposal to end his allegiance to one lord without first securing the protection of another more powerful. There was therefore a strong element of compulsion and the whole institution operated as a combination of insurance and of protection-money. This explains why the obligations of the vassal were greater; there was an invisible premium on his insurance policy.

All four channels were means of transferring goods and services from manual workers upwards to the privileged. As a general principle, the district land and cattle chiefs passed on about one-third of what was collected to the Mwami or his representatives, about two-thirds being kept by themselves and their subordinates in the hierarchy. In the military channel, too, payments were made from below upwards, converging on the Mwami, but depositing substantial benefits on the way with the chiefs of regiments and companies. And the Mwami stood at the head of the feudal structure too; his vassals were the highest chiefs, who in their turn had vassals who had vassals. If, therefore, a traveller, seeing a Hutu peasant milking a cow, asked him whose it was, he might get a variety of replies. The peasant might be the sub-sub-sub-tenant in a ladder leading back to the Mwami, and his immediate lord might be the tenant of some greater lord.

The system of lords and vassals supported the distinction between Tutsi and Hutu in a way curiously oblique and indirect. Not all Tutsi were lords; indeed, all Tutsi were vassals to someone, though it might be only to the Mwami. Most were in a dual relationship—vassal to someone higher, lords to vassals below them, of whom some were Tutsi and some Hutu. Some Hutu too sub-let to other Hutu. But the system supported the superiority of the Tutsi because a poor Tutsi could always save himself from manual work by going to a rich noble and asking to become his vassal. In that case, the superior would let him have the tenancy of a sufficient number of cows to sub-let to one or two Hutu; he would thus obtain servants and agricultural produce. A Tutsi vassal would be given no heavy or menial work; he would come with presents and acknowledge the superiority of his overlord and he might be told to herd cattle or supervise someone else's work or accompany his lord as a retainer on a journey to court. Thus the Tutsi avoided what South Africans know as the problem of 'the poor white'; the superior group is not degraded in the eyes of inferiors by humiliating work or low status.

The whole social system of Ruanda—at the beginning of this century —thus provides a singularly elegant way of solving what, for the ruling group and at one stage of human development, is one of the basic political problems of society. The Mwami and the Tutsi lords are assured of a flow of goods and services from the tillers of the soil; their superiority is confirmed by their training and the myth that they are a different order of being, consuming different food and hardly needing solid nourishment. The Mwami himself is protected against a conspiracy of the Tutsi; he has two representatives in every district; one is likely to report to him any infidelity of the other and even if the two conspired to defraud him, news would almost certainly reach him through an army chief or one of the higher feudal chiefs. At the same time, the Hutu populace can hardly assert themselves against so complex a network of subordination; each man is likely to be in touch with the subordinates of the cattle and land chiefs, and of an army chief as well as with a feudal lord. Any leader of revolt would need to be extraordinarily subtle and persuasive to organize any general dissatisfaction without being betrayed by someone through one channel or another.

But while it would be hard for the Hutu to rebel, there would be much to reconcile them to a system of this kind. The goods and labour taken are about one-tenth of the produce, which is a light tax compared with the one-half or one-third of the produce usually taken by Indian Kings and their officials. The myth of Tutsi superiority is maintained before their eyes; they do not think they can compete with the Tutsi in intelligence. And they are so closely knit into the whole system, so dependent on the Tutsi lord for protection, that they can hardly disentangle any element which they can identify either as a rallying-point or as a general grievance. Many Hutu are themselves minor lords with some vassals and these do not want to end the feudal system; others dare not face a hostile world without a protector. Some are officials under the land or cattle chief. There are various channels in which a Hutu can make some progress though never so much as to imperil the system. The army cuts across the district organization and discourages territorial separatism.

Again, there are safeguards against excessive tyranny. Though a Hutu cannot escape from dependence, he has some choice as to the man on whom he is dependent; a lord who is unreasonable in his demands or brutal in his punishment will not acquire new vassals and his power and prestige will diminish. Further, there is some opportunity for the subordinate to get the support of his army chief or his feudal chief against each other or against the land or cattle chief. But this would be a dangerous game and it would probably be a mistake to stress the point. It was perhaps a more efficacious safeguard that the Mwami would hear through other channels if a lord or official was too oppressive.

A more recent study than Maquet's[1] has stressed the importance of power in this system as against the principle of balance. But the

[1] Helen Codere, 'Power in Ruanda'.

controversy does not seem very fruitful. There can be no political system which is not concerned with power; power is what politics is about. But there must also be an element of balance; a good system of political control is surely one in which the amount of actual force which need be displayed—let alone used—is at a minimum and in which the maximum of co-operation by the public is achieved without force. Judged by this criterion, here was a system of exploitation by a minority, visibly different from most of their subjects, which seems to have been singularly efficient and to have reached its maximum efficiency at the time when the arrival of Europeans began to interfere with it.

It is Maquet's thesis that the society was based on the 'premise of inequality' and his description of some of the consequences of this social structure are singularly reminiscent of Mannoni's findings in Madagascar. 'There is no private sector in the life of the inferior *vis-à-vis* his subordinator', writes Maquet. 'When a European employer avoids intruding into the privacy of a Ruanda subordinate, the latter not infrequently tends to interpret it as a withdrawal from the protective role expected from any superior.' Strict contracts with accurately defined obligations are not possible; they imply equality. The superior group become domineering and authoritative. The inferior group, outwardly compliant, develop extreme skill in dissimulation; it becomes customary to say what you believe will please the superior and the idea of objective truth is at a discount. And this spreads to other fields; in any context, what is said is what the speaker thinks will serve his purpose.

Surely in varying degrees these findings apply wherever there is a relationship of dominance and inferiority. In South Africa, in the Deep South, in India, it was the commonplace talk of the dominant group that those of the subordinate group never spoke the truth and were incapable of gratitude. Arrogance and impatience are commonly attributed by outsiders to dominant groups—and it is what one would expect, because there is no one who dares answer back. What has not been remarked quite so often is the desire to emphasize difference and to deny that one shares human attributes with the subordinates. The Tutsi pretend to eat no solid food; the twice-born castes in India vied with each other in the lists of food they would not eat and the precautions against pollution in preparing it. The Tutsi training recalls Sparta and Rugby; the upper-class English of the late Victorian age gloried in subjecting their sons to rigours which marked their superiority to the lower bourgeoisie. I have written elsewhere[1] of the growth in the English class system of this need to emphasize difference; it was at its maximum just before the First World War and was surely an unconscious response to the threat of equality posed by the French and

[1] Philip Mason, *Prospero's Magic.*

American revolutions. One form it took was the feeling that it was improper for servants to use the same lavatory as their employers.

Let me end this chapter on a personal note. We shall hear more of the relation of patron to client, both in India and South America; all I would here note is that the relationship has about it a special flavour, instantly recognizable. As I read Maquet's account of the Tutsi lord, surrounded by his vassals, with their various functions and the hinterland of undefined rights and obligations, of total protection and total allegiance, I was carried back to India, to villages in Rohilkand, in the North-West of what is now Uttar Pradesh. There the landholders were usually Rajputs, though sometimes Rohilla Pathans. In either case, they prided themselves on being warriors, men with noble traditions and a high sense of honour; they despised meanness, cowardice, and inhospitality. In either case, they were surrounded by a crowd of hangers-on—retainers, vassals, tenants, servants, clients—some of whom had special functions, such as the family priest at the highest end of the scale, but going down through the family potter and washerman to the landless labourers. But all these people acknowledged a Rajput leader as patron or *jajman*, and the relationship cut across the caste system, for there would be Brahmans and Rajputs too among the clients. The Brahman would be priest or cook, the Rajput would be foreman, overseer, head of the retainers, collector of rents from the tenants. To all these people—both the high caste clients and the low— the Rajput head of the house was patron. He gave grain and cloth, the right to work a plot of land, perhaps even money, for specified services, but here too there was a hinterland of unwritten obligation. The patron accorded protection against other landowners and the police; loans in times of special need, at a daughter's marriage or when hail slashed a ripe crop to the ground; backing in lawsuits and quarrels. In return, he expected support in his own lawsuits, sometimes in minor riots and affrays with neighbours,[1] help at elections, as they grew in importance, but much else; the supporters would turn out as beaters for a day's shooting, take messages, support the landowner's prestige. How often in an Indian village have I seen a man hovering attentively near by, and, suspecting that he might perhaps be anxious to put some request or give some information, have asked: 'Who is this and what does he want?' And the answer has come: 'This is no one. This is my man.' He was waiting, not for justice from a British official, but in case his patron had orders for him.

There is one point to add. Dr. Codere, author of one of the latest studies of Ruanda, found that her educated Tutsi friends did not like to be reminded of the French Revolution. They were right to identify the danger which has since overwhelmed them.

[1] I have described one such affray in a novel, *Call the Next Witness* (pseud. 'Philip Woodruff'). But the whole story hinges on this feudal relationship.

# CHAPTER II

# The Revolt against Inequality

## 1 Revolt in Europe

We have been looking at one small society in Central Africa, where a minority succeeded in dominating and exploiting for hundreds of years another people more than six times their number. They had no marked technical or scientific superiority; even their initial conquest seems to have been achieved without any fighting which impressed itself on people's minds sufficiently to be remembered. The conquerors were of a rather different appearance from their subjects and they seem to have established a psychological mastery which was supported by beliefs about their physical and intellectual superiority and by complex administrative and social institutions. The effect of these was to knit the subordinate groups into the whole framework of society and to constitute groupings small enough to be psychologically satisfying yet almost incapable of taking effective steps to split away. At the same time, the system provided just enough possibility of social advance to give openings to the most able subordinates and to give them some satisfaction. Above all, it established a sense of permanence which prevented any thought of rebellion, and a sense of difference between the upper and lower groups so complete that the Hutu did not seriously compare their lot with that of the Tutsi.

The point of dwelling on this small kingdom is to illustrate in a simple and isolated form a stage in human society, when dominance has been so successfully established that it is taken for granted. It achieves stability but it is the kind of stability in which imagination and originality have little hope. It is the tranquillity of stagnation. That some such pattern of complementary dominance and inequality was inevitable in any complex social system was, as we have seen, the almost world-wide assumption which for centuries governed the practice of governments, the organization of society, and the behaviour of most people. It was in contradiction to the fundamental tenets of Christianity, Judaism, and Islam as well as to the Greek idea of equality before the law. But until the end of the eighteenth century, the dangerous idea of possible equality lay for most of the time dormant.

When it was proclaimed in France and America as a principle on which the state was to be organized it was, characteristically, limited in a variety of ways.

It is of course a gross simplification to speak as though the American Constitution and the French Revolution were wholly new, in particular as though they owed nothing to Locke and the English Revolution of 1688. But the English, like the Athenians, had limited their egalitarianism fairly strictly; there was supposed to be equality before the law but certainly not political equality and no one in seventeenth-century England can have supposed that a poor man was actually equal to a lord. Even in its most enthusiastic phase the French Revolution proclaimed political equality rather than economic— and the enthusiastic phase did not last long; the Empire was not exactly egalitarian and, throughout the nineteenth century, France, like the rest of Europe, was a battleground in which the idea of equality fought the practice of stratification, on the whole with indifferent success. The rebellions of 1848 were defeated; the absolute dynastic systems of Austria, Russia, and Prussia survived; in France, in Britain, and in Italy there were successes for a moderate liberalism but certainly no general defeat for the basic principle that a few people should have power and wealth, while most people were very much poorer and had little say in determining policy.

Nonetheless, Europe was a battlefield and the ideas of equality and social justice had been spoken aloud and could not be forgotten. The United States proclaimed them, though making notable exceptions in practice. In Britain, as I have argued elsewhere,[1] formal barriers between classes were reduced as the franchise was extended but, step by step, as formal barriers went down, more rigid barriers went up in the mind; a lady would happily share her bed with a maid in the eighteenth century but not in the twentieth. In the twenty years before 1914, communication between classes in England was probably at its lowest ebb—and the reason, I suggest, was a deep unconscious fear among the upper and middle classes. At the same time, there was the beginning of a social concern, very strong among the most thoughtful of that generation of whom so many were killed in the First World War.

It is, again, an impression, which needs further examination, that there was a marked change in the attitudes of the privileged towards class differences in Britain after 1917 and the October revolution. The fear which had been deep and unconscious came nearer to the surface and became more shrill; it became less possible than before to suppose that class differences were in some way inherent and that they would last for ever. Political power was shifting; the General Strike was defeated but there was a Labour Government, though not yet with an overall majority. The social scene began to change too and domestic

[1] Philip Mason, *Prospero's Magic*.

service was increasingly unpopular; this was partly because of better conditions in factories and the spread of education but mainly because the relationship was felt to be humiliating. It placed people from different classes side by side under the same roof and encouraged comparison between their comforts, their hours of work, and above all the esteem in which they were held.

The comparison was inevitable unless people on both sides of the line accepted the idea that the social order was immutable. But this idea was dead. It was still possible to ignore people on the other side of the line so long as leisure was spent at a distance—but under the same roof the differences were continually brought home. It became necessary to make concessions to the remaining servants that would never have been thought of in 1910. The fear which had first expressed itself in an intensification of social distance now began to take the form of uneasy, often patronizing, conciliation. This is a sequence of attitudes which we shall meet again.

But we have to retrace our steps. We have been thinking of the limited world of Europe—a world on which America was not yet impinging very markedly. It was a battleground on which ideas of equality met only limited success, and until 1917 mainly in the political dimension. Inequality of wealth and opportunity was generally taken for granted. There was another most important limitation on the idea of equality. Just as the Athenians excluded slaves from their democracy, the western democracies excluded their colonial subjects and the Americans their Negroes. The exclusion was not based on clearly conceived principles; indeed, in Britain, France, and the United States, frankly racist theories were not the doctrine of the majority. Britain was paternalist; the colonial peoples were wards under guardianship and would one day attain their majority. France was assimilationist; the colonials would gradually all become French. But for the present it was taken for granted that the relationship could not be one of equality.

In 1917, one state proclaimed the desirability of economic equality as well as political. In the previous century, there had been confusion between the ideological conflict and the national. The build-up of rival systems of power had not followed ideological lines; the liberal democracies had been allied with Tsarist Russia and the liberal monarchy of Italy with two autocracies. In the next phase, too, it was impossible to see a clear ideological conflict between those who sought equality and social justice and those who did not. Nazi Germany and Marxist Russia dismembered Poland, as Prussia and Tsarist Russia had done nearly two centuries earlier. From the battles of the Second World War emerged two supremely powerful states, each proclaiming its belief in 'democracy', but each afraid of the other, and each finding justification for its fear in the other's interpretation of democracy. The United States put its emphasis on liberty and pointed to the authoritarianism of Russia; Russia stressed equality and pointed to the extremes of wealth and poverty in America, but above all to the position of Negroes.

Here was a new situation in the dimension of political ideas. Considerations of power, of security, of economic interest, continued to influence most political decisions, perhaps to much the same degree as before; but now the two most powerful states, with all their differences, professed support for social ideals which had seemed wildly dangerous to the rulers of Europe in the previous century. With the exceptions of South Africa, Spain, and Portugal, the rest of the world followed their lead. The idea of equal opportunity became fashionable. Though there was a great diversity of opinion as to what it meant and a still greater diversity of practice, it was easy enough to see what institutions prevented it and what states encouraged the obstacles and set up new ones. This new fashion meant an immense acceleration of something which had begun almost a century earlier—the spread of the idea of equality to the countries which had been ruled or otherwise dominated by the colonial powers.

## 2 Revolt outside Europe

If an imperial power is itself organized domestically on the basis of what Maquet has called in Ruanda 'the premise of inequality', it is faced with no ideological dilemma in its relations with colonies or vassal states. They are governed by the same authority as the subordinate group in the metropolitan country. Tsarist Russia and Bismarck's Prussia had only a technical police problem to solve. But once the idea of democracy is introduced at the centre, the dilemma is raised in an acute form. How is the group to be defined within which democratic principles apply? Or to put it another way, if, in the mother country, it is believed that even the most ignorant should have some say in choosing their rulers, how is it justifiable to govern another people on completely different principles? There can be only two answers, the racist and the paternalist. The racist answer is that the subject people are inherently different and must be ruled for ever; they are slaves by nature, as Aristotle said. The paternalist view, on the other hand, is that they are for the present wards under guardianship; but they will grow up, they will be educated. Here there is a divergence: the French, on the whole, thought that their wards would become French, because they would absorb French culture, which was manifestly the best; English paternalists, again in the broadest terms, did not suppose their wards would become English, because the essence of being English was not culture but character; they did suppose, however, that they would adopt British institutions and enough British habits of thought to attain independence as an admiring younger brother.

But whether the justification was racist or paternalist, some inhabitants of the colonized country must be taught some of the skills of the rulers. They might for instance be needed as clerks and for that they must go to school. In fact, the main colonial powers—Britain, France, Spain, Holland, Portugal, Belgium—were all in varying ways paternalist and pictured some at least of their wards growing up eventually. This meant that some at least would learn more than the bare minimum that the rulers needed if the colonized people were to work for them. It was not possible to educate boys in the Catholic faith without revealing that God was believed to be the father of all mankind; once the British in India decided to educate in English, and not in Sanskrit or Persian, it was impossible to keep out of the curriculum any reference to Magna Carta, Habeas Corpus, and the Revolution of 1688. Thus ideas of equality, or at least of a possible equality in some respects, were inevitably introduced into the air of the colonized countries.

But such ideas did not at once become active. We have seen how they lay dormant throughout the Middle Ages in Europe; it is possible to give intellectual assent to a proposition but not apply it to oneself. And at another stage, it may be applied in favour of oneself against superiors but not against oneself to inferiors. The followers of Simon Bolivar asserted their right to self-government against Spain; few of them extended the principle to the peons on their estates. In India, for most of the time, throughout the nineteenth century, most Indians were in the first stage; they acquiesced in British rule, and indeed many actively co-operated with it. This is shown by the numbers involved, which were not one to twelve (as in the case of the Tutsi and the Hutu) but more like one to three thousand. The first resolutions of the Indian National Congress are astonishing in their moderation. The tranquillity of stagnation was strong and there seemed no prospect of change. But slowly the yeast began to work; there is no escaping the dialectic of imperialism. The imperialist cannot keep for ever the secrets that have given him his mastery; once he imparts them, he is like a witch in a fairy-tale whose magic wand has been stolen by the impudent little hero.

We have spoken already of the willingness with which the Hutu accepted Tutsi domination and have touched on some of its ingredients —a sense of permanence, the satisfaction to many people of dependence without the need to make decisions, the myth of Tutsi superiority, the difficulty of rebellion but some possibility of rising in the scale in relation to other Hutu. Something very similar is widespread in colonial history; after an initial struggle which is startlingly short, new rulers are often accepted almost as a matter of course. This was partly because the societies of Europe, which, from the Renaissance onwards, were individualist and in process of rapid change, came into contact with societies much less individualist, much more static in social

structure, and usually based on more rigid stratification. If the conquered society was already based, as it usually was, like Ruanda, on
the premise of inequality, it was easy to exchange one set of masters for
another. And, in such cases, the habit of dependence was often so
deeply ingrained in the personality that it would easily be transferred
from one set of institutions to another. The biographies of missionaries,
explorers, hunters, and officers in the nineteenth century are full of
stories of the fidelity of servants, guides, soldiers, who had transferred
to new leaders the total allegiance they had previously given to
ancestors, feudal superiors, or tribal elders. And it is really only in the
light of this habit of dependence that it is possible to explain Pizarro's
conquest of Peru, or the kind of relationships so quickly established by
the British in India and described, in so easy and vivid a style and in
such convincing detail, by men like Sleeman and Meadows Taylor in
the first half of the nineteenth century.

But this acceptance cannot last for ever. The conquerors, as we have
seen, are forced by the situation in which they find themselves to pass
on some of their skills to the conquered, whose help they need, and in
doing this some of their own magic is rubbed off onto the conquered.
Indeed, even without any formal teaching, the mere presence of the
conqueror brings the infection of individualism, of a jealous concern
about time, of competition, of dissatisfaction with self and environment.
Nothing is the same again after he comes. And sooner or later, his
concept of a relationship based on a contract, limited to specific
functions, which can occur only between people basically equal before
the law, is bound to clash with that other concept of total allegiance in
return for total protection. Bitter resentment will follow when the
conqueror insists on a right to a life of his own and withdraws from his
role of total overlordship.

. There are servants, soldiers, the untaught, who rebel when they are
denied the comfort of dependence. But there are also those who have
learned something of scientific ideas of causation, of social competitiveness, ultimately of freedom, and who see with dramatic vividness the
imperial dilemma, which perhaps the imperialists have not yet themselves perceived. They, the leaders of the colonial people, eventually
apply the lessons they have learnt to themselves and demand self-rule
or independence. And of course there is no clear division; it would not be
sensible to suppose that everyone would fall neatly into one or the
other of two categories—educated and wanting independence on the
one hand, or on the other uneducated and pining for a dependent,
feudal relationship. The need for a dependent relationship is usually
unconscious and there are few in whom it does not sometimes well up;
the desire for independence from foreigners who are felt to be cold,
aloof, and uninterested, if not actively cruel, whose overlordship is a
humiliation, is strong even among those whose own psychological need

is to be vassals—but to a lord who understands their needs. There is continual interplay between the two needs, one conscious and the other unconscious; accordingly, in individuals there is ambivalence and inconsistency.

But the broad direction of change is constant. Even the most illiberal of conquerors needs labour, and the concentration of labour for any large-scale enterprise is in the long run likely to be a breeding-ground where ideas of change will grow. It has been argued that, in the short term, industry will not produce a change in race relations, because management will prefer to conform to existing social patterns rather than risk trouble by offending those in political power.[1] This is true in an immediate sense, but in the long term, labour increasingly needs skill, which has to be learnt; labourers cannot be insulated for ever from the ideas and standards of their employers and unless they can be persuaded that there is some divine sanction for their different status, they are bound in the long run to make comparisons. The circles within which they compare themselves will grow wider. And the process is more rapid among the educated, particularly if the ruling group profess liberal and democratic views and are embarrassed by claims that they would make themselves if positions were reversed.

Not only concentrations of labour but a host of other factors have widened the fields in which comparison is made. There is no need to enumerate them: newspapers, radio, the petrol engine, travel by air; movements of troops and population in two world wars; the rapid and cumulative effect of decolonization—all these have spread the radical ideas which in Europe had been fermenting for the previous two centuries. But far more quickly than in Europe, disillusion followed hope. Freedom has not meant food; the vote has not meant the esteem of one's fellows. And esteem is almost as high as food on man's list of needs.

The nineteenth century in Europe meant the progressive realization that freedom has many dimensions, and that as soon as progress is made in one, its hollowness is perceived until the others have been achieved as well. There is first a legal dimension, concerned with the rule of law without respect to persons; second, a political, concerned with means of controlling those who make the laws; the third is economic, and at this stage some means is provided of ensuring that men get a fair return for their labour; fourth, and most difficult of all, is the social dimension, and here the hope is for some minimum of mutual respect, and some opportunity for a man to realize the maximum of which he is capable and to win esteem for doing it. These four dimensions of freedom have only to be stated for it to be apparent that very various emphases have been placed on them by different societies and that a wholly just society, in which freedom is achieved in all these dimensions, has nowhere been reached.

[1] Guy Hunter et al., *Industrialisation and Race Relations*.

To the idea of a just society, we shall return. For the present argument, what is important is that even in England—the example for so long of gradual non-revolutionary change—disillusion has usually followed each step forward. Formal equality before the law is an ancient British tradition; since 1688, some say in choosing the government has been assured, at first to a very small group but one that has widened steadily. But in spite of the repeal of the Combination Acts and the Corn Laws, in spite of Factory Acts, Trade Unions, successive education acts, health insurance, and old-age pensions, no one can say that in the economic and social dimensions equal progress has been made. In the former colonial countries disillusion has been far more vivid and bitter. It was easy to suppose that independence would solve everything; it was a bitter blow to find that it did not. In fact, independence from colonial rule was only a first step towards the first dimension of freedom, the political, and very often it proved in practice to be a step back.

# CHAPTER III

# The Bitterness of Betrayal

## 1 Rejection, Doubt, Betrayal

Once again, we need to turn back in the story. We have looked in outline—the barest outline—at the revolt in Europe against what was felt to be injustice; we have seen successive attempts to peel away aspects or dimensions of injustice and inequality and hierarchical organization. The enemy was very seldom clearly defined by those who fought it. But one thing is clear, that the end has not been reached, even in Europe; at each stage, it has been found that another layer remained. Outside Europe the process began much later; in the colonial territories hopes were focused with sharp precision on a single aim—independence. At the moment when this was attained, there was often a gush of goodwill towards the former colonial power but it could hardly last. The very sharpness of the focus on this one goal was one reason for the disillusion that followed; another was simply that so much remained to be done. But the process of decolonization and the mood that followed independence have a special quality of bitterness, which is due to the nature of the old relationship and in particular to ideas about race. Neither the revolt against inequality in Europe, nor the colonial struggle for independence, nor the Civil Rights question in the United States, can be isolated from each other. But it is the special bitterness of the last two that I now want to discuss.

The subject of this book is the development of relationships which depend on a whole complex of causes, most of them quite irrational. Some forms of behaviour, it is true, are based on conscious calculation of economic interest, but even these are often felt more deeply as slights or humiliations than as physical losses. It is the element of *feeling* and *emotion* that is here stressed because it is apt to be left out of calculations in the study. To some of the deeper causes we shall return in a later chapter; at this stage, it will be necessary to state briefly, as hypotheses, the substance of what is there argued at greater length.

I have already suggested that the success of European peoples in establishing dominance over a great part of the world was largely due to a different social structure, a different view of man's relation to his

environment, and a different set of values. It is a vague and unsatisfactory expression, but let us for the moment call this 'Western culture'.
The second and third parts of the book will consist of an examination
of some of the very varied systems that were established as a result of
people of this culture meeting other peoples. One point that emerges is
the widespread symbolism of colour; in the ancient world of Greece
and Rome, in the three linked religions of Judaism, Christianity, and
Islam, as well as in Hinduism and in much of Africa, there is an
association of moral qualities with light and brightness, while passions
that are deplored and disliked are linked with darkness. This meta-
phorical use of language, with its strong moral content, has been
confused with the biological fact of skin colour, which, however
relevant at earlier stages of evolution, is of little significance in modern
life. The confusion is not recent; it has affected the relationship from
an early stage. It is not rational, but that does not make it less deadly,
and both parties have been affected by the consciousness of it.

It has been argued that feeling of this kind is a by-product of
imperialism and slavery. But this does not fit the facts and it ignores an
important distinction. The feeling is older than colonialism and the
association with slavery; but at an early stage it did not express itself
in the form of institutions. It had not become rigid; there was no
established pattern of behaviour as in South Africa and the Deep
South. But the feeling was there and it influenced behaviour. Let me
illustrate the point—not to go further afield or further back in time—
from Shakespeare's Britain. The early play *Titus Andronicus* depicts an
utterly villainous Moor with no redeeming quality. He is said to be
black and to have woolly hair and I do not doubt that he was thought
of as a Negro. It is not a very good play and there is no light and
shade—in our language this metaphor is inevitable—no subtlety in the
character. But *Othello*, one of the world's great plays, is very different.

Othello himself is a noble character, 'the noblest man of man's
making', Swinburne declared, but he is the object of prejudice;
Desdemona's father is horrified at her marrying a Moor, and Iago
expects this and plays on it. Other points in the play turn on prejudice;
one motive for Iago's malignancy is Othello's colour, but, above all—
and this is essential to the play—Iago's success in wakening his
jealousy turns on Othello's *own* recognition of prejudice. He has an
uneasy awareness that everyone thinks it odd that Desdemona should
have chosen him; it is easy to arouse a horrible suspicion that there was
something unnatural about it and that she is likely to turn to one of
her fellow countrymen. And the passion, the impetuosity, that are part
of Othello's nobility and are also his undoing are exaggerations of
what a white audience expects of 'a coloured man'.

By 1604 then, two years before Virginia was founded, there was
feeling about colour in Britain but it was not expressed in institutions

of a general kind, such as a ban on marriage between races. There was no need. There was, all the same, an order in the last year of Queen Elizabeth's reign, commanding certain 'blackamoors' to be transported out of the country. Now there was no Empire at this time; the Marxist idea that colour prejudice was developed to justify the export of capital and exploitation of subject peoples really will not do. Nor was this the reaction to a threat; the Moors had been expelled from Spain a hundred years earlier and the danger to Britain for at least sixty years had been Spain. The theory that colour prejudice began with the fact of Empire therefore does not fit the dates.[1] Nor was it a product of slavery; *Othello* was first acted sixty years before the African slave trade was an important feature of British life. In the seventeenth century, many white people were sent overseas as 'indentured servants' or practically slaves, while some were captives to the Moors in the Mediterranean.

It would interrupt the argument to mass evidence that colour prejudice is older than European imperialism. But let me call four witnesses to make one point in support of this. In the fourth century A.D., one of the desert ascetics from Alexandria records his temptation by the devil who appeared to him in the form of a Negro; St. Teresa of Avila on successfully resisting temptation saw a small Negro boy chattering with rage at his frustration; James I and VI of England and Scotland in his *Demonologie* tells us that witches' covens habitually met under the presidency of a black man, who was the Devil in person; in the eighth century, Bede argued that the Ethiopian baptized by Philip (as recounted in the Acts of the Apostles) must have turned white on his conversion.

Prejudice about colour in a form not yet moulded into institutions, then, is older, in North-Western Europe at least, than associations with slavery or colonialism. But in the nineteenth century these new associations came to reinforce the older feeling, which was based—I suggest—largely on the symbolism and metaphor of colour. At the same time, a personal need widely felt throughout Northern Europe fused with a national need for justification that was general among the imperial powers. The general or national need has already been outlined. It arose from the difficulty of justifying their rule over colonies by France and England, which professed to be democratic, and also by countries which, without attaching much importance to democracy, were passionately nationalist and would have resisted to the death any attempt by a foreign country to establish a similar overlordship over themselves. As we have said, the *official* justification was paternalist or assimilationist; 'they'—the natives—were wards under guardianship and would one day grow up. But comparatively few people really believed this and let it influence their behaviour. The dilemma of the

[1] All this I have argued at greater length in *Prospero's Magic*.

imperialist democracy was much more happily solved if 'the native' was permanently and genetically inferior. Thus there was a national need for a racialist doctrine and in fact the mid-nineteenth century was the flowering period for theories of this kind.

It is not my purpose here to analyse the beliefs of the nineteenth-century writers about race; they have recently been admirably described by Professor Michael Banton[1] and before that by Professor Jacques Barzun.[2] But their influence was immense and is still wide-spread among people who have never heard the names of those who propagated them. For long, speculation was hampered by a time-scale based on 4004 B.C. as the date of Man's creation, derived from the genealogies in the Bible. Many absurdities were solemnly announced. There was a Principal of Yale University who believed that the complexion of American Indians was due to the secretion of bile, which was excessive because they lived near rivers and in undrained forests and inhaled noxious gases from decaying vegetation. It was widely taken as dogma that there was a Great Chain of Being, in which there could be no gaps; this was a speculation of the Neo-Platonists taken over by St. Augustine and mediaeval theologians. It was now revived in a new form and it was argued that there must be humans who formed a continuum with the primates and 'an orang-outang husband would be no disgrace to a Hottentot female'.

Absurdities apart, there was much writing in the first half of the century which tried to find scientific reasons for the different stages of development which man had reached; some writers were influenced by a desire, not always subconscious, to justify slavery; I can think of none who had any doubt of Western superiority at the time when he wrote. But for our purpose the most important developments were in the second half of the century and they fall into two groups. De Gobineau and his followers, looking at the manifestly different achievements of mankind in different periods of history, attributed success to the 'pure blood' of a master race and failure to the degeneracy which followed racial mixture. This kind of thought was buttressed by 'Social Darwinism', of which derivative forms were very widespread.

The Social Darwinists started from the position that the evolution of animals and man from much simpler forms had taken place by natural selection, which meant that those least fit for survival were destroyed. Surely, then, it was natural—and *right* because it followed the pattern of nature—for a stronger group of men to dispossess, exploit, and indeed destroy, one less fit to survive. So ran the argument. It seemed manifest that evolution had culminated in the people of North-Western Europe and North America, who dominated the world and, in their own eyes, surpassed all others in skill, intelligence,

[1] Michael Banton, *Race Relations*.
[2] Jacques Barzun, *Race: A Study in Superstition*.

beauty, and moral standards. The highest product of the evolutionary process had a duty to rule 'the lesser breeds without the law', to 'take up the White Man's burden' and, without thanks or payment, keep the peace and educate and instruct the lesser breeds until they were more like 'the hereditary nobility of mankind'. There was a choice between 'liberty, inequality, survival of the fittest' on one hand and on the other 'not-liberty, equality, and the survival of the unfittest', wrote one American writer,[1] who clearly included in his concept of 'liberty' the maintenance of considerable privilege for his own class. There were writers of this school who advocated compulsory sterilization of the unfit and rewards for breeding children by those judged 'most fit'.

Thus the national need for some justification for colonial rule produced writing very foreign to the temper of to-day, writing which sought to intensify social distance and to justify social arrangements based on inequality. The substance of such writings reached many who had never read a word of them and unfortunately it was the everyday assumptions of the humbler representatives of 'Western culture'—often embodying such teaching—which 'the native' was made to feel. These doctrines were popular because they were admirably suited to meet a private need as well as the national. 'Western culture' had encouraged a sense of internal conflict, a profound unhappiness, in its children, for whom one way of escape was to be convinced that they were 'better' than others, whom they had a duty to rule and improve.

Again, it is necessary to summarize briefly matters that need discussion at greater length but are an essential part of the argument. The changes which took place in the environment, social structure, and habits of thought of most people in Western Europe and America during the nineteenth century were profound. They were the culmination of movements that had begun much earlier—the Renaissance, the Reformation, the Industrial Revolution, the Agricultural Revolution. We give names to these movements of thought and sections of history but they are all part of the change from static cultures based on life restricted to a small community to life in much larger groupings, in a culture much more individualist, open, and mobile. These changes had given people from Europe a great advantage in dealing with the more rigid and less individualist societies they met elsewhere. Their outstanding advantage in the nineteenth century was an air of self-confidence, and in general they had little doubt that what they brought with them was better than what they found. This was particularly so in Africa, where missionaries as a rule believed African customs to be bad and tried to teach European. But behind the confidence of missionary and explorer was a growing doubt and unease. There was of course a time-lag; thoughts widely expressed among the educated in England would often not reach the missionary in Africa for many

[1] William Graham Sumner, quoted in Michael Banton, *Race Relations*.

years and even within England they would take time to seep down to the less sophisticated. But the uncertainty was at the heart of the century.

One of the most sensitive and musical of Victorian poets, who died a dozen years before the end of the century, wrote of himself and his contemporaries:

> Vague half-believers of our casual creeds
> Who never deeply felt, nor clearly will'd
> Whose insight never has borne fruit in deeds
> Whose weak resolves never have been fulfill'd;
> For whom each year we see
> Breeds new beginnings, disappointments new;
> Who hesitate and falter life away. . . .

He was the son of Arnold of Rugby, one of the great moulders of the Victorian Age. Surely his uncertainty and loss of faith had something to do with the rootlessness of the new urban populations and the beginning of a general loss of any clearness about the purpose of life?

I have suggested that at a much earlier stage in history there had been a marriage of convenience between on the one hand man's awe in the presence of the forces of nature, of infinity and eternity, and on the other a wide variety of far more mundane matters, tabus on incest and on certain kinds of food, provisions about days of rest and the precedence to be given to kings and priests, elders, and parents, the whole structure of society and the family. These had been married off to the sense of the numinous to give them respectability. One of the tensions which began to tear the Victorians was that this marriage was breaking up; the fashion was still conformity but there was doubt not only about the non-essentials, not only about the formulation of dogma, but about the most fundamental assumptions.[1] Intellectual doubt among the educated was often matched among the urban workers by an indifference to Christianity and a complete lack of anything to replace it; they had long forgotten the remnants of animistic religion which still lingered on in the countryside and many were now without any formulated view of life or conception of its purpose:

> The Lars and Lemurs moan with midnight plaint,
> In Urns and Altars round
> A drear, and dying sound
> Affrights the Flamens at their service quaint;
> And the chill Marble seems to sweat
> As each peculiar power forgoes his wonted seat.

[1] If anyone questions the prevalence of this tension among the Victorians, I suggest he looks at *Bishop Blougram's Apology*:

> But, I, the man of sense and learning too,
> The able to think yet act, the this, the that,
> I, to believe, at this late time of day!

Yet Browning's popular stereotype is of the robust and unvarying optimist.

But the dismay of forsaken deities was nothing to the emptiness in the hearts of men.

It is my suggestion—which no doubt will seem far-fetched to many— that the doubt of the intellectuals and the rootlessness, the spiritual vacuum, of the masses—lost in the new liberty of individualism, in the sheer numbers of the great cities—were ingredients in the burst of aggressive imperialism with which the century closed. For it was in the years from about 1880 to 1914 that imperialism became a creed— shrill, brassy, arrogant. Psychological research has generally con- firmed the hypothesis that racial intolerance is often a sign of insecurity; a man who (in an individualist Western society) believes he has failed in life, one who is emotionally insecure, one who has risen or fallen sharply in the social scale, is the man who takes comfort in the thought that at least he belongs to a dominant group. And perhaps a similar insecurity lay behind the shrillness of that brief imperial heyday.

This may be disputed but it can hardly be questioned that beneath the mood of the late Victorians lay the personal need to justify their supremacy. There is a story of Cecil Rhodes waking a friend in a tent one night to ask him if he had ever thought how lucky he was to be an Englishman. It was necessary to assume that one was quite different from the rest of the world if one was to rule it—and quirks of doubt at heart made it necessary to state the assumption more and more loudly. Every sign of outward success was there; all over the world the flag waved, and Englishmen had to take up the White Man's Burden:

> To wait in heavy harness
> On fluttered folk and wild—
> Your new caught sullen peoples
> Half-devil and half-child.

It was all for their benefit; it was necessary:

> To seek another's profit
> And work another's gain.

And they would not be grateful; they would bitterly resent all that was done for them. The logic of national need and the personal need for a quiet conscience alike pointed to a paternalism based on a contemp- tuous, often outwardly jocular, belief that for a long time to come the 'native' would need to be looked after. The relationship with a son or ward is seldom easy; it is even less likely to be harmonious if the parent is self-appointed and regards his ward as 'half-devil and half-child'.

The doubt at the heart of the Victorian period came nearer the surface as the twentieth century began and by the middle of this century, self-confidence was manifestly lost. Few any longer believed that Europe had a way of life, a recipe for living, which could be recommended to the rest of the world. For some in Britain the loss of empire bred an angry resentment; it was strongest in those who had comforted themselves for lack of success in the things they most esteemed by the thought that they were white, that they were British. These formed the extremist political groups who have appeared and splintered and formed again in Britain sporadically since the end of the Second World War. They were the extreme cases, but surely there were many others in whom a soreness at loss of prestige and power combined with a wondering resentment at lack of 'gratitude for all we have done for them'. And surely this is also a strong feeling in the United States, where colonialism was so much detested, where so much aid has been poured out, and where there is so strong a desire to be loved.

This is a sketch of the white side. Let us turn now to the non-white. We have already suggested the more superficial reactions which are to be expected. It is only with an exceptionally wise, loving, and forbearing father that a filial relationship is likely to proceed smoothly and we have seen enough to know that this father, apart from being self-appointed and uneasy about his role, was concerned to justify his authority by emphasizing the dependence of the ward and his unfitness to look after himself. To the ward, the 'benefits' of alien rule were not always so apparent as the disadvantages, quite apart from the fact that no one likes to feel that he ought to be grateful, even for benefits which he recognizes. But the implications of all that had been written had soaked down so deep, the assumption of superiority was so widespread, it was so often expressed in insulting and humiliating language, that one does not have far to look to find reason for resentment on the most direct and superficial level. It must be emphasized again that what often penetrated to the Asian or African was—in the most simple and brutal terms—a confused belief that he was *permanently* inferior, that the colour of his skin showed him to be lower in the chain of evolution, inferior in morals as well as intelligence. And this message was often conveyed by those who to him did not seem particularly good examples of either high morals or artistic achievement. There was, however, something deeper, a double betrayal.

Consider the case of the African, educated perhaps at a mission school. He is a clever boy and his masters praise him. They are not crude racists who think he cannot compete with a white man. But they cannot avoid a subtler form of patronage. He has to face one difficult examination after another; they see that he is uniformly successful. But behind all that they teach him, behind all his efforts to learn, there is an unspoken assumption on both sides that 'Western culture' not only has something infinitely precious which his own has not, but that he can acquire it and that, once he has, he will be accepted as one of those born into it. But when he has passed every test, he finds that he was doubly deceived. He goes to Britain, let us say; he gets his degree, he eats his dinners at Gray's Inn or the Temple, he is called to the Bar. Yet when he goes back to his own country, as late as the 1950s, he would often find that he must live in a segregated quarter, away from his white colleagues, that he cannot join their club, nor take part as an equal in their leisure. These exclusions often coincided with the shattering discovery that his mentors no longer had any faith in what they had taught him.

This is a matter in which—from one angle—there is all the difference in the world between the Negro American, the African, and the Asian from former colonial territory, but in all three cases there has, for a man educated to university level, been some degree of commitment to a culture which he does not feel to be his own. And for each the shock of the discovery that 'they' do not believe in what they have been teaching is like the shock felt by a son who finds his father in a brothel. For the Negro American, there is a special poignancy. He is an American; as has often been said, perhaps the most American of all Americans, because forcibly removed from his own background so long ago. Most of his people at the time of emancipation belonged to a specifically American sub-culture of slavery and poverty; he cannot return to that nor draw on it for anything of value—except such basic virtues as courage, humour, endurance; he has taken a hard road and learnt what seemed to be the means to success, only to find that he is still not an equal and that the people who reject him do not believe in what has seemed to set them apart.

That is why Negro intellectuals write as they do. That is why, for instance, James Baldwin wrote:

And there is, I should think, no Negro living in America who has not felt, briefly or for long periods, with anguish sharp or dull, in varying degrees and to varying effect, simple, naked and unanswerable hatred; who has not wanted to smash any white face he may encounter in a day, to violate, out of motives of the cruellest vengeance, their women, to break the bodies of all white people and bring them low, as low as that dust into which he has been and is being trampled.[1]

That is why Frantz Fanon wrote:

But every time Western values are mentioned they produce in the native a sort of stiffening or muscular lock-jaw. During the period of decolonisation, the native's reason is appealed to. He is offered definite values, he is told too frequently that decolonisation need not mean regression, and that he must put his trust in qualities which are well-tried, solid and highly esteemed. But it so happens that when the native hears a speech about Western culture he pulls out his knife—or at least he makes sure it is within reach. The violence with which the supremacy of white values is affirmed and the aggressiveness which has permeated the victory of these values over the ways of life and of thought of the native mean that, in revenge, the native laughs in mockery when Western values are mentioned in front of him. In the colonial context the

[1] James Baldwin, *Notes of a Native Son*.

settler only ends his work of breaking in the native when the latter admits loudly and intelligibly the supremacy of the white man's values. In the period of decolonisation, the colonised masses mock at these very values, insult them and vomit them up.[1]

That is as much a mood as the quotation from James Baldwin and, violently though it was felt at the moment it was written, it was—one may be fairly confident—not a mood in which Fanon would have persisted every moment of every day. Perhaps it is so violent because he knows he cannot do without what he wants to vomit up. In the next section of this chapter, let us look at some forms of ambivalence towards Western values—often an outspoken rejection while at the same time some special aspects are not merely retained but heavily emphasized. Common to all is the feeling of having been led by deception along a path which has ended in betrayal and rejection; all alike seek some new path which owes as little as possible to 'Western values'.

## 2  The Search for a Pedigree

It is the thesis of the second section of this chapter that there is something in common between a number of different happenings and movements at different times in different parts of the world and that what they have in common has one explanation. I want to point out similarities between many, if not most, of the colonial risings, revolts, and rebellions of the nineteenth century, and the sectarian movements and cults of the poor and neglected all over the world. Next I want to suggest that both have something in common with intellectual movements of our own day and with nationalism in the former colonial nations. Finally, I suggest that all these movements together with what is often called the search for identity—but which I prefer to call the search for a pedigree—constitute an attempt to deal with a real dilemma, and that the attempt takes a number of forms, of which one is despair and very often destruction.

Consider first the physical rebellions of colonial times. These were among peoples who had become subject largely because they took a different view from their conquerors of society and particularly of causation; it is not surprising, therefore, at the most everyday level, that they should rely on magic to help them in a rebellion. But it is surprising to find from all over the world that the same kind of magic is so often expected. For example, in what used to be called the Indian Mutiny, in the Maji-Maji rebellion against the Germans in Tanganyika, in the Hau Hau rebellion in New Zealand, in the Matabele and Mashona rebellions in Rhodesia, in Burma and the Transkei, in

[1] Frantz Fanon, *The Wretched of the Earth.*

Madagascar and Kenya, there are tales of an almost identical belief; on a certain day, or if a certain amulet is worn, or if some prophet's instructions are followed, the white man's bullets will turn to water. Mannoni provides a Freudian explanation for this, suggesting that the white man is identified with the father, the gun with the penis, and the water instead of bullets with sexual impotence. Some will find this more convincing than others will, but the point I wish to stress is the belief that it is by magic that colonial rule is established—something in the realm of 'spirit', 'mana', supernatural force—and that only by magic can it be overcome.

Even more significant and widespread in such movements is the combination of old and new. It is necessary here to recognize that the leader of such a rising is likely to understand very clearly the need for secrecy beforehand and complete commitment when the crisis arrives. If he held a high position in the old hierarchy, he may use the traditional symbols of authority as something to swear by, something that will exact vengeance for disloyalty. But it may well be that the prestige of these symbols has been somewhat tarnished by the conquest that preceded the rising. Again, he may himself be an upstart in the traditional system. In either of these cases, he may insist on his followers binding themselves by acts which cut them off from the old tradition or even which damn them completely in the eyes of those who have not joined the movement. The obscenities of Mau Mau oaths in Kenya were surely of this kind; they put men outside the traditional religious system of the Kikuyu. Secret societies from within 'Western culture'—I add in parenthesis—have sometimes felt the same need before some desperate crime. It may serve the same need if a tabu is broken; in one case reported, the women were told the secrets of the male initiation ceremonies. Thus a break is made with the past and this helps the leader because there is no turning back; everyone who has done such things is now knitted together into a new society.

Every leader of revolt needs unity, secrecy, and commitment. Some need a break with tradition for personal reasons; all, in some degree and to some extent, need also help from tradition but perhaps few— if they were fully conscious of their hopes and able to express them— would not want to add some improvements to the past. There is then a deeper significance than the merely tactical about the breach of tabu; what is taking place is a protest against a total situation in which two social systems are at variance. It is a protest against both, against the traditional society as well as the new ways of the conquerors. The rebels have seen something new and attractive—but it is withheld from them —and they can no longer be content with the past.

It is my suggestion that this quality of protest against old and new alike should be looked for—and will usually be found—not only in colonial risings but in millenarian cults all over the world, and that it is

matched by the ambivalence in the betrayed intellectual. In all these
cases there is a feeling of betrayal and anger against a human group,
usually a dominant group of another race, which arises from the
difficulty, if not the impossibility, of living in two cultures at the same
time. There are moods in which both are rejected, others in which both
are admired; attempts are made to select from each—but then anger
against the dominant group supervenes and their culture is loudly
rejected, even though much of it is still secretly admired.

It will make the point clearer if we look at a group of primitive
millenarian cults and at some similar modern movements in the
United States and the Caribbean. 'Cargo cults' have been widely
reported from the islands of the Pacific. The identifying mark of a
cargo cult is that its adherents expect wealth to come to them suddenly
from overseas in a ship or an aeroplane in the form of Western goods—
bicycles, cameras, radio sets, and indeed whatever they want. It is a
simplified magical escape from a situation with which there seems no
rational way of dealing. There are wants but no way to satisfy them,
no clearly seen way of improving conditions, and indeed there are often
specific obstacles to any improvement. Then the people of an island or
a village or a group of villages bind themselves together to adopt
means of solving the problem which are basically magical and in which
a fantasy is expected to come true.[1] The cults take many different forms;
most are in some degree hostile to Europeans—though it is European
goods that are wanted—some fall back on the traditions of the group's
own past, though often with some modification or rejection of some
aspects; others borrow from another culture; some are militant, some
emotional, some practise a quiet withdrawn ritual. But all appear to
share the quality of expecting some *total* solution, something that will
solve *all* problems, and all are protests against a situation intolerable
at the moment. Most seek for unity under one leader and emphasize
it by a flag, a badge, a uniform, and some have initiation ceremonies
which are meant to ensure that commitment is total, a break with the
past as well as the future. Sometimes the act of commitment is sacrificial; in some cargo cults the devotees throw away their money—their
only means of getting the goods they want. But the money is not enough,
so they demonstrate their faith in their fantasy by throwing it away.
There is an example of this sacrificial commitment in a well-known
episode in South African history, when many sections of the Xhosa
killed all their cattle on the day when their prophetess had announced
that a new age was to begin.[2]

Surely there is much in common here not only with such events as

[1] See Raymond Firth, 'The Theory of Cargo Cults'.
[2] See, for example, Raymond Firth, 'The Theory of Cargo Cults'; Peter Worsley,
'Millenarian Cults in Melanesia'; and Marian W. Smith, 'Towards a Classification of
Cult Movements'.

the Mlimo's rising in Matabeleland but also with modern movements such as the Ras Tafaris in Jamaica and the far more sophisticated Black Jews of Harlem in New York. The Ras Tafaris, like many American Negroes, are combining in one movement their protest at two predicaments: that of the ex-slave who was unprepared for freedom and who in a colour-conscious society cannot extricate himself from poverty and ignorance, and that of the rural labourer forced to come to the town because he has neither land nor capital and cannot find employment. They profess to believe that they come from Ethiopia and will one day go back; they search the Scriptures for words of divine comfort and find (in Jeremiah 8 : 21)[1] that God is black and that Negro women have been abused by white men; that Esau, who was rejected in favour of Jacob, was red and hairy and therefore the first white man—and much more of the same kind. They find authority for smoking hemp in the Book of Psalms and this is one line of escape from a situation in which they see no hope; a second is to turn their backs on a world which does not esteem them, to turn the tables on it by professing to despise it; a third is the fantasy of eventual return to Ethiopia. Like the people of the cargo cults, they see no practical means of satisfying their wants except by fantasy.

The Black Jews of Harlem also find Biblical authority for their belief that they represent part of the lost ten tribes of Israel, that they migrated to Ethiopia, were there captured and then enslaved in America, and that only now have they discovered their true past, their true identity. When described by Howard Brotz,[2] they were setting up synagogues and learning Hebrew in order to mark their new identity and their rejection alike of their own past and of white Anglo-Saxon culture. The Black Muslims, whose official name is, significantly, the Lost-Found Nation of Islam, have much in common. Their derivation from the Moorish Science Temple of America, and their resemblances with some of the black fraternities of the South have been described fully and need not delay us; but there is much about them that is important as a symptom of a far more widespread psychological unease.[3]

First, there is their insistence that they have been lost and are found: the prophet of the Moorish Science Temple gave each of his followers a personal identity card, while the first prophet of the Lost-Found Nation insists that each Muslim must be born again. Everything he had

[1] In the King James or Authorized Version of the Bible, Jeremiah 8 : 21 reads: 'For the hurt of the daughter of my people am I hurt; I am black; astonishment hath taken hold on me.' This text is regarded as important by various Negro sects as well as the Ras Tafaris, but alas! their interpretation disappears in moden translations, which substitute 'I mourn' or 'I go in mourning', for 'I am black'. And even the Authorized Version gives reference to two occasions (in Joel and Nahum) where the same phrase is used and where it clearly indicates mourning.

[2] Howard Brotz, *The Black Jews of Harlem.*

[3] Eric Lincoln, *The Black Muslims in America,* and E. U. Essien-Udom, *Black Nationalism.*

was stolen by the white man—nationality, religion, name—and now he must start again with a new name revealed by Allah, with a new nationality, with a new religion. Once he is born again, the convert has to accept a high standard of personal puritanism; there must be no sexual irregularity, no smoking, no drinking, no gluttony; a member can be disciplined for being overweight. He must work hard and save money. There must be no cosmetics, personal display, conspicuous spending; a third of yearly income must be given to the cause. Muslims must 'buy black', that is refuse to trade with white people; they have been successful in establishing co-operative trading and saving societies. Above all, they must never mix with white people sexually.

There are thus three essential strands in their beliefs: a rejection of the white picture of the typical Negro as lustful, lazy, improvident, flashy; a rejection and distrust of white good intentions; the search for an identity, an intellectual and moral pedigree of their own. All these points are emphasized over and over again; if the white man had really wanted to be just, they argue, he could have done so any time these last three hundred years. He only begins to talk of integration 'when his empires crumble' and he begins to be afraid. But even now what he means by integration is integration at the bottom. As for Christianity, it is hypocrisy; it was this that lynched Negro men and raped Negro women.

Here is much that we have met before. Note the emphatic rejection of *two* cultures; there is a formal rejection of the whole white culture although many of its values are retained and in fact given a new and exaggerated emphasis; at the same time, there is rejection of all those elements of the old ex-slave culture which the legends of the white South had stressed. The movement is much more sophisticated than the cargo cults or the Ras Tafari group; there is a strong emphasis on 'this world' and on economic success by hard work and economy. But it is trying to deal with the same problem and it does not wholly reject fantasy.

It has never seemed likely that this movement would spread very far; it is psychologically satisfying because it enables its adherents to look down on the corrupt and luxurious society which has rejected them, but it demands sacrifices that only a devoted few are likely to make. At the same time, there are elements in the doctrine which rational men will reject, such as that all non-white people are linked by blood and that all are Muslims without knowing it. But many other sects share many of its elements. Eric Lincoln mentions more than twenty bodies in New York City which have similarities. Pentecostal Sects among Jamaicans in Great Britain and among aborigines in Australia share the puritanism which aims at giving self-respect. And the three main strands of doctrine have been taken up by the Black Power movement. This again is a minority group, with aims which are seldom defined in terms which seem to have much political realism. But millions of Negroes who would never join these movements feel sympathy with the three main emotional elements—rejection of white goodwill, rejection of the role which white men have allotted to black, and the need for an intellectual and cultural pedigree. As to white goodwill, the predominant feeling is simply that it is not translated into action which the Negro can feel; the income gap grows bigger, the relative figures for unemployment get worse. White liberals are useless because they will not recognize that a radical reorganization of society is needed; besides, they make it more difficult to hate.

What a majority of Negroes still balk at is the tactic of separatism. How can this help them? It is magic, it is fantasy; it does not make even so much sense as in South Africa, this *apartheid* in reverse. You cannot disentangle a complicated industrial society. And yet the emotional need to reject whiteness is as strong as its reverse in South Africa. Even the best of white culture must be rejected. 'Black music only; no Bach, Beethoven, or Brahms', was the cry raised on the campus of a Negro university in the autumn of 1967. This is surely a reaction to the same emotions as: 'Burn, baby, burn,' the cry that went up in the riots of Watts and Newark.

The Asian, the Negro American, the African are all three in different degrees facing a similar dilemma. In India, it has been present since the end of the eighteenth century. Early in the nineteenth century a great Bengali, Raja Ram Mohan Roy, began to advocate a synthesis of the best in the classical Sanskrit tradition with elements in Christian thought and European scientific knowledge; it has been said[1] that his attitude to the West was one neither of surrender nor withdrawal nor of conflict, but of comprehension. He founded the Brahmo Samaj, a reforming religious society, which was dedicated to working out an eclectic religious philosophy on these lines. But as the century advanced, as tensions and rivalry between British and Indian increased, this happy development became less and less popular in India and the place of the Brahmo Samaj was taken by the Arya Samaj, whose far more militant purpose was to return to the primitive purity of the Vedic scriptures, freeing them from later accretions and foreign influence alike.

Muslims too in undivided India faced a similar problem; if they learnt the English language, English law, and something of Western history and Western thought, they were bound to find themselves at some point in conflict with the fundamentalist *maulvis* who would not go beyond the Qur'an. Indeed, it can be said that every Indian thinker and leader of importance for the last century and a half has in some degree had to struggle to keep the best of his ancient culture and yet profit by what the West had to teach. But this is a much less

[1] Percival Spear, in *Oxford History of India*, Volume 1.

harrowing experience than that of the African or the Negro intellectual. Indeed, for the Asian, one should perhaps abandon the metaphor of the search for a pedigree. He knows very well who are his father and mother, but he does not find it easy to combine their widely different traditions.

But African, Caribbean, and Negro American, all in varying ways, face the dilemma starkly. At one time, it seemed that their answer would be to glory in nihilism; one cannot write on this subject without quoting Aimé Césaire's famous lines:

> Eia pour ceux qui n'ont jamais rien inventé
> pour ceux qui n'ont jamais rien exploré
> pour ceux qui n'ont jamais rien dompté.[1]

That stage has passed; to-day there are new African and Caribbean states in which positive achievement is desperately needed. But the same impatience of the West which produced Césaire's nihilism has sometimes produced a narrow nationalism, sometimes an emphasis on a past which really has little connexion with the present. At its best, however, impatience has turned positive, to a real seeking for something growing on a recognizably African past and yet influenced and enlivened by Western experience.

There is D. K. Chisiza's well-known paper on the African outlook: 'We in Africa belong neither to the East nor to the West. . . . We excel neither in mysticism nor in science and technology but in the field of human relations.' And some of Chisiza's thought has been developed in writings about African socialism by the Heads of two States—Kenneth Kaunda of Zambia and Julius Nyerere of Tanzania—and by Tom Mboya in Kenya. There has been an attempt to analyse and re-state the main strands in Western philosophy as a prelude to constructing a specifically African philosophy with the somewhat daunting name of Consciencism; no doubt this will be the first of many. And there is a growing artistic achievement, poems and novels in French and English from Africa and the Caribbean. Frantz Fanon has expressed the new mood:

> The unconditional affirmation of African culture has succeeded the unconditional affirmation of European culture. On the whole, the poets of Negro-ism oppose the idea of an old Europe to a young Africa, tiresome reasoning to lyricism, oppressive logic to high-stepping nature, and on one side stiffness, ceremony, etiquette and scepticism, while on the other frankness, liveliness, liberty and—why not?—luxuriance; but also irresponsibility.

But it is not easy for the Negro American to share this lyricism. At one time almost every Negro American wanted only to be admitted to white society, white culture, as an equal, without consideration of

[1] Aimé Césaire, *Cahier d'un retour au pays natal.*

colour. To-day, as we have seen, disillusion has set in; he feels himself betrayed and rejected. There is no visible escape by political means; no rational man can seriously suppose that the United States, which fought the bloodiest civil war in history to preserve its unity, will hand over, as the Black Muslims sometimes pretend they hope, certain states to be a Negro homeland. Nor is escape by fantasy a course in which a reasonable man will persist; there was a time when Negro poets wrote with romantic nostalgia of an exotic African home, a land of golden fruit and brilliant flowers, beautiful black women and ancient kings; to-day, too many have been to Africa. The fantasy persists in obscure sects, but not for educated men. Nor is it really a solution to construct a bogus past.

It used to be said that the Negro, in relation to whites, had three paths to follow: acceptance, avoidance, and aggression. Most of the time he accepted white domination; there were times when he could avoid and forget; rarely was aggression a possibility. But to-day hardly one, even in the Deep South, can regard acceptance as anything but a temporary expedient; withdrawal becomes less and less a psychological possibility. The whole tone of world opinion, everything he reads in the newspapers or hears on the radio, is against it. He is involved in the affairs of the most powerful nation in the world; his son is drafted to fight in its war. He cannot feel accepted; he cannot avoid the situation and pretend it does not exist. He has no choice but aggression. And this takes two forms; there is obvious physical violence, the cry of 'Burn, baby, burn!'; 'it was time', writes Eldridge Cleaver, 'for the blacks . . . to riot, to sweep through the Harlem night like a wave of locusts, breaking, screaming, bleeding, laughing, crying, rejoicing, celebrating, in a jubilee of destruction. . . .'[1] But there is also the intellectual's equivalent, to pour out a riot of words, strong, emotive words—words from the streets that for centuries have been forbidden in white literature—proclaiming that black is beautiful, that black is strong, that white is cold, gray, and pitiful; pouring scorn on white folk who have forgotten their bodies and forgotten how to live; clamouring that in sex black is triumphant, that sex is more glorious than any cold pretence of chastity. The gospel of the black phallus is preached by one writer after another; how far it is defensive and how far aggressive does not matter. What is important is that it rejects traditional white ideals of conduct and the traditional ways of avoiding racial conflict. It proclaims separation or destruction. The modern Afro-American cannot in practice separate himself from a society which rejects him and whose rejection still afflicts him. He is left with no escape from the dilemma but despair and destruction. So he says: 'Burn, baby, burn.'

[1] Eldridge Cleaver, *Soul on Ice*.

### 3 A Summary of the Argument

That is really the conclusion of this chapter. But there remain some points to be underlined and a summary of the argument may be a help.

We have been talking about the reactions of groups, not individuals. We shall come back to some personal means of escape taken by individuals. Here it is necessary to underline one of the pessimistic conclusions that are inevitable in the study of race relations, or indeed of any relationship between a dominant and subordinate group who do not communicate easily with each other. There is a tendency in such relationships to be cumulative; as soon as one group forms a picture of the way the other is expected to behave, evidence will be found to strengthen it, partly because evidence that confirms the stereotype will be remembered and the other kind forgotten, and partly because people actually *will* behave as they are expected to behave. This cumulative downward spiral has been the fate of the American Negro ever since emancipation found him untrained for freedom. The latest developments, his despairing reaction to continued rejection, are likely to confirm the dominant group in their hostility.

There is a final point, arising from all that has been said in this chapter. We have looked at a widespread revolt against the dominance of one group over another; in particular we have seen widespread revolt against the dominance established by rich white nations over the rest of the world at the end of the nineteenth century. There is a special bitterness about this because of the confused association of dark skin colour with moral condemnation; this arises from the use of metaphor in all our languages. There is also a bitterness arising from the search for an intellectual pedigree and the lost, betrayed feeling of those who fall between two cultures. In the world to-day all this comes to a focus on two questions which serve as symbols for a vast reservoir of emotion. One is Southern Africa and in particular South Africa, where the principle of inequality and the privileges of a minority—everything at which this revolt is directed—seem to be enshrined. There are many other countries where something in some degree similar does in fact exist, but only in South Africa does the government openly oppose the principle of equality and legislate to keep people apart. Two facts feed the resentment felt about South Africa: first, that no conceivable combination of African powers can match South Africa in military strength; secondly, that South Africa's two best trading partners are Britain and the United States and that neither is prepared to forgo their trade. This confirms the sick anger, the sense of betrayal, which at one time or another every black African—like Baldwin's Negro—must have felt.

The second question is the position of the American Negro. In the non-white world, there is a conviction that it would be better to save money on Viet-Nam and the moon and spend it on re-educating and re-housing the Negro. But to the non-white world, South Africa, Rhodesia, Civil Rights and Viet-Nam, Cuba and Che Guevara are all part of one picture. The rest of this book will be spent in attempting to disentangle the separate parts of this picture and trying to suggest some way out of the impasse we have reached.

# PART II

## CONTACT AND CONQUEST: PROVISIONAL CLASSIFICATIONS

### CHAPTER IV

## Disentangling the Elements

*1 Race War or Peaceful Change*

The last chapter ended on a gloomy note. British and American white society is still complacent and has even now little comprehension of the immense emotional forces that are building up; I have therefore expressed starkly what I believe to be the predominant non-white mood. But I have been using a very wide-angled lens. Perhaps a closer look at the differences between one pattern of dominance and another will reveal more ground for optimism.

The broad lens used so far might well suggest that a race war on a world scale was inevitable. Indeed, that is just the thesis eloquently expounded by Ronald Segal in his book *The Race War*; he does in fact argue that it has already begun. That there is a world conflict of views, I do of course agree. But that is not war, which involves the use of force between sovereign powers. And a general war in this sense does not seem likely on any large scale in the immediate future, simply because of the immense preponderance of power on the rich or white side. This means that however bitter they may feel, the *governments* of the poorer countries will try to avoid war. And a general race war is certainly not in the interests of the richer powers.

The real danger is the spread of something that is already happening —a cold race war with hot points. There is widespread despair and anger at a society which is felt to be quite obviously unjust; in some small and comparatively poor country, a revolutionary party arises whose immediate objective is to overthrow the present system and whose ultimate object is not clearly defined, but which usually includes vaguely communist ideas. It is then a temptation, to the United States more than to any other power because of their nervous obsession with communism, to help the existing régime. Whatever the outcome, one effect of this is to sharpen racial antagonism. And this kind of situation is likely to spread. Wherever there is social injustice and poverty, there is a target for revolutionary infiltration and the temptation to intervene.

At the same time, there is a complex set of factors at work in the international field, which I must not here analyse in detail. One is the growing strength of world opinion and the growing, though limited, sensitivity of the larger powers to this opinion. At the same time, there is a marked inadequacy of international machinery in two respects. There is the obvious inadequacy of machinery to enforce decisions and —partly as a consequence of this, but it is also one of the causes—the failure of governments to act *responsibly* in international affairs, that is to say, as though their votes and speeches would be carried through into action. In matters which are of supreme importance for the continued existence of mankind, racial antagonism—the cold race war —constantly and uniformly operates in a way hostile to fruitful development.

Deeply disappointing though international action still is, one must not underestimate world opinion, nor the extent to which some of the great powers are sensitive to it; indeed, all are to some degree. Contrast the Suez crisis of 1956 with British action in Egypt in 1882, when Alexandria was bombarded by the Royal Navy, while Wolseley marched overland to defeat the Egyptian army at Tel-el-Kebir; the lesson to be drawn is not merely that Britain was relatively much weaker in 1956. That is true in relation to other large powers but it would still not have been difficult to gain a military victory over Egypt. The true lesson is surely that Britain was not prepared to defy world opinion, particularly if that included the United States. Again, put the abortive episode of the Bay of Pigs beside American intervention in Cuba in 1898 and subsequent action in Panama, Dominica, and Haiti. It is surely unlikely that President Theodore Roosevelt would have allowed anything like the Castro régime to become established in Cuba; his America—in contrast with the British example—was relatively much less strong than President Kennedy's but it did not have to concern itself with world opinion. Russia, it is true, has defied world opinion over Hungary and Czecho-Slovakia. This has been possible partly because there is no colour issue involved and because colour and colonialism are such strong emotional issues that they obscure other injustices.

This surely makes it the more important to analyse the racial factors in world opinion and their effect on the international situation, also to consider the nature of racial injustice in various societies. We are agreed that there is a real danger of increasingly sharp division of the world's nations into rich and white, poor and non-white. This affects the fruitful development of international co-operation of all kinds, not only on specifically political matters. It affects the working of technical agencies, the administration of aid, even the growth of international justice. The poorer nations have lost confidence in the International Court of Justice since their decision regarding South-West Africa. But it would surely make some difference to the starkness of the polarization if changes could be brought about in the internal affairs of the societies in which there is obvious racial injustice. To some non-white intellectuals, the international scene sometimes presents the appearance of one undifferentiated conspiracy to maintain a *status quo* which is immensely to the white advantage. But of course there are really many distinctions and differentiations within this landscape which looks so uniform, and it is worth looking at them to see what is worth saving.

I have already suggested that in some societies there may be a prospect of peaceful change while in others attitudes are so rigid, and tension has built up to such a pitch, that change cannot be expected without an explosion. And I have already pleaded a strong preference for peaceful change; it is easy to forget how recent, how fragile, and how hard to rebuild is the underlying social contract, the peaceful convention, by which a complex modern society is ordered—by which trains run without accident, newspapers and food are delivered, some observance of law is maintained, and men perform the varied functions society requires.

What we shall expect to find will be not exactly laws, certainly not laws as predictable in their results as the laws of physics or mechanics, but resemblances and regularities from which predictions can be made as to probable trends. We can draw up schemes into which most patterns of relationship will fit at some point or another. We shall be looking at patterns of dominance in general, whether there is a racial element in them or not, but with a special interest in the racial aspect if there is one. It will be as well therefore as a preliminary to define the sense in which we use the term 'race' and distinguish its biological from its social significance.

## 2 Race, Biology, Intelligence: Distinctions and Assumptions

Historically, the word 'race' has been used with the widest variety of meanings; poets in the eighteenth century wrote of 'the feathered race' and we still speak of 'the human race'. The Victorians often used it of what we should call nationality and even of family, and until quite recently in South Africa—where it is so important—'the race question' meant relations between Afrikaans-speakers and English-speakers; relations between white and black were 'the native question'. In this book I shall use the word to describe a category which has, or is thought to have, some biological significance. But the question in which we are interested is whether or not the category has any special significance. I shall use it to indicate the difference between Indian, African, and European in South and East Africa; between Bushman and Bantu-speaker, again in Southern Africa, but not between Ibo and Yoruba in Nigeria nor French and German in Europe. I shall inevitably use it in a slightly different sense in South America and the Caribbean and to a lesser extent North America; here there has been biological mixture and racial terms are used to put people into social categories which are determined on a number of different grounds such as wealth, education, and profession as well as appearance and descent. There is wide variation between one territory and another, and even between regions within one territory, and the balance between the social and biological aspects is delicate. I shall also suggest that in India 'race' is a factor in the division between Brahman and untouchable, between North and South.

But 'race' is an unsatisfactory term. It is used by biologists of plant and animal populations which belong to the same species but have been isolated long enough to have developed characteristic differences. This would seem at first sight easy to apply to human beings. There is no longer any serious dispute that human beings are all of one species, though this term too is extremely difficult to define. Attempts at definition usually take account of ability to breed together and produce fertile offspring; a horse and a donkey belong to different species and a mule is infertile. Another aspect of the species which a definition would take into account is the possibility of demarcation; can it be precisely distinguished from any other group? On both counts, mankind must be judged one species. Men of course do breed together and produce fertile offspring and there is no difficulty in distinguishing them from any other *living* group, though there is controversy about extinct forms.

But the question of demarcation does present difficulties when the word 'race' is used of human beings, among whom borderline cases are frequent. This is because human beings are the most widely distributed and the most mobile of animals. There is uncertainty as to whether the term can properly be used of human beings where there are comparatively minor physical differences, particularly of a quantitative kind, as between, say, a Nilotic people such as the Dinka and Bantu-speakers such as the Kikuyu. Between these groups there are major ethnic and linguistic differences, and there are physical differences, for example in height and skin colour. These are both quantitative differences which can be measured. The Dinka on average are taller than the Kikuyu but the taller Kikuyu are taller than the shorter Dinka. In other words, there is overlapping. There are also differences which cannot be described in terms of more or less. For example, in the blood-group system most widely known, a human being must belong to one of four groups: A, B, AB, or O. These are distributed differently in different parts of the world; there are more people of group A in Norway than in Germany and more of B in Russia; there are more of group O among American Indians. But if a blood transfusion has to be made, it is the blood group that matters, not the race. It may be perfectly safe to give Chinese blood to an Englishman when blood from an Englishman of another group would kill him.

There are biologists who say that 'race' is a term that cannot be used scientifically of human beings. They are too mixed, such authorities would argue; their history has been a long record of migration, conquest, and trade, interspersed in some cases with periods of isolation, but always followed by mixing. But a majority would agree that, in spite of the difficulty of demarcation, the differences between, say, a typical population from the West Coast of Africa and a typical population from, say, the Swedish countryside are so considerable that some term must be used to distinguish them. 'Race' is thus a term which *has* a biological meaning though it must be used with caution. But I emphasize that it is with the social and political results of its use as a social category that we are concerned.

There is still controversy as to the stage of evolution at which racial differences arose and knowledge of the question is hampered by the fact that many distinguishing characteristics are perishable; you cannot always deduce skin colour from a skeleton. At present, human remains that are distinctively Negroid have not been found which are comparable in antiquity with those which seem to be of caucasoid or mongoloid type. There is therefore no ground for regarding the Negroid type of man as biologically primitive; it seems, on the contrary, likely that they are the most recent. But it is hard to see that this question has the importance for race relations which has sometimes been assigned to it. What is of importance is not the antiquity of a distinct biological type, but the stage any population has reached in the specifically human quality of ability to master the environment. It would be of real significance if there was any scientific indication of a relation between different racial types and different levels of intelligence.

On this question, the consensus of opinion, again summarized in the broadest terms, is that it is extremely difficult to measure genetic aptitude for learning. What can be measured is skill already acquired, ability in displaying it, and to some extent the skill so far acquired in the art of acquiring more skill. But this is not the same as genetic aptitude. This varies even in the case of identical twins—that is, twins from one egg—who may resemble each other so closely in face, eyes, and hair that they are quite indistinguishable to strangers. Experiments have shown that identical twins 'perform appreciably more similarly in intelligence than do fraternal twins'—that is, twins from two egg-cells maturing simultaneously. Fraternal twins resemble each other only slightly more than brothers and sisters who are not twins. Identical twins brought up together resemble each other in performance more closely than those who have been separated, each being brought up in a different environment. But their environment, even when most different, is usually within the same national culture; I have yet to hear of one twin brought up by Australian aborigines and another in Chelsea. Between twins brought up in professional and working-class homes in the same national culture there may be quite considerable differences at the age of twelve.[1]

What is thus beyond dispute is that performance in intelligence tests is governed partly by environment and partly by genetic or inherited aptitude. It is not possible to say precisely how much is genetic and how much is acquired; the two cannot be separated. The difficulty arises from the fact that with human beings there can be no completely controlled experiments. A child starts to learn as soon as it is born; even if we had identical twins available for experiment—and even if they really were completely identical, which they are not—we could not withhold all stimuli from one and supply them to the other. We can find out something of what a child *has* learnt, but nothing precise about what it *might* have learnt in different circumstances. That is why we cannot compare the genetic aptitude of people from quite different backgrounds.

What has emerged, from many studies and much writing—some of it highly tendentious—is a majority opinion on two points. First, within any human population of a fairly homogeneous background, the distribution of aptitude for learning is likely to follow roughly the same pattern, that is to say, there will be an average level, near which many of the population will register scores, while above and below there will be a diminishing number in each grade, until extremes are reached some way above and below the average. The pattern is shown in Figure 1 below. The distance from the average to the two extremes is likely to be about the same for any population of any size which has so far been open to this sort of comparison; one would expect to find it less among people who have been exposed to fewer stimuli.

Secondly, the nearer two populations are to a common background (whatever their racial origin), the nearer the *averages* of intelligence are likely to be, while there is always a large overlap, that is to say, the higher scores of the group that does not do so well are near the top register of the better group and well above their average. 'Background' includes prospects; a child's performance in school is influenced not only by what he learns from his parents but by what advantage he thinks he will get from learning more at school.

[1] Theodosius Dobzhansky, *Heredity and the Nature of Man*. Dobzhansky's figures for correlation of performance in intelligence tests are as follows:

| | |
|---|---|
| Identical twins reared together | 0·87 |
| Identical twins reared apart (but in the same national culture) | 0·75 |
| Fraternal twins | 0·53 |
| Siblings | 0·49 |

Perfectly identical achievement would be 1·00 and this would mean that the measurement was exact and that the aptitude measured depended entirely on heredity and not on environment.

It is possible to say positively that differences between the behaviour and achievements of individuals are due both to genetic inheritance and to environment. But in the case of groups, it seems likely that the *averages* of genetic aptitude, if they could be measured, would be close, while the results of environmental differences are clearly very considerable. It is therefore the general assumption of what follows that differences in the behaviour of human groups are more easily to be accounted for by history, by reaction to environment, by tradition, and by the skills handed down by ancestors, than by any inherited differences of intelligence or temperament. This does not rule out the possibility of inherited differences in 'temperament'; it would be surprising if the processes of evolution, which have produced such differences in appearance, had not produced some differences in the

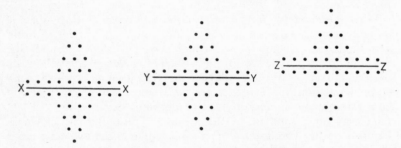

Figure 1    *Average Levels of Intelligence*

XX, YY, and ZZ are average scores in intelligence tests of human populations with similar backgrounds; highly schematized, the pattern of high and low scores that one would expect to find is shown, with considerable concentration near the average, tapering quickly away to extremes above and below; there is considerable overlap between them, the best of X group scoring much higher than the average of Z.

balance between, say, emotion and conscious reflection. But it is not easy to see how such a quality can be measured. The attempts at measurement I have seen do not strike me. as satisfactory and subjective judgments are notoriously erratic; in any case, individual differences are so considerable within any one group that, even if measurement was possible, the results would probably resemble those relating to intelligence.

On this general assumption then, I shall try to draw a rather more detailed sketch of the types of human society in which a class or group or caste has established dominance over other groups, the means by which it has been done and the significance of the ways in which they differ.

## 3 *A First Attempt at Classification: Numerical Proportion*

We are thinking of situations in which there is contact between two groups of people who regard each other as different. We shall not expect to find a smooth chain of types of situation between which one can trace an uninterrupted curve, leading from the barest kind of marginal contact to the extremely complex relationships of modern cities. Nature seldom presents such regularity. Nor shall we expect to find a similar progress in time, a regular succession of certain types of relationship invariably developing in the same order. Various 'cycles' of race relations have, it is true, been described with authority and they have some degree of validity but always, I believe, within a limited field. That is to say, one could, on the basis of such theories, predict what would be the probable sequence of events and relationships if a new minority was introduced into California, provided it was of not more than a certain size and not more than usually exotic in behaviour and appearance. But that cycle or sequence of relationships will not cover past events in other parts of the world.

One cycle which has most illustrious backing[1] predicts that 'contact' will be followed by 'competition', and there will then be two more phases, 'accommodation' and 'assimilation'. This is not, of course, really a cycle, because no one suggests that the whole process would then start again with contact following assimilation. It is an expected sequence of events. But apart from this verbal point, it does not seem illuminating to apply such a scheme to South Africa, where the succession was contact—war—domination; still less to Tasmania, where it was even simpler—contact followed by extermination. Even in the United States, for which the 'cycle' was designed, it is doubtful whether the Negro American is more assimilated than he was twenty years ago. The concept assumes smooth unbroken progress towards harmony but to-day the world-wide revolt against hierarchy and fixed status is everywhere producing movements in the reverse direction.

Much more detailed sequences have been devised, but the more complex and detailed they are, the more closely they fit one pattern, usually American. So we shall be suspicious of any idea that 'cycles' can be universal, though we shall recognize that the sequence of events in one situation may tell us something about the probable sequence of events in a similar situation. There may be a sequence of relationships— though not a cycle which repeats itself—which is frequent in colonial situations; there may also be a sequence of relationships affecting immigrants to an industrial society.

This suggests that there is an overriding difference between situations where the dominant group is indigenous or already established and another set of situations where the indigenous are subordinate. But again there is a complication. The British in India in the seventeenth century were by no means dominant; they were suppliants at the Court

---

[1] Robert E. Park, *Race and Culture: essays on the sociology of contemporary man.*

of the Moghal Emperors. But by the nineteenth century they were a dominant minority. The same change took place in the case of the Tutsi in Ruanda and the Fulani in Nigeria. And the historical dimension adds a relationship to world thought and to world events. Immigrants to England will behave differently in the twentieth century from immigrants in the eighteenth; there may be similarities in the reactions of the indigenous English but the pattern of world thought is different.

What we shall try to establish is a series of certain broad types of relationship which throw some light on as many situations as possible. But there will be borderline cases which will not fit very neatly into these categories, and, even within one category, events will not always succeed each other in the same order in the same kind of way in every situation. And a situation will move from one category to another in the course of history. It is exactly the difference between two situations that resemble each other within the same category that is illuminating. We shall group these broad categories together and compare them and distinguish and note how one melts into another.

Take for instance 'the plural societies of South-East Asia'—Chinese, Malays, and Indians in Malaysia, as one example. At one time, these lived side by side with little communication except that they were part of the same economic framework and held together (as a rule) within a common but alien political rule. But, with modern forms of education, inequality began to develop and the process was made more acute when the imperial power withdrew. This is quite a different history from the patterns of conquest and diplomatic triumph which established dominance elsewhere and forms a third grouping of categories, the first two being the subordinate immigrant grouping and the dominant colonial grouping.

There is no end to the complexities. There is a criss-crossing pattern; certain factors are present in varying degrees in every situation and they run right across any grouping of situations into broad categories. But again, they do not behave tidily. One factor is numerical proportion, but we shall not find, for example, that the smaller the dominant minority the more harshly it behaves, nor the reverse. Nor shall we find that there is a critical proportion—when for example a minority increases from 5 per cent to 10 per cent—at which there is invariably a change in political or social behaviour. Still looking at that one factor of numbers or proportion, we may, however, be able to establish certain limits and certain correspondences within which it is possible for a certain kind of situation to develop. But these correspondences are difficult to represent in the form of a chart or graph.

We need not spend long on considering forms of contact which are so peripheral that they really do not much affect the culture of either people. The classical example is 'silent trade'; Herodotus reports silent trade between Carthaginians and natives of the West Coast of Africa;

the Carthaginians would leave a pile of goods on the beach, retire to their ships, and send up smoke, when the natives would emerge from hiding and put down a pile of gold which they offered in exchange. They would then go inland and the Carthaginians would take the gold if they thought it enough, but leave both piles and go back to the ships if they did not. The same kind of practice is reported from other parts of the world; it argues a considerable degree of commercial confidence, in spite of personal distrust, and it is not easy to see how the parties first arrive at the bargaining convention. But though the economy of the natives would clearly be influenced by this kind of contract, it is not the kind of relationship we are thinking of, in which two peoples live in the same territory, or compete for parts of it. It may perhaps have been on these lines that Chinese and Indian ships first traded with the East Coast of Africa; all we know is that beads and fragments of pottery are found buried beneath the dry-stone fortresses of Rhodesia and that there was a minimum of cultural influence from these ancient civilizations on the empire of the Monomotapa.

Professor Banton[1] has written of peoples who live side by side in what is described as symbiosis, neither despising the other nor acting aggressively. One fully described example is that of the Mbuti pygmies in the Congo and neighbouring Negro groups. The pygmies live in the forest as hunters and food-gatherers, but periodically decide to come to the agricultural, village world of the Negroes, perhaps for a change of diet or because the hunting is not good. They leave behind their whole set of values, particularly their ideas of what is sacred, and behave as the Negroes wish them to, but go back eventually to the forest and resume their old ways and beliefs. This is certainly one step beyond silent trade, but it does not sound like an *equal* relationship; the Negroes do not reverse the practice and accept the gods of the pygmies. It is perhaps intermediate between parasitism and symbiosis. If the Negro population grew and began to extend cultivation into the forest, the pygmies would find themselves threatened and might eventually be forced into the position of the Twa in Ruanda.

Other examples quoted by Professor Banton are between Eskimo Tungus and Cossacks in North-Western Manchuria, between Lapps and Scandinavian peasants, and between Ladinos and Indians in Guatemala. There is some evidence that neither of the latter two relationships are as free from tension as has been suggested;[2] the Tungus

[1] Michael Banton, *Race Relations*.

[2] For Ladinos and Indians in Guatemala, Pitt-Rivers is sceptical about Tumin's conclusions. On Lapps, Whitaker writes: 'From being equals, they (the Lapps) have come to be considered as definite inferiors, indicated by disparaging remarks. . . . There has been a decline in hospitality offered to nomads . . . the peasants have refused Lapps accommodation. This has upset old relationships. . . . The introduction of the money economy has produced a new set of values. . . .' Whitaker, *Social Relations in a Nomadic Lappish Community*.

are a group of 'about one hundred and fifty nomadic reindeer herders occupying some seven thousand square miles of territory', while the Cossacks, who speak Great Russian, are literate and agriculturalists, are only one hundred and fifty persons, and live outside the Tungu territory; it seems obvious that these are conditions in which there is no great pressure on resources, and no great need for hostility. It is hardly typical.

I believe that we need not be concerned with these marginal cases and that the term 'symbiosis' is better used of such people as the Parsis in India and the Syrians in West Africa, perhaps of Indians and Burmese under British rule in Burma, or of Malays and Chinese in Malaysia. This is more in accord with the word's original botanical application to organisms which not merely live together and use complementary elements from the soil but actively help each other or even depend on each other, because one performs functions which the other cannot. These peaceful minorities do throw light on our subject; their position may change abruptly—indeed usually *has* changed abruptly.

Professor Banton does not spend long on the Tungus and their reindeer but goes on to draw up a scheme of typical situations between races. Having excluded 'silent trade' on the same grounds as I do, he goes on to suggest six 'orders' of race relations. He distinguishes in the first place between peripheral contact, in which cultural influence is negligible, and *institutionalized contact*, in which there is a group who are specialized intermediaries between two societies. This is his first 'order'. I can supply first-hand evidence of exactly such a group of intermediaries—though again a marginal one—the Marchchas of Garhwal in the Central Himalayas. These people had their headquarters in villages in passes between India and Tibet, at heights of 8,000 to 11,000 feet; here they would sow a crop of barley and a special short quick-growing millet[1] as soon as the snow melted in May or June. In August they would move over the passes, usually about 17,000 feet above sea level, into Tibet, where they would trade sugar and iron for salt, borax, skins, and wool; they came back to their villages in September, cut their barley, and a few weeks later left their villages, which would soon be buried deep in snow, and moved with their flocks to the plains to complete their trade cycle. They were regarded by the Hindu peasantry of the foothills as untouchable, because they were reputed to eat yak-meat in Tibet—and a yak is a kind of cow—and further as an economic threat, because as they moved down in winter they encroached on the grazing and cut wood for fuel; both grass and wood were increasingly scarce as one moved towards the plains. But they did to some extent combine the Hindu and Tibetan cultures. This was possible because the relationship between the two governments was

[1] It was known locally as Ogil, but I do not know its botanical name.

relaxed. Neither wanted the territory or goods of the other; on the other hand, there were no illusions as to which was the more powerful.

But surely we should disregard fascinations of this kind. In Professor Banton's scheme, *institutionalized contact* means a situation in which the overlapping is only limited and exchange between the two cultures is approximately equal. His next order is *acculturation*, in which one of the cultures is so much stronger that it replaces the weaker; since the weaker group adopt the culture of the stronger, they cease to be distinguishable and this will normally lead to the fifth order which is *integration*. But in Banton's scheme institutionalized contact more often leads either to complete *domination* by one group over the other or to *paternalism*. These two are alternatives. Domination is likely to lead to pluralism of an unequal kind, while paternalism is likely to lead to integration. He displays his system in a diagram of which the following is a simplification:

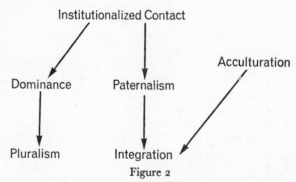

Figure 2

*Simplification of Banton's Scheme of Typical Situations between Races*

I am not sure that I perfectly follow this division into orders. The test comes when one tries to fit in examples and consider the sequences. Muslim rule in India was, I suppose, domination merging into pluralism, but what about British rule in India? This was, first, institutionalized contact—with the servants of the East India Company acting as specialized go-betweens; later, it was paternalism—perhaps the most perfect example of paternalism there has ever been. But it ended not in integration but in withdrawal. Again, in Rhodesia, in the Cape Colony, Mexico, and Peru, there was first some control by the home government and I think Banton would regard these as coming in the paternalist 'order'; but independence from the home government meant a situation much nearer domination. In South Africa and Rhodesia it has surely become complete domination. In Mexico, the relationship between Spanish and Indian in the early nineteenth century was surely what Banton would regard as 'dominance'. To-day, in most of Mexico, peasants of predominantly Amerindian physical type speak only Spanish and are presumably to be regarded as 'integrated'—though as this is the triumph of one culture over another, it is hard to see how it differs from acculturation. It seems to me that the definitions break down as soon as one begins to trace a progress from one to another.

It might, I suppose, be argued that the arrival of West Indians, Pakistanis, and Indians in Britain produced a situation in which acculturation was taking place, with some doubt as to whether it would turn to integration or unequal pluralism. And there are the Maoris, the North American Indians, and the Australian aborigines; the Australians were almost exterminated, but there have been several changes in policy towards them. It was once hoped to assimilate the American Indian; now the policy is a tolerant pluralism alternating with integration and perhaps with a seventh order—neglect. The changing factors have been world opinion, the conscience of the dominant group and their confidence about their own culture. The tides, it seems to me, flow in a much more shifting and intricate pattern than Banton suggests. But any schematic arrangement faces this kind of difficulty; the examples will not quite fit the pigeon-holes and the sequences are far more fluid, delicate, and shifting than any diagram can represent. All the same, every conscientious attempt to classify these types of situation does illuminate them. Banton's is for me a valuable starting-point, but it needs elaboration.

A rather different approach by Professor P. L. van den Berghe[1] suggests that a situation can be usefully placed in a scale between two extremes. It is confusing that van den Berghe uses the label 'paternalistic' for the system Banton calls 'domination'; but, whatever it is labelled, both would include under this head the plantation system of the Deep South or the countryside in the Transvaal, where race is the overriding sign of social position, where there is little chance of escape from fixed status, where elaborate codes of behaviour govern any contact between the dominant and subordinate groups and where the consequences of belonging to a racial group are defined by law.

At the other extreme of van den Berghe's scale is a more fluid situation, which he calls competitive, in which there is probably an industrial economy and much more opportunity of movement in the social scale. In this type of situation there is some degree of overlapping, in that the best off in the subordinate group may be higher in the scale of profession and earnings than the lowest of those in the dominant group; manners are more fluid and there is ostensibly democratic government involving some conflict of values about the whole system. Perhaps New Zealand would be at this end of the scale, but, in spite of van den Berghe's insistence on the importance of wide comparisons,

[1] P. L. van den Berghe, *Race and Racism.*

his schematic outline looks very like the Old Deep South at one end
of the scale and the modern North of the United States at the other.

Brazil, Mexico, and South Africa, as well as the U.S.A., are examples
which van den Berghe has studied thoroughly; of each, he provides a
brilliant and perceptive account which is of great value. It is only his
model that I find unsatisfactory. All have presented, in the past, a kind
of paternalist model not too different from the Deep South, all have,
in some respects, moved to something more like his competitive model.
He does not, it must be said, suggest that there must necessarily be
movement in time from one end of this scale towards the other. If he
did, he would clearly exclude South Africa, which in many respects
has moved backward. He ignores the distinction, which seems to me
real, between dominant and paternalist; it seems to me that South
Africa, at least in the Cape Province, once showed signs of paternalism
but has clearly moved to dominance with competitive elements. Van
den Berghe does specifically limit the application of his model to the
four examples, United States, Brazil, Mexico, and South Africa. But
he does sometimes write as though it could be used with a wider
application, to place a given society at a given moment and also to
throw light on its historical development. And this seems a little unreal
in the case of societies that never had anything like the agricultural
slave society which he puts at one end of his scale.

But there is, it seems to me, a more fundamental objection. Van den
Berghe's two models are opposed in respect of a number of variable
factors, which he lists. Thus the 'paternalistic' type of situation is
agricultural in its economy, while the competitive type is more likely
to be manufacturing; the former will have an 'integrated value system'
and the latter an ideological conflict. All this—indeed, with one
exception, his whole list of variables—seems to me valid as between the
Deep South and the North. But the usefulness of this as a model for
other societies is limited by the fact—which van den Berghe acknowledges—that his variable factors operate independently.

Take, for example, three of his variable factors: numerical proportion,
degree of industrialization, and social stratification. Of numerical
proportion, he says that in the paternalistic[1] type the dominant group
is a small minority, while in the competitive type the dominant group
is a majority. But as soon as one tries to put a society into place in this
scale, anomalies appear. If South Africa is contrasted with Colonial
West Africa, the South African Republic is surely far more advanced
in the organization of labour and in industrial complexity yet far more
rigid, and therefore according to the model more backward, in social
structure. And the numerical proportions are the reverse of what the
scale suggests. The white group in colonial Nigeria was in a much
smaller minority.

[1] I am of course here using the word in his sense, which is neither mine nor Banton's.

In fact, the numerical variable really does not work at all in the way suggested; the British in India were numerically the extreme example of a dominant minority but the social structures of British and Indian were divided by almost vertical lines and great deference was paid by British officials to Maharajas. If we contrast colonial Kenya and Rhodesia, we find Rhodesia more advanced industrially and with a higher proportion of whites, but more rigid socially. Neither in Brazil nor the Deep South was the dominant group 'a small minority'. Perhaps van den Berghe was thinking of the local situation on the plantation, not the general national or regional situation, when he made this point. We shall come back to this question of numbers and look at it in more detail.

In short, as soon as a wider range of examples is set against this model, it becomes apparent that it would be quite mistaken to think of an advanced and a backward society, between which any given society will find a ranking in the scale which will hold good in respect of every factor. One society will develop industrially but may recede socially, as has happened in South Africa. And indeed, all the factors are more complex than this scheme allows. For example, in the 'paternalistic' type of race relations, there is said to be: 'Accommodation: everyone in his place; everyone knows his place: paternalism: benevolent despotism', while on the other side of the scale, opposed to this in the competitive type of society, there is 'antagonism; suspicion, hatred; competitiveness'. But the antithesis is nothing like so simple. Despotism in the Deep South was not uniformly benevolent nor is antagonism a monopoly of the industrial North. Again, the 'stereotype of the lower caste' in the paternalistic type is: 'Childish, immature, exuberant, uninhibited, lazy, impulsive, fun-loving, good-humoured; inferior but lovable'. This is a picture which the Southern American tried to persuade the Northerner, and perhaps himself, that he held of the Negro: but was it really his picture at any period? In Rhodesia and South Africa (of which I know more), there was never a stage at which such words as 'dangerous, treacherous, and unaccountable' should not have been added to the list. I suspect this or something like it was present in Southern minds too. And the Peruvian owner of a hacienda did not usually think of his peons as 'exuberant' or 'fun-loving'.

To revert to numerical proportion, the operation of this important factor is complicated by a number of subsidiary aspects of the situation. It depends on habit and custom; on a sense of permanence in the social system; on outside threat or the possibility of outside help for either party. For example, the South African whites had in most of the nineteenth century to think of a formidable body of warlike tribesmen as well as their African or coloured servants and labourers; on the other hand, there was the possibility of hostility in some circumstances, and help in others, from Great Britain. This was a more complicated set of possibilities than those which confronted the Virginian, who by the mid-nineteenth century had only the slaves and the Northerners to consider. Texas again was more complex, with Indians and Mexicans added to the equation. Quite obviously, the numerical proportion becomes a factor of vital importance in certain societies once the idea of change is introduced. The British in India, as soon as 'Reforms' began in 1919, were in a completely different relationship from before.

Finally—in my list of objections—there are variables which affect the social structure but do not proceed from it. One of the points we shall have to consider is the difference in social structure between Mexico and Peru; one factor, surely, was climate and terrain. In Mexico, the Spaniards centred their rule on the old capital; there was continuity, no abrupt break. But in Peru, they did not want to live at a height of 13,000 feet and started a new capital on the coast. This must be taken into account in any explanation of the harsher division in Peru between the Spanish and the traditional cultures. There were similar factors at work in Africa.

Considering these attempts at classification, I find myself, in general, preferring scales with extreme examples at either end to any system of 'orders' into which actual situations have to be fitted. But we need, I think, a complex set of scales in respect of various factors and a set of groupings against which to display them. It will sometimes help to group our various situations in broad categories from a particular point of view, but not permanently. Let us take, for example, three categories, two of Banton's orders, domination and paternalism, adding as a third van den Berghe's competitive society. Let us, under these three columns, jot down, almost at random, certain situations. Some of these will be described in more detail later, but they are sufficiently familiar to illustrate the meaning of the categories, which we will not at this stage try to define. Then let us consider one factor, numerical proportion, and note the approximate numerical proportion of dominant to subordinate against each situation. It will be seen that a suggestive hypothesis emerges from this arrangement.

It looks rather as though there was a broad range of proportions within which each of the three categories of subordination can occur. There is no overlapping. Paternalism in my sense is limited to ruling minorities which are very small. The three East African territories (in colonial times) are particularly interesting; an American observer[1] classes them very definitely in the order: Uganda, Tanganyika, Kenya: in respect of the characteristics I regard as 'paternal' rather than 'dominant'—that is, concern for the well-being and development of the subordinate group and a greater degree of social respect for them. And this is the order which the numerical proportions would lead us to

[1] Julian Steward, *Contemporary Change in Traditional Societies*, Vol. 1.

Table 1

Numerical Proportion of Dominant to Subordinate

| Category: | Domination | Paternalism | Competition |
|---|---|---|---|
| Situations: | South Africa (1960) 1–4 | British India 1–3,000 | Britain (1968) 50–1 |
| | U.S. South (1960) 4–1 | Nigeria (1952) 1–2,000 | U.S. North (1960) 15–1 |
| | Rhodesia (1960) 1–16 | Nyasaland 1–1,000 (1945) 1–570 (1966) | New Zealand 13–1 |
| | Ruanda (before 1960) 1–6 | Colonial Kenya 1–100 | |
| | Brahman village in South India before 1919 (three-tier) 1 : 2 : 1 | Tanganyika 1 : 450 | |
| | Sparta* 1 : 1 : 2 | Uganda 1 : 650 | |

\* Note on numerical proportions of Spartans (full citizens) to Perioikoi and Helots: Herodotus says that at the Battle of Plataea the contingent from the state of Lacedaemon consisted of 10,000 heavy-armed troops, of whom 5,000 were Spartans or full citizens, the rest being presumed to be Perioikoi. Each Spartan was attended by a retinue of seven Helots (IX, 10); there were 35,000 Helots at the battle (IX, 28). But this does not mean that the proportions within the state were 1 : 1 : 7. Aristotle says the country could support 31,500 troops; he appears to mean heavy-armed troops and therefore to be excluding Helots, and this suggests a total population (other than Helot) of around 300,000, of whom perhaps less than half were full citizens. There is another estimate of the Helots after the Messenian wars at between 175,000 and 225,000. I have suggested a proportion of one Perioikos and two Helots; this is far from certain but it is quite clear that the proportions are well within the limits of the other states classed in my table as giving an example of a *dominant* relationship. I am much indebted to Mr. Russell Meiggs of Balliol College and Professor W. den Boer of the Rijks-universiteit te Leiden for information on which I have based this approximation. I may add a personal calculation: if a Spartan ate rations on the scale of an Indian soldier in the Second World War—and the composition of their food was similar, wheat or barley cakes with a relish of dairy products or some meat—one Helot's tribute of 70 medimnoi should provide the food for eight adults in a year. A Spartan would have to provide for his family and would trade some grain for services. The tribute of two Helot holdings should have been enough.

expect. But the technical resources of the dominant and their readiness to use them ruthlessly will come into the calculation; also, as we have said, the local attitude to change and world habits of thought.

This sample chart is simplified and deals only with a limited number of categories and situations. We have not included, for instance, Algeria or Senegal. They do not fit exactly into the scheme but do bear out the general trend; proportions total approximately one European to nine Muslims in Algeria in 1960; in Senegal in 1960 one European to eighty Africans. Algeria is thus on the borders of the dominant and Senegal of the paternalist categories. The list could be considerably extended. But of all factors, numerical example is the easiest to arrange in a scale. We put the British in India at one end with a proportion of about one to three thousand, and we can move through the French as a colonial power in Asia and West Africa, through the French in Algeria to the Tutsi with their one to six, through the South African whites to the Deep South, where the proportion is reversed and the dominant group is a majority of four to one.

It is a more difficult model to follow with other variables, because these are in themselves more complex and it is not easy to rank them numerically. Some obstinately resist enumeration and indeed so change their nature, at different periods and from one region to another, that comparison in any system of ranking is misleading. But an attempt on these lines will, I believe, present fewer anomalies than either of the others we have looked at. What we need is a number of arrangements in columns, rather like that in Table 1, putting certain situations into categories in relation to one variable factor. But we shall probably need to vary the categories, adopting different groupings with different points of view.

There can be many varied approaches to this problem. To me it seems helpful as a preliminary to add more of the historical dimension. We shall therefore look at some forms of contact and some forms of dominance in the pre-industrial age and the problems which a dominant group faces. I shall then look at the patterns which emerge in the industrial age and consider the variable factors which make them different. These seem to fall into three groups, those from the side of the dominant group, those from the side of the subordinate group, and those arising from climate and terrain. The aims with which the dominant group begin are, of course, soon modified by the circumstances of the territory and by the reactions of the subordinate group and these consequences of contact will form another chapter.

# CHAPTER V

# Before the European Expansion

## *1 Incas and Aztecs*

We can now look at the main kinds of movement which have led to patterns of dominance in the pre-industrial world. The motives which have led people to move have been the search for food, trade, pressure from some other people, or deliberate conquest in order to acquire land or power. There is a significant difference between planned conquest and the other forms of migration. Trade in pre-industrial times did not necessarily lead to conquest or occupation, though it was often used as a form of reconnaissance before conquest, notably by the Aztecs and by the Israelites before invading Canaan. There have been forays, which did not always establish a permanent relationship, for example, by the Vikings on Britain and Ireland, and by the Afghans on Northern India. In these examples, sporadic raids developed into occupations, but they were short-lived. Nomadic peoples have migrated, in search no doubt of better grazing or climate, and have found themselves in country already inhabited, which they have taken. There are many examples from Africa; we have already looked at the Tutsi in Ruanda, but a similar case is that of the Fulani in Northern Nigeria. The Fulani came as nomad groups and lived alongside the agricultural Hausa for some generations before they launched what they called the Jehad or Holy War and established themselves as a dominant group.

There must be many cases hardly known to written history—traceable only from tombs, skeletons, potsherds, jewellery—of migrations which have pushed other peoples into remote and difficult country, or overrun and conquered them. One has only to think of the prehistory of Britain, of the long barrow people overrun by the round barrow people and the successive waves of invasion that followed. Everywhere, in Africa, in America, in Europe, in India, the graves tell similar stories. But it is idle to speculate on these forerunners of the modern American advance westward to California and of the white South African advance northward to the Limpopo. We seldom know enough even to speculate on the relationships that arose. Nor do I propose to dwell on such planned sea-borne conquests as those of the Normans in Sicily and in England.

More interesting from the present point of view are the conquests which gradually built up empires and the methods then adopted by the ruling class in order to keep power. There are many, and it would be fascinating to dwell in detail on several, contrasting the extraordinarily varied means by which rulers have attempted to solve the essential problem of holding together in one political organization groups of whom each has a distinct sense of identity. But the temptation to dwell on them must be resisted; all that is necessary to the scheme of this book is to suggest that the problem has not been basically changed by swifter methods of communication nor even by modern weapons, though this point needs a good deal of qualification; next, that there are many ways of dealing with the problem; finally, that some of the solutions are more flexible and more open to intelligent manipulation than others. I propose to touch very briefly on several examples. My choice from so many is inevitably arbitrary.

The Incas were a small tribe two hundred years before the Spaniards came to Peru, and their main expansion did not begin till Pachacuti was crowned in 1438. Yet by 1532, when Pizarro put Atahualpa to death, they had established their rule over an empire two thousand miles long, covering not only modern Peru but the greater part of Bolivia and Ecuador and the northern tip of Chile. This was in country where communications could hardly be more difficult. The Spaniards were not able here, as they were in Mexico, to make use of native allies only too glad to rise against their masters. This was because the Incas had with extraordinary skill unified their vast empire almost as successfully as the Tutsi did their small kingdom. One may question Prescott's[1] picture of his adoring subjects crowding for a glimpse of their beloved monarch as the Supreme Inca made a tour of his dominions—and yet concede that there must have been very widespread acquiescence in Inca rule. A Peruvian prince is quoted as saying: 'We must spare our enemies or it will be our loss, since they and all that belong to them must soon be ours.'

This, of course, was a Roman maxim: 'spare the vanquished and impose the custom of peace'.[2] The Incas followed both parts of it. They seem to have usually incorporated a newly won country completely into the empire. The first step was to introduce the worship of the Sun, but rather as the Romans introduced worship of the Emperor, as one among many deities; some sacred objects of the previous religion were taken to Cuzco, with some of the chiefs and their sons. Both chiefs and sacred objects acted as hostages; the chiefs were

[1] William H. Prescott, *The Conquest of Peru.*
[2] Hae tibi erunt artes, pacisque imponere morem
parcere subjectis et debellare superbos.

allowed to go home when they had sufficiently absorbed the language, religion, and ideas of the Incas but their elder sons stayed behind. The Quechua language was made the official means of communication everywhere, overriding many hundreds of languages and dialects; a survey of resources was carried out, after which the land was divided into three unequal parts, for the Supreme Inca, for the Sun, and for the maintenance of the people. There was sometimes an exchange of population, colonies of trusted Quechua-speakers being moved into new territories. These moves seem to have been sometimes for economic as well as political purposes.

A system of good roads was introduced with staging-houses and runners for short distances, so that a message could be passed by relay a hundred and fifty miles in a day—a speed probably not equalled in Europe until Napoleon's time—and armies could move swiftly to any affected point. The Inca system of irrigation, with its aqueducts of cut and fitted stone—one was between four and five hundred miles in length—are one of the wonders of pre-industrial civilization; these too must have been a unifying force. To withhold water would be a powerful sanction. Their use of fertilizers—both fish directly applied and guano from the offshore islands—was striking; few African pre-industrial societies used any fertilizers but wood ash and that only incidentally as a result of clearing the ground. It is reasonable to surmise that the introduction of these techniques would be impressive to the ruler of tribes among the newly conquered peoples.

There is no doubt that the accepted policy was to apply one uniform model everywhere and one might expect that this would be resented. But perhaps the whole system was not always introduced immediately; certainly in the early conquests local chiefs were allowed to keep jurisdiction under Inca overlords. And the evidence suggests that the system met basic needs of the people. Justice was swift and without appeal; every case must be settled within five days. There was also a general principle that the members of the community were responsible for each other's behaviour and they might all be punished if one of them committed a particularly serious offence. There was no uncertainty; everyone knew where he stood. He could be in no doubt about his duty.

Above all, there was a highly egalitarian distribution of land. One must suppose that in most cases the land had previously been held in common, by a community, no doubt in very varied ways. The Inca system was of the most radical nature and linked with the most intimate aspects of the social system. Marriage was a duty of the citizen and was prescribed at a given age; choice of partners was limited to the immediate group and further reduced by the fact that no delay was permitted; the marriage must be approved by the families and the seal was set on it by the chief. It was as much a part of the state system as work on the roads. On marriage, a man was allotted land sufficient for himself and his wife; there was a yearly re-distribution to meet the changing needs of a growing or diminishing family.

From the standpoint of an individualist society, this system seems harsh. The householder had to work on the lands of the Sun and the Supreme Inca as well as on public works and on his own allotment, and he might be summoned at short notice for military service. Even within the area of his own community, much of his labour must have been supervised and directed. This is a necessary deduction, because the hills were terraced, and faced with stone walls; in some cases, soil was brought to fill the space behind a stone terrace wall. I have seen just this work in progress in the Himalayas and it is extremely heavy. But there a man was making a permanent improvement which he could leave to his sons. In Peru, where the land was re-distributed every year, a man was not working for himself but for the community when he engaged in this arduous toil. The compensation was that he was taken care of, that he lived with a community he knew and that his place in it was allotted; the system was divinely ordained and it applied to all.

The basic unit of administration was ten householders, one of the ten being the leader and representative; there were higher divisions into fifty, a hundred, five hundred, a thousand, ten thousand. But it seems likely that this rigid numerical division was not always in exact accord with the facts; the ten must often have been seven or twelve. There was a local community tilling the soil before the Inca decimal system was imposed and no doubt in most cases it endured beneath the bureaucratic framework. Grain was stored as a provision against famine, and wool as well as land was distributed to every man according to his need.

Only the Incas themselves were to some extent outside the system; the word in this sense is used of the descendants of each monarch, who were many because there were many wives and concubines. The young men of this royal class were brought up with care, being trained to run long distances, to fast, to wrestle and box and use their weapons as well as being instructed in tradition, religion, and methods of administration. A young prince had to pass severe tests before going through an initiation rite and being accepted into what Prescott compares with an order of chivalry, but what might be better called a high military and administrative service. It was this service or order which provided the Viceroys of the four quarters of the Empire and all the more important military, religious, and administrative posts.

It is probable that all accounts of pre-Columbian Peru are to some extent idealized; indeed, no one can describe a society at all without abstracting from the material of day-to-day life principles which may not be apparent to the people concerned, and which may often be in contrast with their actual behaviour. In the case of the Incas, we have only—apart from archaeological evidence—what Indians remembered and were prepared to tell the Spaniards after the Conquest; even the record of Garcilaso de la Vega, himself the son of an Inca princess, is Hispanicized, not only because he was half-Spanish and a Christian but because he wrote for Spanish readers. But after allowance has been made for some distortion, it seems clear that the Incas followed a policy for the unification and perpetuation of their Empire which may not have been explicitly stated but was nonetheless well understood by every member of the ruling class.

It was their aim to extend over all their territories a uniform system, in which all were provided with a function, duties, and the necessities of life, in which private needs were rigidly subordinated to the general interest, in which justice was swift, harsh, intelligible, and uniform. The system was cemented by a network of rapid communications and by efficient agricultural techniques. It was divinely ordained; it was designed to be permanent. Only the royal rulers were exempt from its normal operation and they were not only descendants of the Sun but they were distinguished from the rest by a long and arduous education.

Much has been written about Peru since Prescott, and an immense amount of archaeological material has been added to the written records on which he mainly relied. This has extended our knowledge of the Peruvian civilization backward into time; we now know that the Incas united into one political and linguistic system a number of peoples whose arts, religion, way of life, had formed an intelligible whole over a period of at least three thousand years before Pizarro. In one region a religious cult or style in art would flourish for a century, perhaps for two or three centuries; sometimes it would spread and a great part of what was later the Inca empire would be influenced. Four hundred years before Pachacuti was crowned, the Tiahuanaco style in pottery and decoration had spread in various forms over most of the area.[1] The Incas therefore found a certain underlying unity among many of their subject peoples, as the Romans did on the shores of the Mediterranean.

But this new information does not invalidate the general conclusions Prescott reached about the nature of Inca rule. In a passage highly relevant to the argument of this book he wrote:

No man could be rich, no man could be poor, in Peru; but all might enjoy, and did enjoy, a competence. Ambition, avarice, the love of change, the morbid spirit of discontent, those passions which most agitate the minds of men, found no place in the bosom of the Peruvian. The very condition of his being seemed at war with change. He moved on in the same unbroken circle in which his fathers had moved before him, and in which his children were to follow. It was the object of the Incas to infuse into their subjects a spirit of passive obedience

[1] Alden Mason, *The Ancient Civilizations of Peru.*

and tranquillity—a perfect acquiescence in the established order of things. In this they fully succeeded. . . . No people could have appeared more contented with their lot or more devoted to their government.

What Prescott could not do was to contrast the rigidity and lack of imagination shown by the pottery and textiles of the Incas with the rich variety of invention shown by some of their predecessors. What material was available to him had not been classified and dated. But the difference in artistic imagination is, surely, what we might expect in the social and political conditions he describes.

Prescott contrasted this empire with that of the Aztecs. Once again, he had far less knowledge than we have to-day of the Aztecs' predecessors, but the history of their immediate past he knew. The Aztecs, like the Incas, were a comparatively obscure group until two centuries before the arrival of Cortés; they too in the course of about ninety years subdued a vast empire in which, with many regional variations of language, of culture, of artistic style, of forms of worship, there was some community of ideas, some exchange, stretching back over thousands of years. Here, too, the Empire displayed a deterioration in artistic imagination. But the social and political contrast between the two empires was as marked as the resemblances. Prescott's judgment in both cases was based on the written records, but in the case of Mexico there are Aztec pictographs to tell the tale of the conquest as well as Spanish writings; the evidence is perhaps not quite so heavily Hispanicized as for Peru. He first contrasts the Inca policy in war, of preserving as far as possible the people they meant to rule, with the conduct of the Aztecs, who, 'animated by the most ferocious spirit, carried on a war of extermination, signalising their triumphs by the sacrifice of hecatombs of captives. . . .' This was no doubt an exaggeration; it was not a war of extermination but, as Pitt-Rivers[1] points out (following Soustelle[2]), included a ritual element; the object was not to exterminate but to capture prisoners for sacrifice and establish superiority. But Prescott was surely right to continue: 'their policy towards the conquered forms a contrast no less striking . . .'; though he again is somewhat carried away by the current of his rhetoric when he writes:

The Mexican vassals were ground by excessive imposts and military conscriptions. No regard was had to their welfare and the only limit to oppression was the power of endurance. They were overawed by fortresses and armed garrisons and were made to feel every hour that they were not part and parcel of the nation but held only in subjugation as a conquered people . . . the various tribes who successively came under the Mexican sceptre, being held together only by the pressure of external force, were ready to fall asunder the moment that force was withdrawn.

[1] Julian Pitt-Rivers, *After the Empire: Race and Society in Middle America and the Andes.*
[2] Jacques Soustelle, *La Vie Quotidienne des Azteques.*

The drawing is harsh, without light or shade. Yet modern scholars, however much they emphasize the achievements of the preceding cultures which the Aztecs inherited, do not present a different picture, though they use different language. The Aztecs or *Mexica* came into the valley of Mexico as barbarian mercenaries; they built their city of Tenochtitlan on an island in the lake, more probably because it was a site no one else wanted than because, as they later alleged, they had divine instructions to settle at a point where they saw an eagle perched on a cactus and devouring a snake. They formed an alliance with the wealthy merchant state of Tlatelolco in which at first they were the junior partners, but they quickly established control over Tlatelolco, and allied themselves with their next most powerful neighbour, Atzcapotzalco, until they felt powerful enough to change sides and destroy this state in its turn. In the next phase they were part of a triple alliance with Texcoco on the far side of the lake and another neighbour, Tlacopan. In this again Texcoco was at first the dominant partner, but Tlacopan was quickly reduced to vassalage and eventually a puppet ruler established in Texcoco. Thus three times within a century the Aztecs repeated the manoeuvre of using an ally until strong enough to devour him.

Once established as imperialists, they seem to have realized quite consciously the need to construct a myth to justify a social reorganization. Itzcoatl, the ruling king at the turning point of their fortunes, decided to reframe the history of what had been little more than a war band. He set down in substitution a highly improbable tale of a bargain, made between the 'nobles' of the tribe and the commoners, before declaring the decisive war against Atzcapotzalco. The 'nobles' had already adopted a pedigree; they, the leaders, were now descended from people of one of the ancient Mexican cultures, the Toltecs (of a branch known as the Colhua) while their followers were still descended from the nomads of the northern desert, the Chichimecs—almost a synonym for barbarians. If they lost the war, the nobles agreed that they should be eaten by the commoners; if they won, the commoners would carry their burdens and serve them for ever.[1] It was not a bargain that would encourage the commoners to see much gain in winning. But the story does suggest that a social change had taken place and was felt to need justification. Further stratification followed; a class of life-peers, like the Roman knights, was created as a reward for successful officials. The hereditary nobles might be rewarded by feudal estates in some of the conquered territories, with serfs tied to the land. There was also a class of slaves—though not chattel slaves who could be sold—below the free men of Tenochtitlan itself.

Thus the Aztecs perceived one of the basic problems of a dominant group; they must establish their superiority over their domestic subjects,

[1] Eric Wolf, *Sons of the Shaking Earth.*

whom they must sub-divide into stratified tiers to perform different functions. But they do not seem to have considered the second aspect of the problem; as Prescott said, they made no attempt to unify their empire by anything but fear. They remained, writes Eric Wolf, 'little more than a band of pirates, sallying forth from their great city to loot and plunder and to submit vast areas to tribute payment, without altering the social constitution of their victims'. This again is an exaggeration; there was an elaborate system of registration for taxes, inherited from Texcoco but continued when the tribute was paid direct to Tenochtitlan, the city of the Aztecs. The truth seems to be that they gave no thought to social organization beyond their own metropolitan limits; they had, after all, only just asserted their ascendancy over Texcoco when the Spaniards arrived. Further, it was not to social organization that they gave most thought; they were obsessed by the need to maintain the sun in heaven and avert cosmic anarchy by feeding the gods with human sacrifice. Wolf writes: '. . . cruel against himself and others, doing battle against doom and yet attracted by it . . . haunted by omens, the Mexica warrior constituted an extreme among possible psychological types, ever engaged in fulfilling his prophecies of destruction by acting upon the assumption of imminent catastrophe. . . .' Something of this fascinated concern with death, pain, and destruction has been mentioned by everyone who has written about the Aztecs.

They form a contrast not only with the Incas but with their allied, and eventually satellite, state of Texcoco. Two kings of Texcoco in the last seventy years before the Spaniards came were poets and philosophers; in contrast with the Aztec state of Tenochtitlan, Texcoco gave nobles and commoners equal representation on their governing council and encouraged merchants and professional bureaucrats to play a part in the affairs of the state. Texcoco enacted a legal code, began to move towards monotheism and restrict human sacrifice. Texcoco was in fact Athens to the Sparta of Tenochtitlan—but it was the militarist, not the philosophical, state which triumphed.

The difference in character between Aztec and Inca rule must have contributed to the difference between the racial situation in modern Mexico and modern Peru. But a paradox is at once suggested; the Incas' more intelligent and enlightened solution to the imperial problem led to a greater rigidity to-day. In Mexico the old empire had to be smashed and it readily fragmented; in Peru, it was simply decapitated and the Supreme Inca replaced by Spanish rule. This, as well as geography, to which we shall return, must be one part of the reason for the extreme psychic withdrawal of the Quechua-speaking peoples in certain areas. Let me emphasize that it is only one part; it is seldom indeed that a social phenomenon can be wholly attributed to the operation of one factor.

## 2 Sparta and Athens

Sparta is better known, at least in Britain, than Mexico or Peru. But it has so long been regarded as representative of a certain kind of state and a general political philosophy, that it is impossible to leave it out of this sketch. The Spartans were one branch of the Dorian invaders of the Peloponnese. They turned the original inhabitants into serfs; the Helots were peasants who worked the land, each Helot paying to his Spartan overlord a fixed due of seventy medimnoi[1] of grain as well as fruit and cheese and other dues. The Spartans were thus released from manual labour and could give their whole time to the public service and to training for war. As everyone knows, a Spartan baby was not allowed to live if born with any defect; Spartan boys left their families at the age of seven and went to live in military messes with others of the same age, ruled over by young prefects of between twenty and thirty; like Incas, Aztecs, Tutsi, and the Victorian English public schoolboy, they were trained by hardship and physical exercises, but the Spartans went further than anyone else in rigid subordination of private life. A young man could not leave the mess and live at home with his wife until he was thirty. At that age he became a citizen and a member of the general assembly. There was a Spartan secret police, the Krupteia, whose duty it was to discover any subversive attitude among the Helots and punish—immediately and by death—anyone even suspected. The Spartan state annually declared war upon the Helots, and thus legalized this practice. There were many Helot revolts.

The original city-state of Sparta was soon surrounded by a ring of conquered and vassal states. The first of them was Messene, which was defeated in war and incorporated into the system, the inhabitants being reduced to the condition of Helots and their land divided up into lots for the Spartans. But they worked on different terms from the original Helots, sharing the produce half and half with their overlord. Other states had been allies and became vassals; their inhabitants were the *perioikoi* or neighbours; they were not citizens of Sparta but, as individuals, they were free, not enslaved, and citizens of states which continued to exist although under Spartan hegemony. Thus there were three main classes: the Spartans, who alone were full citizens, and who provided the armoured infantry; the *perioikoi*; and the Helots. It was believed that they were of different descent—race is hardly the word. The Helots were the aboriginal inhabitants and the *perioikoi* were Achaean invaders, while the Spartans were Dorians, both invaders who came in successive waves.

There are several points here which are relevant to the general argument. First, the Spartans appear at one stage of their history and

[1] A medimnos is nearly twelve gallons; in barley probably about ninety pounds weight.

at first glimpse to reverse the general trend towards greater stratification; there was a period when they consisted of nobles and commoners; it was later that they became a uniform group whose proud boast was that they were all 'peers', or equals. But this was not due to any idea of general equality; the change in social structure seems to have arisen from a change in military tactics. The Spartans found that heavily armoured infantry, of high morale and discipline, in close formation, could beat cavalry[1] and light infantry. Military success called for a body of picked men, highly disciplined, regarding each other as equals; military victory made possible a social structure which could provide just such a force. It was a form of tactics which demanded a widely defined aristocracy. But as the ruling group was enlarged, so it was re-defined, not only against the Helots but against the *perioikoi*. And there can surely be little doubt that for a Spartan 'peer' the system produced keen psychological satisfaction; he could feel that he belonged to a group which was superior to all others, trained by rigid discipline in complete unity, simplicity, and utter devotion to the state. Within the group, there was equality, mutual respect, no conflict of duty, and above all no one to envy. It was a life which to those who practised it had an austere beauty. For this it was little to give up luxurious living, which was suitable perhaps for barbarians but ugly in itself as well as debilitating to mind and body.

Such a system would not encourage artistic imagination or be receptive to new ideas. Indeed, the Spartans were caught in a trap of their own making, and one from which there was no escape. It was the Helots who released the Spartans from such ignoble occupations as trade and agriculture; it was they who made it possible for the Spartans to lead a life of public service. But it was the Helots who made it necessary to live in an armed camp, constantly on the alert against revolt. The subjugation of the *perioikoi* added factors to both sides of the equation; their tribute strengthened the state but their rebellion was one more danger to provide against. It was a trap; there is no escape from such a system once it has reached a certain stage. They had a wolf by the ears; they dared not let go. And it was of their own making; they had decided—at some stage and by what process one can only guess— that the Helots should remain separate and without rights for ever. They made themselves the bravest of the brave but fear was not to be driven out; they set up a statue to Fear in the market-place[2] but she was not to be propitiated.

We should perhaps not remember the Spartans if it were not for the Athenians on whom in the end they inflicted defeat and humiliation. But, utterly different as the Spartan spirit was from the Athenian, it

---

[1] Their cavalry had no stirrups and were therefore not much use except as scouts or in pursuit.

[2] See Plutarch, *Life of Cleomenes*: I am indebted for this point to Sir Robert Birley.

would be a mistake to suppose that their social and political systems were different from the beginning. What is remarkable is the speed, yet the continuous fluidity, of Athenian change from one system to another. At the beginning of the seventh century in Athens, there was a king and a group of nobles, the Eupatridae or well-fathered, and two other classes of free citizens, rural and urban; one consisted of the farmers or substantial peasants and the other of the bourgeois, the merchants and master-craftsmen. Apart from slaves, each of these two classes stood above a lower class of rural landless labourers (who were sometimes share-croppers on the extremely harsh terms of keeping one-sixth of the produce[1]) and employed artisans; neither of these were citizens. The state thus consisted of nobles—two classes of free citizens—two classes of free men not citizens—and slaves.

But by the end of the century, the voters were ranked in three classes, by wealth not birth; the wealth was expressed in terms of the corn, wine, and oil annually produced by an estate, but it was not apparently necessary to own land. Only those with an income of more than five hundred medimnoi could hold the highest public offices; there was an intermediate class of those with more than three hundred, to whom other offices were open, and the third class of voters consisted of those with more than two hundred. These classes had officially taken the place of the old ranks, which were reckoned by birth, but descent was still important and no doubt for a long time it was valuable to be 'well-fathered' as well as to have an income of over five hundred. Below an income of two hundred medimnoi—three times what a Helot paid his Spartan overlord—there was a class of citizens, the *thetes*, who had no political rights—the smaller peasants and town artisans; this lowest class of citizen still did not include the landless labourers and journeymen.

In the sixth century, the vote was extended to this fourth class of the *thetes*, though at first they were still unable to hold office. And a most far-reaching democratic measure was introduced, courts drawn by lots from this fourth class, who could enquire into any man's conduct while in office when his term expired and who could punish him by death or banishment for any misconduct of public affairs. The powers of these courts were less at first but they gradually increased until they became a serious impediment to executive action.

Very quickly, then, in the course of about a century and a half, Athens moved from being an aristocracy of birth to being first a wider and more fluid oligarchy based on wealth and later a democracy in which all the citizens could play a part, though there were still a considerable number excluded from citizenship—women, immigrants, landless labourers and journeymen, slaves. It was here that full

[1] So Bury says, but it seems almost unbelievable. In India half-and-half or *nisfi batai* was regarded as harsh.

expression was first given to ideas of equality—equality before the law and consequently trial by ordinary citizens, not skilled speakers of the law, and a share by ordinary citizens in the management of the state. It was in fact too large a share for any but a very small state. Nonetheless, Athens still lives; men still visit her buildings, gaze at her statues, read her poets and philosophers, and act her plays; in a thousand ways, the thoughts of Athens still influence men's lives. This flowering of art and thought surely had something to do with the Athenian solution of the internal problem of rule; instead of limiting the privileges of living in a community to a few and deliberately keeping that privileged body separate, as Sparta did, Athens widened the circle of the privileged and allowed movement between the ranks. But Athens was not so good at solving the problem of ruling others.

This first democracy did not extend to allies and vassals the right to determine their own fate and the attitude of Athens became extremely severe when she was fighting Sparta in the thirty years' war which threatened her very existence. The expansion of Athens began with the formation of a confederacy of equal states, who supplied contingents of ships and men to fight beside the Athenians. The next stage was to enlist in the confederacy cities who merely subscribed to the Athenian treasury the cost of ships which Athens built, controlled, and manned. But a third process accompanied these two; other territories were made subject; they lost their freedom and were compelled to pay tribute, not as confederates but as vassals. And increasingly, allies were persuaded to move from the class who supplied contingents to the class who paid tribute; this increased the size of the navy over which Athens had complete control. And the voluntary system became increasingly compulsory.

There was little sympathy for states which attempted to leave the confederacy. One island, Carystos, wished to be neutral, but, lying at a strategic point, was compelled to become not merely a member of the confederacy but a subject of Athens; Naxos attempted to secede from the confederacy but was reduced by force and also made subject to Athens; Thasos, an island with a considerable fleet, revolted but was defeated, handing over to Athens all their ships and control of a gold-mine on the neighbouring mainland. This was before the war with Sparta, but as that war dragged on, the attitude to defection became even more severe. When Scione revolted, not only was the town destroyed but all the male inhabitants were put to death; when the island of Melos persisted in refusing to join the alliance—now clearly an empire—the town was eventually taken, the men of military age were put to death, the other inhabitants enslaved and the island colonized by Athenians. This was fifteen years after the beginning of the war with Sparta, when, although Athens still had command of the sea, Spartan supremacy by land was such that Attica was year after year invaded right up to the walls of Athens; it was not a time when tolerance would be popular. Ten years earlier, when the war was younger, the Athenian Assembly had pronounced the same sentence on the citizens of Mytilene, a city in Lesbos which had attempted to unite the whole island under its own rule—as Athens had united Attica—and to leave the alliance. But Athens had repented and sent a second ship to countermand the order; in one of the most dramatic moments of history, the second ship arrived just as the executions were about to begin.

## 3 African Empires

Many African states built up empires in a way not very different from the initial stages of the expansion of Incas and Aztecs, Spartans and Athenians, each of whom had first to consolidate the immediate area from which the expansion began. With these African empires we shall be dealing at greater length in another part of the book. But here it is necessary to say that there is a certain pattern among them, some elements which make them recognizably different from anything else. We have already looked at Ruanda, an African state, which had established with considerable skill an internal system of dominance. Others, too, had achieved internal stability in which there were often very complex systems of consultation between different groups. The network of relationships and the social and political structure of the Lozi[1] (or Barotse) in Zambia is particularly interesting; there were three councils representing the King's relatives, the greater office-bearers and nobles and the junior office-bearers; consensus between them was the ideal that was sought in any important question.

In general, the African societies which had reached the stage of primitive states set a high value on consultation and consensus of opinion. Also, they showed a remarkable ingenuity in grouping people together in groups small enough to feel at home in, but yet linked into a unity by other groupings which cut across them. Their social structure was almost always segmented vertically in lineages, clans and the like, that is to say on a basis of descent, but was frequently also divided by horizontal divisions. There were sometimes age groups who were peers for education, initiation, and military training; sometimes there was a military organization into regiments which lasted after initiation and cut across descent. Sometimes there was another overlying vertical network, like that of the patron and client system in Ruanda; sometimes also there were horizontal divisions similar to what some American sociologists call castes, which are settled by birth and outside which

[1] African tribes have often an Anglicized name more familiar to English readers and a more correct name used by anthropologists. 'Ba-' is a plural prefix and so the two names are almost the same.

marriage is not usual. The division of Ruanda into Tutsi, Bahutu, and Twa was of this kind; among the Ndabele,[1] who broke away from the Zulus in Natal and migrated through the Transvaal to the Western part of Rhodesia, there was a similar stratification between the descendants of the original Zulus from Natal, the descendants of other South African groups such as the Sotho and Tswana who had joined at later stages of the migration, and—the third and lowest group—the Shona peoples whom they had found in the country round Bulawayo when they arrived. To this last group were added the captives from raids eastward among the Shona after the kingdom was established. These divisions were distinctly caste-like; not only was intermarriage unknown (before the conquest and break-up of the old system) but it was impossible for the lowest group to eat with the others; they were virtually serfs—hewers of wood and drawers of water.

Another frequent feature of the African empires is an inner ring of close neighbours who pay regular tribute, and an outer ring who are subject to sporadic raids. The Lozi, who prided themselves on their ability to rule others and build an empire, distinguished between the young people sent as part of the tribute from this inner ring, whom they called 'the honoured', and those brought back after raids among the less organized people to the east, whom they called 'the seized'. But both 'the honoured' and 'the seized' were brought up in the family with Lozi and were absorbed into the system. In West Africa, too, the kingdoms of Benin, Dahomey, and Ashanti display an inner ring of vassals and an outer ring of territories which are raided. Sometimes it is felt that the outer ring, the raided folk, are in some way the *property* of the central kingdom; this is 'our' raiding territory, it is felt. A raid might mean that a heavy tribute was exacted, usually in cattle and young people; more often it was like an operation of war, from which some no doubt successfully escaped, but, of those who were taken, the very young, the old, and the men of military age were killed, while women and boys were taken to the metropolis. This concept of the hunting territory which 'belonged' to an African state was later used by Europeans, notably in Northern Rhodesia, but also in Southern Rhodesia, as a fiction enabling sovereignty to be transferred. A great part of Northern Rhodesia was assumed to be within the 'sovereignty' of Lewanika, king of the Barotse, and transferred by Treaty to the British South African Company.[2]

Thus it can be said that over much of Africa before the coming of Europeans there were coming into being African states, which here and there were beginning to coalesce into empires, in ways sometimes

---

[1] The Ndabele in the plural becomes Ama-ndebele; the English called them Matabele.

[2] Terence Ranger, 'The Rewriting of African History during the Scramble: the Matabele Dominance in Mashonaland'.

reminiscent of Greece as well as of pre-Columbian America. These
states had frequently achieved a high degree of internal unity by very
complex organization into smaller groups in a variety of overlapping
systems. Some had systems of internal stratification and of dominance
by a minority, usually believed to be of different descent from the
majority. But none had achieved anything like the widespread empire
of the Incas.

Later in this book we shall look at the conquest and occupation of
India by the Aryans, the Moghals, and the British, and shall compare
the results. One notable empire on which it would be interesting to
dwell is the Ottoman, which was ruled by a civil service of slaves,
recruited from Christian countries in the Balkans. It was not lawful to
enslave a fellow-Muslim and so the slaves had to be taken from the
Christian countries; they were chosen with great care for their beauty
and intelligence. They were usually converted after enslavement; a
man remained all his life the property of the Emperor though he might
be Viceroy of a province or Wazir—Prime Minister, Chancellor,
Adviser—for the whole Empire, and might possess slaves of his own.
And the Ottomans had an ingenious system of religious federalism by
which a religious group had some degree of local autonomy. But we
must return to the main purpose. These rapid glances at some forms of
primitive empire are enough to show the extraordinarily varied means
employed to solve essentially similar problems. It is time we moved on
to European expansion and the forms it took.

# CHAPTER VI

## The European Expansion

### *1 Another Broad Classification: Conqueror or Immigrant*

In his monograph on Ruanda, M. Jacques Maquet[1] remarks that a conqueror has to choose whether he will take the honey he finds in the hive in the manner of a bear or adopt instead the policy of the bee-keeper. The previous chapter has endeavoured to illustrate this point; the Incas, like the Tutsi, were essentially bee-keepers who had organized their honey-taking so that there would be a crop year after year. But it has also been suggested that the conqueror has a second choice, whether to keep rigidly separate from the conquered or to permit a fusing. A gradual mixture seems to be the course of events most likely to occur unless the conquerors determine from the start to keep themselves separate and apply severe sanctions to any breach of the prohibition. In pre-industrial societies, the Spartans, the Inca royal clan, the Tutsi, the Matabele of Zulu descent (the Zansi), the Aryans in India, to name only some of those we have touched on, kept themselves apart in this way. On the other hand, some great conquerors positively encouraged fusion; Alexander in Persia, Akbar and Albu-querque in India, made this a policy.

We can now look at the expansion of the peoples of North-Western Europe, the results of which influence every aspect of the world scene to-day. We are hoping to classify or analyse the results of this expansion, which have proved so different in, for example, Brazil and South Africa. And we have made a preliminary decision to insist on no hard-and-fast classification into 'orders' but to try rather to make temporary groupings of situations which resemble each other, when looked at from a certain point of view, and then to consider the application to these groupings of one variable factor. (See Table 1, on page 64.)

The first task, then, is to construct some provisional or experimental grouping of the kinds of relationship which arise in modern times, mostly from European expansion. We may make other groupings later, but in making this classification, let us think in terms of the choices open to those who initiate the contact. Let us adopt a new metaphor and

[1] *The Premise of Inequality in Ruanda.*

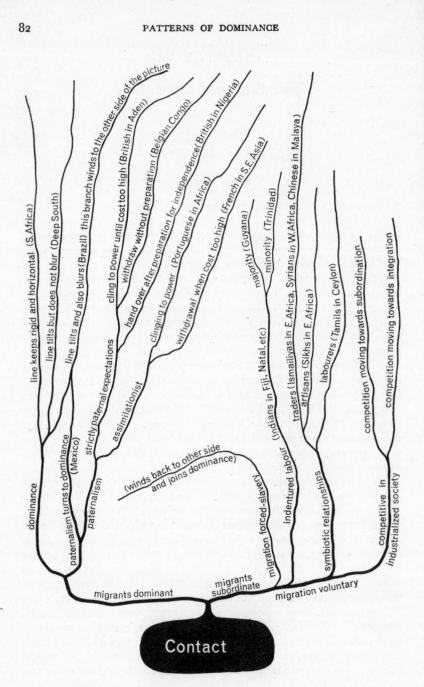

Figure 3   *Relationships Which Arise from European Expansion*

visualize these varied situations as growing and branching like a climbing rose. At the base is a single stem, growing from the soil of the first contact. There is a bifurcation at once; in one kind of relationship the migrants are a dominant conquering group, in the other they come as suppliants. Cortés came to Mexico with every intention of winning an empire; West Indian immigrants to the United Kingdom to-day have quite different aims. But, as I have already pointed out, one situation may develop into the other, as in the case of the British in India; the rose-tree would represent the actual facts more accurately—as well as being more like a rose-tree—if its branches crossed and intertwined and gave out a tangle of side-shoots. But the object is to simplify and clarify.

The left-hand branch, which represents the migrants as dominant and conquering, again forks very soon into two main branches, representing two broad groupings, those of dominance and paternalism, and the sense in which these words are used must now be explained. The distinction is between the relationship of father and son and that of master and slave. It is seldom an absolute distinction, because there will often be a strong paternal element in a situation which I class as one of dominance. But the first characteristic of a father is, or at least ought to be, that in what he does in connexion with his son's up-bringing, he believes he is acting for the son's good. Secondly, a father very commonly assumes that as his son improves or grows up he will share his father's tastes, admire him, and wish to be like him, even though he will perhaps never quite succeed. And finally he supposes that at some distant date his son will be independent—though he probably does not agree with his son as to when the moment for independence has come.

In all these respects, the relation of dominance is different; the master does not try very hard to persuade himself that he is acting for his servant's good, he does not picture the servant growing up to resemble himself and he means the relationship to be unchanged for as long as possible. I repeat that the situations merge into each other, that there are often elements of one in the other; nonetheless, there is a very distinct difference between the relationship of British and Indian in the former Indian Empire and that of white and non-white in South Africa to-day. There was not much paternalism in the relation of Spartan to Helot and the typical plantation-owner in the Deep South before the Civil War did not suppose that the slave would ever be very like himself.

Still keeping to the left-hand shoot of the rose-tree, the dominant type of situation again branches, this time into three. In the most rigid form, the line between the groups is not only insisted on as an absolute social barrier, it is kept horizontal in the sense that in *all* relationships the dominant group is on top. But in some circumstances the line tilts; in the Southern states to-day, a black doctor may have his car filled at a petrol-station by a white attendant. (The example is Professor Banton's.) There is still a stiff social distinction and it is much better to be white than black, but at least in this one relationship a richer and better educated black man is served by a white. Or again, the line may both tilt and blur, as in Brazil; it may not be easy to classify every individual as falling precisely on one side of the line, yet at the same time some classification by race is an element in social ranking. This shoot, from the basic stock of dominance, ought really to wind across to the other side of the picture.

Let us go back to the shoot of paternalism. The different *spirit* of paternalism has already been defined; a rough working guide by which paternalism can often be distinguished from dominance is control by the home country. Thus the Spanish—or at least the Spanish in Spain—are usually paternalist about the Amerindians until the beginning of the eighteenth century. They were deeply concerned to convert the Indians; some of them hoped to 'improve' and educate the Indians in secular affairs. The Crown of Spain did usually try to protect the Indians, though not very successfully. But the independence of the South American countries ended the Crown's interference and for most of the nineteenth century the Indians of Mexico and the Andean countries were dominated and exploited by the owners of *haciendas* or *fincas;* these were men who belonged to the Spanish culture and most of whom regarded themselves as being mainly of Spanish descent. In Mexico, this period came to an end with the revolution of 1911, when the lines of differentiation both blurred and tilted. I have therefore shown a shoot from paternalism winding back towards dominance but eventually grafted (by a rather eccentric gardener) into the shoot of blurring and tilting lines.

But in spite of exceptions and difficulties, the broad division is clear. Algeria and Rhodesia fall under the head of dominance; Senegal and Nigeria (before independence) were paternalist. In the shoot labelled paternalism, there is a fairly early bifurcation between those who believe that the dominant group has a civilizing mission, which will end with the *assimilation* of the subordinate, and those who follow the paternal analogy more closely, believing that one day the boy will come of age. The French and Portuguese were assimilationist, the British more literally paternalist. The Belgians too were paternalist, but in a peculiarly empirical way of their own, it being their declared intention not to look far ahead.

In the years since the Second World War, both the paternal shoot and the assimilationist have branched again. Some of the assimilationists have decided that—once the colonial bluff has been called—the cost of holding power is too high or can be attained better by financial than by military means. Others are still holding on. The

French in Indo-China were outraged at the rejection of their civilizing mission and determined to stay by the use of force. But they were convinced by defeat that the cost was too high. The Portuguese, however, still cling to power in Africa. Of the paternalists, Britain in most cases went through an uneasy period of preparing for independence, giving some ministers experience of office, agreeing on a constitution and trying to allay the fears of ethnic and religious minorities. But here and there, for strategic reasons, Britain too held on till the military cost became too great, as in Aden and Cyprus. Belgium left the Congo almost without preparation.

The right-hand branch of the rose-tree consists of those who come to a country where a stronger, or at any rate more numerous and established people live, usually asking permission to work or trade. But immediately there is a fork, dividing those who move to some extent by their own will from those who go at the will of someone else, as slaves; the slavery branch winds back to the other side of the tree and ought to be grafted on to the shoot labelled dominance.

Next comes a shoot which represents indentured labour. When slavery came to an end in British possessions in 1834–8, there was an acute labour shortage in a number of territories, particularly the sugar islands of the West Indies and the sugar country round Durban. Various solutions were proposed; at various times, the solution of indentured labour was tried, labourers being recruited from various parts of India—in most cases no doubt under some pressure from officials and landowners. They usually came on an indenture to stay and work for five years and sometimes stayed on for a second period and then indefinitely. This was the origin of the Indian population in Trinidad, British Guiana, Fiji, Mauritius, and Natal; in Natal, the Indians are one of South Africa's minorities (to which we shall return), but in the other four territories they have grown until they are either a majority or nearly a majority of the total population.

Indentured labourers were sometimes accompanied by traders or priests catering for their special needs; the East African railway line to Uganda was built by Indian labourers who went back to India when it was finished, but left behind them traders, clerks, artisans, petty officials. It has never been seriously disputed that these people were of considerable importance in the economic development of East Africa; they had skills which Africans had not and were prepared to operate small retail shops for a scale of profits that Europeans would scorn. In the early history of Kenya, they were symbiotic to Europeans and Africans in a way that provides a good analogy with the classical symbiotic relationship of algae and lichens. Similar functions were performed by the Chinese in South-East Asia and by Syrians on the West Coast of Africa; they formed an intermediate group, tolerated by both the subordinate and dominant group because they were useful.

But with independence, groups of this kind usually come under heavy pressure. They flourish under imperial protection but, in a young democracy which is strongly nationalistic and in which there is underemployment, their prospects are bleak. These symbiotic groups are shown on the rose-tree as a branch from the stem of voluntary migration by a weaker group.

The next shoot is one of great importance. It differs from the last in two respects: it is migration to an industrialized society, and the migrants are not distinguished from the people they find by any special skill which the natives have still to learn; rather, it is the immigrants who have much to learn. This represents the immigration of West Indians, Indians, and Pakistanis to Britain, and the internal migration of Negroes from the Deep South to the urban North in the United States; of the Irish, the Italians, and the Puerto Ricans to the United States. The characteristic is that the migrants are pushed by unrewarding conditions at home and attracted by the prospects of a better life at least for their children. They are not legally differentiated from the majority. It is a competitive society—but is the competition fair? Immigrants of this kind have usually understood that they themselves will have to suffer disadvantages—in housing, in employment, in esteem—but the crux comes when their children, born in the new country, leave school. If they, or a fair proportion of them, move on to better houses and better jobs, there is hope of a trend towards a healthy relationship which we may call integration; this may conveniently be defined in the words of Mr. Roy Jenkins when he was Home Secretary[1] as 'equal opportunity'—for education, employment, housing, and other benefits of society, 'accompanied by cultural diversity in an atmosphere of mutual tolerance'. But if the second generation do not get equal opportunity, the trend is towards a double standard, in which one group is expected to be subordinate.

This completes the classification of situations seen from the dimension of the motives of the migrations and the intentions of the dominant group. It provides an outline chart to which we shall be able to refer later when we consider some situations in more detail. It displays four main groupings—relationships which may be classed together as dominance, paternalism, competition, and—rather smaller—symbiosis. Its usefulness is simply as a reminder that we are not thinking only of the internal situation in the United States and Britain, nor of the colonial world, but of both; of the aftermath not only of slavery, but of voluntary migration; of Asia and South America as well as Africa. We shall now experiment a little further with the consideration of one variable factor in relation to these loose groupings.

[1] On 23 May 1966 to the Voluntary Liaison Committees at the Commonwealth Institute.

## 2 Sexual Attitudes

Let us now, with this rough classification in mind, try to apply another 'variable factor' to various situations and see whether any interesting results emerge. Let us choose as our variable factor attitudes to various forms of sexual union between different groups and attitudes to the offspring of mixed unions. It is not easy to use exactly the pattern we followed with 'numerical proportion' as a variable, because to reduce sexual attitudes to numerical symbols is unreal and misleading, and because the general attitude of a social group to sexual matters expresses itself in various different relationships, of which I choose four—marriage, concubinage, exploitation, and paternity. We can look at these relationships in various societies at various periods, and we can, in listing these societies, bear in mind the groupings we used before—dominant, paternal, competitive—and contrast differences within these groupings.

As soon as one begins to classify and put into charts, it becomes apparent that some falsification is taking place. Fine shades of difference are destroyed; the subtlety and delicacy of real life are lost. Nonetheless, a preliminary attack with this rather blunt instrument will reveal some questions to be asked.

The first distinction is between those who take a negative view of the genes of the subordinate group and those who take a positive view of their own. The first—white South Africans, white Americans in the South, for example—regard the genes of African descent as a kind of stain which condemns the offspring of mixed unions to the lower group. There have not been many who have taken the positive view which is completely opposite and think that their own genes raise their offspring to such an extent that they are wholly and immediately acceptable; when this has happened it has usually not lasted much longer than one generation. But there have been many who regard the offspring as in an intermediate position—with many variations, largely depending on class and wealth. The son of Cortés by an Indian mother became a Marquis of Spain; the father's prestige contributed to this. But with each generation after the Conquest, complete acceptance becomes less common, until the reverse current set in about the time of the Mexican Revolution. On the other hand, there is always some degree of intermediacy, even among those who make the most absolute distinction; in the slave-owning South, the mulatto was usually a house-slave rather than a field-hand, sometimes a steward. But the broad difference is clear enough when one contrasts the extremes of attitude. There is also a stage when the offspring for most purposes follow the position of one parent, usually the father. It might here be convenient to look at Table 2 on page 90.

There is another preliminary point which is important. Writers on

Brazil, and particularly Gilberto Freyre,[1] often seem to imply that sexual freedom between the races is, in itself, and without qualification, a relaxing element in the racial situation. It does at least admit common humanity and one cannot wholly despise—the argument seems to run—what one desires. But this is surely bad psychology and quite out of accord with the facts. To take one clear example, in the early days of white presence in the territories which are now Zambia and Rhodesia, there is a consistent body of evidence from the few white men who were concerned to find out what Africans thought. Such men report that there was bitter anger and resentment at the freedom with which many white men took African women. This was the main African grievance, some reported. White freedom with African women was coupled with sensitivity to any suggestion of sexual interest by an African in a white woman.[2] In plantation Brazil, we are told that the white plantation owner frequently used his female black slaves for enjoyment, that his son had his first sexual experiences with them, and so on. But this does not imply equality. If he had a white wife, the plantation owner applied very different standards to her. The Brazilian system, to which we shall be coming back in Part III of this book, was much less rigid than any British society in Africa but here too 'sexual freedom' cannot sensibly be discussed without considering 'sexual equality'; there is a dual standard between the races, and a dual standard between the sexes. White 'freedom' is male; it does not indicate respect but, on the contrary, a profound contempt both for the black man and for the black woman. And though resentment was seldom recorded when the servile group was inarticulate, can anyone seriously doubt that it was often felt? It was not felt *always*; dominance breeds servility and sometimes servility reached such a pitch that a man rejoiced that his woman should share his master's bed, because of the benefits it brought him. That is a measure of the degradation. The point remains that it is only when *marriage* between people from two groups becomes socially accepted that one can suppose that there is equality of esteem.[3]

But there is a half-way house between marriage and the casual use of a social inferior for sexual pleasure. In some societies, it has been quite usual, and socially condoned if not accepted, for a man of the dominant group to take a concubine from the subordinates and for her to live with him in domestic felicity for a long period. Burma and India are here contrasted; concubinage of this kind was a feature of British life in Burma throughout the whole period of contact; in India, it was very unusual, although, particularly in the early days, the English in

---

[1] Gilberto Freyre, *The Masters and the Slaves*.

[2] See Philip Mason, *The Birth of a Dilemma*.

[3] Roger Bastide, 'Dusky Venus, Black Apollo'.

Bengal often kept female servants with whom their exchanges seem to have been confined to the bedroom.

It seems then that any attempt at analysing social attitudes to sex and race must take into account four dimensions or relationships— *marriage* across a group frontier, long-standing *concubinage*, temporary *exploitation*, and the position of the *offspring*. But the attitudes cannot always be expressed with simplicity; concubinage in Burma, for instance, was officially disapproved of but socially condoned by most English men. Sometimes the Burmese lady would disappear if there were white guests; sometimes only if there were white ladies. Again, intermarriage in this society did occur, and Burmese wives went to Government House—but was it approved or merely accepted? There were everywhere exceptions; there was a famous character in Northern Rhodesia who had been a district commissioner. He retired and lived on in the country with two African wives; he was a hospitable man and had many white visitors but on these occasions, his wives would not be seen.[1] He made no attempt to conceal their existence but did not wish to embarrass his guests. His case was unusual in that part of Central Africa; it was not parallel to the frequent pattern in Burma.

It is already clear that the different patterns of behaviour are due to a variety of causes. The British who went to India and those who went to Burma are not easy to distinguish; indeed, the Burma Commission was recruited largely from the Indian Civil Service and the Indian Army, and for some time Burma was administered as an Indian province. The difference lay largely between Burmese and Indian—a difference in their social structure and attitude to life. It is therefore unreal to suppose that—without serious loss of sensitivity in the analysis— one can excise one 'variable factor' and treat it in isolation for more than a temporary demonstration. It at once leads to others.

Again, sexual attitudes differ very markedly from one period to another. They must be related to changes in the world in general, to changes in the country of origin of the dominant group, and to the growth, in the subordinate group, of the sense of injustice that arises once comparisons begin. Further, what we are concerned with is very complicated; we are thinking of the interplay of at least three factors in at least two societies; we are concerned with the generalized attitudes of each society to sex in general and to individual relationships between sexes across class frontiers and across ethnic frontiers, and in each of these three dimensions—social attitude—sex relationship— ethnic relationship—there will be many delicate shades of difference. Nonetheless, as a stage in preliminary clearing of the ground, let us try to tabulate some broad distinctions. The scheme used is shown in Table 2. How it is used becomes apparent in Table 3.

[1] J. E. Stephenson, *Chirapula's Tale. A Byeway in African History.*

Table 2

Social Attitudes to Sex, First Table:
Four Relationships Classified

| | Marriage | Concubinage over Long Periods | Temporary Sexual Exploitation | Paternity: Status of Offspring |
|---|---|---|---|---|
| 1 | Forbidden by law or tabu | Forbidden by law or tabu | Forbidden by law or tabu | Offspring excluded from higher group |
| 2 | Regarded as disgraceful | Regarded as disgraceful | Regarded as disgraceful | Included in various intermediate groups |
| 3 | Condoned | Condoned | Condoned | Follow one parent, usually father |
| 4 | Accepted | Accepted | Accepted | Raised to higher group |
| 5 | Encouraged | Encouraged | Encouraged | — |

It would be possible to use numerical symbols, such as M1 for marriage forbidden by law, M2 for a marriage that is frowned on or regarded as a disgrace. But I believe that to do this would rob the discussion of reality and gives it a spurious air of scientific validity which may seriously mislead. To use the scheme at all involves many hard choices and always slightly falsifies reality. For example, South Africa is the extreme example in modern times of a society determined not merely to preserve but to increase the rigidity of separation. There can be no doubt that in the first three columns of my chart the word to use in South Africa's case is Forbidden; not only is intermarriage illegal but any sexual contact can be punished under the Immorality Act. But at the last column, there is a moment of hesitation. In theory, persons classed in South Africa as white or European are supposed to have no coloured blood, but in fact it is well known that some long-established families have coloured ancestors. And undoubtedly there is an intermediate category in the Cape Coloured. All the same, the decision must be that South Africa heads this column too. A South African has to be white or non-white. This kind of difficulty arises in almost every line of the table that follows:

## Table 3
### Social Attitudes to Sex and Race, Second Table:
### Various Societies Classified in Respect of Four Relationships

| | *Marriage* | *Concubinage* | *Temporary or Casual Union* | *Paternity: Position of Offspring* |
|---|---|---|---|---|
| South Africa (1968) | Forbidden | Forbidden | Forbidden | Lower group |
| Deep South (1960) | Forbidden | Disgrace | Condoned (in most states) | Lower group |
| Brahman village (1910) | Forbidden | Forbidden | Forbidden | Lowest group |
| Tutsi (1960) | Disapproved of | Condoned | Condoned | Higher group if married |
| British India (1780) | Accepted but rare | Accepted but rare | Accepted | Intermediate |
| British India (1880) | Disgrace | Disgrace | Disgrace* | Intermediate |
| British India (1945) | Accepted | Disgrace | Disgrace* | Intermediate† |
| Burma (1880–1930) | Condoned or accepted | Accepted | Condoned | Intermediate† |
| British West Africa (1955) | Accepted or condoned | Condoned | Condoned | Intermediate† |
| British East Africa (till 1960) | Frowned on | Frowned on | Frowned on | Lower group† |
| Portuguese Colonial Empire | Officially encouraged; in practice condoned if not too dark | Accepted | Accepted | Intermediate |
| Mexico (time of Cortés) (Spanish-Indian) | Accepted [but baptism necessary] | Accepted | Accepted | Accepted |
| Mexico (seventeenth century) | Condoned | Accepted | Accepted | Intermediate |
| Mexico (1950) | Accepted | Accepted | Accepted | Accepted |
| Victorian class system | Disgrace | Disapproved (but tolerated for nobility) | Disapproved | Follow father if acknowledged |
| New Zealand | Unwillingly accepted | Disapproved | Disapproved | Follow one parent |
| Britain (1968)‡ | Disapproved by relations | Disapproved | Disapproved | Not yet known |

* For officers but not for 'other ranks'.

† But in last phase follow one parent or the other if wealthy.

‡ Unusual in that the marriages are nearly always between women of the dominant majority and men of the subordinate minority.

The classification is varied slightly from Table 2 in order to approach a little more closely to the shades of difference which are present in reality. An additional dimension which is omitted for the sake of simplicity is the extent to which disapproval is greater when the sexual link is between a woman of the higher group and a man of the lower.

The table, for all its imperfections, does draw attention to some interesting points. In the first place, there is a difference between South Africa and the Deep South. South Africa and seventeen states of the American South forbid marriage between the races by law. South Africa has an Immorality Act which forbids any sexual contact between the races;[1] only two American states, Alabama and Mississippi, go so far, but regular concubinage—in the sense of living harmoniously together without a legal tie and sharing something more than sexual experience—is rare in the Deep South. The real difference arises in respect of casual exploitation or temporary use of women from the subordinate group. The literature suggests that this was once common and indeed approved in South Africa; young men—who had usually been looked after and often suckled by black or coloured nurses—had their first sexual experience with coloured girls. But the tide turned against it; the conscience of the Dutch Reformed Churches has always been tender on this point and the twentieth century has seen a hardening of opinion against it, the passing of the Immorality Act, and a number of prosecutions. Clearly, no one passes an Act against a practice unless it is thought to occur and prosecutions suggest that it does—but now comparatively rarely. There are allegations—seldom amounting to proof—that the police exploit Bantu women in this way as a form of corruption; the multiplicity of technical offences puts every Bantu man or woman in a position very easily exploited. The same allegation is made about police in the Deep South and there the evidence I have seen suggests that casual intercourse, though much less frequent than it once was, is condoned to a much greater extent than in South Africa.

Indeed, while the consensus of white South African opinion is overwhelmingly against any sexual contact across the racial line, in the Deep South it seems to be still broadly true that the objection is not

[1] In 1967, the states which forbad marriage between Negro and white were: Alabama, Arkansas, Delaware, Florida, Georgia, Kentucky, Louisiana, Maryland, Mississippi, Missouri, North Carolina, South Carolina, Oklahoma, Tennessee, Virginia, West Virginia.

At the same period, fourteen states had abolished similar laws: Arizona, California, Colorado, Idaho, Indiana, Michigan, Montana, Nebraska, Nevada, North Dakota, South Dakota, Utah, Wyoming.

There are some curiosities in these laws: Mississippi classes as incestuous fornication between persons whose marriage is prohibited by law by reason of race; Missouri puts interracial marriage in the same class with incest and marriage with imbeciles; North Carolina has a specific prohibition for marriage between 'a Cherokee Indian of Robeson County' and a person of Negro descent.

so much to sex as to equality in sex. There are, I believe, two reasons for this; first, the numerical proportions and the seriousness of the threat to Afrikanerdom—the national existence of the people who speak Afrikaans. They are outnumbered four to one and by people whose culture is wholly alien; if there is fusion, it is we—they say— who will be absorbed, not the Bantu; we must put up every barrier. This danger is much less in the United States, where there is no separate culture, at the most, a sub-culture. The second reason is psychological and arises from the religion of the Afrikaners and the nature of sexual contacts in the early days of the occupation of the Cape. With this we shall deal in the third part of this book.

There is not much difference between the attitude of South Africa and the Deep South to the offspring of mixed unions. Both exclude them from the dominant group; both regard the genes of the subordinate group as a stain. Both are concerned about what can be *seen;* the South African law now provides that every person must be registered and his race officially defined; the criterion to be applied in a doubtful case is common repute. It is commonly said that many of the older Afrikaner families have in fact some African genes but if they have been regarded as white for some generations, they are legally white. In America the definition varies between the states; a fairly common definition is that a person is a Negro if it is known that he has one Negro ancestor in three (or four) generations inclusive. Since this has been the common criterion at least since the Civil War, it really means that anyone whose grandfather was known to have had a Negro grandfather is a Negro. It is said that the tendency of the Courts in Alabama is to hold that 'one drop of Negro blood' is sufficient to create the offence of miscegenation. In Georgia, it is provided that 'the term white' shall include only persons of 'white or caucasian race who have no ascertainable trace of Negro, African, West Indian, Asiatic Indian, Mongolian, Japanese or Chinese blood in their veins'.[1] Virginian law provides that 'white' shall apply only to those who have no trace of blood other than Caucasian—but persons who have one-sixteenth or less of the blood of American Indian and no other non-Caucasian blood shall be deemed white. But enough has been said to show that in both countries, to be *known* to have Negro or African blood is a stain and that only in very exceptional cases is it possible to pretend that the stain is not there.

One other difference between South Africa and the Deep South is not shown in the table. In the Deep South, white mobs frequently took the law into their own hands and lynched, that is murdered, a Negro who was believed to have made sexual approaches to a white woman. Proof was sometimes completely lacking; a rumour of the offence was sometimes enough and sometimes what was alleged was of the most

[1] Martindale Hubbel, *Digest of State Laws 1968.*

trivial kind.[1] Sometimes the murder was particularly cruel and brutal, the offender being burned alive. Sometimes it seems to have been felt that a Negro had to be murdered—whether he was guilty or not—and an offence had to be expiated—whether it had actually taken place or not. But lynching was almost unknown in South Africa—though sometimes white crowds came near it and very similar emotions are recorded. It has been one of the arguments used for the Immorality Act and the severity of the laws about marriage and rape that without strong laws lynching would take place.

I have put one example from the Indian caste system next in the list—a Brahman village in South India at an arbitrary date, 1910, chosen simply to indicate the stage when the system was probably at its most rigid. Such a village is described in André Béteille's *Caste, Class, and Power*; the Brahmans, who were about one-fifth of the village —about two-fifths being non-Brahmans and two-fifths untouchables— had almost a monopoly in ownership of land, in religious and social prestige, in education, in opportunities of employment, and in such political power as existed. Their rules about sexual contact were not enacted as law but had the force of ancient custom and any breach was punished by excommunication if the offender was a Brahman—and it is almost impossible to exaggerate the seriousness for a Brahman of being put out of his caste. Breach would be punished in a variety of ways—which might go so far as murder—if the offender belonged to one of the subordinate groups. That is not to say that Brahman men never formed what was usually referred to as an illicit connexion with women of lower castes, but it was a matter of shame, to be kept secret, and neither marriage nor regular concubinage was possible.

The Tutsi are included as a fourth example of a dominant group. As described by Maquet, the standard of behaviour normally expected was clearly defined; marriage was usually between Tutsi and Tutsi, between Hutu and Hutu; both groups were insulted by the idea that marriage with a Twa was even possible. It was common for a Tutsi lord to make use of a woman from the family of one of his Hutu vassals; but the possibility did exist of a poor Tutsi marrying the daughter of a rich Hutu. The Tutsi admitted with reluctance that it might occur but clearly felt it as a reproach; the Hutu tried to convey that it happened much more often. In the case of marriage, the offspring would be regarded as Tutsi; if the encounter was casual, the child would be regarded as belonging to the maternal grandfather. The words used on the chart for the Tutsi are (as usual) not quite appropriate because the attitude of people in Ruanda to sexual functions was different from either European or Brahman; sex was regarded

---

[1] See John Dollard, *Caste and Colour in a Southern Town*, and William Faulkner, *Intruder in the Dust*. But there are few books on the South which do not have some mention of this.

(Maquet found) as a natural part of the human condition, and its regular enjoyment was necessary, both for man and woman; if the husband was away, it was proper for his wife to be regularly consoled by a male cousin.

Relations between the British in India and Indians varied very markedly over the period of nearly two centuries in which the British were a dominant group. They were much more free in the eighteenth century than later. Job Charnock, the founder of Calcutta—who reigned there 'more absolutely than a Rajah'—married the widow of a Brahman whom he rescued from her husband's funeral pyre, and until about the time of Lord Cornwallis, such marriages were fairly frequent. They were perhaps excused rather than accepted. Up country, there was an occasional adventurer who set himself up as a minor prince with a following of retainers and who lived as an Indian, in marriage or permanent concubinage with an Indian woman, or women. This went on well into the nineteenth century but the numbers were not large. As I have already said, female servants were kept in the time of William Hickey for purely physical reasons. Nor was a mixture of genes regarded as a disqualification for a man of courage, who might command a regiment of irregular cavalry.[1]

But as the nineteenth century advanced, social distance grew, first in the three Presidency towns—Calcutta, Bombay, and Madras— which were the seats of government, and later in remoter parts. Richard Burton in Sind in the 1840s describes a society like that of Calcutta in 1780. Each generation speaks of an increase in social distance since their fathers' time; it grew as communications with England improved, as home leave became more frequent, as more English women came to India. But there was more than that. There was the Evangelical movement, strong among the families who sent sons to India; there was the concept of dedicated, impartial service, which appears surprisingly early; it was felt that to be truly impartial it was necessary to be aloof.[2]

The taste—it was as much aesthetic as moral—of the English upper and middle classes changed between 1780 and 1830. It was the difference between *Tom Jones* and *Pride and Prejudice*; a change in taste which affected behaviour. Attitudes to sex changed in England even where there was no difference between the parties either of race or of class—but the change affected attitudes to race and class as well. Indeed, it is my hypothesis that in all three cases—sex, race, class—the change was due to nervousness about the hierarchical position and the

[1] Donald Pierson (in *Negroes in Brazil*) mentions the fact that in 1678 the East India Company encouraged soldiers at Fort St. George in Madras to marry Indian women. But he is wrong in supposing this was a consistent policy and it was abandoned before British rule in India began to expand in the middle of the eighteenth century.

[2] See Henry Roberdeau's diary, 1804–9.

danger of admitting that the upper group shared a common humanity with the subordinate.

By 1880, as I have suggested elsewhere,[1] the distance between British and Indian was coming into its worst period. The British in India fell into two quite distinct social groups, those who belonged to the club and were invited to Government House, and the rest. The first group were mainly civil and military officials, with some business men in the big cities, and in some areas—parts of Behar, Assam, and Bengal, parts of the South—a few planters. They sent their children to England at seven or eight years old, and retired there themselves in their fifties; it was very rare for anyone from this group to marry an Indian.

But sometimes an unwary young man 'straight from home' was imprudent enough to become entangled with a girl from the other group, who was 'of the country'. This did not always mean of mixed genes, though it might; there were British soldiers—'other ranks' not officers—who had taken their discharge in India, sometimes with British wives, but more often with an Anglo-Indian wife from the railway community. The predicament of a young man who became attached to a girl from such a family is a frequent theme in early Kipling stories; the friends who do not want him to ruin his career by an imprudent marriage go to great lengths to prevent it. Concubinage—in the sense of a comparatively permanent union—was rare in the upper group and kept as secret as might be; again, there is a Kipling story, 'Without Benefit of Clergy'. 'Other ranks' commonly resorted to prostitutes but this was not thought proper for officers; the strong Victorian emphasis on the value of sexual restraint[2] was reinforced and emphasized by the need to maintain aloofness, to display no weakness, to have nothing in common with the alien race.

Of course there *were* people of mixed blood and the more high-minded officials felt they had some duty to those whom their erring brothers had called into existence. The railway service, the opium department, and various other special spheres of employment were filled with Anglo-Indians—but only the most senior and successful were asked to dinner. But again there are exceptions; in small stations, the rules were relaxed and the socially approved felt it proper to take notice of those who were not quite so senior—people who at head-quarters could be left to find their own level. It should be added that the attitude of the official classes to Indians of birth and wealth was quite different; they belonged to another society, while the Anglo-Indians or Eurasians were the lower tiers of British society. Some British officers were slightly obsequious to Maharajahs.

By 1945, the end of the Second World War, things had changed

---

[1] Philip Mason (pseud. Philip Woodruff), *The Men who Ruled India.*
[2] Peter T. Cuminos, 'Late Victorian Sexual Respectability and the Social System'.

completely. In the Indian Civil Service, the intake had been half British and half Indian for a quarter of a century; the slower start in the Army had been greatly accelerated during the war. Officials in India knew that independence was coming—but they believed their pensions were reasonably safe and they had in any case always meant to retire to Britain; their attitude was not at all like that of colonists in Rhodesia or Algeria. And in English society attitudes to sex had relaxed, while on the subject of class, most intelligent people expected that after the war there would be a far more radical and more rapid approach to equality than in fact occurred. There was no longer much point in keeping up the pretence of being quite different. The myth had served its purpose and could be discarded. Marriage across the racial line was more frequent and was entirely acceptable; the children usually chose to follow one culture or the other. Concubinage and prostitution were both regarded with disfavour; there was thus a reversal of the rule so common in a dominant society, that sexual contact is condoned as long as it does not imply equality. It had been accepted that dominance was at an end and in this untypical society, when independence was in the air but no one knew how close, sexual contact was permissible so long as it *did* imply equality.

I have already suggested that the very different atmosphere in Burma must have been largely due to the difference between Indians and Burmese. The British came basically from the same backgrounds. There was some choice open to officials in the All-India services when Burma was a province of India, and perhaps those who volunteered for Burma in the first place were more adventurous or more impatient of convention than those who stayed in India; perhaps unconventional behaviour had in some cases made it expedient for a young man to get away from his immediate superiors and start again. Some members of the Burma Commission were recruited from professions that were not official. And Burma was remote from the Viceroy and the Government of India. But these are not sufficient to account for the marked difference in attitudes.

Even at the time when the British in India were most rigidly aloof, marriage between British and Burmese was accepted, socially with only the slightest reservation, officially with none at all. Concubinage, for a district officer in a lonely place, was widespread though frowned on officially; the relationship was quite different from that with the 'female servants' of Hickey's day in Calcutta; it was really a short-term marriage. 'It was pleasant, after a day of hard work in the courts, to come home to a pretty little Burmese girl, who looked after the house and mended one's socks and talked about what had been happening at home all day. They loved each other—but it usually ended when the man went on leave; he was going to come back, perhaps with an English wife, almost always to another district, and his Burmese friend would marry a

Burmese man with no feelings of reproach'—so the relationship was
described to me by an informant who clearly knew what he was talking
about. But it is hard to sum up in a word the position of children of
mixed blood; those from a marriage between an official and a Burmese
woman would—in the earlier part of the period—almost certainly be
brought up as Europeans. At a later period, they would choose their
culture. As in India, there were official niches for the Anglo-Burmese.
On the whole, 'intermediate' is the classification.

Why were relations in Burma so different from India? Mainly
because Indian society was different from Burmese. The caste system
lays great emphasis on marriage within the group; although one aspect
of Hinduism has idealized procreation, the higher reaches of Hinduism
emphasize brahmācharya, which means control of all sensual appetite
and particularly of the sexual. Remarriage of widows was prohibited
for the higher castes in the traditional system and the idea of marrying
a girl who was not a virgin—let alone one who had kept house for an
Englishman—would be inconceivably repugnant to a Hindu of the
twice-born castes. Indeed, British aloofness was partly a response to
the Hindu idea of ritual purity, which was destroyed by *any* contact
with a person who—to name only one disqualification—had ever eaten
beef. At the same time, the ideas of caste were infectious; few English
who spent long in India did not absorb them to some extent and the
idea of sleeping with an untouchable has only to be put in words to
appear repugnant. And only untouchables were usually available.

West Africa was more like Burma than India. One reason for this
was the nature of the relationship at the beginning; the country was
thickly populated when the British first came and there were powerful
chiefs; the first traders were suppliants. This affected the whole
relationship, which was quite different from the South African. Later,
when British rule began, neither officials nor traders were usually
accompanied by white women; white children were unknown until
some control of malaria was achieved, as late as the 1930s. And the
African attitude to sex was more like the Burmese than Indian. In
British East Africa, there were differences between the three territories,
Kenya having far more white residents, but, until independence was
in sight, the impression is of relationships more like India in 1880 than
Burma or West Africa.

The Portuguese colonial empire shows, like the British, many
variations both in time and space and I have not attempted to show
all these in the chart. There are differences between West Africa and
East, between Brazil and India; there is a marked difference between,
for example, the attitudes displayed in the Congo in the time of first
contacts in the early sixteenth century and those which developed a
century later. Tolerance and politeness marked the first meetings; a
Congolese prince was invited to the Court at Lisbon, stayed for two

years and was treated with courtesy. But a century later the slaving era had begun and there was a deterioration in Africa. There can be little doubt that the Portuguese encouraged mixture of the races because they were short of manpower. This was the official policy in India of the great Albuquerque, the conqueror of Goa, but he made it clear that he meant women of Aryan descent—'white and of good appearance'— and not low-caste or dark women. And no one questions that there was everywhere much miscegenation outside marriage with slave women. Nor is it in dispute that there were in all the colonies some marriages with women of the indigenous group; they do however seem to have been more frequent in India than in Africa and in all areas much more frequent with those of mixed descent than with the unmixed indigenous. A typical sequence in Brazil was that in the first generation both concubinage and exploitation took place with Amerindian women and a variety of intermediate relationships; in later generations, the same relationships continued, with marriage added, but for marriage those of mixed descent were preferred. African slave women in Brazil were used as concubines by their masters but marriage in colonial times was almost unknown. What is to some extent in controversy is the degree of esteem in which mixed and indigenous wives and their offspring were held.

To me the case presented by Professor Boxer is convincing; there is, for example, the classification of the population of Goa reported by an Italian Jesuit in 1580; he said there were some European-born Portuguese, mostly illiterate soldiers; a very few born in India of European parents—who are weak, vicious, and idle, having been brought up by slaves; and then three classes, those with a white father and a mixed mother, those who are of mixed origin in about equal proportions, and finally those of mostly Indian blood. All the three latter classes are 'treated by the Portuguese with the greatest contempt'. By the end of the sixteenth century, all the Religious Orders refused to admit Indians or those of mixed blood; a few were trained for the secular priesthood but kept in subordinate roles.

A serious attempt was made to end the colour bar in Portuguese Asia and East Africa by the Marquis of Pombal in a decree of 1761. This proclaimed that Asian subjects of the Portuguese Crown who were baptized Christians must be given the same legal and social status as white persons; the decree made it a penal offence for white Portuguese to call their fellow subjects by a variety of insulting racial terms, which are specified and seem to have been in general use. At the same time, Pombal ordered the establishment of a seminary for the training of coloured clergy at Mozambique; his instructions were shelved, and nearly two centuries later, in 1954, it was sadly noted that no native priest had yet been ordained in Mozambique (though this was by no means the case in Angola). As I have already suggested, there are so many variations between territories and periods that it is hard to generalize, but it seems broadly true that although marriage with local women was officially encouraged in India as far back as the time of Albuquerque, though many such marriages took place, though there were many edicts enjoining equality of treatment, in fact there was throughout the Portuguese empire a gradation of esteem based largely on race. Edicts by the Crown enjoining equality of esteem for all Portuguese subjects seldom received much attention on the spot. Men from Portugal made free use of local women and outside marriage often preferred brown to fair but, for marriage, they preferred someone from Portugal if she could be found; if not, the lighter her colour the better. There is equality neither between sexes nor races.

The picture is one to which there are continual exceptions. But a hierarchy of gradations, in which colour is an important element, is certainly the rule. Among many examples quoted by Professor Boxer, one is outstanding; in the last quarter of the eighteenth century, the viceroy of Brazil ordered the degradation of an Amerindian chief because he 'had sunk so low as to marry a Negro woman, staining his blood with this alliance'. And one of his successors made a distinction between white and coloured officers of the militia, shaking hands with the whites but permitting the coloured only to kiss their hands to him from the door. To the distinction made by both Spanish and Portuguese between Amerindian and Negro we shall return.

Mexico comes next on the list. Relationships here have been even subtler than in Brazil and we shall be looking at them in greater detail later. But a brief anticipation of the fuller account is necessary. At the time of the Conquest, the Spanish conquistadors constantly referred to themselves as the army of Christ accomplishing his purposes; the speeches of Cortés refer also frequently to glory, less often to gold. But their difference from the Indians the Spanish expressed primarily in religious terms; they were happy to take Indian wives if they would be baptized, and Cortés owed much to his faithful Doña Marina (or Malinche) his secretary, interpreter, and mistress; an almost equally important part in the conquest was played by Doña Luisa, a Tlascalan princess, given by her father Xicotencatl to Alvarado, one of Cortés's principal lieutenants; 'their posterity intermarried with the noblest families of Castile'.[1] So for a brief period, the Spanish accepted their offspring as their equals.

But this did not last. They continued, generation by generation, to mate with Indians and with those whose genes combined in increasingly complex combinations the Spanish and the Indian; but, probably because of their own history in relation to Moor and Jew, they distinguished between the combinations. They made legal distinctions to which privileges were attached. But these became too complicated to

[1] William H. Prescott, *The History of the Conquest of Mexico*.

be remembered, fell into the limbo of obsolete historical survival, and disappeared at independence. The general pattern persisted of a social scale based on descent, though capable of some modification by achievement. Early in the nineteenth century, the most widespread social grouping was dual; there were landowners, of mainly Spanish descent, a dominant privileged group in a semi-feudal relationship with a peasantry of mainly Indian blood, so crippled by poverty and debt that they were virtually tied to the land. But the pattern was changing all through the century; the Revolution of 1911 was not so much a sharp break as an acceleration of progress in the direction of a new social and racial structure, of which the basis was a central group, more than 80 per cent of the total, who would describe themselves as *mestizo* (or in some regions as *ladino*), who would refer as a matter of course to their own Indian ancestry but use the word '*indio*' as a term of abuse, meaning primitive, dirty, and ignorant, and who in fact would be proud of European physical characteristics. In attempting to put this Mexico into the chart, we must first recognize that it was important for Mexicans to establish their *machismo* or virility in the eyes of the world, so that attitudes to sex are not those of either Hindu or Englishman; at the same time, there is the cult of *indigenismo*—a theoretical admiration for a romanticized Indian past—and an inconsistent admiration for fair skin and light-coloured hair. Thus—throughout the central *mestizo* group—there is less general disapproval of sexual relations outside marriage, whether or not there is any consciousness of racial or class distinctions, nor is there the intense consciousness of shades of colour that is so important in the Caribbean and which affects choice in marriage. When these factors are combined with the strong inclination towards equality which dominates political thought, or at least political utterance, it is understandable that the attitudes for Mexico on the chart are permissive. But they do not apply to a small group of former estate-owners, of mainly Spanish descent, at one end of the scale, nor at the other end, to the larger group of those who speak an Indian language and live in an Indian community.

The difficulties, experienced all through this section, of fitting a single word to an attitude becomes even more acute when we come to the 'competitive' types of society, such as Britain or New Zealand. But, before we look at racial patterns in these two countries, it is worth glancing at the British class system in the nineteenth century; here—in sharp contrast with Mexico and Brazil—there was strong social disapproval of any sexual relations outside marriage. But to err was more permissible in the aristocracy than in the middle classes, and much more permissible for a man than for a woman. The earl who kept a flat for a lady of the chorus was regarded with indulgence—though *she* was not; it was a much more serious matter to *marry* a girl of working-class origin, even if she had achieved the accolade of success on the stage. Even to marry a girl from the upper middle classes was serious for a nobleman.[1] For a woman of the aristocracy or upper middle class to marry a working-class man was regarded—by the upper classes of both sexes—as something deeply shocking. But—just as in Rhodesia and South Africa—there were occasional whispers of some deeply depraved lady who seduced the footman or the gamekeeper. In general, each class married within its own range—a little above or a little below—and the extent to which this was possible was the backbone of the English novel; relations outside marriage were disapproved of, whatever the class of the parties, but might be condoned if the male came from high in the system and the woman low, but never in the reverse case; lust was permissible only in the male. The marks are those of a dominant rather than a paternalist society.

New Zealand, like Brazil, has been held up to admiration as the perfect society, wholly free from racism. This of course is exaggerated; the Maoris, a Stone Age Polynesian group, were defeated and expropriated from most of their land, but no rigidly defined legal colour bar was established against them; it was not necessary. For long, it was possible for a Maori either to live at home in a Maori community, speaking a Maori language, and voting as a Maori, or to come out into the world of the Pakehas where he would earn his living and vote with them; his son would go to school with them. In effect, the kind of jobs he would hold would be as a sheep-shearer or as a manual labourer on the docks or in the building trade. White men have not objected to working alongside him or drinking with him, but there is a prejudice against a Maori neighbour and still more against a Maori partner in marriage.[2] Parents and family on both sides disapprove—but the disapproval can be overcome by personal qualities. On the other hand, general social attitudes to sex are those of middle-class Britain forty years back. But there are signs to-day, on the white side, of a romantic idealization of the past (and some atonement for past wrongs) shown by a readiness to claim Maori ancestry; on the Maori side, there are indications of a determination to take pride in a distinct Maori identity.

Britain to-day is passing through a fluid stage, in which the native English have not yet adjusted themselves to the presence of Indians, Pakistanis, and West Indians in appreciable numbers. There seems little doubt that there is usually disapproval by relations if a white girl decides that she wants to marry an immigrant from one of these groups. On the other hand, it does happen. What will become of the children is one of the great questions that hangs over us. But there is something here which we have hardly seen elsewhere. It is rare for a girl from one

---

[1] The novels of George Meredith are very revealing on this, particularly *Evan Harrington* and *Lord Ormont and his Aminta*. But see also Trollope, Surtees, Thackeray.
[2] John Harré, *Maori and Pakeha*.

of the immigrant manual worker groups to marry an English man; all three main groups of immigrants were however at first predominantly male and there was a sprinkling of marriages with English girls. These girls, in spite of initial opposition by their families, have often helped the man to adapt himself to new conditions, to find himself accommodation and work. General social resentment at these marriages has not been strongly expressed, except by a small minority; on the whole, the resentment which has been expressed much more widely has been directed simply at the presence of these groups in the United Kingdom.

At this point, the question will perhaps be asked whether Table 3, on page 91, should not have included a fifth column, indicating the strength of the feeling against a woman having any sexual contact with a group generally regarded as socially inferior. But the complexities seem to me too great to make it worth while. Account has to be taken, first, of the distinction between peoples who regard sex as on the whole a proper and enjoyable human activity and those who have put a strong emphasis on sexual restraint; there is also the extent to which women are subordinate in the social system. The societies that fall into the dominant group have the strongest sense of outrage at a woman marrying down. The paternalist societies are only slightly less vehement in this respect; the Victorian British in India felt almost as strongly as the white Southerner. It is less strong in the competitive societies, but here again distinctions have to be made. In Britain, attitudes are still transitional and fluid; in New Zealand, cross marriages often occur among the better educated and there is still a generally lower level of education among Maori women than Maori men, therefore, among the educated, more contacts between Maori men and white women and more marriages of this kind. In the Northern United States, the marriage of a Negro man to a white woman is rare outside university circles. Still, the provisional hypothesis does emerge that in these competitive societies resentment at this situation is generally less.

Another important distinction has emerged between the societies where a breach of class and race rules is more important than a breach of sex rules and those where the order is reversed. In the former group, sex relations for a dominant male with a subordinate woman are permissible *outside* marriage but not *in*. But with the assertion of new pride in the group that was formerly subordinate this becomes bitterly resented.

The list in Table 3 does not include the Caribbean, which is more like Brazil than anywhere else, and says nothing of the symbiotic group of societies. On the whole, it seems best to deal with these elsewhere. The nuances between attitudes in the Caribbean islands and between the islands and Brazil do not lend themselves to classification in a word or phrase.

## 3 The Nature of the Territory

We have used the term 'variable factor' of something that distinguishes between situations, but clearly not all these variable factors are of the same kind; some are *causes* and some are *manifestations* of the form the current relationship takes. The intentions of the conqueror are a cause; the sexual attitudes which eventually emerge are manifestations, though the attitudes of the conquerors to sex in general are often an important cause. The nature of the territory is clearly a factor in the relationship that arises; is it in fact a cause? If so, can it be isolated and be said to *determine* the results that follow?

The movement of peoples was for a long period most frequently from a harsh environment to one where it was easier to grow food. Highlanders raided the plains, desert nomads the fertile crescent. But with the growth of wealth, and specialization of function, trade became at least as powerful a magnet as land, and later minerals became as powerful as trade. Trade however presupposes people; areas of dense population were attractive to traders, while the farmers in the first place wanted land they could possess with as little opposition as possible, though they often hoped for a supply of cheap willing labour once their farms were established. At every stage, the natural resources of the territory interact with the needs of the newcomers and the reactions of the native population. In the current stage of history, there is a strong reverse flow; people move towards industrial employment rather than towards agriculture. This has sometimes meant migration from a favourable to a harsher climate. But in this case the change of physical climate has been much less important than the change of social atmosphere.

Before we come to consider the main interactions of population and geography and their effect on group relations it is worth mentioning two preliminary and almost incidental points. There are in the first place certain almost exactly opposed features of South-East Asia and Middle America. In Middle America and the Andes, the more advanced cultures developed in the highlands; the lowlands were usually barbarian territories occupied by primitive tribes. But in South-East Asia, social geography was reversed; the high cultures arose in the plains and it was in the surrounding hills that the barbarian tribes persisted. No doubt rainfall was an important element in this; in South-East Asia, there was too much rain in the hills; in Mexico, not enough rain in the plains.

Clearly the nature of the country will affect military movements. It has often been alleged that in Nigeria the Yoruba checked the Hausa-Fulani advance when it reached forest country unsuitable for cavalry; a defeated group has often been able to take refuge in wild mountainous country where the conquerors cannot move easily and where settlement is less profitable than in easier country. This accounts for pockets of aboriginal peoples such as the Hos, the Mundas, and the Sonthals in India and for the different distribution of blood groups in Wales and England. An aboriginal population in an isolated and inaccessible country of this kind is liable to be a nuisance to a more settled group in easier country nearby; they are apt to steal cattle and sheep if no worse; the Welsh border was turbulent for some five hundred years and in India an observer in the early nineteenth century wrote of the Sonthals, an aboriginal hill tribe in Chota Nagpur: 'A deadly feud existed till within the last forty years between them and the cultivators of the neighbouring lowlands; they being untamed thieves and murderers, continually making forays and the Mohammedan land-owners killing them like mad dogs or tigers whenever they got them within gunshot.'[1] Even when such a state of affairs had ended, contempt and hostility are likely to survive between two such groups for almost so long as they continue to be distinguishable. In Burma, when the British left, hostility flared up between the settled central Burmese and the highland groups of the perimeter; in Spanish America the threat from the wild or jungle Indians who surrounded them sometimes made the subjugated Indians of the centre more ready to be Hispanicized than they might have been otherwise.

In the colonial period, the nature of the country becomes of even more importance. The dominant group, the newcomers, have come with a variety of motives, but one motive always present, though in varying degrees, is economic advantage. Gold—already dug, already portable—was a magnet to the Spaniards in Mexico and Peru; in South Africa and Rhodesia it was gold beneath the surface, still to be mined, that drew the Victorian British. In the twentieth century, oil takes the place of gold, but there is an immense difference; in the nineteenth century, one man could pan for gold in a river; in early days in Rhodesia, he could dig a hole in the ground and mine gold by himself or with one partner. But oil to-day may demand a hundred million pounds of investment before any substantial results are achieved. Minerals are increasingly intensive of capital and skill rather than labour; they may be found beneath the sea or the desert, so that they need not involve the loss of much agricultural land. But the skill and the high capital cost of extracting minerals in the mid-twentieth century import a special element into the racial and political scene; contrast Zambia, which has copper, with Malawi, which has not. National policy is basically different; attitudes to racial questions are emotionally very similar but one country can afford to express them in politics, the other cannot. Consider also the effect oil has had on the politics and group relationships of Iran and Iraq.

We are here on the verge of a basic factor in world affairs—the rich

[1] Bishop Heber, *Indian Journal*.

white nations have the skill and the capital required to extract minerals, but are dependent on the acquiescence of much poorer nations beneath whose territory the minerals often lie. A complex relationship thus arises; an oil or mining company must pay heavily for permission to extract and is at the mercy of the country where its product lies; on the other hand, this territory is often dependent on its oil or copper revenues. Each is dependent on the other and it is the nature of man that dependence is usually resented. It is a relationship that calls for— but does not always receive—the tolerant symbiosis of algae and lichens.

A very different relationship arises when the territory is primarily agricultural and it is for control of land that the invaders have come. Their agricultural techniques may be much more advanced than those of the natives, but it is only in their own eyes that this is any justification for what happens. Loss of land is far more than the loss of 'income', of 'capital', of stocks and shares. It means losing the graves of one's fathers and the home of one's childhood; the sense of community, of the ordered pattern of nature, of the continuity and meaning of life, are destroyed. When people lose their land, there can only be deep and bitter resentment. The relationship, where a group of newcomers means to possess the land and expropriate the former holders, is usually quite simple; it is one of unmitigated hostility until one group is in a position to impose its will on the other.

But there are two important bifurcations here; there is a distinction between countries where population is sparse and cultivation extensive and those where population is dense and the cultivation already intensive; there is also a division between temperate and tropical countries. These distinctions overlap; it is broadly true that the densely populated countries were tropical but not true that all the tropical countries were densely populated.

Can we with any advantage construct a chart or diagram of the effect on group relations of the nature of the territory? It is not easy because the nature of each of the two populations affects the relationship; the density of the population comes into play as well as the resources, and we have to bear in mind, as the classification proceeds, the groupings already attempted, particularly those in Figure 3, into dominant, paternal, and competitive. It becomes necessary to change the categories as one proceeds along the forks or branches and the whole construction is lamentably lacking in logic or symmetry. Nonetheless, it does bring out some contrasts and put some order into our picture if we do once more adopt the metaphor of a climbing rose-tree with the branches disentangled and displayed, rather like that in Figure 3.

The diagram is meant to illustrate the effect on race relations of the economic resources of various territories. The branches near the ground

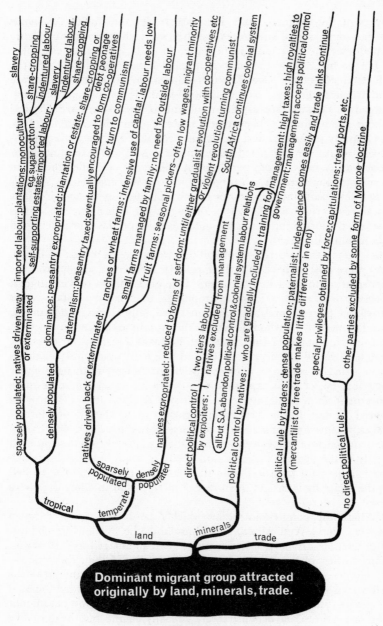

Figure 4

*The Nature of the Territory: Economic Magnets in the Colonial Period and their Effect on Group Relationships*

represent the magnets, land, minerals, trade; the tips of the shoots suggest some kind of human relationship, even where it is not explicitly stated. But the diagram will be easier to understand with examples.

Let us first follow the branch marked 'land', which leads to the left-hand side of the page. The first bifurcation is between temperate and tropical climates. This distinction is made because people from temperate climates are usually reluctant to undertake hard physical labour in hot climates. The tropical shoot at once splits again into two, the sparsely populated and the densely populated. Where the population is sparse (or organized in primitive ways) it is exterminated or driven away into remote parts without difficulty, and the land taken over by the new arrivals, who organize it either in feudal estates of a self-supporting economy or perhaps later in plantations specializing in a single cash crop, such as cotton or sugar. In either case, labour is needed; the local inhabitants are not available and slaves or indentured labour must be found.

In Jamaica, the original inhabitants were exterminated; in Brazil, they were pushed back into the forest. In both cases, slavery was the first solution to the labour problem. One alternative—or sometimes a successor—to slavery is share-cropping; that is, the estate-owner provides a piece of land, and sometimes seed, implements, and fertilizer, to a labourer, with whom he shares the crop in an agreed proportion. But not all crops are easily dealt with in this way; coffee, for example, does not bear till it is five years old and thus locks up capital; tea needs to be dried in a factory with expensive machinery. Both need either an estate-owner with capital *or* a co-operative society or some more extreme form of joint enterprise, such as a Kibbutz, that can provide shared capital.[1] In the West Indies, Brazil, and the Deep South, former slaves became sometimes share-croppers, more often hired field hands. In many parts of Spanish America, and elsewhere, the estates consisted partly of the owner's demesne and partly of small holdings for which the tenants paid by working on the demesne; they were often so tied to the estate by loans at a high rate of interest that in effect they were serfs.

Where the country was more thickly populated, as in parts of Mexico, Peru, West Africa, and Nyasaland, the previous inhabitants were neither driven away nor exterminated, but reduced in status, from 'owner' of the soil—however they understood their ownership— to tenants, squatters, or serfs. Often it had been the community—the tribe or its chief as a representative or trustee—who regarded the land as 'theirs', subject sometimes to the overlordship of some paramount authority; the actual occupiers were virtually tenants but the dues they paid for their tenure were often hardly felt as a burden: they were

[1] Tea begins now to be possible as a peasant crop but was long thought to be essentially a plantation crop.

respect and obedience to chiefs or elders, conformity with tribal traditions, ceremonial presents. Under the new dispensation however they became tenants to an authority who seemed wholly alien and who demanded dues that were very substantial. This, for instance, happened to many inhabitants of Nyasaland; they had been cultivating a piece of tribal land with the permission of their chief; he—often with no comprehension of what the transaction was supposed to be about— sold a large stretch of tribal land to a white man, sometimes for a few yards of cloth or two or three flintlock guns. The tenants were then suddenly informed that they were living on the white man's land; they must either leave or work for him, three days a week.

Here a distinction arises of a rather different order. Nyasaland was a paternalist rather than a dominant society; at a very early stage, many transactions of the kind just mentioned were declared void or modified in the tenants' favour by Sir Harry Johnston. He made it a principle that village sites or land actually cultivated should be excluded from such transfers, but, since cultivation was shifting, people were continually moving on to land which their fathers had cultivated but which now 'belonged' to a white man. In spite of Johnston's reforms, this remained a serious problem, indeed a central problem to the history of the territory. Continual attempts were made to regulate this feudal arrangement, but it persisted until the 1950s. It was in principle not much different from the peonage of Peru.

The Anglo-Egyptian Sudan and India also provide examples of tropical possessions under paternalist rule but they are very different from Nyasaland. Here there were no settlers—and in the Sudan there were not even the planters who in some parts of India spent part of their lives. In neither was desire for land the reason for British presence so they are out of place on this shoot. But the contrast must be underlined at some point. The peasantry in both countries remained in general in possession of their lands. In India they had always been taxed; they paid tax now to a government instead of to a Raja; collection was more systematically enforced but the amounts due ceased to be arbitrary. Their status was not basically modified. Indeed, it was sometimes modified in their favour; the definition of occupancy rights and the liberalization of the terms on which hereditary tenants held their land, in for example what is now Uttar Pradesh, were in the end a definite advantage to the tenant, though it took a long time to work them out. In the last days before independence, the tendency was to promote the formation of co-operative societies and such enterprises as the Gezira scheme in the Sudan.

Where the climate is temperate, there is again a distinction, if a blurred one, between areas of dense and sparse population. Tasmania is the extreme example; a scattered and primitive population were exterminated. Much the same is true of the greater part of Argentina.

In the Western Cape, Hottentots and Bushmen survived but the Hottentots ceased to exist as organized groups. In the Northern parts of North America, the American Indians were hunters but also agriculturalists, loosely organized in tribal groups; they were too primitive to make comfortable neighbours for white settlers but at the same time they were not too many to drive back and they left wide spaces open as a perpetual encouragement to the settlers to advance. At this point, it becomes clear that sparse habitation and primitive organization tend to coincide and it is not solely the sparseness of the population nor solely its primitive nature that is responsible for the severity with which they are treated; both contribute. In fact, density of population and a higher degree of organization are bound together; the population will not become dense until it has found a fairly advanced form of organization—and density imposes such an organization upon it.

When land was the attraction and the previous population sparse and primitive, the economy that results is built on plentiful land and scarce labour. The ranches of the South-Western United States, the great wheat-farms of the prairie provinces, the sheep farms of Australia, use very little labour in proportion to land. The aboriginal population is not there; what remains of it is secluded in reserves. There is no internal problem of race relations, indeed there is virtually no problem of labour relations. In very different country, the small farms of New England employ little labour outside the family. It is only fruit farms that demand seasonal labour and look for temporary workers, often migrants of another group.

There are not many temperate areas where the population was relatively dense, but the highlands of Mexico, Peru, Ecuador, Bolivia, and Kenya do perhaps fall in this category. It cannot be said that the natives fared much better here than in the tropical areas of comparative density. In Mexico and the Andes, the native population was highly organized and suffered a change of masters—but it became a feudal, dominant type of society; Kenya was different in that 23 per cent of the whole territory remained African reserve, while exclusive white occupation was limited to 5 per cent.[1] Kenya must be classed as paternalist because the British government kept enough control to enforce its will in the end, but at one stage it looked very like becoming a dominant society of the Rhodesian kind.

We come to the second main branch, minerals. Here aims are more limited; it is not, in the nature of things, a necessity to control a territory politically in order to extract minerals. A favourable government is certainly an asset but even in the nineteenth century it was

---

[1] The actual figures are: total area: 224,960 sq. m.; White Highlands: 16,233; African Reserves: 52,040; but these figures are slightly misleading. The white area includes forest reserves (2 per cent of total). The total includes both lakes and deserts.

not regarded as essential; Chile, Bolivia, Peru, and Mexico are examples of countries where mining was carried on by foreign companies. But there is a difference in atmosphere between the territories which are directly colonial and those which are not. In the self-governing countries in the nineteenth century, there is a strong hierarchical system, whether of class or race; labour will typically consist of a small number of highly skilled imported men and a larger number of unskilled locals; management will consist of highly qualified imported financiers, engineers, and accountants, but at a much earlier stage than in a colony, the natives of the upper class will begin to be associated with the management, perhaps as decorative members of boards, perhaps in ways even more remote. Chile, Peru, Bolivia, in the nineteenth century, were semi-colonial; the great foreign firms were usually in alliance with the upper classes who formed the government and their joint object was to preserve the existing state of society. But in the twentieth century, the kind of revolution which began in Mexico in 1911 spread rapidly, particularly after the Second World War. It became necessary to encourage a much more than token association of local people with management and to play a much reduced part in the affairs of the country.

In colonies directly ruled, the exclusion of natives of the country was usually more complete in the pure colonial period; they often played little part except in the lowest ranks of labour. But as the colonial period drew towards its end, many large enterprises looked ahead and foresaw a stage when the territory would be independent. They sometimes perceived that the new government would be determined to assert its independence by revising all existing relationships. In Northern Rhodesia, now Zambia, management of one of the great copper groups consciously decided that it would prefer an independent government with popular backing—however inexperienced—to a colonial government perpetually engaged in a delaying action with nationalist forces. The other copper group, having large interests in South Africa, was compelled to appear more conservative. But both, in varying degrees, were in difficulties with the white highly skilled labour who saw their position threatened by the increasing advancement of Africans.

But however different was the line of development between colonial and independent in early stages, where the main foreign interest was minerals, the two types of territory in the later stages became much more alike—with one exception. In Zambia, Iran, and Bolivia to-day, the exploiting business interests and the government are uneasily dependent on each other and neither can wholly disregard the other's interests. The labour force is small in relation to capital employed and becomes increasingly skilled; training of local people aims at eventually replacing foreigners; management can take no important step without considering the political implications; high taxes and royalties must be paid to the government. The shoot on the chart which represents direct political control by the exploiters is thus shown as winding back to be grafted on to the other which represents nominal independence. The exception of course is South Africa, which has kept—and indeed does all its government can to intensify—the colonial form of labour and social relations.

The last of the three main branches represents trade. No one trades with an empty country and almost by definition this category concerns countries of dense occupation and comparatively developed economic and political systems—India, China, South-East Asia, West Africa, the Ottoman Empire, Persia. Everywhere, in the colonial period, European traders found that their ideas of justice and public administration were in conflict with those of their neighbours and they devised various means of dealing with this difficulty. In India and West Africa, and parts of South-East Asia, they gradually assumed political control; in China, the Ottoman Empire, and Persia, they obtained by force special privileges for themselves—Treaty Ports in China and in all three areas the right of their citizens to stay outside the normal jurisdiction of the territory and to be tried by the consuls of their own countries. Another development was to proclaim a sphere of influence and keep out foreigners.

The final result seems to suggest that special privileges were more bitterly resented than alien rule. But the important point emerging from the consideration of this branch is that the traders resemble the miners and oil-seekers; political control is not an end they desire for itself and they will abandon the territory to a native government much more readily than the agriculturalists. But in another sense, politics is overriding for both traders and miners; they will generally fall in with the political and social system of the day and of the territory, provided they can secure their primary aims.

One other point becomes clear from this chart, that the climate and resources of the territory, though important elements in the whole relationship, cannot be isolated from the intentions of the dominant group nor from the reactions of the subordinate. Clearly something in the nature of the conquered society contributes to the final situation. In the next section of this chapter we shall consider whether any regularities emerge from looking first at the subordinate side of the equation.

## 4  The Nature of the Conquered Society: Maori and Pakeha

Their expansion between the end of the fifteenth and the middle of the twentieth centuries brought Europeans into contact with many different types of society. In broad-terms, these fall into three groups, of the first and third of which one can at once perceive that their stage of development influenced the way they were treated. But the intermediate group consists of peoples who although at somewhat similar stages of social development meet very different fates. Our task at the moment is to see what contribution to this difference comes from their side.

The first group consists of primitive societies at an early stage of social development, living in desirable territory. They are usually exterminated or driven away into remote deserts or mountains. Examples are the Tasmanian and Australian aborigines, the Bushmen, the Caribs and Arawaks of the Caribbean, the Indians of Argentina. The Eskimos do not come into the category because their territory is not coveted by anyone else as a place in which to live.[1] In earlier times, as already mentioned, the same fate befell the more primitive peoples in India and indeed many human populations all over the world.

The intermediate group, because it is the most interesting, we will leave for the moment. The third group consists of highly developed cultures; sometimes of ancient civilizations in temporary stagnation, as in South-East Asia, sometimes of young empires founded on a long history of artistic and social achievement, as in Mexico and Peru, sometimes of powerful chiefdoms beginning to develop into primitive empires, as in West Africa. In all these, alien rule is superimposed on the existing structure; the mass of the people are accustomed to paying taxes and obeying the orders of chiefs or officials; all that happens—after the initial clash—is that they now obey a new class of official. There is often an early period of acquiescence and acceptance before the beginning of that general revolt which is the whole subject of enquiry in this book. The relationships that eventually emerge are varied, but it seems a fairly widespread feature—common in varying degrees to Mexico, Peru, India, West Africa—that they tend, in the last stage, to be expressed, when put into words, in cultural rather than racial terms. The point is most clearly demonstrated by Pitt-Rivers[2] and can be seen in Southern Mexico, where 'an Indian'—which is a derogatory term—means a person who belongs to an Indian community and speaks an Indian language; in contrast, a man who speaks Spanish and lives in Spanish style is classed as a *mestizo* or *ladino* even though all of his grandparents may have been known as 'Indian'. In the other areas, the transfer was nowhere so explicit, but a man who had given up most of his own cultural background and had been through Western forms of education was, though not called a European, at least treated outwardly as one. In other words, an individual, at some sacrifice and to some extent, could make himself one of the dominant group.

These two first very broad generalizations suggest that the cultural

[1] But the Eskimos are increasingly threatened by the exploitation of oilfields.
[2] Julian Pitt-Rivers, 'Mestizo or Ladino?'.

distance of conquerors from conquered is in some way related to the relationship that eventually arises. But looking at the intermediate group, it is clear that the relationship cannot be expressed as a simple curve; it is certainly not true that the greater the gap the more rigid the relationship. Consider the cases of the Maori, the North American Indian, the Bantu-speaking tribes of South Africa, and, in East Africa, the Masai, the Kikuyu, and the Luo. Of all these peoples, the most technically advanced and the most highly organized socially were the Bantu-speakers.[1] They had the use of iron and, as we have already seen, some complex political mechanisms and a closely-woven corporate life. But the relationship of whites with Bantu-speakers is to-day the most rigid of those we have looked at. Why—to take two as samples—have things developed so differently for the Maori and the Bantu-speakers?

There are differences which affect the white side—numerical proportions, external threat or support, religion and ideology—and we shall come back to these later. But we are trying to see whether any significant factors emerge from the side of the native society, and this is an aspect which has been neglected, it having been sometimes assumed that the relationship has been determined entirely by factors on the dominant side. It seems worth looking a little more closely at the Maoris and the history of their relations with the Pakeha or white man.

There can be no better authority than Raymond Firth, who summarizes the history of Maori contact with white culture as falling approximately into four distinguishable phases.[2] Contacts in the second half of the eighteenth century were few and marginal; the characteristic was an immediate recognition by the Maori of the value of European goods, particularly axes and muskets. His carving in wood is immediately attractive to European taste, but his tools were of stone; he recognized the superiority of metal at once. His was a world in which war was frequent, and muskets of course transformed the nature of war. But, at any rate in the interior of the island, Maori society remained basically Maori; transactions were of 'merely a spasmodic nature' (writes Raymond Firth); a ship would anchor in the bay and trade iron, axes, and cloth for flax and fresh provisions. Even as late as the 1820s, the natives of Southern New Zealand were not much in contact with white men. But increasingly there were less sporadic contacts; whaling ships began to call regularly and Maoris signed on with them as hands; missionaries—from 1814—and white traders came to live in the country. By 1830 there were about 150 Europeans in New Zealand and by 1837 eleven mission stations north of Taupo. Firth mentions that in 1814, 150 baskets of potatoes and

---

[1] There is no single satisfactory term for these peoples. There is no such language as Bantu; it is a family of languages. The South African Bantu-speakers like to be called 'Africans' but Hottentots, Bushmen, and Afrikaners are Africans too.

[2] Raymond Firth, *Economics of the New Zealand Maori.*

eight pigs were traded for one musket and not long after—more ominously—two hundred acres of land for twelve axes. The first phase was beginning to merge into the second.

Firth's second phase, covering approximately the twenty years in the middle of the century, was one of enthusiastic acceptance of European customs on the Maori side, a definite and deliberate intention of colonization on the white side. The rapid spread of Christianity, the almost equally rapid alienation of land, are the two most obvious marks of what was happening. Maoris began to wear European clothes, to grow wheat, to set up mills for grinding wheat, to buy horses and bullocks, carts and ploughs. Some tribes jointly owned sailing vessels for coastal trade. It would have been understandable if an optimistic observer had argued that here, if anywhere, the course was set for a happy outcome of the meeting of two peoples.

But in fact there was another side to the picture. Maori society had slowly evolved over the centuries its own system of checks on behaviour and responses to its environment; how could it alter all its ways without loss? The social system of the Maoris (writes James Ritchie)[1] was based on three concepts: of *tapu*, which is approximately 'sacredness'; *mana*, which on the lowest level means 'prestige, honour, reputation', but also 'psychic force', and carries the implication 'favoured by heaven'; and *utu*, which means 'atonement' or 'satisfaction', something more positive than 'revenge'.

*Tapu* meant the personal sacredness of a chief, which must not be lost by pollution or misuse or lack of respect; it meant the sacredness of natural resources which must not be wasted or improperly used. Like many such concepts, it had its absurdities; the head has more *tapu* than the rest of the body and a man's hat, which shares this quality, must not be put on a kitchen-table, associated with food, which is common or unclean—a neat reversal of the reason a European housewife might give for the same prohibition. A man had more *tapu* than a woman, a chief than a commoner; thus *tapu* acted (as Firth says) as a social cement, holding in place chief and commoner, man and woman, young and old. A tree had *tapu*; it was a valuable asset which was not to be wantonly mutilated but only felled after due consideration and proper ceremony. Thus *tapu* achieved by natural, evolutionary means the purpose of preserving the forest and ensuring a fair distribution of its products—a purpose which I remember trying to achieve more clumsily in the Himalayas by setting up forest committees in the villages of the foothills. A meeting-house would have *tapu* while under construction, perhaps so that the women would not come and hinder the work with their chatter, but it would have to be de-consecrated when it was finished so that everyone could use it—again a neat reversal of European practice. But enough has been said to explain the

[1] James Ritchie, *The Making of a Maori*.

value of the concept. To the idea of *mana* we shall come back; for the moment, the point to be made is that *tapu* was bound to be undermined by the coming of a dominant group whose ideas were enthusiastically received; the weakening of its influence was bound to produce discord and unhappiness in Maori society.

Demoralization of every kind is always likely to occur in a transitional stage when every feature of traditional life is being changed by new ideas. But the loss of land alone might well have been enough to produce the bitterness and the disillusion which made the other side of the medal in the period of 'enthusiastic acceptance'. The Treaty of Waitangi in 1840 transferred to Queen Victoria 'sovereignty', a concept which to Maori chiefs was probably not very precisely defined. The Chief Tamati Waka Nene expressed his view of it in these words: 'Remain for us a father, a judge, a peacemaker. You must not allow us to become slaves. You must preserve our customs and never permit our lands to be wrested from us. . . . Stay then, our friend, our father, our Government.'[1] But to English lawyers sovereignty included the principle that 'unoccupied' land vested in the Crown and that the Crown had a pre-emptive right over all land. These Crown rights were perhaps the most serious of the legal ideas about land which were foreign to the Maori. Their results may be simply recorded in figures: the Treaty of Waitangi acknowledged as Maori preserves 66,400,000 acres, of which 28,400,000 were in the more densely populated North Island and 38,000,000 in the South Island; but by 1891, these figures had shrunk to 11,079,486 of which only 250,000 were in the South Island. The Maoris had been almost totally dispossessed from the South and were left with two-fifths of their holdings in the North. By 1911 their holdings had fallen to 7,137,710 acres and by 1937 to 4,545,765.[2]

These are lands held as reserves, and do not include individual holdings; from at least the time of the Native Land Court of 1866, the Government adopted a deliberate policy of individualizing the tenure of land. But the effect was that a whole countryside, which to a Maori group had been 'their' land, was now developed, and mainly by white farmers. A few plots remained but the rest had not been 'unoccupied' in their eyes; this was where they had dug for fern-root; this was where they had cut leaves for thatching or grass for lining a house. Figures tell something but not the heartbreak of a people whose identification of themselves with mountain, lake, and river seems to have been very close; Firth[3] quotes from Elsdon Best his picture of an old chief gazing at a wide and beautiful landscape, all now in the hands of an alien people, pointing to the landmarks famous in the history of

[1] Keith Sinclair, *History of New Zealand.*
[2] A. Grenfell Price, *White Settlers and Native Peoples.*
[3] *Economics of the New Zealand Maori.*

his family and ending sadly with the words: 'very great is my love for this land'.

There must surely have been many who, from early in this second period, felt premonitions of the evils that would come from abandoning the ancestral ways: the evils came, though for reasons that we should class as social, economic, and psychological rather than magical. They made a formidable total and resentment grew steadily. In the third period, it was expressed in cult movements of the kind referred to in Chapter III of this book—Paimarire or Hau Hau, the Te Kooti movement, the Maori King movement. There was a period of war, four campaigns, in all of which the Maoris were 'defeated, though not overwhelmed'. But this third period, opening with armed action, grew from feelings that had formed an undercurrent from early in the period of acceptance.

Despair is the characteristic of this third period. Defeated in war and dispossessed of land, beliefs, and pride, the Maoris lost heart as a people. It was a view widespread among Europeans at this time that more primitive peoples could not exist in contact with 'higher races', by which was meant people of the more industrialized cultures. 'Up to the end of the Nineteenth Century', writes Grenfell Price, 'almost every well informed student agreed with the verdict of Archdeacon Walsh who stated in 1907 that the Maori race was sick unto death.' And this the Maori seem to have accepted themselves. Firth quotes a proverb that 'as the *pakeha* rat has driven out the *maori* rat, so will the Maori die before the white man'. Maori numbers had long been believed to stand at about 40,000 and the numbers recorded in 1896 were 42,113; but at the time of this pronouncement the tide had probably already begun to turn. There is some uncertainty, because in the earlier stages the methods of the census were less accurate than later, but the census of 1926 showed an unmistakable increase to 63,670, on which the Government statistician remarked complacently that 'it presents an almost unique spectacle of a native race living with a white race of overwhelmingly superior numbers and yet able to preserve in no small degree its individuality and strength'. By 1951, the census recorded 115,676 and the forecast is 224,000 by 1975.

The wars had come to an end by 1872 and a period of withdrawal and rejection followed. Some Maori groups had in fact been on the white side, but, though their economic position was not as desperate as that of the defeated, the psychological attitude (writes Firth) was much the same. The Maoris had lost confidence in themselves; they believed that by abandoning their old observance of *tapu* they had lost their *mana*, here meaning psychic force or divine favour. And they had no more confidence in the white man—his word, his religion, his good intentions—than in their own future. They met him with sullen distrust.

But from early in this period—as in the last—a contrary tendency began to appear. The rapid advance of colonization, in the sense of white ownership and development of land, brought white men to farms in the interior and farms brought stores, creameries, little townships, opportunities for employment, which were increasingly accepted, and there began to arise the characteristic attitude of to-day—a very complex relationship of attraction and at the same time distrust. In the economic field, the old ways have given place entirely to the new; barter has given way to a money economy, traditional clothes to European, hand-made tools and utensils to goods from the store. But the psychological atmosphere is more divided.

Among intellectuals, one manifestation is 'Maori-tanga', which corresponds to something we have met already as *négritude* among French-speaking Africans and West Indians and as *indigenismo* in Mexico and the Andes. This is the re-discovery of a heroic past, the glorification of tradition, in art, folklore, all that contributes to the specific individual quality of a people's spirit. Sir Apirana Ngata, a leading exponent, spoke of the elements in it as the language, the sayings of the ancestors, traditional songs and dances, traditional art, the traditional house, and the customs and ceremonies of the meeting-place, above all the prestige and nobility of the Maori people. No doubt this rather artificial return to the past helped to restore the lost self-confidence of the Maori, particularly because it was regarded as respectable by educated white people. But it did not extend very deep among the Maori themselves; for most of the young people among the Maori to-day it stands for something from which they want to escape.

In a modern study of a fairly remote agricultural and forest district in the North Island, with a high proportion of Maoris, Dr. Ritchie[1] has written of their predicament with sympathy—but in terms sadly reminiscent of many other minorities, many deprived classes. Most Maori parents value 'education', as something they have not got themselves, something which helps people to get on in the world. But, being in most cases themselves very poorly educated, they do not know how to help their children; they think it is enough to send them to school. At the more advanced stages, they do not understand the need for quiet in order to study at home; but in fact many children from such homes will be in difficulties before the stage when homework begins. On the first day at school, a narrow range of vocabulary and of abstract concepts will put them at a disadvantage compared with those from middle-class or professional backgrounds; for the Maori children in Dr. Ritchie's 'Rakau', this was one stage worse than for the children of unskilled workers in England or the United States, because many of them spoke Maori in the home. It was only occasion-

---

[1] *The Making of a Maori.*

ally that a prejudiced teacher used such a phrase as 'lazy Maori', but there are many teachers who expect that the Maori child will not do so well as the white, and there are few children who do not know how their teachers regard them. The Maori in Rakau does not do well at school because he feels he is not expected to; he tends to leave school early because he has not done well; he believes that his Maoriness has held him back and condemned him to the kind of life his father led, probably in the lower ranks of farm or forest workers. He must deal (says Dr. Ritchie) with a white man who looks down on him because he is a Maori and with his own elders, who look down on him because he is less of a Maori than they are. He lives in a circumscribed world— which he sees to be narrow, which he knows is boring, which has the interest and the compensations neither of the Maori world, now hopelessly lost, nor of the white world of the cities which he cannot reach. He can escape only at the expense of his Maori-tanga, by becoming a brown Pakeha.

This is a simplified and highly abridged statement of the dilemma as it is seen in this single remote area; it will not apply in quite the same way to the Maori who has reached the city. But there too most Maoris are in poorer jobs than most white people; it is appreciably more difficult to get out of the ruck. It is the tale of the slum child in Britain but with the difference that he is defined and labelled for life. But it is all the same a *mixed* and complex definition; it would be easy to find authority, in the writings and even the everyday speech of white New Zealanders to-day, for a very favourable picture of the Maori; they are friendly, spontaneous, gay, artistic—skilful in carving, naturally musical—wise in ways that Europeans are shallow; they are physically brave, if child-like and simple; they are warm, affectionate, and intelligent. It is a picture of the noble savage, and if it had once a certain correspondence with reality, it has not much to-day. And it is a picture held usually by the more comfortably placed Pakeha, who applies it to the 'real Maori'—the Maori in the country, who is still unspoilt—not to the Maori daily labourers who live in the same city. They are more likely to conform to the other picture of the 'native', one that we have met before: he is dirty, lazy, improvident, irresponsible, and incapable of sexual restraint.

Of course, there are many white New Zealanders who are far too sensible to hold either view, but the evidence suggests that the unfavourable picture is held by a few all the time and that parts of it are held by many people for part of the time. But it must be added that it is an article of New Zealand faith that there is no colour bar, and it is true that all have an equal opportunity of going to State schools, that Maoris are specifically represented in Parliament, that they have risen to high rank, that intermarriage is frequent. As we have already noticed, intermarriage is often opposed by the families on both sides, but quite often the generalized opposition to 'a Pakeha' or 'a Maori' disappears when the actual person is seen and his amiable qualities appear.[1] It is, in short, a competitive society in which the Maori has a bad start; he belongs to a handicapped minority and expects some discrimination; but he is much less rigidly separated from the dominant group than the Bantu-speaker in South Africa.

We come back to the question of why this should be so. In all questions of race relations, what is thought to be the case is sometimes more important than what is really the case; we have noticed too the cumulative effect of the opinions people form of each other. What then were the first impressions which Europeans formed of the Maori? Like the more recent, they were mixed.[2] The first visitors were explorers with scientific interests; they belonged to the Age of Reason and in the idyllic islands of the South Seas, far from the malign influence of priests and kings, they had some expectation of finding the Noble Savage. Much that they found accorded with this idea; they noted the favourable traits but hardly dwelt on them—they were expected. Their friendliness and hospitality above all things, but also their skill in music, their intelligence, their courage, industry, and fine appearance are recorded—but it is on the disappointments that the first voyagers dwell more persistently. The greed, laziness, treachery, lack of sexual restraint, and cannibalism of the islanders were shocking—and there was as yet no one to point out that most people to an outsider appear sometimes idle and sometimes industrious, according to their needs and the customs of their society.

As contacts increased, these first impressions were repeated again and again in varying forms. Dr. R. N. Erwin, in his study of these early stereotypes, notes that on the whole men of some education laid more stress on the favourable aspects of the Maori character, further that there is a growing tendency to attribute to missionary influence all the good—even the friendliness and hospitality noted by Cook before any missionaries set foot in the islands. The views of missionaries themselves of course were influenced by the strong Victorian conviction that the moral principles of nineteenth-century middle-class England were divinely ordained and that any deviation was wicked. The missionaries were therefore more often than not censorious of those they had come to save; it was not typical of the age to look for the social reasons for strange behaviour. More and more often it was the case that the newcomer to New Zealand came predisposed to views of the Maori he had already heard or read, and these continued to alternate between the Noble Savage—as he was thought to have been before the white man came—and the idle, improvident, and demoralized loafer who might be seen on the quayside when the visitor stepped ashore.

[1] John Harré, *Maori and Pakeha*.
[2] See R. N. Erwin, in James E. Ritchie (ed.), *Race Relations : Six New Zealand Studies*.

The fact that the favourable picture existed beside the other no doubt had some influence on the development of racial policy in New Zealand, particularly as it was an image stronger among the educated, the class who made policy, than among the manual workers. But they would hardly have kept such a mental image unless it had to some extent been *demanded* by the situation. And in fact the situation did demand, from men anxious to remain kindly and humane in their own eyes, some atonement for the destruction of Maori culture. The picture of the Noble Savage was near enough the truth to make it out of the question to condemn altogether a people against whom the odds had been so heavy, whom all admitted to have been struck down by the white man's diseases and demoralized by his vices as well as defeated in war. It was some salve to the conscience to acknowledge with admiration his good qualities and to make a virtue of equality before the law—once it was securely established that in wealth and numbers and power the white man was securely on top.

It was not only myth but a matter of fact that the Maori wished to display qualities which in most of the Old World, as well as in the high cultures of the New, have been regarded as 'noble'. Nobility—a concept to which we shall come back—can only be recognized by a corresponding generosity and, as we have seen, not all visitors to New Zealand perceived it. But some did see that the Maoris gave their admiration freely to the kind of person admired in the Homeric poems and in the Norse sagas, by Rajputs at the time when Tod recorded their annals, and by the Spaniards who conquered Mexico. Courage, hospitality, fidelity to friends and kinsmen, the chivalrous gesture to a noble adversary; a concern for honour rather than ease or safety or even life; wise counsel and resolute action—these are the qualities that are praised. Hernando Cortés and Odysseus would both have made good Maori chiefs. The Maori also admired something less usual, a leader's personal involvement in necessary work. Firth quotes a proverb which praises a chief 'with short finger-nails'—one who actually works with his hands. These are perhaps some of the qualities of which Dr. Ritchie is thinking when he says that their Victorian rulers shared many values with the Maori. 'It is more accurate', he writes (rejecting some early missionary views), 'to see the two cultures as very similar in their concepts of character and in their patterns of status, economic values, and warfare.' Governor Grey and the first Maori King, he goes on, would have understood each other very well.

Is this really more true of Maori and British in New Zealand than of their contemporaries in Africa? We shall be looking at South Africa in detail later but one or two points are inevitable here. In the first place, there was no talk of the Noble Savage when the Dutch arrived at the Cape; Rousseau was not yet born, but I do not think that is the sole reason why no European speaks well of the Hottentots, of whom such words as 'brutal' and 'stinking' are habitually used. The Dutch at the Cape had formed their picture of what 'natives' were like before they met the Bantu-speakers—to whom they did, nonetheless, ultimately extend some grudging admiration. But on the whole they transferred to the Bantu-speakers most of the attitudes they had already adopted in relation to a much more primitive people. There was too the question of numbers and the whole black continent hanging over the first Afrikaners like a cloud. There was certainly some understanding of each other's responsibilities between such opposed figures as Lobengula and Dr. Jameson, more between the missionary Coillard and Lewanika; those who met Moshesh of the Ba-Sotho admired him—but there were oceans of misunderstanding between them. There is also a hint of the white New Zealander's double image in the affectionate picture of the old coloured nurse or the African herdboy, which persisted for long, particularly in the Western Cape. But on the whole there can be no doubt the South African had a far less favourable picture of 'his native' and less understanding of his ideas. The failure to understand was perhaps partly due to a difference in the relationship between the individual and the group. The Afrikaner thought of himself first as an individual; the Bantu-speaker was first a member of a group. It is worth considering how far this was different among the Maoris.

I have already suggested that their individualism was one of the great advantages possessed by Europeans from the sixteenth century onwards in their dealings with other peoples. First impressions of the Maoris suggest that as against Europeans they were at the same disadvantage as Zulu and Xhosa; the individual among them, says Elsdon Best,[1] was lost in the group—in the first place, in the *whanau* or extended family, that is, usually the descendants of one man either still living or fairly recently living, and, secondly in the *hapu* or lineage and in the tribe. Raymond Firth questions this as an overstatement; he points out that it is in conflict with Best's own description of the democratic nature of their society, of the readiness of the whole gathering to discuss a plan of action proposed by a chief; it is inconsistent with the system of *tapu* with its sanctions against individuals, which would clearly be unnecessary if the individual did not sometimes act of his own volition and against the interests of the group. Indeed, a state of affairs to which so absolute a statement applied is difficult, if not impossible, to visualize. Where is the society in which there are not, as Firth says, 'divergences of behaviour, conflicting interests, personal ambitions, bickerings, misappropriations, and acts of downright opposition to group policy'? Certainly in the African tribes which have been described in detail by anthropologists these conflicts exist; some of them are, for example, indicated in Max Gluckman's readable

[1] Elsdon Best, *The Maori*.

account of law among the Barotse.[1] But, from outside, many societies look far more monolithic than they are. The question is whether in this respect there was a real difference of degree between Southern Bantu groups and the Maori.

It seems to one who has only second-hand knowledge of either that, with many similarities, there was a good deal more scope for individual volition, as against the group, for the Maori than for most of—to take an example—the Nguni group in South Africa. The Maori were organized in *whanau*—extended families or households—which again were linked in *hapu* or clans, which were also descended from a single ancestor but further back than the *whanau*. The extended family and the clan were the most important groupings; the *whanau* was the basic economic unit but the *hapu* had joint rights, of fishing in certain waters, of hunting in certain forests, and of cultivating certain land, which it would maintain against other *hapu* and subdivide between its own *whanau*. The tribe, the grouping above the *hapu*, defended the land within its own boundaries and above this was sometimes a loose confederation of tribes which might combine in war. But it appears that the functions of the social group grew less as the common ancestor receded; it was the *whanau* first and the *hapu* second that came into the ordinary man's life and if all went well it would be only occasionally that the larger organizations would affect him.

But it is relevant that a common ancestor was the basis of every grouping. Excluding slaves, who were usually members of other groups captured in war, every one in the *hapu* or tribe was in some degree related; the chief was the eldest son of a line of elder sons and thus everyone could speak to him and express an opinion; there was no grovelling, as before Tshaka, Msilikatse, or Lewanika. Further, there is the idea of *mana* which is in many of its aspects very individualistic. It is not an inherent quality, an essence; it is something which can be increased or lost. A man may lose his *mana* and live; he may increase his *mana* by success or popularity or wealth, like a boxing champion, a film-star, or a Prime Minister.

It is perhaps of this that Dr. Ritchie is thinking when he writes: 'An individual had as much *mana*, as much *tapu*, as much land, as many allies, as he could validly claim by evidence of his daily actions. In one sense, this was a more anarchically individualistic conceptual system of rights than that of the European. . . .' He goes on to speak of the 'granular' nature of Maori society. To-day, he suggests, there is continuity with this old granular principle, so that Maori society 'follows opportunistic rather than formal lines of structure; that groupings are defined by situation; that individuals value their autonomy and enter into organisation only to express and protect it (autonomy); . . . that, in the hierarchy of loyalties, the individual

[1] Max Gluckman (ed.), *The Judicial Process among the Barotse of Northern Rhodesia*.

stands high and the group low'. Perhaps this view is somewhat over-
stated to counter the traditional attitude of Elsdon Best; undoubtedly
part of what is to-day observed is due to a century of deliberate
individualization by the Government. But when that has been said it
seems probable that the Maori's social structure was more individualistic
than that of most Southern Bantu peoples and that he did therefore
more easily accommodate himself to Pakeha ways.

But if this was a factor of real importance, should we not find that
the more loosely organized African tribes were more acceptable to
white people in Southern Africa? As less of a military threat, they
should arouse less apprehension, and as less closely woven into a wider
group, they should accept the values of white society more readily.
But this is not at all the case. Indeed, to take two peoples living side
by side, the former military kingdom of the Matabele (Ama-ndebele)
and the very loosely organized Mashona groups, it is for the former that
most white Rhodesians will express a preference. The point, however,
is not conclusive; the Mashona belong to small units and were not a
military threat but no one who knows them has thought of calling them
individualists or using of them the kind of language just quoted from
Dr. Ritchie.

The conclusion which the examination suggests to me is that if the
Maori had been quite a different kind of people—sharing fewer ideals
of conduct with the Europeans or more closely integrated into their
tribal groups—they would have found it more difficult to fit in to New
Zealand white society. But the overriding factor in the white readiness
to receive them has arisen from the relative strength of the two groups;
it was when their superiority in numbers was assured that the Pakehas
began to treat them with more generosity. Further, the whites on the
spot were confident at the crucial stages of the friendly power of
Victorian England in the background. The Dutch at the Cape had
first met very primitive groups of whom they formed very unfavourable
opinions; they later met numerous and formidable enemies who
greatly outnumbered them; to them the imperial power seemed always
alien, at best unsympathetic, often hostile. I believe that if we were to
spend as long on considering the other intermediate peoples mentioned
at the beginning of this section we should reach a similar conclusion:
that the qualities of the people conquered play a part in the outcome,
but that it is only a secondary part.

## 5  The Nature of the Dominant Society

The underlying purpose of Part II of this book has been to examine
one by one the variable factors in a number of situations in which one
group, usually a racial group, has been regarded as superior to another.
We have looked in turn at the numerical proportions between the two

groups; at the sexual attitudes and relationships which develop; at the nature and purpose of the migration; at the nature of the territory and the economic attractions which draw visitors to it; and, in the last section, at the nature of the subordinate society. Looking in turn at each of these factors in a number of situations has thrown some light on the degree of importance to be attached to each; it has told us something about several situations which we might not otherwise have seen. But the difficulty of isolating one factor from another has not diminished; there is always something artificial about the attempt and a sense of the uniqueness of each situation grows.

This sense of uniqueness does not diminish as we come to look at the remaining variable factors, which seem to be all on the side of the dominant group. The social structure of the conquering society seems likely to be important; is it aristocratic or egalitarian, in fact or in intention? What assumptions lie behind it? What are its professed and actual intentions, in the conquered territory and at home? What kind of person does it send abroad? Are they men who work with their hands, officials, or feudal lords? Does it train them for a special task in the conquered country? Do they mean to stay there permanently? Does their religion or philosophy affect the relationship? Are they severed from the mother country and its culture or is there a strong umbilical cord? How effective is the political control of the parent society?

These questions really involve an imaginative understanding of the parent society as a whole. And this should lead to an attempt to understand as a whole the conquered society and then—as a whole— the fused society that results. Some attempt at this kind of approach will be made in the third part of the book. In this section we will continue the method of Part II, looking one by one at the factors just set out in the form of questions, and relating them to broad groupings, as we did with numerical proportions.

The broad groupings of societies which we then used were three: Dominant, Paternalist, and Competitive. It seems necessary now to add a fourth, which would cover those societies in which an original clear line of demarcation between races has first tilted and then blurred. This has continued until eventually racial characteristics, such as skin colour and hair formation, no longer determine social position absolutely, though they may be included among other marks which are used for identification, such as clothes, manner, and accent. It is not true that in such societies race is unimportant; in some Caribbean islands, colour is almost an obsession, but as a means of grading in a social spectrum, not as a rigid barrier. It may be that in such societies there is less chance to rise in the world than in a competitive society such as the United States, so that they are not, in any absolute sense, more fluid, but they are more fluid in respect of race as an indication of social status. It is not a wholly satisfactory term, but we might call them Societies of Fluid Racial Definition.[1]

Let us begin then by a rough grouping, similar to that in Table 1, on page 64.

Table 4
Societies Grouped in Four Categories

| Dominant | Paternalist | Competitive | Racially Fluid |
|---|---|---|---|
| South Africa (1968) | British India | U.K. (1968) | Mexico (1968) |
| Rhodesia (1968) | (1880) | U.S.A., North | Jamaica (1968) |
| Deep South (1910) | Mexico (1530) | (1968) | Brazil (1968) |
| Mexico (1840) | Jamaica (1880) | New Zealand | Peru (1960) |
| Ruanda (1900)* | British West | (1968) | (in Lima) |
| Brahman village | Africa (1930) | | |
| (1910)* | Peru (1550) | | |
| Sparta* | | | |
| Brazil (1880) | | | |
| Peru (1960) | | | |
| (in *sierras*) | | | |

* Pre-industrial

To be considered in relation to the following variables:
a) Social structure of parent society
b) Tendency to devolve or centralize power
c) Permanent residence of ruling group
d) Presence of manual workers of dominant group
e) Attitude of parent and colonial to manual labour
f) Strength of political link with parent society
g) Strength of cultural link with parent society
h) Religion of parent society

This is more complicated than Table 1, not only because there are four categories instead of three, but because (arising out of the discussion of Figures 3 and 4) we have put one society in different groupings at different periods, notably Mexico. Peru is something of a problem; in Spanish colonial times, it can just be classed as paternalist because the Crown of Spain exercised some control for the benefit of the inhabitants and at least professed to be actuated by the intention of saving Indian souls. After independence from Spain, Peru, like Mexico, became primarily a feudal society, the landowners of large estates having by means of debt established a control over the peasants who worked for them which made most of them virtually serfs. This I class as dominance, and there was a strong racial element in it; the serfs

---

[1] This category was not useful in Table 1 because numerical proportion is hardly of much significance in countries where the stratification is fluid and there is a gradation rather than hard lines of division.

were nearly all biological Indians, though with a scatter of Spanish genes, while, among the landowners, Spanish appearance was prized and all were Spanish by courtesy. In Peru, there has been nothing corresponding to the Mexican revolution of 1910. To-day the Government is cautiously Liberal; there is no open discrimination on racial grounds and in Lima almost everyone (except for foreigners and a small group of white aristocrats) is assumed to be of mixed origin; there is a colour gradation, but of a somewhat intangible kind. They are classed as *mestizo* but in the *sierras*, on the estates, for the most part the peasants are Indian or *cholo*, which, broadly, means an Indian who is becoming absorbed into the Spanish culture. Here, in the *sierras*, where the reforms have hardly begun, Peruvian society is still stratified and almost feudal, though the stratification is not openly expressed in racial terms. On the whole it seems nearest the truth to class the *sierras* as a society of dominance and Lima as 'racially fluid'.

Again, Barbados fits awkwardly into the classification. While Jamaica in 1865 reverted to the status of Crown Colony and was ruled paternally by officials, Barbados kept its seventeenth-century constitution for three and a half centuries; it was ruled by the planters, of whom a high proportion were resident in the island. In Barbados, alone of the Caribbean islands, there was a formal colour bar; though it operated in certain contexts only, Barbados in the height of the Victorian period must be classed as a society of dominance; to-day it is probably moving into the category I have labelled 'racially fluid', like Jamaica, but such changes are not made overnight. To the reasons for this difference from Jamaica we shall come back later.

The lists in Table 4 are intended only as examples but there are enough to illustrate the extent to which the variable factors that remain are significant.

*a. Social structure of parent society.* First, let us consider whether the social structure of the parent country is an important element in what has happened. The three pre-industrial societies included under the head 'Dominant' are left there mainly as a reminder that this kind of relationship was not invented by Europeans, but was in fact the most common condition of developed societies for most of history. But clearly most of the factors we are now considering do not influence these pre-industrial relationships because there is no parent society with which they retain links; the whole of one society is in contact with the whole of another. So for the present purpose we can ignore these three.

Let us look at the rest of the column headed 'Dominant'. The three outstanding examples are South Africa, Rhodesia, and the Deep South, all having past ties with Britain, which, until the 1880s, may be reckoned an aristocracy with bourgeois support and some social mobility. It was certainly not a general belief that all men were equal; in practice, they obviously were not. But English society was nonetheless shot through with ideas about equality and there was a kind of outspoken egalitarianism in speech and behaviour which persisted from Tudor till late Victorian times. In theory men were equal before the law and there was a belief that the ruled should have some control over the rulers. Spain on the other hand was a centralized monarchy; though there were *local* privileges, by which certain cities and corporations had rights against the Crown, it was a society more rigid than England in its stratification. But more of the Spanish colonies fall into the category 'Racially Fluid'. Why is this?

There are, I believe, deeper causes to which we shall come in Part III, but from the present point of view there are certain paradoxical points which can be stated fairly shortly. The centralized and autocratic quality of the Spanish Crown made it essential to hold a balance between feudal nobility, Church, and people; the Crown was in general the ally of Church and people against nobles; in the New World, as at home, the Crown was concerned to prevent estate-owners from setting themselves up as an aristocratic governing class; it tended therefore to be protector of the Indians. And it tried to keep a centralized control. The British Crown, on the other hand, increasingly the captive of a much more loosely defined aristocracy, devolved some degree of power more readily to local squires and plantation-owners. The Anglican Church was even more ready to decentralize than the Crown; in Virginia, the parson was the servant of his parishioners.[1] The society which at home was the more fluid for that very reason permitted its colonies to set up a structure that was more rigid.

This is the briefest of glances at something very complex. But it is clear that the structure of society in the parent country, though it will affect the colonial situation, will not automatically reproduce itself in a colony. All the European societies which established colonies before 1789 were built in varying degrees on the premise of inequality; they differed in whether their formal structure was monarchic or oligarchic, but in the colony the most important difference was whether the parent tended to devolve or centralize power. But whatever its intentions, in fact the parent could never fully control its offspring and there was always a conflict between the interests of the local leaders and those of the parent.

*b. Readiness to devolve power.* It has been argued, in relation to British colonial history, that control by the imperial government was always a liberalizing force and that to devolve power, to South Africa for example in 1910 and to Rhodesia in 1923, was the beginning of evils which might have been avoided. But this is only true as long as control can be enforced; if the interests of local leaders are too starkly in conflict with those of the parent, they will find ways of evading control or, in the last resort, they will revolt. British experience in America in

[1] Herbert Klein, *Slavery in the Americas.*

the eighteenth century created a distaste for colonial wars with white colonists; the South African War reinforced this distaste. Rhodesia to-day illustrates the point; what is vital is not constitutional procedure at Westminster but power to impose Westminster's will. If Rhodesia had not declared independence, the British government would have been in an even worse position than at the time of writing, because their responsibility would have appeared even greater, while their impotence would have been no less. Nor does India support the view that the home government always represents the forces of light; in 1879, it was the home government which insisted on removing the duty on imported cotton, to the benefit of Lancashire and the detriment of Indian manufacturers. The Government of India, consisting of officials, was overruled.

The broad fact remains that control from the parent country is more likely to establish a relationship that is paternal rather than dominant; but it has seldom been enforced for long except by officials who do not intend to settle in the country they are ruling. British colonial history certainly underlines this point. The decision to make India and Ghana independent could be taken by Parliament without any danger of local opposition, because the country was ruled by officials and there were virtually no white inhabitants who were committed to the country. But the difference went deeper than this; officials were paternalist, often no doubt misguided parents, but usually justifying their actions as in the ward's interests, seldom having any direct economic interest at variance with the ward's. Men committed to the country on the other hand were employers, usually interested in cheap labour, often in acquiring cheap land.

*c. Permanent residence.* Nothing could be more different than the models of India and Rhodesia. In British India, the highest class of civil servant consisted of a small service, originally paid very highly and selected by a rigorous competition, trained in England, forbidden to own land in India, and expected to retire to Britain. They could only be displaced by the Secretary of State in Britain. They were admirably placed to be impartial between the native inhabitants of India, and often took their part against the comparatively few planters and businessmen. There were hardly any white manual labourers. Contrast their position with that of a Native Commissioner in Rhodesia, usually recruited and often born and educated in Rhodesia or South Africa; he was answerable to a Minister in a white Rhodesian parliament and expected on retirement to live as a member of the dominant group, whose interest it was that Africans should come to work for low wages. In the early days a great deal of his time was taken up by this question of labour. He might be impartial between Africans but it was very difficult indeed for him to be impartial between Africans and his fellow-whites.

This point need not be laboured. The two situations are clearly quite different. India and the Anglo-Egyptian Sudan were the extreme examples of countries ruled by small cadres of highly-paid and carefully-chosen officials who were not permanent residents; an important feature of the system was that all minor officials, and some of the higher, were natives of the country. The French, in contrast, in their colonial empire encouraged minor French officials and petty traders. The task of disengagement thus became more difficult.

But while we can be confident that it is better, from the point of view of future developments, that officials in a colony should not mean to live in the territory, there is another quite different point about residence. Intention to stay permanently is one of the two main distinguishing marks between the dominant and the paternalist type of society. But the racially fluid countries, with the exception of Jamaica, share this characteristic with the dominant. Jamaica is something of an anomaly; the absenteeism of landlords was for long one of the worst features of Jamaican society and Jamaica cannot truly be classed as 'racially fluid' until independence came in sight. The Colonial Service officials, who would move elsewhere as their careers developed, were reduced to three some years before independence became formal, and although there were still 'expatriates' in banking and business, the emphasis on commitment to the country grew steadily as independence drew nearer. But though intention to stay distinguishes both the dominant category and the racially fluid from the paternalist, it does not explain why Mexico is so very different from South Africa. For this we have to go to other variables.

In competitive societies, intention to stay is a factor which is of only marginal importance. The dominant majority are a permanent part of the population; the minority who have come to the Northern towns of the United States or to the United Kingdom may have some romantic dream of going home eventually which may delay their adaptation to their new surroundings, but the pressure of events is against them and experience suggests that most of them will in fact stay permanently.

d. *Presence of manual workers.* I have already mentioned the French tendency to encourage 'petits blancs'. This is not quite the same as the concept of 'poor whites'. But the presence of either may operate on a racial situation, and in a variety of ways, and this is connected with attitudes to manual labour. In the first place, there is likely to be economic rivalry between groups who, increasingly, are distinguished by physical appearance more than anything else. Early in the colonial situation, the white manual workers, in the Deep South and in Africa, are so much more highly skilled that comparisons hardly arise. But the gap in skill begins to decrease and there is then a struggle to keep it wide open. The white upper classes can afford to be detached and can take paternal steps for the instruction of the natives—but this is hard for the carpenters and bricklayers whose inflated wages will drop if the gap disappears and if the market is free. At the same time, there is closer contact than if white artisans were not there, miscegenation usually takes place, there is more possibility of a social spectrum; it is only by conscious effort, as in South Africa, that the rigidity of differentiation can be maintained. But on the whole, their presence is more likely to be inflammatory than not.

*e. Attitude to manual labour.* The attitude of the dominant group to manual labour is a matter in regard to which one is bound to rely to a large extent on subjective impressions but they do suggest hypotheses which could be tested. As we have seen already, human societies in general, once they have emerged from the most simple forms, tend to stratify; it seems usually necessary to establish some kind of myth which prohibits the ruling group from manual labour; to certain Brahman groups in India, for instance, it was pollution to touch a plough. In the Middle Ages in Europe, the nobles who bore arms were sharply distinguished from those who worked for them in the fields and, as the old rhyme implies, the gentleman was one who did not delve. But as the Middle Ages drew to an end, the towns became increasingly important and here master and man often worked together; the Lord Mayor of London was more likely in Tudor times than to-day to have once worked with his hands. As is well known, the English system of primogeniture often forced younger sons, at least of the smaller landowners, to earn their living and merge with the middle classes.

The Spanish colonies in America established their traditions a century earlier than the English, and Spanish society, only just emerged from the wars with the Moors, was less urbanized; middle-class virtues were less admired. Honour—and this often meant military honour—was of the first importance. The object of many of the Conquistadors was to win military honour and the gold to support it, to buy back the ancestral estate in Spain or improve it. Their ideal was the *hidalgo*, the noble for whom other people worked on the land. Their attitude to agricultural labour, in fact, was very like that of the Tutsi of Ruanda. Two studies of Spanish-speaking America speak of attitudes to work among the *ladino* or *mestizo* populations in Colombia[1] and Guatemala;[2] both regarded it with great disfavour, one speaking of work as 'God's punishment' and preferring to go hungry rather than incur it. But the Indian-speaking populations praised and admired a man who worked hard. Here a difference of attitude is clearly an obstacle to better living and to any integration of the two communities.

The English colonists who went to New England came from a society that had already become far less feudal; it still had roots in the

[1] G. and A. Reichel-Dolmatoff, *The People of Aritama.*
[2] Melvin M. Tumin, *Caste in a Peasant Society.*

countryside but its aims were increasingly middle-class. The typical settler in New England was neither a peasant nor a noble; he was more likely to be the son of a trader, a yeoman, or a skilled artisan. He had often a sturdy contempt for those who did not work with their hands. He was therefore much less concerned with the need for labour which dominated so much of colonial history.

The point could easily be exaggerated. In Virginia the younger sons of squires tried to re-create the life of an English country gentleman and their plantations depended on Negro labour, not their own. There was interaction between the social and the purely geographical factors; to some extent the climate imposed the nature of the crop and the structure of the economy and then attracted a certain class of settler; to some extent also the settler's outlook influenced the economy. Officials of the Dutch East India Company at the Cape recorded their disgust with peasants from the Low Countries who soon after arrival conceived a dislike for any kind of manual labour; here it was clearly the colonial situation which influenced the attitude to work rather than the reverse.

Perhaps we have given this factor the wrong name. It might be restated as 'demand for labour'. Where there was no demand for labour—whether because of the class or the ideals of the original settlers—there has been no economic incentive to exact work from the original inhabitants, who often fared the worse for that reason. But excessive admiration for the *hidalgo* and the gentleman sometimes left in its wake a problem not directly racial—the contempt for manual work of the first generation of the natives who have been educated in the ways of the dominant.

No clear hypothesis emerges from consideration of the two last factors. Those accustomed to working with their hands, as in New England, Australia, and New Zealand, have been inclined to exterminate or dispossess the indigenous inhabitant rather than enslave him; at a later stage, the distaste of a dominant group for manual labour may help released slaves to earn their living as artisans and contribute to a social spectrum, as in Cuba and Brazil, instead of a rigidly stratified system; once industrialization begins, the competition of manual workers from two races is liable to cause friction. But in any attempt to construct a general law, operating in a way that could be illustrated by a smooth curve, exceptions at once appear.

*f. Political links with parent society.* What is the effect of political links with the parent society? We have already glanced at this and noted that a distant imperial government usually finds it easier to be disinterested than settlers on the spot—though there are exceptions. Far from restraining them, King Leopold incited his agents in the Congo to more extreme rapacity. Nor were the Directors of the East India Company notable for disinterested detachment in the first days of rule in Bengal. But as they became used to political responsibility they grew rapidly in the enlightened use of power. From the appointment of Lord Cornwallis as Governor-General, they may rank with the Crown of Spain in South America and the British Government in the Cape Colony; all three provided an ameliorating influence. But in the case of the two latter, it could be fairly easily circumvented in practice. Any government which tries to rule a colony with permanent settlers from a distance will face a divergence of interests; the more centralized and efficient it is, the more acute the divergence will become and the more likely, in the end, the chain is to snap.

The man on the spot has the immense advantage of being desperately in earnest; the issues affect his life. The man far away in an office tends to put an awkward case on one side till next month. The odds are on the settler; he can wear down his opponent or evade his restrictions. Even within the United States, it proved after the Civil War impossible to rule the South from the North; how much more difficult to liberalize Peru from Madrid or Johannesburg from Westminster! If the settler is forced into war with the parent, he still has an advantage, though perhaps not so great. He knows the country and the kind of operations it will permit; he is at home with the climate, the diseases, the food; he has in short the advantages of the guerrilla.

These are some reasons why the political links with the parent country are less important than they appear at first sight. Britain's ideological commitment to 'freedom' and a mild form of democracy in the nineteenth century was no help at all to the Tasmanians and the Australian aborigines; in South Africa and Rhodesia it has operated in a very complex manner, and it is arguable that the political link has been as much an irritant as an emollient.

*g. Cultural links with the parent society.* The cultural link works differently; it is not so often felt as bondage and if it is accepted at all it is usually with goodwill. Australia's cultural links with Britain have been strong and the growing liberalization of policy towards the aborigines owes something to the climate of opinion in Australian universities, so long closely connected with those in Britain. This was a predisposing factor which could exercise little influence until Australian whites felt secure in relation to the aborigines; it was no doubt also helped by an uneasiness in respect of Asian opinion on racial matters. The same kinds of predisposing influence have been present in New Zealand.

But a strengthening of cultural links may have the reverse effect. In the early days of the British connexion with India, the voyage might take a year; the death rate was high and a young man who went to India might never come back; even if he survived he would not expect to see his family again for fifteen or twenty years. He lost touch with Britain and adopted many Indian customs. But the invention of steam, the overland route through Egypt, the Suez Canal, gradually changed this; the telegraph, the improvement of aircraft continued the process. Men who had always hoped to retire to Britain went there on leave far more often, lost touch to a far less extent, and were correspondingly more aloof from the country in which they lived. Each generation makes the point in contrast to the one before. In all kinds of minor ways, the fashion, the style of living, changed; English ways were imitated by Indians as well as English. This is perhaps a minor influence compared with the intellectual climate of universities, which was strongly committed to the liberalism of nineteenth-century Britain.

But this factor is perhaps of more importance in South Africa than anywhere else. Here there was a population of white farmers, fruit-growers, traders, and artisans before British officials replaced the Dutch. Cultural links had been with Holland; the considerable Huguenot elements were estranged from France. But from the Napoleonic Wars onward the links were broken and the official language became English; the Low Country dialect which became the Afrikaans language was contemptuously known as the 'taal';[1] people who spoke it were cut off from their own cultural background and felt themselves rustic and backward in their own country. This combined with the circumstances of a frontier society to isolate them mentally and in Victorian times had already contributed largely to the rigidity of the pattern of dominance. In the early years of the twentieth century, a determined and conscious attempt was made to fuse the two white societies by anglicizing the Afrikaners; this produced a sharp reaction which has been even more important in hardening attitudes. Cultural links can operate, then, either favourably or unfavourably to a relaxed and harmonious situation.

*h. The religion of the dominant.* Finally, there is the important question of the conquerors' religion. There is an obvious association between the column in Table 4 headed 'Dominant' and Protestant forms of religion, particularly the extreme forms prevalent in South Africa and the Deep South; equally, the 'racially fluid' group includes a number of Catholic societies. Dr. Arnold Toynbee has emphasized this association, sometimes attributing to the racially fluid societies a far more harmonious relationship between different groups than I believe really exists, and sometimes implying that religion has been the main causal factor in the different formulation of racial attitudes. I have no doubt that it has been an important influence; Cortés brought to Mexico a universal religion with a central authority, asserting that the justification for conquest was conversion. Thanks to the Church, the question of the treatment of Indians[2] was thoroughly argued out in Spain, and if the Church's influence on events was intermittent and sometimes ineffective it was never wholly absent. And it could not permit the development of

[1] 'I can patter the taal', says a character in one of Buchan's early romances.
[2] Lewis Hanke, *Aristotle and the American Indians.*

attitudes so narrow and hard as those which arose in South Africa from identification with the Chosen People and the more intolerant passages of the Old Testament about the destruction of the Canaanites. I believe also that the whole psychological atmosphere was stiffened and hardened by the rigour of Calvinist views about predestination and original sin, while on the other hand it was relaxed by sacramental confession and absolution. Nonetheless, to my mind there are three reasons for questioning too sharp an emphasis on religion as the main differentiating factor.

In the first place, South Africa is distinguished from the racially fluid countries by several other factors, some of which are extremely cogent: the strength of the threat from the Bantu-speaking tribes, the primitive nature of the Hottentot groups which the first Afrikaners encountered, the numerical proportions, their cultural isolation, pressure from Britain. But it might to this be replied that the Deep South, which in racial structure is much more like South Africa than it is like Brazil, Mexico, or the Caribbean, shares with South Africa only the religious factor and pressure from the North (corresponding to pressure from Britain). On the other hand—and this is my second reason—the British Caribbean islands, in spite of their religion, are to-day more like Brazil than they are like South Africa. Here again, there is a counter-argument; the dominant group were usually absent and it could be said that any religious influence on the situation was negligible until the nineteenth century. Nonetheless, on these two grounds alone I am brought to the conclusion that, though of great importance, this difference in religion must be regarded as one among a number of other factors influencing racial attitudes.

My third reason is thus superfluous; it will be less convincing to some. But it is surely necessary to push the question one stage further back. There was a period when England and Spain were part of one cultural and religious system; it was a short period, because Spain expelled the Moors and became wholly Christian only a third of a century before England became involved in the anti-clerical revolution which combined with various political and personal reasons to establish a national Church. What was there in the national culture which led us to formulate our beliefs in terms so different from the Spanish? Perhaps there was more often an English refusal to formulate, while the Spanish accepted with enthusiasm an exact formulation. Some reason for the divergence must be assumed, and it must surely go back far deeper into time than the end of the fifteenth century. If I am right in thinking that there is a deep social and cultural difference beneath the immediate occasions of the English breach with Rome, surely this, as much as its manifestation in religion, underlies the difference in social and psychological attitudes regarding race?

*i. Conclusion.* In this section we have considered how far the factors listed below Table 4 on page 126 have determined the nature of the societies loosely grouped under four categories. All of them have some influence, but none is of overriding importance in determining the society's development. It will now be useful to turn to a rather more detailed study of the nature of certain societies and the processes of their development.

# PART III

## SOME SYSTEMS OF INEQUALITY

### CHAPTER VII

# India: Traditional Structure

*1 The Mythology of Caste*

Of all systems of human inequality, the Indian is the most ancient, the most highly systematized, and the most complex. It has lasted more than two thousand years and is still strong; it has astonished every newcomer to the country who has taken the trouble to be interested. At its height—it is undoubtedly on the decline—it embodied a differentiation between people more extreme and explicit than is to be found even in the plantation slavery of the Southern United States or in South Africa to-day.

The origins of the caste system are obscure. One may guess at probabilities; they will certainly be controverted in some particulars by scholars of repute. What is possible with some degree of certainty is, first, to describe the system in its heyday from two angles, as it was thought of and as it really existed, and then to consider how far it has been changed. It is not easy to choose a precise moment in time for this description, because the system—solid and enduring though it appears in comparison with almost any other society—is in continual flux and different parts of it are changing at different speeds and even moving in opposite directions. And it is different in North and South, in town and country. But we will try to look at the system as it was thought of and as it existed before Western ideas had made any serious impact. In most country districts, this will mean before the mid-thirties of this century.

There is bound to be an element of mythology in the way an ancient institution is commonly regarded. And mythology is seldom rational or consistent. The popular account of the origins of Indian society starts from two propositions, of which the first is racial. Aryan invaders from the North-West—tall, fair men—came into the country and defeated and ruled a smaller, darker, flat-nosed people. That is the first proposition. Among the beliefs of the Aryans is the second, that from the time of the world's creation man has been divided into four orders—priests, warriors, merchants, servants—and these must not mingle. The two ideas are combined in a somewhat confused way; it is thought that the Aryans reserved for themselves the ranks of the three higher orders—priests, warriors, and merchants—and that there is some mixture of aboriginal blood among the fourth order, which split up into a very large number of smaller groups. But there are also the people excluded altogether from the four orders—to-day more than sixty million of them—who were in the traditional system untouchable; these are in the main the descendants of the aboriginals. The Aryans—so runs the popular myth—spread from the Punjab first into the Gangetic plain and later over the South, which they conquered and converted to their religion. Their descendants remain in the South as Brahmans—the first order—but the great mass of the people in the South are either of the fourth order or untouchable, outside the caste system altogether, and both are, in varying degrees, of aboriginal blood.

So there is, first, a general idea, all over India, that to be fair and long-nosed means to be high in the social scale, while to be dark and to have a short blunt nose suggests aboriginal blood and a low place in the scale. And, secondly, the North at least believes that in the South there are far more dark aboriginal people, who are to be despised.

There is clearly a good deal of fiction in this. The four orders or *varnas*[1] are part of a creation myth, so they must—to be consistent—have been in existence before the Aryans arrived in India. But we have a picture of the Aryans in their own literature and they are much more like the Greeks of Homer's epics than like Hindus. They are a military aristocracy, the nobles fighting from chariots, drinking mightily after the battle and feasting on beef; they sacrifice animals and show no signs of being divided into castes. No one can seriously doubt, then, that the orders came into existence after the Aryans came into India. There is another anomaly, pointing in the same direction, that the Punjab, where the Aryans must have been racially most free from indigenous blood, later acquired a taint of ritual impurity; the heart of Brahmanism, but not Aryanism, lies between the Ganges and the Jumna.

We now know, from archaeological techniques, a good deal about

---

[1] I dislike using words that are not English when they can be avoided. But there has been such confusion between the mythical four orders and the actual caste-groups that it becomes dangerous to use the word 'caste' as a noun. 'Order' is ambiguous and so is 'estate', so I shall most often use *varna* for the mythical four orders of mankind. The actual caste-group within which a man must marry is called *jati*, but this I have sometimes translated caste-group, where the sense is clear, though usually adding *jati* as an alternative. There is a third word needed, for a group of *jatis* usually known to an outsider by a common name, such as Kayastha or Bhangi. The distinction is not clear in the spoken language of Northern India. *Varna* means colour but it is also used to describe the four stages of a Hindu's ideal life—student, householder, mendicant, anchorite. It thus can mean grades or stages. I am not convinced that it has any more to do with complexion than the Buffs and Blues at the Eatanswill election or the factions in ancient Byzantium which were named after the colours used in chariot-racing.

the Indus civilization which existed before the Aryans came; whatever their complexion or the length of their noses, their delicately carved signets and their highly organized city life suggest a civilization more advanced than that of the Aryans. They worshipped the bull and the phallus and it is probably due to them that these interests became part of the Hindu system. No doubt much else that seems characteristically Hindu came from the Indus people and not from the Aryans, perhaps including the tight social compartments, the caste-groups, as they exist in historical times. It is possible—but this is surmise—that the Aryans found a social framework that was already cellular, divided on a basis of trade or occupation; if so, it is possible that they adapted this to their own purpose, of keeping themselves distinct from the conquered, by superimposing the three higher orders on top of a fourth order of occupational castes.[1]

It is part of the mythology that the Aryans alone were 'civilized'. This ignores not only the Indus civilization in the North but a considerable Dravidian civilization in the South, which may in fact have a common origin. There is also, one may be fairly confident, a good deal of myth in ideas about purity of ancestry. There has been more mixing than is commonly supposed; nonetheless, the distribution of blood groups shows that castes—by which is here meant *jatis* or in-marrying groups—have been genuinely isolated from each other for many centuries.

## 2 Caste in its Heyday

Whatever its origin, a caste system was noticed by Greek observers about 300 B.C., some twelve hundred years or so after the Aryans arrived. About a century later, an unknown editor put together the laws of Indian society, which were attributed to a mythical law-giver Manu; by this time, the small caste-group known as a *jati* was well known and was distinguished from the four orders or *varnas*. Hinduism had by now developed into what is recognizably the system of manners and religion found by French and English writers two thousand years later—something quite different both in spirit and in detail from the culture of the Aryan invaders. The principle of *ahimsa*—non-violence, the abstention from taking life in any form— was by now well established as an ideal, together with reverence for the cow and the Brahman. Vegetarianism and abstention from liquor were essential for a Brahman, and were virtues for every Hindu.

[1] This 'surmise', highly probable in itself as the only plausible explanation of the fact that the Aryans were manifestly not Hindus, will be greatly strengthened if the language of the Indus civilization proves, as is claimed, to be 'proto-Dravidian'. A group of Finnish scholars at the Scandinavian Institute of Asian Studies believe they have found the key to this language.

The caste system is very complex indeed and it is misleading to simplify it. In all that follows in this section, I am describing the caste system as it was in its heyday. The best introduction for an English reader that I have found was written more than sixty years ago. The writer apologizes for his 'vivacious language', which he feels unsuitable for 'a scientific purpose', and it is true that there is a note of flippancy in his description, but the application of the names of one society to the ideas and structure of another seems to me as accurate as such a thing can be. Let us listen to Sir Herbert Risley:

Let us imagine the great tribe of Smith, to be transformed by art magic into a caste organized on the Indian model. The caste thus formed would trace its origin back to a mythical eponymous ancestor, the first Smith who converted the rough stone hatchet into the bronze battleaxe. Bound together by this tie of common descent, they would recognise as the cardinal doctrine of their community the rule that a Smith must always marry a Smith, and could by no possibility marry a Brown, a Jones, or a Robinson. But over and above this general canon three other modes or principles of grouping within the caste would be conspicuous. First of all, the entire caste of Smith would be split up into an indefinite number of 'in-marrying' clans based upon all sorts of trivial distinctions. Brewing Smiths and baking Smiths, hunting Smiths and shooting Smiths, temperance Smiths and licensed-victualler Smiths, Smiths with double-barrelled names and hyphens, Smiths with double-barrelled names without hyphens, Conservative Smiths, Radical Smiths, tinker Smiths, tailor Smiths, Smiths of Mercia, Smiths of Wessex—all these and all other imaginable varieties of the tribe Smith would be as it were crystallized by an inexorable law forbidding the members of any of these groups to marry beyond the circle marked out by the clan-name. Thus the Unionist Mr. Smith could only marry a Unionist Miss Smith, and might not think of a Home Rule damsel; the free-trade Smiths would have nothing to say to the tariff reformers; a hyphen-Smith could only marry a hyphen-Smith, and so on. Secondly, within each class enquiry would disclose a number of 'out-marrying' groups, bearing distinctive names, and governed by the rule that a man of one group could in no circumstances marry a girl of the same group. In theory each group would be regarded as a circle of blood-kindred and would trace its descent from a mythical or historical ancestor like the Wayland-Smith of the Berkshire hills, the Captain Smith who married Pocahontas, or the Mr. W. H. Smith of the railway bookstalls. The name of each would usually suggest its origin, and marriages within the limits defined by the group-name would be deemed incestuous, however remote the actual relationship between the parties concerned. A Wayland could not marry a Wayland, though the two might come from opposite ends of the kingdom and be in no way related, but must seek his bride in the Pocahontas or bookstall circle, and so on. Thirdly, running through the entire series of clans we should find yet another principle at work breaking up each in-marrying clan into three or four smaller groups which would form a sort of ascending scale of social distinction. Thus the clan of hyphen-Smith, which we take to be the cream of the caste—the Smiths who have attained to the crowning glory of double names securely welded together by hyphens—would be again divided into, let us say, Anglican, Dissenting, and

Salvationist hyphen-Smiths, taking regular rank in that order. Now the rule of this series of groups would be that a man of the highest or Anglican group might marry a girl of his own group or of the two lower groups, that a man of the second or Dissenting group might take a Dissenting or Salvationist wife, while a Salvationist man would be restricted to his own group. A woman, it will be observed, could under no circumstances marry down into a group below her, and it would be thought eminently desirable for her to marry into a higher group. Other things being equal, it is clear that two-thirds of the Anglican girls would get no husbands, and two-thirds of the Salvationist men no wives. These are some of the restrictions which would control the process of match-making among the Smiths if they were organized in a caste of the Indian type.

There would also be restrictions as to food. The different in-marrying clans would be precluded from dining together, and their possibilities of reciprocal entertainment would be limited to those products of the confectioner's shop into the composition of which water, the most fatal and effective vehicle of ceremonial impurity, had not entered. Water pollutes wholesale, but its power as a conductor of malign influence admits of being neutralized by a sufficient admixture of milk, curds, whey, or clarified butter—in fact, of anything that comes from the sacred cow. It would follow from this that the members of our imaginary caste could eat chocolates and other forms of sweetmeats together, but could not drink tea or coffee, and could only partake of ices if they were made with cream and were served on metal, not porcelain, plates.[1]

In this vivid picture, Risley is really describing one of the great orders and his 'Smiths' are very like the Brahmans. But of course Smiths would be a *Sudra* caste—that is, be graded in the fourth *varna*—because their traditional occupation is artisan. They would be what I have called a 'group of *jatis*', like the Brahmans or the Kayasthas, and within the in-marrying *jatis* there would be out-marrying clans like the Wayland-Smiths who would properly be called *gotras*. But it is the *jati* that is the basic unit and the most easily definable. The essential point about it is that it is endogamous; no one may marry outside it. It must be defined in relation to marriage, because although often linked with a hereditary occupation, this is by no means always the case, while members of one *jati* may follow different sectarian traditions in worship. It is essential to marry within the *jati*, but many *jatis* are divided into *gotras* or clans, which are exogamous; a man must marry a woman from a *gotra* not his own, and sometimes, though not always, from a *gotra* counting as lower than his own.

Further, as Risley says, there are territorial divisions; the inter-marrying unit lies within a normal travelling distance that can be covered in a reasonable time. A bride will want to visit her mother's house—and the distance regarded as reasonable will depend on the wealth of the family and the means of travel at their disposal. Land-owning Rajputs in Rohilkhand would in the twentieth century go to

[1] Sir Herbert Risley, *The People of India*.

the next district for a bride, involving a journey of a hundred miles with a change of trains in the middle and a bus journey at either end; a man from one of the humble but respectable cultivating castes—say a Kurmi, a group who were essentially cultivators with small holdings in which they were usually tenants—would arrange a marriage within twelve or fifteen miles, a distance he would expect to cover in one day in a bullock-cart.

There are probably no human groups which do not prove, on a closer inspection, to be far more sharply divided within themselves than they appear to be from a distance—but perhaps Indian castes are the supreme example. Risley's illustration brings out the point admirably, although it is confusing that he calls the Smiths a tribe; they are really a group of *jatis*. A group of *jatis* may at first look like one structure; this is true even to-day. A recent study from South India by André Béteille[1] describes a village of 349 households. It is a village in which some generations ago a ruling sovereign endowed a community of Brahmans, whose duties were to study the scriptures and pray; until lately the Brahmans owned most of the land. At first sight, there are three groups in the village—92 Brahman households, 168 non-Brahmans (or, as the Brahmans would say, Sudras, people of the fourth *varna*), and 89 Harijan or 'untouchable' households. But on examination, each of these main groups is divided, the 92 Brahman households into no less than twelve *jatis*—groups who marry within the group—the 168 Sudras into 26 *jatis*, and the 89 'untouchables' into four *jatis*. Something of the kind would be found in most Indian villages.

It is rules about marriage that define the *jati*. An occupation is usually associated with a *jati*, but not all of that occupation will belong to that *jati* and in many cases all of one *jati* will not be of that occupation. This is particularly true of the larger caste-groups; the Chamars of Uttar Pradesh, who are 13 per cent of the state population, are traditionally skinners and leather-workers, but in fact form the bulk of the landless labourers; probably three-quarters of them have nothing to do with leather.[2] The younger sons of the cultivating caste-groups turn increasingly to other occupations if they can find them and the growing break-up of the old semi-feudal relationship of patron and follower—to which we shall return—has put an end to the occupation of many of the specialized service caste-groups who hung round the households of the larger landowners. One large group who must be looking for other occupations are the Kahars, who traditionally carried the palanquin of high-born travellers. They were Sudras and menials but a Brahman could drink water drawn from a well by a Kahar—

---

[1] André Béteille, *Caste, Class and Power.*
[2] The Chamars are traditionally untouchable and outside the *varnas*, but like other untouchable caste-groups observe strict caste rules among themselves and will not take water from a Bhangi or scavenger.

and this of course made them useful on a journey in a thirsty land. There are not many palanquins now—but long after the palanquin was superseded they were employed as domestic servants to fetch water, to dust the furniture but not the floor, to carry messages. But a Brahman cannot accept cooked food from a Kahar, while a Kahar would be degraded from his caste-group if he swept the floor. So his usefulness is limited.

Each *jati* then is a self-contained group which must marry within the group, though usually outside the sub-group or *gotra*, and in Northern India outside the village. Each *jati* has its own code of what its members may or may not do. This will include ceremonial observances, rules about food and about relations with people of other groups. The Brahman is supposed traditionally to visit water—preferably running water—three times a day; this he must do first thing in the morning before and after defaecation, and again before his mid-day and evening meals. On each occasion, he must bathe and change his clothes, repeating Sanskrit prayers and verses which take about one and a half hours each time; indeed, if a Brahman observed every day all the ritual that he *should*, he would have time for little else.

Traditionally for each caste-group there was a *panchayat*—literally a committee of five but not necessarily five in practice—who adjudicated on breaches of the rules of the group. Some rules would be disregarded by everyone but an eccentric few; others—particularly those which lower the group in relation to others of a similar status—meant the offender was excommunicated. 'His pipe and water are shut' is a literal translation of the expression generally used in Uttar Pradesh; no one could smoke with him, take water from him or give him water or permit him to draw from their well. He could expiate his offence by complicated and protracted ceremonies, some of which would be extremely distasteful to anyone not a Hindu, and by the payment of fines to the Brotherhood and, in the case of the higher castes, fees to Brahmans as well. Incidentally, in Northern India the word used colloquially to describe the group in this context means exactly 'brotherhood'.

The weakness of Sir Herbert Risley's illustration now begins to be clear. The cement which holds Indian society within the framework of caste contains an ingredient not present in British society. In both, men seek the approval of their fellows, who may be pictured in a series of concentric rings, concern being more acute about those closest. But in Hindu society, and not in British, concern centres on ritual pollution; the caste-group or *jati* consists of a brotherhood who observe the same rules about pollution and therefore can intermarry. Risley is flippant because he regards the idea of pollution as ludicrous.

In the broadest terms, one might say that there would be a considerable agreement about the order of ranking between two lists, one showing the caste-groups or *jatis* ranked by the esteem in which they are traditionally held, and the other showing the same groups ranked by the austerities and privations imposed on them by the code of their group if they are to avoid pollution. But neither list would be easy to draw up and there would be wide exceptions. The various caste-groups who are generally agreed to belong to the second *varna*—the Kshatriyas or Rajputs or Warriors or Rulers[1]—rank above the third *varna* known as Vaish or Baniya, the merchants, but are far less concerned about ritual abstentions and ceremony. 'As well make a bow out of a pestle as an ascetic out of a Rajput', says a proverb. The Vaish abstains from meat and alcohol, while the Kshatriya or Rajput will eat meat, particularly wild game, even the flesh of a wild boar, though not domestic chickens or pigs nor of course the flesh of any animal remotely bovine—as for instance the antelope called a Nilgai or blue cow which is not really a cow at all. And anyone who has lived long in India will recall instances of persons so holy or so highborn that they could ignore all rules—except that no Hindu can eat beef.

It is reasonable to think in abstract terms of a list in which caste-groups are ranked in order of esteem, but as soon as a beginning was made of actually writing down such a list, difficulties would arise—and the more detailed the greater the difficulties. The broad principles might be grouped round food and water; a Brahman may take water drawn by a number of groups; he may accept uncooked food—oranges, raisins, or betel-nut—from other groups and cooked food—rice and its accompaniments—as a rule only if it has been cooked by a fellow Brahman. Indeed, in the modern study already referred to, André Béteille mentions certain Southern Brahmans who can eat no cooked food unless prepared by the eater himself or his wife. As late as the Kaiser's War, there was an infantry battalion of Brahmans in the Indian Army who could eat food only if cooked by themselves and who must remove all polluting leather equipment before they could eat or cook. Twice a day they took off belts and boots and lighted six hundred little fires to cook their meals. There is a proverb making fun of this tendency: 'Three Kanaujia Brahmans means thirteen fireplaces to cook at.' I recall further a group of Rajputs among whom the men had to marry into a *gotra* classed as lower than their own and who assured

[1] I found it very confusing before I went to India that the word 'Rajput' should have sometimes a caste and sometimes a regional meaning; I fear there is no way of avoiding this difficulty. There is a further confusion, in that it sometimes means '*varna*' and sometimes a group of *jatis*. The *varna*, the second order of warriors and rulers, is best called Kshatriya, but Rajan or Rajput is sometimes used with this meaning. Rajputana or Rajasthan is the land in which Rajputs were the dominant caste; throughout Moghal and British times it was divided into princely states, each ruled by a Maharaja, with a group of feudal nobles or Thakurs. Throughout many other parts of Northern India, notably Uttar Pradesh, land was often in the hands of people referred to as Rajputs or Thakurs. But they did not marry into Rajputana. The Kshatriyas in any region were divided into a number of exogamous clans. The highest ranking of these were hypogamous, that is to say, the man had to marry a woman from a lower class.

me that in theory they could not eat food cooked by their own wives or mothers; they had to employ a Brahman cook. But they were beginning to disregard this absurdity.

A ranking list would take account of who may take food from whom, but would soon find differences between theory and practice, differences between one region and another, and changing practice even within one region. I remember going into a mountain village in Garhwal where all the inhabitants were Brahmans, except for a handful of aboriginal outcastes who lived away from the main village. In the laws of Manu, the Brahman must not touch a plough. So I asked them how they managed to plough their small and stony terraced fields; there was far too much work for the aboriginals to do it for them. They assured me they did not do it themselves; they were true Brahmans. They got help from neighbours, they said, evasively and somewhat implausibly. There was much laughter when I repeated this conversation to Rajput officials born in the district. Everyone knew that these Brahmans *did* plough; it was part of the prevailing religious snobbery that they would not confess it to me.

Caste-groups would not only struggle to achieve higher status by adopting some new privation but would split, to separate themselves from a section who carried out a degrading task. In Uttar Pradesh, at one stage, those Chamars who did not skin animals or work in leather attempted to split from those who did; the purer branch began to call themselves Jatavs but the distinction may now have been abandoned. There are many points in a ranking list at which conflicting claims would be encountered, each of two groups claiming priority.

Nonetheless, a spectrum can be constructed in which, though the bands of colour melt into each other and blur at the edges, there is a real difference between the two ends. At one end is the Brahman—or rather, the collection of caste-groups who are jointly known as Brahmans. Ritually, there is no doubt they come at the head of the scale; it is the duty of every Hindu to revere and cherish Brahmans. It is an act of piety for a rich merchant to feed five thousand Brahmans, like founding a monastery in the Middle Ages in Europe. But, whatever his religious duty, a Rajput landowner would in certain contexts entertain for the Brahman the contempt that a soldier in all societies sometimes feels for a man of peace, while lower castes look on him as a leech, a parasite on society. Dozens of proverbs rub home the point: 'The Brahman and the vulture watch for a corpse'; 'Give a Brahman the corner of your veranda and he will have the house'; 'A Brahman who says no to a bribe, a cat that won't touch cream.'

But ritually, the Brahman is at the head of the scale. At the other end, beyond the Sudras, outside the pale of the *varnas*, come the people who used to be called the untouchables, now more politely in

Mahatma Gandhi's phrase the Harijans, or children of God. Their touch, even their shadow, was pollution. They live apart, away from the houses of the 'twice-born' (the three higher orders). It is pollution to take a coin from the hand of a Harijan; it must be put on a table. His wages must be thrown on the ground for him to pick up. 'When I was the adjutant of an Indian Army battalion in the First World War', a British officer told me, 'I was the only person who would give a sweeper his wages or his paybook.'

I myself recall telling a sweeper that a dog who was suffering from the heat of May ought to be clipped. He agreed.

'But who will do it?' he asked.

'The horses were clipped with a machine only last week,' I said.

'But the man who clipped them belongs to the same brotherhood as the grooms,' he replied, 'he cannot touch a dog.' Grooms were just touchable. Then his face brightened.

'The man who cuts *our* hair will do it,' he said. The scale for animals overlaps the scale for men; the cow, the peacock, the monkey, and even the horse (which is more of a Rajput than a Brahman like the cow) come high above the sweeper.

To value a man less than a horse is not confined to India. It was often implied in the contrast between the stables and the labourers' cottages on the estate of some nobleman of eighteenth-century England. But only in India was it built so explicitly into the social structure. In Béteille's village already referred to, a Harijan as late as 1961 could not walk into the Brahman street of the village to bring the grain he had to pay as rent if he were lucky enough to be tenant of a piece of Brahman land. Not merely his touch but his proximity was still polluting.

I have already suggested that to be a Harijan was worse than to be a slave in Virginia. It is true that the Harijan could not be sold; he was nearer to being a serf than a slave. But the Southern house-slave cooked and mixed drinks for the masters, nursed and suckled their babies, played with them as children. All these human links were sharply denied by the hammer of the auctioneer; in law the slave was property. And after slavery there was lynching. If the Negro raised a hand to a white man or an eye to a white woman, he might be snatched out of the hands of the law and burned alive. Against this passionate assertion of human rivalry but utter denial of equality, it is hard to weigh the concept of pollution. But the man outside caste must cross the road if he sees a Brahman coming; to me it seems that, of the two, pollution was perhaps the more consistently degrading.

## 3 A Network of Inequality

The Indian social system is permeated with inequality. Inequality is reflected even in grammar; the plural is traditionally used of himself by a superior when speaking to an inferior, who is referred to in the singular, and who in reply is expected to use the singular of himself and the plural to his superior. It may not be possible to say precisely and without risk of dispute in what order the groups are to be ranked, but rank is inherent in the whole concept. And it is, basically, rank in terms of ritual purity on the one hand, pollution on the other. Caste is entirely a matter of birth; it is sometimes claimed that the caste-group or even the *varna* of an individual can be changed in his lifetime, but if an example is quoted it is usually two thousand years old. Mahatma Gandhi did not become a Brahman.

Since it is based on birth, the institution suggests a proposition that would be the creed of the most extreme racists, that whole groups share a genetic inheritance so markedly different from each other that they ought rightly to hold quite different places in the social structure. But here there would be a misrepresentation; the Hindu does not think of 'genetic' inheritance. The Harijan brings with him an *ethical* heritage of misdeeds in a past life and it is therefore legitimate to treat him without pity.

Let me quote from a writer, who certainly cannot be called popular nor representative of anyone but himself, but whose unpopularity in India is partly due to his outspokenness in saying what is believed but not generally voiced. Nirad C. Chaudhuri writes:

there are really only three physical types in India . . . the Blacks, the Browns, and the Yellows . . . they are clearly separated from each other by their geographical distribution. . . . These three ethnic groups furnish the key to one of the oldest human conflicts in India, that which has existed between the civilized Browns on the one side and the Yellow and Dark primitives on the other. . . . There is fear and hatred of their Hindu rulers among all the Dark aboriginals. . . . Outside the tribal areas, the conflict between the Darks and the Browns has taken the form of a revolt of the lower, and especially the un-touchable castes against the higher. . . .[1]

These sentences are taken from a passage covering several pages but they do fairly summarize the author's thoughts, which in this case are widely held among those he calls 'the Browns', ideas to which I have already referred as part of the mythology of caste. Again, V. S. Naipaul, a Trinidadian of Indian descent, on a visit to India meets a Sikh who refers to South Indians in the language of extreme racialism; 'blackies', 'niggers', he calls them.[2] He is not typical, but where one tortured and unhappy man expresses emotions with such violence it is likely that there will be others who feel them in a milder form and normally repress them.

Proverbs constantly express the view that a Brahman is expected to

[1] Nirad C. Chaudhuri, *The Continent of Circe.*
[2] V. S. Naipaul, *An Area of Darkness.*

be fair and the lower castes dark; a departure from the rule is to be distrusted. 'A black Brahman, a fair Chamar—don't cross the river with either', is one example.

Caste then is spoken of in terms of physical appearance and descent, but it is *justified* in terms of rebirth and misdeeds in a past life. We now need to consider its *effect*.

Caste—the system of ranking, the institution—is one aspect of social structure and the distribution of privilege. It was never the sole aspect; in the traditional world, as it was pictured in ancient treatises on state-craft, political power belongs to the Raja who by definition belongs to the second *varna*, that of the Kshatriyas or warriors and rulers; wealth belongs to the third order, the Vaish or merchant. On the other hand, the Raja's chief minister will be a Brahman; it is the duty of the successful merchant to endow communities of Brahmans. And there was little of either social esteem, political power, or wealth for the Sudras—the fourth *varna*—and still less for the Harijans, the people beyond caste. Let us look for a little, not at an ideal state, but at the distribution of benefits in the actual life of a village, say forty years ago; we start with a village in the North.

Control of land is the most important economic factor. There is an ancient Indian tradition that all land 'belongs' to the sovereign but in a different sense it 'belongs' to the person who pays Land Revenue for it to the sovereign. In a typical village of Rohilkhand, it was likely that for most of the village the Land Revenue would be paid by a group of connected families, probably Rajputs; further West in Uttar Pradesh, they were likely to be Jats, who are by tradition substantial peasants, but who also have a military tradition and sometimes claim to be Kshatriyas, though Rajputs would not concede the claim. In the village we have chosen, which we will call Anantpur, the landholders are Rajputs; there are a dozen or fifteen households, and they have land in neighbouring villages as well. Some of their land they manage themselves and till through labourers, most of whom are in fact Chamars—the traditional leather-workers, outcastes; much more of their land is let out to tenants, many of whom have hereditary rights and cannot be evicted unless they fail to pay the rent. These hereditary tenants will pay a cash rent, in theory about two and a half times the Land Revenue due to Government—but in fact they seldom pay in full and what is collected will usually be about twice the Land Revenue. The rent is supposed to represent about a tenth of the gross value of the produce of the land. There are other tenants who have less security and pay a rather higher rent.

The tenants belong to the cultivating castes among the Sudras; strong among them are Kurmis, who are cultivators, and Gujars or Ahirs, who are traditionally herdsmen; in some of the other villages where the Anantpur Rajputs hold land, there are Rohilla Pathans, but there are no Muslims in Anantpur. Not far off, the largest landholder is a Rohilla Pathan and his tenants are very like those of the Rajputs. One might say, in the broadest terms, that in this area, the likelihood is that the landholder will be a Rajput or Rohilla Pathan; the permanent hereditary tenant may also be a Rajput or Rohilla Pathan, but he is more likely to belong to one of the higher cultivating castes, while the tenants without hereditary rights and the sub-tenants will be from the lower cultivating castes. To explain the situation is necessarily to simplify; for a given field, the landowner will seldom be an individual but often a group, among whom the shares may have been subdivided over several generations. The same is likely to be true of the tenancy; a tenant in one plot may be a landholder in respect of another. But with many exceptions and with complexities of baffling ramifications, caste and control of land follow roughly the same pattern—Rajputs are likely to be landholders and Kurmis to be tenants, while Chamars are sure to be landless labourers.

There are others in Anantpur whose main means of livelihood is not the land—a Brahman household or two, as family priests to the Rajputs, and carpenters, ironworkers, potters, barbers, washermen. These are occupational caste-groups, and the three last rank low among the Sudra categories. In a Brahman household, anything that has been washed by the *dhobi* has to be rinsed again when it comes back. All these, and the landless labourers, are attached by convention to the household of one or another of the landholders. There is no contract enforceable at law, but they are expected to do any work he wants. He will give them grain at harvest-time, a length of cloth, a few rupees at certain intervals. In Rohilkhand at the time I am thinking of, a Chamar ploughman would get a piece of cloth and two rupees (three shillings; less than fifty cents) twice a year. He would 'belong' to one patron, not that he could be legally sold or transferred or forced to leave the village, but in the sense that his patron had the first call on his time and would use him, not only to plough and weed, but as a beater when he went shooting, as a messenger, or occasionally to help him to assert his will by force. It was the relationship we are familiar with in Ruanda—certain clearly defined services on one side in return for benefits that seem of less value, with a background of total protection and total allegiance.

The same kind of relationship would often apply to the lesser tenants. A landholder in the 1920s and 1930s would still sometimes assemble a small army of tenants and retainers to punish or oppose a political opponent or personal rival, though it was an enterprise to be embarked on with some care and with regard to the probable attitude of the police. In return for these varied services, tenants and retainers would be protected by their patron, as far as he could, against anyone else.

While the Chamar ploughman usually has one patron, the carpenter, the potter, and the barber have several and are thus in a stronger position economically, while socially and ritually they start in a higher rank than a Chamar. But they would be helpless if they incurred the anger of the Rajput landholding group; the police-station is seven or eight miles away and in any case the police would be reluctant to be involved in direct opposition to the landholders. The village headman at Anantpur is a Rajput; the same man is Chairman of the *panchayat* or village Committee. Of the six other members, three are Rajputs of his own group. The chairman has the ear of the officials of Government; the Rajputs are the dominant caste.

It remains to add that although the Chamars are untouchable, outside the four *varnas*, being by tradition eaters of dead cattle, they are not the lowest of the low. In every village, there are sweepers and scavengers, removers of night-soil, a group of ten *jatis* known generally as Bhangis, who have their own caste committee and their own code of what they may or may not do. A Chamar would not accept food or water from a Bhangi. And outside the village, somewhere in the neighbourhood, camping in the waste sandy land near the river where nothing grows but tamarisk, or in the mango-grove of a friendly land-holder, there will be a nomad group like the gypsies of Europe, Nats or Khanjars or Luneras, outside the *varna* system, untouchable, disliked as dangerous neighbours likely to steal fruit or anything else they can lay hands on, but whose presence is not so deeply polluting as a Bhangi's.

This was the traditional system—a hierarchy of groups defined exactly by birth; marriage confined to the group; the lower ends of the scale a walking pollution to those at the other end—and this hierarchy corresponding broadly with the distribution of wealth and political power. Those at the bottom end of the scale were dependent on the favour of their patrons but were also protected by them and the relationship was usually hereditary.

I have been describing Anantpur, and more generally Rohilkhand, in the early 1930s. Recent anthropological accounts suggest that at the same period a similar structure, though with many local variations, was fairly widespread. In the South, too, the basic fact is that wealth and power were then in the hands of the caste-groups who ranked high in the ritual order of precedence. In André Béteille's Sripuram, the three main caste-groups are the Brahmans, the non-Brahmans, and the Harijans or untouchables. Broadly speaking, the Brahmans thirty to forty years ago held the land and ran the village; they had something not far short of a monopoly in land, education, and power. In the region as a whole, they had a majority of government posts. And, again broadly speaking, the non-Brahmans were tenants or artisans, the Harijans landless labourers. There were sometimes Brahmans without land or non-Brahmans who were landholders, but in general there was a considerable coincidence of caste, class, and power.

## 4 Conflicting Forces

This traditional system was strong and almost universal thirty years ago but already disturbing forces were at work on it. They had begun more than a hundred years earlier; they were economic, religious, legal—indeed, they affected every aspect of life. But it is easiest first to disentangle the economic forces that were disruptive. I saw these at work in the first few months that I spent in India. Some of the Chamars in a village near the Jumna, which here divided the Punjab from Uttar Pradesh, had left the village to look for work; this they had found in a neighbouring town in a shoe-factory, where of course no one higher in the scale than a Chamar could work without pollution. They worked there for wages but had not settled in the town; the village was still their home. When they came home to visit their friends, they told them to refuse the degrading task of removing dead cattle and to demand regular wages for all they did. This of course was to attack the basis of village society and when the Chamars acted on this advice, the Rajputs beat them with shoes.

The British system of law did not recognize the semi-feudal relationship of patron and follower; the Rajputs had no redress but force, and when they resorted to force they laid themselves open to the charge of causing simple hurt under the Indian Penal Code and were brought to the law courts. Here the Rajputs, with their greater wealth, better legal advice, and a crowd of suborned witnesses, tried to prove the charge a fabrication. The Chamars tried to prove that far more serious and sensational offences had also been committed. This was a pattern of dispute in village life that became increasingly frequent until Independence. It was due in the first place to the economic pressure which sent the landless labourer to the towns, but secondly—and really more profoundly—to a basic conflict between the assumptions underlying traditional society and those underlying the British Indian system of law—and indeed, all the institutions of the modern West. The law was codified and admirably clear; it made no legal distinction between any of Her Majesty's subjects[1] and was based on the *laissez-faire* doctrines of Bentham and Mill current in mid-Victorian England.

Another and similar conflict frequently arose in the more sophisticated parts of the hill district of Garhwal, where members of the untouchable aboriginal community known in the hills as Doms began to aspire to a privilege previously confined to the higher castes. Among Rajputs, it was a custom that the bridegroom should ride to his wedding on a horse. For a Dom to ride a horse was unthinkable, but the Doms

[1] This is not quite true because the Code of Criminal Procedure did make special provision for members of 'criminal tribes', certain nomad groups whose hereditary profession was stealing. These might in certain circumstances be kept in settlements, usually run by the Salvation Army, an early and crude kind of reformatory for adults.

began to do it and the Rajputs obstructed and beat them. The Doms
went to the courts, where the decision revealed a second underlying
conflict; this was between the Western concept of law and the aims of
those administering it.

The Doms were His Majesty's subjects and no one had a right to
obstruct them when proceeding on the highway by any means they
chose. There could be no doubt about this legal principle. On the other
hand, no one could force the owner of land to permit anyone of whom
he disapproved to trespass on it. These two points were combined in
one judgment and, since all the land was owned by higher castes, the
wedding procession was therefore confined to the highway and could
not reach the bride's home. This happened because very few British
officials wanted to make active changes in the customs of the country;
it was an ancient tradition not to interfere with religion. Customs
linked with religion—and in Hindu India that meant most customs—
were therefore respected unless the conflict with European ethical
standards was too sharp. Thus, at the beginning of British rule, the
custom of burning a widow with her husband was strongly disapproved
of but not actually forbidden; officials were expected to remonstrate
and persuade, but if the widow insisted that she was willing to burn,
she could not legally be stopped. But this tolerance decreased as
British power became more established; many individual officers took
the law into their own hands and forbade the practice in their own
areas, and the custom was generally forbidden in 1829. But though it
was worth risking a riot to save a woman's life, it was much more
doubtful whether that risk ought to be taken to permit a Dom to ride
to a wedding. Hence, one must suppose, a judgment in which juris-
prudence and conservatism seems to have been nicely balanced.

But the conflict of principle is clear enough. It is part of a double
process in which the institution of caste had been involved for a century
and a half by the time of Independence. On the one hand, there was
still at work a process nearly three thousand years old, which Professor
Srinivas has called Sanskritization.[1] This might be called the struggle
to move upwards in the caste system, of which instances have already
been mentioned. Part of a group will split off from the rest, renounce
some degrading practice, and adopt some new privation that carries
status; they will change perhaps from demanding a bride-price to
giving a dowry—an immense step in the social scale; they will forswear
the re-marriage of widows or turn vegetarian or renounce onions (as
the Brahmans do) and will take a new name. This was the process of
ritual snobbery by which the Dravidian South was Sanskritized;[2] it is
still happening to tribal groups. It is fascinating to contrast F. G. Bailey's

[1] M. N. Srinivas, in Philip Mason (ed.), *India and Ceylon: Unity and Diversity.*

[2] According to the myth. But I suspect that the Dravidians some thousand years
earlier had converted Aryans to the practices later called Sanskritic.

account of the Konds[1] in modern Orissa with the writings of British officers a hundred and thirty years earlier; Campbell and Macpherson were engaged in the suppression of human sacrifice among these people when they were unquestionably a tribe, outside Hinduism, an aboriginal mountain people with an animistic religion. To-day they are three-quarter Sanskritized, in process of becoming a caste.

In the mountains of Garhwal, I saw a similar process almost complete; the majority of the population had eighty years earlier been usually called Khasiyas; in the neighbouring country of Nepal Khasiyas are supposed to be the offspring of Rajput men and Mongolian women. Only the aristocracy would have called themselves Rajputs a century ago. But the Khasiyas made good soldiers; they were recruited for the Gurkha regiments; they were formed into a regiment of their own, several battalions strong. They became Khas Rajputs; then they became Rajputs, each with Singh after his name, and, for the polite, with Thakur as a title before it. Bride-price was still paid in the villages, but to high-caste Hindus in the plains this is a primitive and degrading practice—virtually selling one's daughter. To make the change to giving a dowry instead of receiving a bride-price was a big social hurdle. An educated man would give a dowry and there was a growing segment of society in which in fact a bride-price would be asked, but the father would be ashamed to admit it to a stranger—like the Brahmans with their ploughs.

But while among the lower ranks this process of Sanskritization was spreading the caste system over a wider area—bringing in tribes to whom it was unknown and extending Sanskritic customs among the lower groups—an opposed tendency was at work, particularly among the higher castes. It had been a settled conviction of the British administrators in the mid-nineteenth century that modern education would kill Hinduism, which they saw as an absurd superstition. Could it really be supposed, they asked, that a man who had graduated in mathematics or physics or had read Hume and Gibbon would wish to spend an hour and a half three times a day in bathing and reciting charms? And although they were wrong in expecting mass conversions to Christianity, they were right in thinking that what Europe had brought would undermine the system.

There are many strands in the process. First, as the Victorians had expected, the study of the subjects taught in European universities—though often aridly presented—did induce a bracing and invigorating scepticism about much in the Brahmanical system. In the early part of the nineteenth century, this produced in the best Hindu minds an urgent desire to combine the best of two systems of thought. The most notable example is Raja Ram Mohan Roy of Bengal, who (as mentioned on p. 43) founded the Brahmo Samaj, with the object of reconciling

[1] F. G. Bailey, *Politics and Social Change*.

Hindu religious philosophy and Western thinking. But the first rapid gains of Western thought—coupled perhaps with the arrogance of Western manners—soon brought a sharp reaction. The Brahmo Samaj wasted away and was succeeded by the Arya Samaj, a reforming Hindu movement. This was ostensibly fundamentalist, going back to the Hindu scriptures. In fact, it was influenced by the West in, for example, its renunciation of caste and its advocacy of education for women, but it claimed to be centred on its own Aryan culture, which was now still further mythologized to show that there need be no borrowing from anyone else; the Aryans had known—it was sometimes absurdly claimed—how to fly and make motor-cars too. This was a part—and an important part—of modern nationalist India and it is one of the paradoxes of the situation—though a very natural one—that it is Western forces that produce the reaction against the West.

Thus in India forces are at work which are a good deal more complicated than those where a less highly developed society was in contact with the West. Among the Maori, for instance, we saw Maori culture at all social levels being replaced by Western, the process being only marginally influenced by a slightly sentimental admiration for old Maori customs. But in India, while traditional Hinduism in its most orthodox form is being abandoned among the most highly educated, it is still gaining ground at the lower end of the social scale, just as it has throughout the centuries, and, at the same time, by a third quite distinct process, a re-thinking is at work and people are trying to synthesize the two systems.

The conflict and paradox are admirably illustrated in Mahatma Gandhi's attitude to caste, described by Dennis Dalton in *Unity and Diversity*.[1] Gandhi was cautious at first about rejecting tradition and throughout his life tried to reconcile his understanding of the Hindu scriptures with what he had learnt from the West. He held for most of his life that it was right that mankind should be divided into orders or *varnas*, for whom there were appointed tasks and duties; the duty of performing your proper function in the appointed order—the virtue known as *varnashramadharma*—remained for him one of supreme value. But the in-marrying group—the *jati*—he denounced as a modern innovation not to be found in the Vedas and a social injustice. At one stage he even went so far as to proclaim it as a duty to marry an untouchable; he told those who lived in his *ashram* that they must do the work of a scavenger and clean their own latrines. He clung, in short, to the idea that it is a duty of man to perform his divinely appointed function in society but rejected the concepts of pollution and cellular particularism.

The conflict is not merely between social tendencies; it is between systems of thought. Yet each has helped the progress of the other.

[1] Dennis Dalton, in Philip Mason (ed.), *India and Ceylon: Unity and Diversity.*

Improved communications, from railways to broadcasting—both Western products—have spread both the Sanskritizing process at the lower end of the social scale and the Westernizing at the top. No one will be surprised that Western ideas have been spread by these means among the sophisticated. But it is surprising that at the lower end of the scale, awareness of wider horizons has promoted an opposite effect, an increase in religious snobbery—the ambition to rise in the social scale by competitive privation—but also a new sense of community with groups in other regions who belong to the same group of castes.

We have already given examples of low castes and tribes becoming more Sanskritic. The best example of a group of castes coming closer to each other has been in the South, where the Brahmans—a group of many distinct *jatis* who did not marry or eat together—in the first quarter of the twentieth century had, as we have seen, almost everything in their hands—land, education, government posts, political influence. But the spread of Western or modern ideas produced resentment among the non-Brahmans and this was expressed in a variety of political forms by the Justice Party, the Self-Respect Movement, the two Dravida parties (the D.K. or Dravida Kazhagham and its offshoot the D.M.K. or Dravida Munnetra Kazhagham)—all of which in varying degree aimed at breaking up the Brahman hold on land, power, and education. This they did very effectively, but in the process also unified the Brahmans.

I have already mentioned that included within the community of Brahmans in Sripuram were twelve in-marrying caste-groups. Now that the Brahmans have lost control of both village and state politics, they begin to close their ranks. They are more conscious of their identity as Brahmans, less insistent on the differences between them. Groups who would neither eat nor smoke nor drink together will now sometimes eat at each other's weddings though they will not intermarry; groups who are closer and would eat with each other but still would not marry will now agree that marriage is possible. The Brahmans have drawn together, just as the immense number of non-Brahmans have drawn together against them. But the distance between Brahman and non-Brahman is—at this stage—perhaps sharper than ever before. What becomes clear, as one considers this process, is that Western ideas are continually eroding the concept of pollution, which formed a vital ingredient in the traditional system, but that new economic and social pressures are building new ties and divisions, much more closely resembling those of class and often linked with political parties. But these questions require a separate chapter.

# CHAPTER VIII

# India: The Discovery of Self

## 1  A Changed Decision

A recent book on housing in Britain[1] emphasizes as a main thesis that the 'movement of population within a city is something controlled by the city itself'. The writer is thinking of a modern city, Birmingham, controlled by a Mayor and Corporation, democratically elected; it is less easy to understand the complex processes by which corporate decisions are taken when a society has a less explicitly formulated system of authority. Yet it is one of the premises of anthropology—and of this book—that customs and institutions do not grow up haphazard but in response to a need—though they often outlive it. This implies a process in the past which at least resembles what is generally called taking a decision. Indeed, a gardener will sometimes speak of a climbing plant 'choosing' to follow one line of growth rather than another, but there is a world of difference between mere response to stimulus and a conscious choice between courses of action that are perceived and identified; somewhere between those extremes one must reckon the 'decision' of the Aryan invaders of India to adopt the institution of caste.

Whatever the processes by which it occurred, something that may loosely be called a decision was reached at some stage between the arrival of the Aryans and the comments of Greek observers in the fourth century B.C. It provided one of the most ingenious and stable solutions that has ever been found to the basic problem of any group who see themselves as rulers distinct from the people they rule. It arranged that the rulers should be kept permanently separate from the ruled and that the ruled should be divided up into groups who could not intermarry, small enough to give the individual a homely feeling of belonging to something intelligible, yet not large enough to be a political threat; it linked these in-marrying groups with function, so that the work of the society would be carried out; it persuaded rulers and ruled alike that the system was permanent because divinely ordained; it provided as a kind of social cement[2] the concept of

[1] Philip N. Jones, *The Segregation of Immigrant Communities in the City of Birmingham*, 1961.
[2] The phrase is Raymond Firth's.

pollution, involving serious sanctions for any breach of the system; it laid down the dutiful performance of function (*varnashramadharma*) as one of the supreme virtues; it provided a moral escape route against any charge of earthly injustice by the doctrine of rebirth, according to which present misfortune is the consequence of past misdeeds. Further, by allotting esteem and spiritual rank to Brahmans, military power to Rajputs, and wealth to Vaishes, it gave an interest in maintaining the structure to a wide variety of groups.

Contrast this solution, so similar to Plato's, with the Spartan, based on naked force, rigorous training for the rulers, and the secret police, the Krypteia; it does not seem to have been backed by any mythology which the Helots accepted and Helot revolts were frequent. The Hindu system was far more efficient; it lasted two millennia and a half, and there is no tradition in India of popular revolt against the social system. And let there be no mistake—it was a system of dominance with little paternal benevolence about it. It must be emphasized that I am speaking of the success and stability of the *social* system, supported by its unique social mythology. Periodically, political systems arose which used methods similar to those of the Spartans; the Maurya emperors too had their secret police. Empires rose and fell but the social system remained—a system of rigid allotment by birth to a prescribed status, with many local and regional variations, but usually displaying, in any given area, a concentration of wealth and power in the hands of one group. The key to its success was that it was thought of as permanent, indeed timeless.

How the social system spread to the South is not known. What is known is that by the time of Asoka—say, 270 to 230 B.C.—one political empire extended over the greater part of India, though not the extreme South, and that long before this, the Brahmanical system had reached the whole of the South. But there is a marked difference in the social form of Brahmanism in North and South. Plato, it will be remembered, put political power in the hands of the golden caste, the philosopher Guardians; his second, or silver, caste of warriors was under the orders of the golden, the philosophers. The Hindu system agrees in putting Brahmans at the head of the scale and enjoining reverence for Brahmans on every Hindu, but differs in making the Rajputs or Kshatriyas or warriors the kings and landowners as well as military leaders. But traditionally there is a Brahman Prime Minister. If one regards the system as inspired by the Brahmans, it must be supposed that they were content to let the Kshatriyas appear to rule while they preserved for themselves the realities of power. There is good evidence too that they encouraged a liberal interpretation of what made a Kshatriya; ancestors who drove chariots and who spoke an Aryan language seem to have been allotted in retrospect to anyone who commanded physical force and it seems probable that early Hindu kings in the North were often of Mongolian descent. The solution of the rulers' problem adopted by the Brahmans in the North was thus subtle and far-sighted.

But in the South, even the idea of Kshatriya was unknown. It was a society in three main tiers, not five; there were Brahmans, non-Brahmans, and untouchables, the many castes of non-Brahmans being generally regarded as Sudras, that is, of the fourth or menial order in the theoretical Northern scheme of four *varnas*. The Brahman of the South, belonging to the only twice-born caste, exacted an additional reverence from the rest, who must be more obsequious to him than they ever were to a Brahman in the North. At the same time, the untouchables of the South were treated with an ignominy considerably more extreme than was ever enforced in the North, where it was unknown for any group to be compelled to keep at a distance of a hundred paces from any other person—as Dubois[1] says the Pulias were compelled to do.

It is not difficult to suggest a reason for this difference between North and South; in the North, the Brahmans had the backing of the Kshatriyas, the men in power, who commanded the military machine; the social and religious system placed the two together on a pedestal in isolation. In the South, the Brahman had no similar ally; he had to rely on ritual prestige, which he must emphasize by every possible means. Even to-day, Béteille says that the Brahmans of Sripuram pride themselves on their fair complexions and their clear-cut features which they regard as signs of Aryan ancestry, marking them off from the cultivating castes who surround them and whom they believe to be aboriginals. They were isolated, colonists, alone among the natives. They had no military advantage in weapons or tactics. They must therefore emphasize the myth which assured their dominance and exaggerate every distinction of diet, of ritual, and of social distance. The concept of pollution was the first weapon in their armoury.

Having spread, with many regional differences, over a considerable sub-continent, this unique social system proved itself by surviving two periods of foreign rule, to each of which it responded differently, though in both cases with characteristic tenacity and subtlety. The Muslim invasions of India followed the Aryan route from the North-West but were at first of the nature of raids, sometimes longer, sometimes shorter; it was only in the last quarter of the twelfth century that an Afghan empire of any permanence was founded. It expanded for about a century and a half, till the middle of the fourteenth century, when it extended almost to the limits of Asoka's. For the next two centuries, the centralized empire lost ground to Hindu rulers, and to Muslim rulers who threw off their allegiance to the centre. On this confused background was built the empire of the great Akbar, the first of the four

[1] Abbé J. A. Dubois, *Hindu Manners, Customs and Ceremonies*.

great Moghal Emperors, whose realms eventually spread to about the limits of Asoka's.

Akbar came to the throne in 1556, his reign coinciding approximately with that of Queen Elizabeth I of England; the fourth Moghal Emperor, Aurangzebe, died in 1707, but the Empire was already showing symptoms of decline in his last years. Thus, in much of Northern India, Muslim rule lasted at least five centuries; and Muslim dominance in a variety of forms survived after the Empire's central power had gone, notably in Oudh and Hyderabad. In the South political rule was more intermittent in time and geographically more sporadic. But even in the South, the rulers over great stretches of country were for several centuries Muslim.

Hindu princes fought and were, on the whole and as a rule, defeated;[1] Hinduism bowed—'in patient deep disdain'—and retaliated by infecting, undermining, and subtly converting Islam. The institution of caste was a protection against Islam; the tightness of the in-marrying social group kept the invader from mingling with Hindu society just as it had, at least in theory, kept the conquering Aryans from mixing with their predecessors. I am writing about social definition; about what was *thought* to occur. The biological exchange of genes between Aryans and the people they found had surely sometimes taken place; it did sometimes take place between Hindus and Muslims. But the institution, the method of social definition, set up to prevent mixture, did make it impossible for there to be a fusion of Hindu and Muslim as defined groups; a Hindu could not marry a Muslim without ceasing to be a Hindu.

Caste then was a defence against Islam and as soon as Muslims came to live permanently in India it mounted its own secret and unobtrusive counter-attack. It was not a complete defence; there can be no doubt that in fact massive conversions to Islam did take place, particularly in Eastern Bengal. Frequently, the conversion was of an entire in-marrying group. But wherever this happened, and in many other cases too, caste responded by taking the offensive. To Islam, nothing can be more foreign than the concept of caste. Islam is an egalitarian religion, though at the same time authoritarian; men are equal before God but on earth political and religious authority is deputed from above. But in India the idea of caste was so strong that by the nineteenth century most Muslims in India regarded themselves as belonging to a caste. In hundreds of hours of court hearings, and while organizing a district census, I recall no case of a Muslim party or witness protesting at the questions always asked in court: 'Name? Father's Name? Caste?' Hindu reformed sects such as the Arya Samaj, on the other hand, did protest at such a question. It is true that the word used for caste normally addressed to a Muslim is an Arabic word originally meaning 'tribe', but the reply given excluded any idea of 'tribe', and was often directly connected with occupation: there were Muslim butchers' castes, weavers, iron-workers, and many others. They were in-marrying groups, in almost every respect corresponding to a Hindu *jati*, often governed, in cases of dispute about caste rules, by a *panchayat* just like a Hindu caste, and excommunicating a member for the pollution incurred by any breach of the rules of the brotherhood. The words *bhaibandi, baradari, jat*, and *qaum* were used by both religions indifferently of the in-marrying group.[1] Two of these words are Hindi, one Persian, and one Arabic.

The Indian social system thus recaptured from within and from below what it had lost on the battle-field. This is one example of that success in one dimension and failure in another which is a characteristic of Indian society. Indian armies were constantly defeated by invaders; in spite of vast manpower, knowledge of the territory, shorter lines of communication, personal gallantry, and skill at arms, they were beaten in the field by resolute Western adversaries from Alexander through the Afghan and Persian invaders until British times.[2] This was partly due to military conservatism, in particular a belief in tactical dogmas which were valid only so long as both sides observed the same conventions—and, to particularize still further, a pathetic belief in the value of elephants in war—but partly to something in the social structure. This was the very factor which enabled Hinduism to defeat its conquerors from within—the strength of the in-marrying group—coupled with the weakness of wider groupings.

The military value of the Indian Army organized by the British, on the other hand, was partly due to the fact that it was built at the lowest level on the in-marrying caste group, and for this structure of small firm units provided a formal disciplinary framework which linked companies and battalions into a whole. Armies brought together by Indian princes never achieved this translation of the in-marrying group into military terms nor the linking of smaller units into a whole by any framework that would hold in time of stress. Ties above the in-marrying group were personal and when the leader fell the army broke up.

The strength of the in-marrying group and the extent to which ties of kinship and near-kinship affect all relationships may easily lead one to underestimate the element of anarchy in Indian political thought and in Indian society. In relation to the next invaders—the Europeans and particularly the British—Indian society was at a double disadvantage. There was a lack of strong loyalties at any level above the in-marrying group; at the same time, the individual was still deeply imbedded in the family and caste-group. Nothing is more striking in the

---

[1] I never heard *jati* until I started to read anthropology.

[2] An exception was the defeat of Alexander's former general Seleucus Nikator by Chandragupta in 305 B.C.

early history of both French and British in India than their advantage in both these respects. They could count on the loyalty of individuals to the regiment or to something as remote as the East India Company. At the same time, they could count on the self-reliance and initiative of men brought up in a society that was based on the individual and on the belief that every effect has a cause if one can find it. These advantages ensured immediate success, but, with the British, as with the Muslims, military and political victory over the Indian system was followed by a moral defeat, but of a quite different kind.

Hinduism could not be so successful as it had been with the Muslims in infecting the British with the caste system. Some success of this kind it did achieve; few British who lived long in India and had any contact with Indians could wholly avoid being influenced by twice-born attitudes to untouchables. And a delicate nose for social attitudes would perhaps detect among the British in India an even sharper tendency to social division and discrimination than in Britain; there was a perception of truth in the jokes which compared the police, the engineers, and other services with castes. But they were not endogamous groups; soldiers' daughters married civilians, policemen took wives from the forest service, and men in the Indian services found wives in Britain who had never been to India. Caste could not invade the British in India as it had the Muslims because of the peculiar nature of the British occupation. As I have already emphasized, the British ruling group sent their children to Europe to be educated and settled there themselves when they retired.

What then was the essence of their function in India? What did they achieve historically? The answer to these questions reveals the subtlety of the Hindu counter-attack. One answer which was often given at the height of Victorian power was in terms of roads, of railways, bridges built and acres irrigated. But we are thinking of the social and political contribution and in this dimension the Victorian claim would be political unity, impartial and impersonal justice, discipline and stability, peace, low taxation. There is another side to some of these contributions, but even if they are taken at their face value, as the British Victorians saw them, they were accidents of the system, not its essence, so long as they were imposed by the British and had not been taken into the Hindu system and digested. This did in fact happen to a very considerable extent in the case of one complex set of ideas, largely because it provided the Hindu system with an infallible means of counter-attack.

We have already dwelt on the dilemma which faces an imperialist democracy; if it is right for the mass of the people to choose their rulers at home, why not abroad? This is only part of what Pitt-Rivers[1] calls the imperial dialectic, by which imperial colonists inevitably pass to

[1] Julian Pitt-Rivers, *After the Empire: Race and Society in Middle America and the Andes.*

the natives of the country they occupy their own skills, thus destroying their initial advantage, and sowing the seeds of unrest and revolt against themselves. But the democratic imperialist faces the difficulty in a much sharper form than others, and particularly the Victorian British. They had been taught that, in Magna Carta and in the Revolution of 1688 and on various other occasions, they had asserted a right to freedom which they could not very logically deny to others. As I have said, they had to choose between a frankly racist assertion that freedom was not for Indians and the paternalist attitude that it was not for Indians yet. And having preferred the latter, as the official doctrine, it would have demanded consistent cynicism over a long period to deny Indians the right to prepare themselves for freedom, that is, to be educated in Western ways.

Frank cynicism does not long flourish in English political life. Indeed, the whole argument about education between Macaulay and the Orientalists, who wished Indian education to be directed to Sanskrit, Arabic, and Persian, was conducted on benevolent paternalist assumptions. Was it better for the pupil to be educated in the language of Newton and Locke, alien to his own culture, but conducting him to a rational view of science and of the universe, perhaps even to Christianity? Or was it more suited to his own temperament and genius, more likely to produce by evolutionary methods an integrated personality—the terms of course are an anachronism—to help him to grow from the roots of his own culture, just as Newton and Locke had grown from the study of Latin and Greek? As everyone knows, Macaulay won and the way was opened for a Hindu counter-offensive which used English political and legal concepts.

All this is obvious enough except that it is not usually emphasized that Hinduism, essentially hierarchic and stratified, used against the British egalitarian ideas, derived from Greek and Jewish sources, brought to India by the British, and basically opposed to social stratification. By using them in this way, leading Hindus absorbed them and made them their own, quoted them on a thousand platforms. The conflict inherent in Western culture for two thousand years was thus brought into the texture of Indian thought and society far more intimately than would have been the case if these ideas had not been used as a political weapon. The debate or conflict with the British—it alternated between the two—was at its height from, say, 1885 till 1947. During these sixty years, three generations of young men grew up with whom Western ideas were constant tools employed against many aspects of the imperial system in which they found themselves. When independence came, the main stream of Indian intellect had either to reverse its own current or to endeavour as best it could to change the 'decision' of two thousand years before.

The presence of the British in India has therefore had an effect very different from the presence of imperial powers elsewhere. Its effect has been profound, modifying every aspect of Indian life and thought, education and political organization. Yet, in a sense, the presence of the British themselves was marginal; they were here, they have gone. Their importance lay in the Hindu reaction to them, which involved the use of ideas foreign to Hinduism and brought Hinduism face-to-face with itself. It was one reason for British success in India that there was an official determination to interfere as little as possible with the religion of the people; in a profoundly religious population, and one in which religion and society were inextricably blended, this was also, from an imperialist view-point, a weakness. There could be no interference with institutions that were the gravest hindrance to social progress. But in the long run, and for the world, it was a valuable weakness. It knocked the bottom out of the Victorian moral justification for the British presence in India; it forced Indians themselves to attack what they might easily have defended if the British had moved against it. In short, it forced India, when she came face-to-face with her own problems, to adopt a radical and critical attitude, to make an attempt to reorganize the most distinctive features of her own society.

## 2 Unity and Diversity: Religion

We have been concentrating on social structure, and particularly the institution of caste, because this is a feature of Indian life that is unique. It has survived two great conquests and to-day one of the most important questions for India is how successful she can be in reversing her ancient decision. In a sense, the two past conquests are irrelevant or at least marginal to what is happening, although a consideration of the British presence in India as a historical event has already thrown some general light on the reasons for change. But before we go on to the present problems of India it is worth pausing to sketch very briefly the settlement that followed the first of these two conquests—the extent to which the two societies accommodated themselves to each other.

As we have seen, caste invaded Islam in India. Apart from the occupational Muslim castes—iron-workers, weavers and the like—there were four major Muslim groups in the United Provinces, Sayyads, Moghals, Pathans, and Sheikhs; it was a popular saying that Sayyads were not really descendants of the Prophet (as they should be in Arabia) but converted Brahmans, while the Pathans were not really immigrants from Afghanistan but converted Kshatriyas. This was mythology but these groups were certainly caste-like in many respects. But caste was only one part of the cultural borrowing, the steps towards fusion, that had taken place. Akbar made it deliberate policy to reconcile his Hindu subjects to his empire, marrying several Rajput princesses, employing Hindu ministers, remitting the poll-tax on non-

Muslims, and actually trying to evolve a synthesized religion. The policy was less positive under his successors but until the time of Aurangzebe it was still tolerant. Aurangzebe by his intolerance probably contributed to the break-up and decline of the Moghal Empire, but the influence of one religion on the other was a continuing process not everywhere reversed.

After the death of Aurangzebe, the Empire ceased over most of India to be an effective centralizing force, but many living fragments remained in being; there were great provinces such as Oudh, Bengal, and Hyderabad, under Nawabs who were virtually independent kings; there were many lesser princes, diminishing in size and power and their degree of independence, until they merged imperceptibly with landlords who did not claim sovereignty but only feudal privilege. The ruler or landlord—though this term does not mean just what it means in English—would be surrounded by a group of lesser landlords, officials, retainers, servants; the relationship of patron and client, which the Hindus call *jajmani*, was understood just as well by Muslims. These clients or feudal inferiors would mostly be Muslims, but just as Raja Todar Mal—a Hindu—served Akbar as Revenue Minister, there would be Hindus in high office at many smaller courts. At Oudh and Hyderabad more than 90 per cent of the higher officials would usually be Muslim.

Synthesis of a kind was everywhere taking place, not of the two groups, which remained defined and separate, but of their institutions. Urdu, which became the general language in Northern India, was a mosaic in which Persian and Arabic words and phrases were inserted into a syntax of simple Hindi; it gradually replaced Persian as the official language and developed into a supple and elegant means of communication with a very wide vocabulary and a literature that is not to be ignored. Each religion borrowed from the other; if the Muslims took caste, the Hindus took purdah. A mixed culture grew up, to which both contributed, in dress, in cookery, in clothes, in such customs as the *mash'ara*, in which poets meet to recite their verses and to compete with each other in composing a succession of stanzas, each of which must be fitted to a refrain which caps each appropriately. More deeply, there was an approach of thought; Persian sufism took a new flavour in India, borrowing something from the Hindu school which emphasized *bhakti* or the spiritual unity of all creation. It is not easy to say whether the verses of Kabir are nearer to *bhakti* or sufism; they repudiate the Qur'an and the Vedas alike and borrow from both.

At a lower level, in the villages, men of two faiths lived side by side for long periods, tolerating if not understanding each other; the peace —it was more than a truce—lasted so long as there was some illusion of permanence, or at least no prospect of violent change. Hindu and Muslim peasant both borrowed from the Hindu money-lender for marriage ceremonies or to pay the Muslim landlord; Hindus would lend a shoulder to support the images of the tombs of Hasan and Husain which are carried in procession in Moharram. The differences of Hindu and Muslim have been so heavily emphasized that these long periods of toleration are forgotten. The forces which encouraged the exchange of customs and mutual toleration were reversed from time to time by bursts of fanaticism on either side; they were also liable to be upset by anarchy and uncertainty about the future. But they were never wholly extinguished and it was notable that in the British period the princely states were far less prone to communal trouble than districts ruled directly by the British. In a state, the ruling house belonged to one religion or the other, most of the ruled knew that the interests of one group were paramount, and no change seemed likely. Where an attempt was made at impartial administration there was uncertainty and strife.

For the best part of five centuries, Muslim rule—imperial, princely, or feudal—covered a great part of India. It was the rule of one group by another, the two being distinguished formally by religion rather than by race or culture but with elements of all three differentiations. Does it fit any of the categories we looked at in Part II of this book? In the early days, and periodically later, it resembled the rule of the Spanish in America in being fiercely missionary. The worship of idols was an abomination and early Muslim rulers destroyed temples and broke idols; the heathen must pay *jizya*, a special poll-tax on non-Muslims—though they could escape it by formally accepting Islam. To these practices Aurangzebe returned in the seventeenth century, but the missionary spirit was, as we have seen, intermittent and there were long periods of passive tolerance, and even, under Akbar, of active tolerance.

Muslim rule in India does not, in fact, precisely fit into any of the temporary categories we have erected. It was certainly not paternalist in the sense we have used; the Moghals did not imagine that they would be succeeded by Hindus. In Akbar's time, the policy was that of the bee-keeper rather than the bear; he saw (as one of the earlier emperors, Sher Shah, had done) that it was wisdom to regulate the demands made on the peasants to a level which they could bear and which would encourage them to stay on the land and work. He took great pains to devise a reasonably just system for assessing and collecting the revenue. But his successors seem to have been interested only in the maximum amount that could immediately be extorted. Nonetheless, it is hard to class the system as one of dominance in quite the sense in which we have been using it.

The essence of the societies we categorized under this head was that membership of the dominant group was fixed by birth and could not be changed, and that the dominant group established rules, laws, or myths to maintain their separate status for ever. But although birth was of importance in Islam—and noble upbringing as important as pedigree—the idea of equality before God has always been strong, also its counterpart, the romantic idea of the poor boy who becomes rich or the beggar transformed overnight into an Emperor. And a Hindu had in theory only to say one sentence to be accepted. It was from the defeated side, far more consistently than from the victorious, that continued separation was enforced. In fact, of course, upbringing, tradition, family, a hundred differences in the whole approach to life, kept the two groups apart as well as the social definition which is one of the essential marks of Hinduism. But the relationship was very different from one defined in racial terms.

We have already seen that the British occupation of India had a peculiarly temporary character which differentiated it from most colonial systems and made withdrawal possible. We have also seen something of the changes in the relationship of British to Indian that took place over the approximately two hundred years of British rule. To try to assess or even summarize all the effects of British rule would expand this section of the book intolerably; I must concentrate on the results of the essential achievement of forcing Hinduism to face itself.

There are five internal relationships which India to-day is trying to adjust in accordance with principles consistent with her own struggle for independence. They concern the Muslim minority; the linguistic groups and the basic division of North and South; the tribal minorities; caste and the former untouchables; and finally the relationship of educated leaders with the masses. It is not here contended that these are India's first dangers; but population, food, external defence, balance of payments are dangers of a different order, threats that no politician can fail to see. The structure of the nation, even more difficult to perceive and to manipulate, may however ruin all attempts to deal with these looming perils.

Of the five relationships here mentioned, it is easiest to speak first of the Muslim minority. As Professor Spear[1] has pointed out, there have always been two strands in Islam in India, the tolerant and the intolerant. The divergence became increasingly acute from about the time of the foundation of the Indian National Congress in 1885; this date is taken arbitrarily to mark the beginning of Hinduism's use of Western ideas for the counter-attack on the British. The Muslims of India, formerly the dominant group, now equally with Hindus subordinate to a new ruler, had to decide whether to join the Hindus in their essentially Western secular struggle; if this was successful, they would be at a serious disadvantage in the new state, not only outnumbered by the Hindus, but already behind them in Western education. The struggle within Islam continued; it had been represented in

[1] Percival Spear, in Philip Mason (ed.), *India and Ceylon: Unity and Diversity*.

the Moghal period by the conflict between Dara Shikoh, who followed the tradition of Akbar, and his brother Aurangzebe. It continued till the moment of partition, when it was typified by such men as Maulana Qalam Azad, a Muslim scholar but a leading member of the Congress Party, on the one hand, and Muhammad Jinnah, on the other.

At partition, this conflict came to a head in an agonizing choice. There were two states where there had been one; a man must be Indian or Pakistani. Those Muslims whose homes had been in India were able to make a choice if they were of the middle class, if they were employed by the state, or perhaps if they lived near the new border. But for the most part, there was no open decision made; a peasant in the eastern part of Uttar Pradesh was unlikely to have any assets but hereditary tenure of his land, his bullocks, and cart; how could he set out for Pakistan on a journey of hundreds of miles? He had no certainty of what he would meet at the other end, and many perils were certainly on the way; by the mere fact of going, he proclaimed himself an enemy of the new India. He stayed, and by staying became, whether he knew it or not, an adherent of the conformist tradition. There was no room in India, after partition, for fiercely intolerant Muslim attitudes; the educated and more prosperous, if they stayed in India, and so long as they counted themselves Muslims, had really no choice but to back the secular state; it was their only hope. Of course a man who no longer thought of himself as Muslim could become a communist, but a Muslim as such had really no course open but some degree of attachment to the Congress Party.

The considerable mass of Muslims in India—now thought to be in the neighbourhood of fifty million—are conformists; informed Muslim opinion wants, in the words of Professor Spear, 'nothing better than the liberty to work out its own destiny within the Indian secular society'. It has good reason to fear that it may not be permitted; the Hindu Mahasabha, a powerful body of militant Hindu opinion, expressing its views through a vigorous political party, the Jan Sangh, rejects the idea of the secular state. Pakistan is regarded in India as a hostile nation whose sole reason for existence is rejection of the ideal of the secular state; the Pakistani Press can hardly avoid picturing India as a country where Hinduism is triumphant and the secular state a mere pretence, where Muslims are inevitably oppressed. These attitudes, freely expressed, still more such a grievance as Kashmir and in 1963 actual war, are bound to affect attitudes to Indian Muslims. There is thus a constant uneasiness at the back of Muslim minds. And no one who knows India can doubt that there is real difficulty for the humble Muslims over appointments to minor Government posts and, indeed, on all the many occasions on which official favour can be a help; it is a society in which the personal counts for much and among Hindus the web of kinship and the ties of the 'brotherhood' are still strong.

It is a different story for the Indian Muslim of ability and education; he may indeed enjoy some advantage over Hindus if he is willing
to co-operate, because in a high position he flies a flag for the secular
state. The Government of India since partition has been controlled by
the Congress Party, who are officially committed to the secular state,
and they have found high posts for Muslims; there can be no doubt
that they have tried to damp down communal animosity. But it is not
easy for a government, however long it stays in office, to make its views
permeate throughout a whole society, particularly when they run
against a tendency that is two thousand years old. The Muslims of
India are at present in no sense a direct threat to Indian society; they
want peace and toleration and equal treatment. But if the central and
provincial governments were for any length of time controlled by
militant Hindu groups, or even if the local network of kinship and caste
loyalty grew stronger under a cover of quite different official professions, then Indian Muslims might become a danger in quite a
different sense. It must be a danger to society if there is an element in
the population that feels itself excluded and unjustly treated, particularly if it is so strong as 10 per cent of the whole and formerly
ruled the country where it is now a subordinate minority.

## 3 Unity and Diversity: Language

It has already been suggested that all India's divisions are linked with
ideas about descent. This is perhaps least applicable to the Hindu-
Muslim division; some Indian Muslims did—before partition—think
and even speak of themselves as settlers or colonists in the midst of a
people to whom they were superior, but most of such people have left
for Pakistan and the distinction is now formulated almost entirely in
terms of belief and culture. There is slightly more ambiguity about
language differences, because Hinduism is strongly enmeshed in the
myth of Aryan descent, because there runs through the social structure
so strong a hierarchical feeling and so strong a sense—at least in the
North—that the Northern higher castes are nearer to the Aryan stock
and that their Sanskritic language expresses this. But language is a
subject of sufficient emotional force even without this undercurrent
and India's linguistic problems are unique.

The Linguistic Survey of India gives one hundred and seventy-nine
languages and five hundred and forty-four dialects.[1] But most of these
are spoken by very small numbers of people. There are fourteen, or by
another reckoning sixteen, major languages; of these Hindi is spoken
by the largest number of people—133.4 million in the 1961 census,
which is just over 30 per cent of the total population. This does not
tell the whole story; many whom the census records as Hindi speakers

[1] W. H. Morris-Jones, in Philip Mason (ed.), *India and Ceylon: Unity and Diversity.*

are unintelligible to each other; it is a somewhat arbitrary decision to say what constitutes a language and what a dialect.[1] But the 'Hindi-speakers' can most of them with a little care be made to understand simple sentences in basic Hindi. Linked with Hindi, as derivative from Sanskrit, are twelve out of the sixteen, but some of them are as different as English from German or Spanish from French; Bengali and Marathi, the two next largest groups, have each over thirty million speakers. Then there is the southern family of four Dravidian languages, utterly different in construction; together they have over one hundred million speakers. All these fourteen are written languages with a literature.

Superimposed on this complicated problem is the fact that for nearly two centuries English has been the language of higher education and the official language for the whole country. This was a unifying factor in the period of British rule but it has left a peculiar legacy. English was more widely used in Madras, Bengal, and Bombay than in the Hindi-speaking North; this wave of invaders had come from the sea, not over the mountains. The Madrassis and Bengalis had some advantage over Hindi-speakers in examinations; so at least the Hindi-speakers believed. But independent India—it was felt—must have a national language, not a relic of foreign occupation; the only possible candidate was Hindi, directly Sanskritic and spoken by a much larger group than any other single language. But to adopt it would give the Hindi-speakers a much greater advantage over the Bengalis and Madrassis than the latter had had in the past over the Hindi-speakers. Further, scientists, diplomats—many others—would need to learn English in any case; modern Hindi was by no means the most developed of Indian languages, its literature not comparing in volume with, say, Bengali; at the same time, it was faced with an internal crisis of its own. Urdu, with many Persian and Arabic words in ordinary use and also a Persian literary convention, had been the polite, and also the popular, language of the towns throughout the heart of the Hindi

---

[1] It is not easy to convey the ramifications of language and dialect to anyone who has not experienced them in a society with poor communications and a low level of literacy. But a note from personal experience may help. I held charge from 1936 to 1939 of the hill district of Garhwal, which then provided the Indian Army with four battalions of infantry and a number of subsidiary troops. The infantry regiment made up by these four battalions had a very strong corporate spirit and a high reputation; their official language was 'Hindustani', a simplified form of Hindi with a minimum of Persian and Arabic words, the lingua franca of North India and of the Indian Army. The officers maintained that if they permitted the use of Garhwali, orders were misunderstood because the dialect varied so much from valley to valley. I camped over the whole district, in which in those days there was no wheeled traffic, supervising the making of field maps on a scale of 32″ to the mile. I found that the dialect did indeed vary greatly from one valley to the next, but there was nonetheless a basic Garhwali, spoken by my court clerks and messengers, which almost every peasant could understand, which differed from written Hindi rather more, it seemed to me, than Chaucer's English from current modern English. But it was very rarely written.

country; now these Persian and Arabic words must be excised and a pure Hindi built up based on Sanskritic derivations. It was not quite as unreal as the adoption of Irish as the official language of Eire, but it was of that order, part of the movement for particularism to which we shall return at the end of this book.

Thus to about two-thirds of the people in India, the only possible alternative to English as an official language was not only foreign but less modernized than their own; the whole controversy was further embittered by the quasi-racial feeling between Sanskrit North and Dravidian South. But this is to oversimplify; there were two conflicts, the first about the official language for India and the second about the official language for each state; the boundaries of the state did not exactly coincide with linguistic boundaries. The second conflict was at first treated with a certain arrogance by the Congress leaders, who after partition had overwhelming strength at the centre; to concede linguistic states would be, they felt, a step towards splitting India. If the problem was ignored long enough it would disappear.

But this was to disregard the strength of the emotion with which men regard their language. The means by which a man expresses himself is after all near to the core of his being; it moulds and flavours his thought; his skill with language shapes the image he presents to the world. On another level, it is the means to education, to progress in the world, to choice of profession, and to satisfying ambition. It would have been wise to have conceded from the start some redrawing of boundaries and, at least within the state, the principle that as many as possible should be able to use their mother tongue in school and court.

It will throw light on this subject, and also on the subject of caste in politics, if we dwell in rather more detail on a case-study by Professor Selig Harrison[1] of elections in the years after partition in the Andhra delta. This is an area where people speak Telegu, but it was formerly part of Madras State, in which the majority were Tamil-speakers, while there were large numbers of Telegu-speakers in two other states. There was agitation for a separate Andhra or Telegu-speaking state; in the years after partition the ruling Congress Party did not take the agitation seriously. In the election of 1951, the Communist Party gave their unqualified support to the idea of an Andhra State. At the same time, they put into the campaign a very efficient party organization and succeeded in getting the backing of the great majority of the Kamma caste, a group of rich cultivators, owners of land or prosperous peasants, who through their wealth and control of land have much influence. The proportion of untouchables, who are also landless labourers, was at this time as high as 37 per cent in the delta; paradoxically, their tradition of voting as the dominant Kammas directed seemed also a

[1] Selig S. Harrison, *India: The Most Dangerous Decades.*

vote for equality and freedom. The local Congress Party had been locked in faction for the four years since independence and for reasons of personal resentment or frustration many dissident Congress groups voted against the Party. The Communists won the election, taking twenty-five seats against the Congress ten. Of the thirty-five seats, seventeen went to Kammas, fourteen to Communist Kammas, and only three to the Congress. What exactly the Kammas thought communism would do for them—except provide the Andhra State—is not clear.

This was a severe blow to the Congress, who took the matter seriously. They conceded the Andhra State in the first place and thus removed a considerable grievance; secondly, they turned the full force of their powerful electioneering machinery on to the area; thirdly, they made a determined attempt to win the influential Kamma vote. They were so successful that in 1955 they were able to beat the Communists by sixty-three seats to nine (the number of seats had been greatly increased). The Kammas had twenty-five seats, and of these twenty-four had the Congress nomination. By 1959, the Kammas were divided between three parties, Congress, Communist, and Swatantra, the party of liberal property-owners.

There are no longer any serious demands for linguistic states and no major grievance over state languages to be met. But there are still some groups who are in the wrong linguistic state and twenty-five million people whose mother tongue is not one of the major languages. The constitution lays down safeguards for them but they must be at a disadvantage.

The problem of the official language for the Indian Union remains. It aroused violent passions and rioting in 1965, when the Dravidian-speaking South believed that the Hindi-speaking North was forcing Hindi upon them with arrogant disdain. A temporary arrangement was reached by which an educated boy with any ambition must have some proficiency in three languages—Hindi and English and his state language, or, if that is Hindi, the language of another state. Perhaps a lesson has been learnt and this compromise, with all its imperfections, will be allowed to continue. But the controversy is still potentially explosive and is essential to an understanding of Indian society.

## 4 Unity and Diversity: The Tribes

This quick look at problems of language suggests that caste, politics, regionalism, and power form a closely woven mesh. Indeed, the more one studies India, the more inseparably interwoven with each other the problems of social unity and diversity seem to be. The tribal minorities, for instance—to whom we now turn—can best be defined in terms of their relation to caste; they are non-Aryan groups who have not been absorbed into the caste system. And, of course, there are border-line cases; some of them begin to be more like castes than tribes. The flow of Sanskritic culture washed impotently against great bastions of wild impenetrable country on the North-Eastern and Eastern boundaries with Nepal and Burma; it divided and flowed round smaller islands of difficult hill country throughout Central and Southern India. These islands have all of them in the last century and a half been influenced in varying degrees by Sanskritic if not by Western culture; some have been virtually assimilated. Typical are the Konds of Orissa, who are particularly well documented for two periods. In the 1830s they attracted the attention of British administrators because it was an essential part of their animistic religion to sacrifice human beings in times of drought and pestilence. There was a special class of potential victims; most villages kept one or two of them, reared at the general expense. It was essential that they should have been bought by exchange of goods with another community; they were kept until the emergency arose, when one would be selected and sacrificed by successive slashes from the whole group, his blood and fragments of his body being divided between as many fields as possible to bring fertility. The Konds, living in wild hilly country little penetrated by anyone else, were then unquestionably a tribe, entirely beyond the pale of Hinduism. To-day, a modern anthropologist writes that the Konds 'say they are Hindus like everyone else, but they make a sharp distinction between themselves and the Oriyas who live in their midst'.[1] Professor Bailey sometimes speaks of them as a caste and it is clear that they are rapidly becoming an in-marrying caste-group within the Hindu system.

When this happens, the former tribal group is usually low in the caste scale but regarded with less aversion than the untouchables—and this for a variety of reasons. They are not, in the first place, associated with such degrading tasks as skinners and sweepers. But there is a deeper reason. There was really no need to keep the tribal folk at a social distance so long as they kept to their mountains and jungles; they were usually neither a social nor a military threat. The most that was to be feared from them, and that only by their nearest neighbours, was an occasional raid on a cattle-byre. The untouchables on the other hand by their mere presence were a continuing threat to Brahman supremacy; for reasons central to the argument of this book, it was essential to emphasize their permanent inherent difference.

There is an obvious parallel with the American Indian and the Negro in the United States. The Indian, at least from the middle of the nineteenth century, might be a local threat, in the sense that he might steal cattle or kidnap an individual, but he was not a national threat and, as Pitt-Rivers has pointed out, as soon as he left his tribal background and came among white men, he ceased to be an individual

[1] F. G. Bailey, *Tribe, Caste and Nation.*

threat. The danger he presented when he was part of his tribal group arose from his different culture; when he left the tribe he became a suppliant for Western culture. But the Negro, who had been robbed entirely of his own culture, was already within the white culture as an individual, and, like the untouchable, he was a perpetual threat because he might demand fair treatment. The comparison cannot be carried beyond a certain point because the United States is in so many respects an open society completely at variance with Hinduism.

As Professor von Fürer-Haimendorf[1] has pointed out, the extent to which Hinduism is imbued with caste-separatism has on the whole been a help to the tribal folk. In the past, no Raja wished to convert them; in the present, no Brahman fears that they will marry his daughter. The system is too tightly built, too self-confident. These tribal folk of the cultural islands, the Sonthals, the Bhils, the Hos, the Mundas, the Gonds of Central India, are still in the process of wanting to become more Sanskritic, more Hindu, and it is unlikely for some years to come that many of them will pass through this phase to the next. This is the stage when snobbery flows in the reverse direction and, instead of trying to show how scrupulously you observe rules about avoiding certain foods and certain contacts, it becomes important to display your freedom from superstition and from prejudice about religious trivialities. They are not likely, then, to be a divisive force because they are tribal; they are likely to be on the fringes of the society, near the bottom of the caste system like the untouchables, a danger only in certain specific circumstances. With these circumstances we shall deal when discussing the untouchables.

It is a different matter with the tribal folk of the great Eastern and North-Eastern bastions, who were never surrounded by Hinduism, the Nagas, the Mizos, who used to be called the Lushai, and the people of the North-Eastern Frontier Agency. They had been very loosely administered indeed by the British; in the British period, the central authorities had no missionary zeal to develop or convert them and were on the whole rather cynically prepared to leave them alone so long as they were not too obtrusive in such practices as head-hunting. On the other hand, British administrators who had anything to do with them usually liked them as they were; they liked them far too well to want to see them changed. This extreme form of paternalism for primitive peoples, very common among the British, has often caused trouble after independence. It is fascinating and romantic to spend twenty years among head-hunters if you mean to retire to Devonshire; if you live near by in the plains of Assam, you are more inclined to regard these wild folk as a reproach to your own civilization.

The Indian Congress Party in the years immediately after

---

[1] C. von Fürer-Haimendorf, in Philip Mason (ed.), *India and Ceylon: Unity and Diversity*.

independence was dominated by Nehru, and its mood was earnest, Benthamite, rather humourless; it seemed proper to drag such people as these quickly into the twentieth century. The strategic picture too had changed since the Second World War; the British had never supposed that any threat from China or Burma could develop across that tangled web of mountain and jungle. But this did not weigh largely in the early days of relations with the Nagas, when Nehru still believed that Asian powers were never aggressive. It is of course very important now.

This is not the place to examine in detail the story of the mistakes made, the ill-informed assumptions on which initial contacts proceeded, the concessions made too late. But it is perhaps useful to emphasize the likelihood, almost the certainty, of a gap between the spirit of the instructions issued by the Government and the manner in which they would be carried out on the spot. Few Indian administrators shared the British affection for primitive people and isolated places; their wives had seldom been brought up to believe that solitude for long stretches was an offering they ought to lay on the altar of imperial duty; their children were not sent to boarding-schools for the term and to aunts for the holidays. They were firmly urban in outlook. Many regarded it as a punishment to be sent to a post which to many British officers had seemed a reward; many no sooner arrived at an isolated post than they began to scheme to get away. They were often impatient with a culture utterly different from their own but not so remote as to be idealized. And the tradition of Indian government servants has always been firmly authoritarian. The evidence suggests a progressive loss of tolerance from the centre to the state, from the state to the district and sub-division and towards the lower reaches of the official scale.

Of the three groups we have mentioned, relations with the Nagas and Mizos degenerated into rebellion—or looked at from the other side a war of independence—before concessions were offered which would have permitted them to order their lives as they wished in a reasonable degree of autonomy. Complete independence, in view of relations with China, it is not reasonable to expect—but the atrocities which always accompany war have embittered relations to such an extent that the tribal folk will now accept nothing less. The group of tribes included in the North-Eastern Frontier Agency had even less coherence among themselves than the Nagas and the Mizos. It is only quite recently that the Nagas acquired a common name which would distinguish them from everyone else; for the Mizos this is still more recent and the N.E.F.A. groups have no such word and probably little sense of common identity. There was perhaps also less immediate eagerness to reform and develop them willy-nilly. A code has been drawn up for their administration and a special cadre of administrators allotted; here there seems a reasonable hope of a gradually developing relationship. With the Nagas and Mizos, there seems little hope of breaking the deadlock except by some dramatic act of renunciation on India's part—but such an act demands a leader of the stature and with the national appeal of Nehru.

It is one of the basic difficulties of the situation that India regards this as an internal problem. It is wounding to Indian official opinion that the Nagas, who were startlingly and movingly loyal to the British in the Second World War, should reject so brutally and decisively what the present Government feels to be the far more benevolent and enlightened attempts of independent India to bring them the benefits of civilization. From this it follows that any outside advice or offers of mediation are liable to be resented, most of all if they come from Britain. Only an international gesture would have any chance of success, and that only if conducted with the utmost delicacy. The method of reaching a settlement is obscure; the broad lines on which a settlement would have to be made on the other hand are clear. Autonomy within the Indian Union would have to be bought by a temporary withdrawal of Indian troops; this might perhaps be the preparation for a negotiated return, if it is strategically essential—but it seems at a distance arguable that Pakistan's decision at the other end of the sub-continent was a wise one. Pakistan solved the Frontier problem by abandoning a punishing terrain to its inhabitants and recognizing that an enemy who chose to exhaust himself by advancing through such territory would be the weaker when he emerged.

## 5 Unity and Diversity: Caste and Politics

We come now to caste and in particular to the untouchables. Here in India is a vast nation of five hundred million people, divided at birth by an immensely strong and very ancient culture into many hundreds of groups, whose members must neither marry, eat, drink, nor smoke with anyone outside the group. Further, some seventy million are set even further apart, so that their mere presence is pollution, only to be removed by elaborate penances and ritual. For twenty years, the ruling party has tried by ordinance and decree to overthrow the tradition of two thousand years, but there are parties within the state who oppose this determination and—what is more important—there is the great inert mass of custom to be overcome in a society still largely illiterate. These broad facts are clearly dangers to the entire political and social structure. Can the social structure be radically changed without overthrowing the political? Let us look first at the effect of caste on those within the traditional system, leaving the untouchables till later.

A glance at the Andhra delta has already provided a clue as to the part caste can play in politics. When the majority of a powerful land-owning caste can be stirred by a cause with wide emotional appeal, the combination is hard to resist. But it occurs less often than might be supposed and any account of an election in India usually involves a very complex analysis of a wide variety of factors.

The course of events in Aligarh in Uttar Pradesh from independence in 1947 until the elections of 1962 will throw some further light on this complexity. This account follows the admirable study by Paul Brass in his *Factional Politics in an Indian State*.

Aligarh is, except in one respect, a fairly typical district of North-Western Uttar Pradesh. The main landowning castes are Brahmans, Rajputs, and Jats; a number of Muslims also hold land. The most numerous single caste is that of the skinners, the Chamars, untouchable landless labourers. All this is typical; what is unique to Aligarh is the Muslim University. This was originally the centre for Westernizing Muslims, eager to catch up the long start the Hindus had gained, and opposed in spirit to the traditional orthodox theological college at Deoband; it became the intellectual nurse before independence of the Muslim League and of the idea of Pakistan. Muslims in the district as a whole are 12 per cent of the population, but in the city they are 35 per cent.

At the time of Independence, there was virtually no opposition to the Congress; the more militant Muslims left for Pakistan and those who remained saw in Congress their best hope—the secular state was clearly to be preferred to anything offered by the militant Hindus of the right or by the more extreme Socialists and Communists on the left. The landless labourers too supported the Congress; it was opposed to caste and privilege and would end their centuries of subjugation— so argued the more articulate—while the rank and file no doubt found it comfortable that for once the high-caste landowners who were their patrons gave them the same advice as their leaders. The landowners had been committed to the Congress cause during the struggle for independence and many continued to adhere to it simply by habit; many had not fully considered the implications of its egalitarian and secular doctrines. Thus two considerable minority elements in the population, together making up more than one-third of the whole, were behind the majority; it is not surprising that in the elections of 1952 the Congress swept the board, winning every constituency in the district—all ten seats in the State Assembly and both seats in the central Parliament. They were also overwhelmingly strong in local government bodies and in the co-operative societies, which play an important part in local politics. In 1957, there was little change except that one Assembly seat was lost to an independent.

But in spite of this apparent unanimity, there had been bitter factional fighting within the Congress Party. It arose in the first place from personal antagonism between two Congressmen in the district, both leaders in varying degrees in State politics and one a quite considerable figure in national affairs. The younger man, a Brahman, was the more successful outside the district; the other, a Rajput, was a veteran leader inside the district. Their personal animosity led to the formation of factions, to some extent divided between Brahman and Rajput.[1] Warfare between the two factions became acute, not only for every State and National seat but for every office of local government and for such posts as chairman and secretary of the local co-operative society. As Brass points out, factional fighting within a party tends to be more bitter than strife between parties; since it is personalities not principles that are at stake, no compromise is possible. Each faction in the district was linked with a faction at the headquarters of the State; fortunes ebbed and flowed as one group or the other held power in Lucknow. Criminal charges of embezzlement were answered by civil suits for defamation; murders occurred and one faction alleged that the other had conspired to bring them about—and again there were civil suits for defamation. Finally, there was a split in the Rajput faction over the nomination to an important post in district politics—and as a result of this a sub-faction was formed to oppose the ruling faction's candidates for Parliament and the Assembly at the coming elections.

Meanwhile, another cause of tension arose. The Muslim University, once the power-house for the Muslim League, had after partition turned to the task of conciliation and synthesis, but in 1961 the more conservative elements gained control of the university. In a predominantly Hindu city, the university had always been an object of suspicion; this suspicion now increased and was fanned by the jealousy of three colleges within the city which lacked the status of a university and were predominantly Hindu. There was rioting, in which a number of people were killed; the conservative party among the Muslims felt that they had not been protected and decided to throw off their allegiance to the Congress—which was ineffective because of its internal divisions.

At the same time, most of the Chamars were brought to a similar decision by a leader of unusual energy and ability. While the Chamars, like the Muslims, had at first seen no profitable course open to them but to support the Congress, they too had always contained a small vocal element who saw in this bourgeois party of the caste Hindus their natural enemy. Those of this way of thinking had formed the Republican Party, which previously had had no success in Aligarh. But the extremes of faction in the Congress Party now coincided with the decision of the conservative Muslims to break away, and the

[1] Paul Brass specifically says that in one part of Aligarh the factional strife reflected Brahman-Rajput tension; it is my deduction that this was more widespread. But it seems impossible to avoid; everyone Brass mentions as belonging to the faction of Malkhan Singh has a Rajput name.

leader of the Republican Party saw his chance to construct a Grand Alliance against the Congress. It was an improbable coalition, because the three elements—conservative Muslims, untouchables, and Congress rebels—had nothing in common but distrust for the ruling Congress faction. But it lasted long enough to produce a landslide against the Congress in 1962. In 1952, they had held both Parliamentary seats and all ten Assembly seats; in 1957, they had lost one seat of the twelve; now they lost nine out of twelve. An element in this devastating defeat was not only that the Congress were fighting each other but that the more conservative caste Hindus, who normally provide a strong element in the backing of Congress, were so alarmed by the combination of Muslim and Chamar—both eaters of beef—that they formed a cow-protection society and diverted votes to that.

This brief account shows how minorities may find a sudden opportunity to assert themselves and also illustrates something of the influence played in politics by social grouping in contrast with policies or platforms. One more such account will round out the picture. This also comes from Paul Brass's book. It concerns the district of Meerut, also in the North-Western part of Uttar Pradesh.

This too is a fairly typical district, the special feature in this case being the predominance of one caste, the Jats. They are not the most numerous group in the district, coming third to the Muslims, who, if they are taken as one group, are a quarter of the total population, and to the Chamars, but the Jats own a quarter of the land and cultivate over 30 per cent. Meerut has always been predominantly a peasant district, with no very large landowners and the great majority of the land in the hands of small proprietors. The Jats are a farming caste, careful saving people, usually cultivating their own land, sometimes tenants to others; the proverbs which refer to them[1] emphasize the stereotype of the peasant, proud of his own plot and village, unaware of wider issues, careful of money, not noted for sharp wits. But they have contributed an important element to the Indian Army and have a high reputation as soldiers; it was the Jat caste who formed the backbone of the Sikh armies and the majority of Sikhs are of Jat origin. Those who are still Hindus—and in Meerut this means virtually all of them—would like to be reckoned in the *varna* system as Kshatriyas, but Rajputs would say they should be reckoned in the Sudra group, the fourth order. In Meerut they outnumber the Rajputs considerably.

Another important group in this district are the Tyagis, who, like the Jats, are prosperous peasants on the upward grade, but their ambition is to belong to the first order and be reckoned as Brahmans. There is thus material here for a four-sided conflict between the two dominant landowning castes and the two castes generally reckoned of

[1] Sir Herbert Risley, *The People of India.*

the highest social and religious grade. This might be seen as likely to provide opportunities for a combination of the two most numerous groups, Muslims and Chamars. Or again, it might seem likely that there would be a grouping under Jat leadership of rather similar castes, such as Gujars and Ahirs, both agricultural castes, both supplying some men to the armed forces and occasionally claiming Kshatriya status, though with even less justification and conviction than the Jats. But in fact neither of these combinations has taken place; there has usually been a working alliance of Jats and Tyagis, held together by the conciliatory attitude of the Jat leader, who backed Tyagis for important posts and by the same kind of means was usually able to manipulate a local situation so as to secure the goodwill of other groups too. What emerges from Brass's account of politics in Meerut is that the candidate likely to be successful is the man who can appeal to the widest number of groups.

Here too Muslims and Chamars have usually supported the Congress, on the ground that it is better than any alternative that seems at all plausible. But the Jats and Tyagis have never been able to take for granted the allegiance of Muslims and Chamars, or even their own alliance. In any constituency, the entire pattern of grouping has to be considered and the personality of the candidate and his background of local service taken into account. In one constituency, in 1962, a Congress Muslim candidate won against a Jat Communist and a Gujar Independent; he had the solid backing of most Muslims because he was a Muslim; of most Chamars, because he was Congress; of many Jats, because he and his uncle had for many years 'helped Jats' in various ways—he was a local man—and because he was a Congressman; and of many Brahmans, Rajputs, and other caste Hindus because he was a Congressman and not a Jat.

Another constituency in the same election proved even more interesting. This is the only constituency in Uttar Pradesh in which one caste has an absolute majority over all others put together, the Jats being 60 per cent of the population. Yet a Jat candidate with the official Congress nomination was defeated by a Rajput without it. This appears to have happened because all those who were not Jats decided to vote for the one candidate who was not a Jat, while there were seven Jat candidates who split the vote.

There is clearly no space in a book of this kind to cite more examples. What emerges, certainly, is the importance of caste as an element in almost every election. Most people, unless there are reasons to the contrary, will vote for a man of their own community. But no one can count with certainty on this, because in some circumstances people may calculate that their vote will thus be wasted, or there may be more than one candidate of their community, or the majority of the community may decide that they can apply more leverage by transferring their block vote to a candidate who makes some specific promise. Or faction, arising from personal ambition or antagonism, may split the caste-group just as it frequently splits the party.

The first generalization that seems to emerge is that a candidate is likely to be successful if he can get a wide backing from groups other than his own, particularly if he can keep the backing of his own group at the same time and if that happens to be a dominant landowning group like the Jats of Meerut. To this may be added a second: that in politics the importance of caste is greatest when the election is at the level of the smallest unit and diminishes as it rises to the district, state, and national levels.

A few years ago, foreign observers of India were inclined to predict that Indian politics would increasingly come to be governed by caste. But the important unit in caste is the *jati*, that is to say the in-marrying local group, which is too small to be effective in politics even at the district level; it would therefore be necessary to establish first caste-associations—the argument ran—and then groups of caste-associations which could manipulate large numbers of votes. A pioneer of this kind of view was Professor Selig Harrison whose book *India: The Most Dangerous Decades* is essential for anyone who wishes to study this subject. He suggested, for example, that a model of what was likely to happen was provided by an alliance of Ahirs, Jats, and Gadariyas—known as AJGAR which means a python or some mythical creature such as a dragon. This he believed to be likely to be of increasing influence in the politics of Uttar Pradesh, but by the time Brass wrote, five years later, this combination had disappeared from the political scene.

In general, the caste-association has not prospered as a political force. It had no place in the traditional caste system; there was no structural link between the many local in-marrying groups known by the same name. It is a modern development and it has usually flourished for a caste which wants to improve its status; it has linked the different groups together, urged them to adopt certain customs which may enhance their prestige, represented their case to the government and the press. There was, for example, a caste-association for Chamars who no longer skinned dead cattle; it urged its members not to eat beef or marry widows and tried to persuade other people to use the term Jatav instead of Chamar. But when caste-associations have tried to go beyond this sphere of improving their religious and social position they have had insufficient strength to hold groups together, usually even at the district level and certainly at the state or national level. Politics is a matter of power, jobs, patronage; what is important is who is chairman of the District Congress Committee, who is secretary of the co-operative society, whether money can be found to bridge the water-course which grows to a torrent in the rains and cuts off three villages. Only the local group is interested in this, not people of the same name who live a hundred miles away.

Alliances of several caste-associations have even less chance of success in politics, partly for the same reason—that local affairs are paramount —but also because by their essential nature caste-associations are bound to be rivals rather than allies of similar castes. The caste-association of Ahirs exists mainly to demonstrate that Ahirs are better than Gadariyas and very much closer to Jats than most people suppose— and interests of this kind are paramount with all three groups. It does not provide a firm basis for an alliance. There are some interests which Jats, Ahirs, and Gadariyas have in common—the price of grain and fertilizer, marketing facilities, dues on canal water for irrigation— but these are the kind of interests for which a party, not a caste, is likely to be most useful.

Harrison was right in thinking that the structure of Indian society cries out for some framework to bind together the small in-marrying groups. They cannot be politically effective on the state level, still less on the national. Where he was wrong was in thinking that for purposes of national politics the binding structure would be of the same kind as the ties that bind people together into caste-groups. Brass, writing five years later, perceived that they are in fact different; the faction cuts across caste links. The Congress Party, he considers, is 'organizationally, a collection of local, district and state factions form- ing alliances and developing hostilities in a constant struggle for positions of power and status'. The faction, though it splits the party, has acted as a unifying link between levels of politics—village, district, state—and has weakened the influences of caste by cutting across it. Relations within the faction are personal between the leaders and followers; they resemble the old village relationship of *jajman* or patron and his retainers, with its obligation of total protection and total service, but there is a stronger element of contract; they can be terminated more easily. The follower can split away and form a faction of his own; also, the contexts in which this personal relationship operates are surely becoming fewer, the higher one goes in the structure. Members of a faction will expect support in litigation, because in India this is frequently one of the weapons of politics; above the district level they are year by year less likely to be expected to add prestige to the marriage of a leader's daughter by acting as unpaid retainers.

Caste in fact becomes increasingly only one of a number of dimensions in which status is reckoned. This has always been true to some extent; indeed, one writer, Dumont, defines caste as a system where 'disjunction between status and power exists'. He is thinking of the traditional Hindu society where the Raja is a Kshatriya and the Brahman is his Minister, or perhaps of such a village as Anantpur in Uttar Pradesh (see Chapter VII, Section 3), where the rich land-owners were Kshatriyas and a Brahman might be a cook or a nurse in the household. In both cases, there is some degree of 'disjunction' of status and power, but not in the South Indian village described by Béteille; here power and status were both in Brahman hands. But to-day the division increases. Wealth can be acquired by men of low caste and so can political power; these confer status but it is status in a different *dimension* from that of caste, which is derived from birth and the continued observance of ritual precautions.

Earlier in this book, in the general argument of Part I, we touched on the concepts of equality and social justice and the dimensions in which they might be reckoned. There was first the dimension of legal equality and then three more in which some guaranteed minimum seemed to be required—dimensions of wealth, of power, and of esteem. In Indian society, there is a fifth dimension—caste—which must be added; it can be separated entirely from wealth and power, but not from esteem; it is a component of esteem but not the only component. Wealth and power are also components of esteem; whether wealth or power or caste is foremost in the reckoning of a given person's esteem for another at a given moment will depend on the social con-text. A poor Brahman with no political connexions may be an important man at a wedding; a Kurmi—a cultivating caste of the fourth order or *varna*—who belongs to a powerful faction in the Con-gress and has ingratiated himself with other groups may become Chairman of the District Board or Member of the Assembly and will have power and patronage; or, without any political pretensions, such a man may become wealthy and will be respected for his wealth in a certain context or social setting. This separation of the dimensions in which esteem is earned is becoming more and more apparent.

Faction is one of the means by which power and esteem may be earned, not exactly irrespective of caste, but from outside the traditional caste-structure, by manipulating caste and other groupings. It is a word which in English has usually been derogatory, a word used in politics of one's opponents. Here it has been used to mean a sub-division within the party, admittedly a sub-division based more often on personal allegiance and animosity than on broad questions of principle. But it was inevitable that there should be faction within the Congress so long as this party retained the virtual monopoly of power which it acquired through its prestige as the party which had won independence.

In the first twenty years of independence, politics took a curious form; one sequence constantly recurred. The Congress, being in effect the only party in a given district or region, became over-confident about the possibility of opposition from outside and split into factions whose hostility overrode loyalty to the party. Minority groups or parties would then seize their chance, ally themselves with Congress dissidents, and score a victory. But, until the elections of 1967, the last stage of the sequence was usually that the Congress hierarchy at the state or national level then stepped in, reproved the local dissidents and healed their breaches, brought overwhelming forces to bear on the local scene and recovered the lost ground. This sequence, so common in the past at a district or regional level, might suggest that Congress losses in 1967 on the national level will also be retrieved, but this does not necessarily follow; there is no higher level to appeal to. It is, however, no part of the purpose of this book to forecast the trend of political events; the object is rather to disentangle those elements in the social structure which suggest healthy development.

And in the relation of caste and social structure to politics, there is much that is lively and may become constructive. The Congress was described by Brass as *'organizationally'* a collection of factions at various levels; but there was an ideological content as well and it was also a collection of 'interests', drawing support at one time from mill-owners as well as mill-hands, landowners as well as tenants and landless labourers, from a majority of the higher castes as well as untouchables and Muslims. This was partly due to the momentum of inertia; almost everyone supported the Congress before independence and they continued from force of habit; it was the universal second-best. If the party now begins to resolve itself into a number of parties representing these interests more specifically, that is surely healthy, if also dangerous. In the meantime, Indians have revealed themselves as among the most political of mankind. Two millennia ago their leaders solved with unrivalled success the problem of persuading the masses that it was proper for them to perform degrading and unpleasant duties in return for a minimum of esteem and the bare means of existence. To-day, over the whole country, and at every level, they display solutions to the classical problem of the politician who is extending his following and rising to new levels. Whether he starts as leader of a trade union, a village, or a caste-group, the moment comes when he must go forward if he is not to go back; but how can he extend his appeal to a second village, trade union, or caste-group without losing his grip on the first? Skill in this art is displayed in Indian politics in a very high degree. Even when the motives or the means are corrupt and unworthy—as they very often are—this is nonetheless democracy in practice; it is a very far cry from a society in which power is exercised by inherited right or ascribed status.

This has been written with Northern India mainly in mind; in Southern India (of which I have no first-hand knowledge) my chief authority is André Béteille.[1] Here there was a classical three-tier system of dominance, headed by the Brahmans—whom for the

[1] *Caste, Class and Power.*

moment we regard as one group though, as we have seen, for purposes of marriage they are many. The Brahmans had a near monopoly of land, of social and ritual prestige, of education, and of power. The non-Brahmans, also divided into many in-marrying groups, acted as intermediaries between the Brahmans and the landless untouchables. If one of these landless labourers offended his masters, they would order their non-Brahman tenants to tie him to a tree and beat him; they could not touch him themselves. To-day all this has changed; the non-Brahmans are in power politically, usually at all levels. The Brahmans, who are being forced to coalesce into something much more like one group than before, are now reduced to the position of a minority, like the Muslims of the North; the non-Brahmans, like the caste Hindus of the North, have to contrive among themselves for each situation such a combination of caste-groups, interests, and personal followings as will defeat any other combination. 'Power', writes Béteille, echoing Brass from the North, 'is no longer a monopoly of any single caste in the village. It has to some extent detached itself from caste, and one has now to consider the balance of power between different castes (or groups of castes). This balance is unstable and factors other than caste play an important part in maintaining it....'[1]

These developments are surely healthy; another is not. In the passage just quoted, the castes to whom power is open are the non-Brahman castes. Politics, Béteille suggests, is really quite different at the village and state levels; at the village level it must depend on consensus, and in Sripuram there is none. There are still for social purposes three communities, living each in a separate quarter. The Brahmans used to manage the *panchayat* or village committee, but now they are in a minority. The Chairman is a non-Brahman who in 1950 led a triumphant procession of non-Brahmans and untouchables through the Brahman quarter, polluting and humiliating all the inhabitants; to-day the Brahmans, who are in a minority on the *panchayat*, seldom attend its meetings, while the untouchables are still virtually excluded. The *panchayat* has an increasing number of functions but at least for the moment the village has exchanged the domination of the Brahman minority for that of a bare majority, the non-Brahmans. In such a situation the value of faction is at once apparent; the majority has only to split into factions for the two minorities to have the opportunity of allying themselves with one or the other.

## 6 *Unity and Diversity: The Untouchables*

But it is the untouchables who have been excluded by the ancient social system from power, wealth, and esteem; it is on their behalf that the new state has concentrated its attempts to reverse the decision of

[1] *Caste, Class and Power.*

two thousand years ago. These attempts have been social, religious, political, and educational.

The constitution forbids 'the practice of untouchability' and though this may not be very easy to define, it is quite clear that it is no longer legal to refuse, for example, entry to a temple, or the use of a well, on account of caste. But it is a very different matter to ensure that the law is obeyed in everyday life, still more, of course, to ensure that contempt is not conveyed in a variety of subtle ways. In his study of Sripuram, Béteille writes that the five Harijan or 'untouchable' members of the village *panchayat* are still required to sit separately when they attend; they are often not told of a meeting till it is over, their thumb-marks being affixed to the necessary documents without their having taken any part in the discussion. This implies of course their acquiescence; they could legally insist on being treated with due consideration. But the older men of these communities (for they too are divided into in-marrying groups) have so long been cowed into subservience that they find it hard to change. Many still shrink from accepting a coin from a Brahman's hand, even if he is ready to give it, and they would not venture into the Brahman quarter, except perhaps in a demonstration with companions. Yet the village school has been established just within the Brahman quarter, and to this their children are now admitted. When they grow up, these children will surely be more prepared to assert themselves.

At present, it is still often dangerous to assert civil rights guaranteed by the constitution. The Government's committee on untouchability[1] reported in 1968 that three ex-untouchables had been shot dead in Madhya Pradesh for daring to curl their moustaches upwards as though they were Kshatriyas. In some streets of Mysore, people of these groups are forced to carry their shoes in their hands and in some villages they have been prevented from riding bicycles. But, as the report rightly states, the fact that incidents occur and are reported is a step forward; it is not long since untouchables throughout the South were forbidden to wear sandals on any occasion, and none would have dared to curl his moustache. Already the prohibition on women of these groups wearing an upper garment has gone[2] and it seems fairly safe to predict that these minor differentiations in dress and behaviour will one by one be abandoned.

To-day the Harijan has the vote; he has seats reserved for him on the village *panchayat* and at higher levels too. He has so far usually used his vote on behalf of the Congress because this has been a strong party with a prospect of power and it is committed to the cause of ending caste-discrimination. But we have already seen, in Aligarh, one case of the

[1] Government of India, Commission on Untouchability, *Report*.

[2] See the account of 'the bosom controversy' in Lloyd I. Rudolph, 'The Modernity of Tradition: the Democratic Incarnation of Caste in India'.

Harijans seizing the chance of combining with others and asserting themselves against the Congress. This possibility is bound to occur again at the local level; against it must be set another possibility, that the Congress will break up into its component parts. The chief opponents of any rise in status for the Harijans are the groups immediately above them, those who are low in the fourth order of Sudras, but who, like poor whites in the Deep South, feel that they must stand for the one privilege they have. The Congress Party may reach a stage when they will feel they must weigh the possibility of a backlash from these Sudra groups against any move for the more rapid assimilation of the Harijans. Indeed, there are signs that this point has been reached.

The preferential treatment already given to make up for past discrimination is considerable, particularly in scholarships. In 1944–5, the number of post-matriculation scholarships awarded to members of the Scheduled Castes (the official designation of the Harijans) was 114; in 1954–5 it was 10,034 and by 1963–4 it was 60,165. The total was estimated in 1967 to be half a million.[1] At one time, posts reserved for Harijans in the highest administrative service could not be filled because there were none qualified; to-day this is no longer the case.

Nonetheless, the system of special scholarships and reserved jobs, though undoubtedly a necessary stage in putting right the centuries of inequality, does emphasize and underline the status of untouchable. The scholarship holder must proclaim his status in order to hold the scholarship. It is still extremely rare for him to marry outside his own community; as a student or young professional man he will often still meet the kind of difficulties in getting lodgings that a West Indian meets in Britain. Harold Isaacs has a story of a boy from one of the Harijan castes who left his village with a scholarship, made good, and achieved success. He became a Member of Parliament. On one occasion he visited a village, in his constituency, where he was asked to take tea at the house of one of the leading men, a man of higher caste. The party would probably be held in the central courtyard round which the house was built. He was pleased and impressed by his treatment, until, as he left, he found at the back door his caste-fellow who had brought the brass vessels from which he had drunk and who was waiting to take them away.

It is not surprising that the educated and successful in these communities often turn angrily away from Hinduism and from the ideal of Sanskritization which still inspires the ambitious members of the lower Sudra groups. 'The religion that asks its adherents to suffer the touch of animals but not the touch of human beings is not a religion but a mockery', said B. R. Ambedkar,[2] in 1936, and he led some of his followers into Buddhism, as others had turned to Christianity, Sikhism,

---

[1] André Béteille, in Philip Mason (ed.), *India and Ceylon: Unity and Diversity.*
[2] Quoted in Harold Isaacs, *India's Ex-Untouchables.*

or Islam—though not always to escape from segregation and humiliation. But it is clear that for the Harijans there is no true escape along the lines of Sanskritization. They may eschew beef and degrading occupations but they will then become at best a part of a society still hierarchically organized in closed groups of which they are the bottom. Their hope lies in Westernization and the gradual weakening of the whole caste system.

But for a long time to come, those who escape by Western education will find themselves cut off from their own people, their kin and caste-fellows, by culture, by interests, by habit of life—yet forced to turn back to them at every crisis of life. In India, however far you go, you need the help of your caste-fellows at birth, marriage, and death; even the man, far from home, who has contrived to hide his origin will be forced to reveal it on such occasions as these.

It seems possible then that there will be increasing divergence between those former untouchables who see their hope in a clean break with Hinduism and the 'Uncle Toms' who think they will become acceptable if they stop eating beef. This will sharpen the conflict between the more radical young leaders of untouchables and the 'clean' cultivating castes, those just within the hierarchy of the *varna* system, who are perhaps for some time to come likely to be Sanskritizers rather than Westernizers. This is a conflict that may become dangerous, particularly in the South. We have seen how in Sripuram—where the proportions of the three-tiered society were approximately 1:2:1— the power has passed to the middle group. A coalition between Brahmans and untouchables seems improbable; the non-Brahmans are therefore likely to divide power between themselves, fighting in factions so long as they are secure, but closing their ranks if assailed by any serious threat. In such a situation, the non-Brahmans do not seem likely to make startlingly radical concessions to the Harijans, either in respect of land or political power. But it has already been conceded that they should go to school; the ancient myth on which their degradation depended has been shattered by the non-Brahmans themselves, who are now in the same dilemma as the whole of India after independence. The weapon they have used to obtain their liberty from the Brahmans is now ready to the hand of those whom they still exclude from freedom.

This danger seems less serious in the North, where there was never so sharp an opposition as in the South between the Brahmans and the rest. In Uttar Pradesh, an end has been made of *zamindari*, which was not quite ownership of land but the nearest thing to it. It has been abolished by the State. In Anantpur, the Rajputs, who used to be the principal landholders not only in their own but in all the neighbouring villages, still keep holdings of limited size which they cause to be cultivated through landless labourers, but their former tenants are now legally masters of the land they till. 'But they still listen to us and do as we say',[1] I was told when I last visited Anantpur. The Rajputs are in a much stronger position than the Brahmans of Sripuram; they were less distinct from the middle-class group of castes within the *varna* system, their monopoly of power and esteem was much more local, and there was no state-wide combination against them. There was a social spectrum rather than three sharp tiers. Far from being an oppressed minority, the Rajputs are still influential and provide political leaders at various levels. But it is probably true in the North, as well as in the South, that the point of balance in politics, the central weight of numbers, lies near the middle of the social range. Power is with groups inside the *varna* system who are unlikely to let the untouchables in; it lies with holders of small plots who were formerly tenants and do not want any further division of holdings that will let in the landless labourers.

This is in the country areas, still 80 per cent of India. In the towns, the untouchables have brought with them something of their old rural organization; their in-marrying groups persist and the *mohalla*—which is the part of a town where a community dwells, the ward, the *barrio*—has its own system of social discipline and mutual help.[2] They are perhaps not so utterly helpless as the poor of the English towns in the Industrial Revolution seem to have been. But they have lost the protection as well as the domination of their former patrons; wages are low, work is scarce. In a country where food is short, with so vast a population growing so quickly, the town labourers obviously present a point at which unrest is likely to begin. India has known anarchy, war between princes, and banditry on a scale hardly distinguishable from war; religious riots and massacres have been frequent. But *class* war, in the shape of peasants' revolts, or *caste* war, in the shape of revolts of the untouchables, have so far been unknown. But now that the cementing mythology has been destroyed, the danger becomes real. There is an extra turn to the screw when to poverty, hunger, unemployment, and the appalling squalor of Indian city life is added a stigma which is inescapable—a form of social definition which welds men together almost as firmly as colour can do. Public proclamation that it has ended when it is still experienced makes it more bitter still.

Until lately, the untouchables have, as I have said, generally voted for the Congress. But this would stop if widespread hunger and unemployment convinced them that the Congress had little to offer, or if the Congress began to break down into its elements and become manifestly a party of the middle ranks, forgetting alike the Whig radicalism of Nehru and Gandhi's saintly paternalism and giving way to the Sudra backlash. Then there might be born among the untouch-

---

[1] *'Ham ko mānte'*—the word *manna* means 'respect, acknowledge the superiority of, obey'—but it is not quite so strong as 'obey' by itself.

[2] Owen M. Lynch, in Philip Mason (ed.), *India and Ceylon: Unity and Diversity.*

ables a despair and an anger comparable to that of America's Negroes. They would surely then be joined by many of the tribes who are in process of becoming castes.

The best hope of avoiding the chaos and loss involved in such a national split lies surely in a recovery of its strength and sense of purpose by the Congress Party. For centuries, India had a religion and a social structure curiously similar, their institutions closely entwined and their philosophical background identical. Since Independence, for twenty years, power has been in the hands of a political party which seemed to translate into political terms some of the most valuable aspects of Hinduism, not in its traditional and most orthodox form, but as it is to-day, profoundly modified by the Greek and Jewish ideas of equality and justice. It had the political virtues of inclusiveness, of being reluctant to embark on definitions and formulas, essentially a working machine meant to include all classes and interests. Just as Hinduism has brought into its fold primitive forms of animism as well as transcendental philosophy—the ritual slaughter of goats at Dasehra as well as *ahimsa*, the principle of not taking life—so the Congress has tolerated men of the most profoundly different political outlook. Insofar as it had an ideology it was Western, mildly egalitarian, socialist in the manner of Nehru rather than utopian and anarchic in the manner of Gandhi. This ideology owed little to Hinduism, but the Congress has always shown a remarkable ability to express Western ideas in a Hindu idiom. It has been possible, until 1967, to regard Congress as uniquely representative of a nation attempting, as I have said, to reverse a decision two thousand years old. With many set-backs and much opposition, this has been the conscious aim. The question now arises of how in the next few years the nation will define itself.

India is a democracy in which numbers constitute power. But the use of power by a democracy can only be just if the people define themselves, the nation, in such a way that a consensus is possible, that even the minorities are represented. Indian thought, the Indian social structure, in the past centred—if so protean a system can be said to have a centre—on *varnashramadharma*, the performance of duty in the appointed sphere within the social system. Hindus, better than most people, understand diversity within a unity in the dimensions of religion and social structure; until independence they had been much less successful in translating into *political* terms the idea of unity above a diversity. Their politics were based on the premise of inequality and their society was manifestly unjust except in terms of reincarnation. In politics, *varnashramadharma* was a principle of conduct which applied to the subordinate. Christian princes in Europe have not always been conspicuous for charity towards their neighbours and Indian rulers have not usually given much consideration to any reciprocal obligations to their subjects arising from *varnashramadharma*. The question now before India is quite simply how to define the 'we' who constitute the state—and the greatest danger is that it will be so defined as to exclude the untouchables, the Muslims, and the tribes.

# CHAPTER IX

# Whites in Southern Africa

## *1 Colonial Beginnings*

To describe in detail the development of race relations in Africa would be to write a history of the continent. And it is virtually two continents, North and South of the Sahara. The two chapters that follow will be limited to Africa South of the Sahara; they will deal mainly with differences between areas which were at one time British possessions, though they will touch on Portuguese, French, and Belgian colonies. They will lay considerable emphasis on South Africa, because, to many people, South Africa stands as a symbol for a system that is hated and rejected; because South Africa influences the outlook on world affairs of every state in Africa; and, finally, because South Africa is the extreme surviving example of a pattern of racial dominance.

In India, we have looked mainly at the effect on to-day's society of something I have loosely called a decision, taken more than two thousand years ago, and embodied in the caste system. No one knows how this process of 'decision' occurred in India, but in South Africa we can see something of how racial attitudes hardened and developed and it will be one of the objects of this chapter to suggest reasons for the differences and resemblances between these attitudes in different parts of Africa.

The first point to be stressed is the *isolation* of Africa South of the Sahara until quite recently. It need not be dwelt on at length; much has been written about it. But although both Europeans and Asians knew of the existence of a vast continent beyond the desert, and indeed ships from the Mediterranean had sailed round it before the time of Herodotus, penetration into the interior was slight. The African peoples had been subjected to rather more influence from outside the continent than the Americans, but to nothing like the constant exchange which took place round the Mediterranean. It is true that Indonesian food crops have reached Africa; that there are Indonesian elements in the population of Madagascar and South Arabian in Ethiopia; the influence of Meroë, the last outpost of Egyptian civilization, trickled Southward and Westward; there were caravans across the Sahara. But most of the interior was developing with far less exchange of ideas than took place between the basins of the Indus, the Euphrates, and the Nile.

Secondly, within this comparatively isolated area, human societies were developing—until violently interrupted by the arrival of Europeans—on lines of historical sequence not dissimilar from those in other main areas of human settlement such as Middle America, the Indus Basin, and the Eastern end of the Mediterranean. The stages of development were not contemporary; the Middle East had a lead of some three thousand years over America; Peru and Mexico were in advance of Africa; but three thousand years is not much in terms of man's development from the earliest users of tools. In each of these areas—America, Africa, the Middle East—small food-gathering groups like the Bushmen of the Kalahari desert formed the most primitive societies. At the next stage, we see tribal rather than family groups, some nomadic and pastoral, others settled and agricultural; pottery and metal in turn begin to be used; tools become more complex, but even more marked is the advance in social organization; tribes begin to extend their range by conquest and merge into primitive states; sometimes a new weapon, new tactics, a leader of genius, or a particular form of social organization give one group so decided an advantage that a confederation or a primitive empire is established, like that of the Aztecs or the Incas or the Monomotapa, and sometimes these have produced great cities, imposing monuments, enduring works of art.

Information is still coming to light about African cultures that were unknown to the first European colonists. They are of increasing antiquity; the boundaries of knowledge are being pushed further and further back. These early cultures are of relevance, because in the nineteenth century Europeans in general believed that Africa 'had no history' and this belief contributed to the relationship which grew up between European and African, to contempt on one side and lack of confidence on the other. Recent discoveries have added to African confidence, but at the beginning of the relationship, neither party had any knowledge of such ancient cultures as that of Nok in Nigeria, and there were only shadowy legends of far more recent political organizations such as that of the Monomotapa in what are now Rhodesia and Mozambique.

Towards the end of the Middle Ages in Europe, examples of many stages of development were to be found side by side in Africa. There were food-gatherers of the most primitive type, Bushmen in the South and pygmies in the forests of the Congo; there were Hottentots, organized in larger groups, keeping cattle and tilling the ground. There were the many Bantu-speaking groups, still spreading in general Southward and Eastward over the continent, all of whom were agriculturists, cattle-keepers, workers in iron; sometimes they were organized in small tribal groups, sometimes in primitive states; here and there, such primitive states were beginning to conquer their neighbours and establish primitive empires; some such empires had crumbled and decayed. There were the Negro Kingdoms of the West Coast, casting bronze heads with techniques in advance of any in Europe; there were city-states in the Sub-Saharan region. The points to be stressed are, first, that this was not a unique stage in human history; on the contrary, it was one through which the Middle East, Europe, and Middle America had passed. Secondly, although there were great differences between these various political organizations, it was true in the smallest as well as in the largest that social life was not simple. We have already glanced quickly at some of the primitive empires and states that arose in Africa and noticed that everywhere there was an elaborate network of duties and rights to other people, a strong sense of precedent, of justice, and of propriety. But life was dangerous and uncertain; disease, famine, and witchcraft were always threats and to these must be added, in the case of the smaller groups, raids for captives by the more powerful.

In the mediaeval period and later, the Arabs on the East and Portuguese on the West established coastal fortresses or factories, and sent explorers, traders, and slaving expeditions inland, but neither established a lasting influence away from certain coastal strips. When the Dutch, Danish, and English established posts on the West Coast, in more thickly populated country, their objects were much the same as those of the Arabs and Portuguese—trade in whatever was profitable. But the density of the population led to development with a different emphasis. It was necessary to establish a point at which goods could be collected in readiness for a ship's arrival and this had to be to some extent defensible. It was also necessary to act through African agents or middlemen, who in their turn had to be able to defend their property. Since a principal item of trade was slaves, the agents had to be strong enough to prevent the slaves from running away, as well as to deal on equal terms with powerful chiefs inland and to protect their adherents. Thus the internal balance of power was upset and the first contacts, however peripheral, from the start made it inevitable that the new arrivals should adopt some of the attributes of sovereignty.

This was true in varying degrees whatever the motives with which the invaders came. It was frequently said in the nineteenth century that trade followed the flag. But the reverse was more often true; certainly on the West Coast the flag followed trade. There were areas, notably Southern Nyasaland, where the Bible came before trade or flag. Missionaries came with a conviction that their errand was benevolent. Daniel Lindley in Natal, Robert Moffatt in Bechuanaland and John Moffatt at Bulawayo, Livingstone in his journeys throughout Central

Africa, Coillard among the Lozi—all these men and many others came to Africa to improve, to instruct, above all to change, the African. But these Protestant missions are late; there was little missionary enterprise of this kind before the late eighteenth and early nineteenth centuries. By this time, the missionary spirit which had inspired the Portuguese in their first contacts on the Congo had died away to something much feebler, while in the Southern parts of Africa the Arabs do not seem to have tried to convert Africans with anything like the vigorous intention they showed on the shores of the Mediterranean. With the exceptions of Nyasaland, and the first encounter of the Portuguese, the motive of colonization was not even professedly conversion, as it was in New Spain. Nor was the motive in the early days usually conquest. To most European rulers, sovereignty over African territories did not at first sight present itself as attractive. Slaves, ivory, gold, oil—these were usually the magnets.

But whether trader or missionary came first, and however radically opposed their motives, two general results were almost bound to follow the arrival of Europeans who set up any kind of post or station. Their leader had to enter into some kind of relationship with African chiefs or leaders, and he thus became a factor in their politics; he became in effect a chief in relation to them. And secondly, he would be forced, sooner or later, to act as a chief or sovereign power within the area over which he had control. He had to enforce some kind of justice. He thus added internal jurisdiction to foreign policy. The point is obvious, though on a small scale territorially, in respect of forts on the West Coast. But the missionaries in Nyasaland, who answered Livingstone's passionate appeal to help Africa, who came to teach and heal, equally found themselves compelled to perform sovereign functions. If a fugitive from a village raided by the Yao took refuge with missionaries, they must either protect him or hand him over; if two inhabitants of their settlement came to blows, they alone could settle the dispute. The antagonists had left their traditional culture and excluded themselves, at least temporarily, from the jurisdiction of traditional authorities. So different were the basic assumptions of the two cultures that the seeds of colonialism were inevitably present even in those whose motives were furthest removed from the Marxist account of colonialism.

However benevolent the intention, then, a colonial situation came to Africa with the first representatives of a society that was already increasingly individualist in its social structure, rational in its approach to causation, and industrialized in its system of production. Neither missionary nor trader could avoid a political function, and once they embarked on a political relationship, it was bound to develop. There were withdrawals. The first Anglican bishop in Nyasaland was faced by an intolerable dilemma; he must either allow a party of slaves recently captured to be taken away to the coast or he must intervene. His intervention was disastrous and his mission withdrew to Zanzibar. The Church of Scotland, in default of any other sovereign, exercised sovereign rights over a supposed criminal, but the missionary in charge, untrained in law and with no experience of government, left the case to a European artisan, whose behaviour was prejudiced and cruel. There were protests from Scotland, resignations, a withdrawal, a fresh start. On the West Coast, we find traders acting as arbiters in the succession to a chiefship. The situation could not be static; if missionaries and traders were to enter an African territory, there were bound to be 'incidents', which sooner or later would create a demand for political intervention.

The situation could not be static. There was bound to be advance or withdrawal, whether the motive was trade, flag, or Bible. On the European side, these three motives occurred in different proportions in different areas; but they also found different degrees of development in the African societies they encountered and the interplay of these factors set up a series of widely differing relationships. During the first three-quarters of the nineteenth century, the flag was in general reluctant to move in; official opinion in Britain was hostile to commitments which were bound to be expensive in a continent which promised little in return. But trade and the Bible were strong and continuous motives, sometimes in opposition and sometimes in alliance; more justly, they should be called economic and idealist, because both include a wider range than the more picturesque terms. Trade was the first, and for long the sole, motive on the West Coast, in gold, slaves, ivory, and oil. In the South, land was very soon the attraction.

The first settlement at the Cape was established by the Dutch to provide fresh provisions for ships on the way to the East. Cattle and vegetables might be grown or traded for, but in either case they involved a relationship with land and with the population already present. Here the African set of variable factors comes into play; it was a very different matter to establish a settlement at the Cape and in the Bight of Benin. European writers have stressed the difference of climate and the importance of disease—malaria, yellow fever, sleeping sickness—and it would be wrong to underestimate these factors. Casualties from tropical disease were appalling; life on the West Coast was never attractive to European emigrants. There was truth in the contrast between the popular phrase 'The White Man's Grave' applied to tropical West Africa and 'White Man's Country' applied to Kenya, Rhodesia, and South Africa, though there were heavy losses in the early days in Rhodesia. But differences in African social and political development were elements in the relationship too.

The Oil Coast, the Gold Coast, the Ivory Coast, the Slave Coast were comparatively thickly populated, and by groups with a much more highly developed political organization than any near the Cape; the first European settlements were established where there was little or no opposition and developed at first by alliance or contract or bargain with African agents. But at the Cape, the country was sparsely inhabited and there was no powerful group remotely comparable with the Kingdoms of Benin or Ashanti. Wandering tribes of Hottentots were not willing to part with their cattle; 'it is very vexing to see such fine herds of cattle and to be unable to purchase out of them anything to speak of' is an entry in an official paper dated 13 December 1652. On the other hand, as a military force, they did not present a serious obstacle; they proved later to be uncomfortable neighbours because they stole from the settlers, but their organization and equipment were so primitive that they were never a serious threat. It has lately been shown that Bantu-speakers had reached points much further South in the seventeenth century than had been generally supposed but it remains broadly true that the early contacts of the Afrikaners were with more primitive groups, Hottentots and Bushmen.

In the nineteenth century, African political structures could not withstand European force. The Zulus, the Matabele, the Ashanti, the State of Benin were conquered. Ethiopia in its mountain fastness alone survived until attacked by Italy after the First World War. At that stage, then, the nature of an African society could not save it from conquest. But the degree of political development on the African side at the time of first contact did affect the relationship throughout. The real differences that arose between South Africa and the West Coast were not simply the result of climate but were due also to this difference between the people encountered. Let us look in rather more detail at developments at the Cape.

## 2 The Cape and the Frontier

The Dutch officials at the Cape were instructed by their masters in Holland to behave circumspectly, not to antagonize the natives, to endeavour to win them to trade, to civilization, and to Christianity. But their first contacts were with the 'Strandloopers', an extremely primitive group who lived by gathering food on the beaches; even the more organized Hottentots had no 'wants', refused to trade, and inspired increasing anger and disgust. Since trade was refused, the purpose of the newcomers could only be met by taking land. The record is one of steadily deteriorating relations, until, by the end of the eighteenth century, there were hardly any tribes of Hottentots still autonomous, while individual Hottentots were usually servants and subject to vagrancy laws which made it almost impossible for them to leave service without the consent of their masters.

A distinction can be perceived at an early stage between the society which grew up in and around Cape Town and the 'Frontier' society, which was pushing steadily outwards, Eastward and Northward. The seaport, the 'Tavern of the Seas', grew into a rich medley of races and nations. The officials of the Dutch East India Company and the original settlers from the Low Countries were reinforced by French Huguenots and other Europeans, mostly staunch Calvinists. Like the Portuguese in Brazil, they found the local population unwilling to work, and indeed quite unaccustomed to the idea of regular labour for an employer; they therefore imported slaves from other parts of Africa and from the East Indies. There was a considerable excess of males among both the European and the slave populations, and miscegenation by both groups with Hottentot women not surprisingly occurred, so that there was soon a variety of racial mixtures—European males with East Indian or African slave women; European males with Hottentot women; East Indian or African male slaves with Hottentot women. In the next generation the offspring of such encounters increased the variety by a new set of combinations.

Cape society did not—as the Spanish in the New World did—attempt from the beginning to categorize these mixtures and attach distinguishing privileges and disabilities to them by law. In a later chapter, we shall see something of the *castas* in the viceroyalties of New Spain and Peru in which distinctions of this kind were supposed to be embodied. But the Dutch did feel the need for social definition; the first distinction they made was between Christian and non-Christian. In the earliest days the Hottentots were automatically defined, because they were members of tribal groups; slaves were few—only ten slaves to one hundred and thirty-four Europeans in 1657—and it was accepted that if slaves were baptized they must be freed. But as the number of slaves increased, attitudes changed. Slave-owners opposed conversion if it meant manumission and it began to be argued—and eventually became law—that a slave might be baptized without being set free. So a Christian might be a slave. That distinction was thus blurred, although for two more centuries at least 'white' and 'Christian' were commonly used as synonyms in conversation.

Nor was the distinction of slave and free of much value to a people who saw themselves surrounded by alien cultures and wished to keep themselves from infection; it did not correspond with the distinction between cultures. By the end of the seventeenth century there was a class of 'free blacks', with whom it was permissible for white persons to sit and drink, to share a meal, or to quarrel as man to man. Freed slaves from the East Indies married Europeans and in the seventeenth century no serious stigma was attached to such marriages, but only one case is reported of marriage—as opposed to cohabitation—with a baptized Hottentot woman; she bore a number of illegitimate children before marriage and again after becoming a widow and did nothing to enhance the reputation of her people. She, and other Hottentot women, who in spite of baptism, were notoriously promiscuous, were regarded as 'brutal aboriginals' by the race who had made use of them, and their final degradation was taken as evidence that the Hottentots were irreclaimable.

Thus the Hottentots, to the early settlers at the Cape, seemed manifestly more primitive and degraded than their East Indian slaves, and since the Hottentots were not as a rule legally slaves, the distinction between slave and free clearly could not become the main dividing line in society. This need for a dividing line seems to have been felt more strongly by the settlers at the Cape than by their fellow-Europeans in other parts of the world. Harshness of treatment is recorded from every colony in the New World, but social definition was far more rigid in South Africa and in the Southern British colonies in America than elsewhere. In Virginia, a freed slave had to leave the colony within six months; he was an anomaly, an offence to the whites who wished to keep social categories distinct. But in Cuba, and indeed in all the Spanish colonies, Church and State alike encouraged manumission. Why was this need for definition so much stronger?

No one can be dogmatic as to the reason but it seems likely that the Calvinist religion on one side and the primitive stage of development of the Hottentots on the other were important factors. Calvinism lays a sharp emphasis on the distinction between the saved and the damned; salvation is predestined but not written in men's faces and it is not a difficult step to assume unconsciously that those who look different are damned. Again, Calvinism is stern in condemnation of sexual acts outside marriage and provides no comfortable means of healing a bruised conscience; there can have been little companionship or shared interests in cohabitation with Hottentot women and it seems likely that shame and repugnance would rapidly succeed desire. There was no means of sacramental absolution and the guilt continued to cause remorse. This is surmise, based on some written evidence; what is beyond dispute is that increasingly a sharp dividing line was drawn and that increasingly it was not between Christian and non-Christian nor between free and slave but between white and non-white. But, at the same time, the whites had come to stay; there was a society at the Cape of which white, coloured, slave, and Hottentot made up the parts.

Where two races have mixed genetically and one is socially dominant, there are, as we have seen, two broad attitudes to their offspring that the dominant may take. They may regard their own genetic contribution as 'raising' their children or they may regard the 'blood' of the subordinate group as a kind of taint. At one time, it seemed that the white settlers at the Cape, like the Spaniards in the New World, would follow the first line; in 1671 there are instructions that children of Europeans and slave women were to be educated so that they might in due course 'enjoy the freedom to which, by the right of the father, they were born'. But a century later it had become essential, in order to become enrolled as a burgher, to be born free, of free-born parents who were themselves of Christian descent; objections were raised to serving in the militia alongside a person described as 'of a black colour and of heathen descent'. As in Virginia, African 'blood' had come to be seen as a taint; this was the dividing line. And the Cape was by now a slave-owning society in which, as the officials of the East India Company continually complained, those of white descent would not engage in manual labour.

But there was a difference, as we have said, between Cape Town and the 'Frontier', a term which obviously must have a different territorial meaning from generation to generation as European expansion pushed out from the Cape. It seems likely that the pioneer would usually be a simpler and less sophisticated person than the citizen; certainly the life he led was likely to produce an attitude more given to hard-and-fast distinctions. No one at the Cape could fail to be aware of gradations of colour and class. But those who established themselves as cattle-farmers on three thousand morgen (more than six thousand acres; the standard size for a farm) lived a patriarchal life in which the farmer seldom saw anyone but his wife, children, and servants. Traditionally he felt it was time to move on if he could see his neighbour's smoke on the horizon. He did not have many slaves; he lived simply, often reading no book but the Bible. His servants were Hottentots; he waged constant war, at first, and in the Northern parts of what was later the Cape Colony, with Bushmen; these people he regarded as vermin and shot at sight. Later and further East, he was engaged with more formidable enemies, the Bantu-speakers, in a succession of 'Kaffir Wars'. It is not surprising that he often thought of the Cape as corrupt and luxurious, in morals, in religion, and in the attitude to the heathen. Yet the two societies reacted on each other. The frontiersman had gone out from the slave society of the Cape; his life sharpened and hardened his attitudes, and the result was continually fed back to the capital.

Once a line of cleavage on racial lines is established as a social barrier, the effect is cumulative; every association reinforces it. They are poor, they are ugly, they are dirty, they are improvident and promiscuous—these are the observations frequently made by the upper group, who quickly persuade themselves that the difference in manners and attainments is due to inherent genetic qualities or their lack. The subordinate group find themselves constrained to conform to the role allotted them; they have nothing pleasant to look forward to, so they live in the moment and squander any windfall that comes their way—thus confirming the bad opinion of their master. The vicious spiral circles further down in each generation.

From the viewpoint of the Cape, the Frontier and its sharp distinctions were far away. There was no need to divide the world into 'us, the people' and dangerous enemies, the Bushmen with their poisoned arrows, the Xhosa and the Zulu with their assegais. There was a gradation of rank, status, and wealth among whites; some free blacks had property. The influence of Europe was perceptible and was an influence for moderation and conciliation. There was much to suggest a development similar to that of Brazil, where racial origin, though important, is only one element in social identification. But, perhaps due to the influence of the Frontier, perhaps to remorse and sexual shame—Calvinism's interaction with the primitive nature of Hottentot society—the line, as we have seen, did not blur but hardened. But there was still a possibility that the line, though hard, might not remain horizontal, by which is meant that the lowest white person in the scale might not always be superior to the highest non-white.

This possibility seemed at first to become more likely when the Cape changed hands in the Napoleonic wars and became British. As we shall see, it is misleading to see the conflict between white people as lying between English-speakers and Afrikaners. Dutch officials in the past had in many ways more in common with their British successors than they had with the Frontier Afrikaners. Nonetheless, there was a change of emphasis. The attraction which the Cape offered to the British was much the same as to the Dutch; it was a staging-post on the way to India. But the British did not have to face the same difficulties as van Riebeeck a century and a half earlier; there was an established agricultural economy and people ready to trade. Governors from Britain and their officials did not have to live down early associations with 'brutal aboriginals', nor were they linked by kinship with the Frontier or even with Cape society, which on the whole they despised; they were birds of passage to a greater extent than their predecessors. In contrast with the residents, they were in touch with movements of thought in Europe, they were under orders from Britain, but above all, they seldom had a personal interest in maintaining the colour line as a social and economic line as well.

The first English officials were no doubt remote, superior, paternalist, but they were also distrustful of legal discrimination on grounds of race. They came from a society where class distinctions, though very strong, were not legally defined and were fluid in the sense that money acquired by trade might be used to buy land; it became respectable, if there was enough of it, in the second generation and the taint of trade might be very nearly forgotten in the third. The English almost by instinct visualized a racial society like their own class society, in which 'the best' of the 'natives' would become prosperous and educated and would be happy to accept invitations to Government House instead of agitating for startling change. This might be some time away, but it was the aim.[1]

The British attitude was expressed in a key sentence by Sir Theophilus Shepstone in 1850:

Whilst humanity and . . . the injunctions of our religion compel us to recognise in the Natives the capability of being elevated to perfect equality, social and political, with the White Man, yet it is as untrue as it would be unwise to say that the Native is, . . . in his present state, capable of enjoying or even understanding the political rights of the White Man.

This is to be contrasted with the provision made in 1858 in the Constitution of the Transvaal which embodies the Frontier view: 'The people will admit no *gelijkstelling* (that is, putting on an equal basis) between the White and the Coloured inhabitants either in Church or State.'

This contrast between Cape and Frontier attitudes came to be seen as a clash between English-speaking and Afrikaans-speaking, but in fact the former, less clear-cut, distinction was for long the overriding difference among the whites. The line between British and Afrikaner was perhaps at its sharpest in the period after the South African War when Milner's policy of assimilation was at its height. In attitudes to Africans, however, there was much in common between both groups; until the Jameson Raid in 1895, a substantial number of Afrikaners were on the side of gradualism, of blurred distinctions, of a tilting line, while at first the British enacted Vagrancy Laws which in practice meant that coloured persons were in danger unless they were employed by a European. But even the Vagrancy Laws were not framed in terms of colour, and by outlawing slavery in 1834–8, the British provoked the Great Trek, the movement of the more Frontier-minded Afrikaners away from the Cape.

British rule thus accentuated the distinction between the two attitudes. It is worth repeating the comment of Anna Steenkamp, the sister of Piet Retief; one reason, she said, for the Trek was:

the shameful and unjust proceedings with reference to the freedom of our slaves; and yet it is not their freedom that drove us to such lengths, so much as their being placed on an equal footing with Christians, contrary to the laws of God and the natural distinction of race and religion, so that it was intolerable for any Christian to bow down beneath such a yoke; wherefore we rather withdrew in order to preserve our doctrines in purity.

[1] If the comparison between English social distinctions and Cape racial distinctions seems far-fetched, I suggest re-reading George Meredith's *Evan Harrington*. The hero, brought up as a gentleman, was the son of a tailor; he could pass for a gentleman unless the taint in his blood was known. But this was not true of all his relations. There are a number of South African novels based on a similar situation; usually a brother or sister is darker and has to be hidden. In the middle of the century, the comparison between social and racial exclusion is made explicitly by G. O. Trevelyan on p. 21 of his *Report on India: The Competition Wallah*.

British rule must also be regarded as encouraging the presence of missionaries who were not in the Calvinist tradition and who looked at the South African scene with fresh eyes. The most famous of these was Dr. John Philip, whose attempts to educate Africans roused bitter anger and indignation. Those with the Frontier mind felt that his attitude was a kind of treachery; he was deliberately making a hole in the defences and letting in the savages. He was trying to reduce the real difference in culture and skill which served as an unconscious excuse for maintaining a dividing line based on the colour of the skin.

This broad distinction between the Cape and the Frontier was for some time symbolized by the political divisions of South Africa. The Cape Colony was 'colour-blind' in its legislation; the vote was restricted, as in England, by educational and property qualifications—not by colour—and by the end of the nineteenth century there were Africans who had the vote, who were merchants; there was one who owned and edited a newspaper. This was in marked contrast with the Frontier societies of the Transvaal and the Orange Free State. No doubt the difference was partly due to the stage of development the two societies had reached; it was nonetheless real.

Natal again was markedly less liberal than the Cape; Durban was predominantly British and urban, but one factor had from the start been different. The Zulus were a powerful and aggressive military people strongly established before any Europeans came. The Trek brought Afrikaners into contact with the Zulus; by this time, what Afrikaners wanted was land not trade, and there could therefore be no question of trading through African agents, as where there were powerful kingdoms on the West Coast. The first relationship was one of war. The Trekkers moved first into the Transvaal where they met Zulu armies under Msilikatse, the people who were later to move to Bulawayo and become the Ndebele. Groups of Trekkers were attacked, some were massacred, others succeeded in defending themselves; there were savage reprisals. The Trekkers moved into Natal and met the main Zulu kingdom and here the killing of Piet Retief and the battle of Blood River established a focal point in South African history, still celebrated by a national holiday. Thus, before Durban became a great commercial centre, the Frontier spirit was influential and Durban grew under the shadow of the Zulu kingdom. The Zulus were a serious threat; the Zulu War of 1879 began with the formidable defeat at Isandhlwana, when a British battalion was exterminated without a survivor. Fear and hostility were therefore realities in Durban as they never were in Cape Town; the Frontier was closer, the feed-back of Frontier attitudes more continuous.

## 3 Birds of Passage

To the development of some strands of South African policy we shall return in the last section of these two chapters. For the moment, we must contrast this sketch of the growth of relationships in South Africa with an even briefer account of societies that were developing in other parts of Africa. On the West Coast, as we have said, trade was the motive that first brought Europeans. It is true that the Portuguese had always recognized that Africans had souls and had never quite lost their early missionary spirit, but by the late eighteenth century the Portuguese were virtually limited to the Leeward Coast, that is the area South and East of the mouth of the Congo River. On the Windward Coast, that is North and West of the Congo mouth, until near the end of the century, trade was the only motive. There was conflict between the different European nations as well as between chartered companies, who maintained forts, and interlopers or private adventurers, who did not. But all alike came for trade and all were forced to operate with African agents or allies. They were confronted by societies of very varied political and military strength but by few which could be treated lightly as a military threat. On the other hand, no trader or official wanted to stay permanently on the Coast and make his home there. Time on the Coast was an interlude; it might cover the period between boyhood and retirement, it might include a local wife or any number of local concubines but it never included a white wife and white children. White women did not come because of malaria and yellow fever and so the necessity did not arise of preserving them from the contamination of an alien culture. The mixture of races was not often by formal marriage but neither was it always a hurried and brutal affair of half an hour; there is evidence of long and amicable cohabitation, in which the local wife set up house in a European style. The Itsekiri, near the mouth of the Niger, a people long noted for the beauty of their women, are also known for the Victorian interiors of their houses—their pianos, armchairs, and crocheted antimacassars—and many show unmistakable signs of European ancestry.

The Old Coaster, the slaver, the 'Palm Oil Ruffian', could live his life on the Coast and take up another when he retired to Boston or Bristol; there was no need for him while he was in Africa to establish and define a hard line of social division. There was sometimes extreme cruelty, more often indifference amounting to cruelty, by both black and white, towards those in their power; there was often ignorance of African custom and contempt for African ways. But there was often trust, without which there can hardly be trade; there was sometimes liking. The white trader was dependent on Africans for his living and had to humble himself before African chiefs. There were feasts when trader and King would get drunk together; there were quarrels, reconciliation, intrigue, and bloodshed—one group betrayed to another as in the Massacre at Calabar—but until the nineteenth century, the Europeans were on the fringe of an existing African society of which they were not part. They had no desire to be part of it nor did they want to change it; it suited them as it was.

But missionaries followed the traders and the missionaries did want to change African society and for that reason were bound to become part of it. Governors followed missionaries and traders, and the forts grew into colonies; the colonies expanded from the seaports and their immediate surroundings to wide territories. Nonetheless the pattern of relationship which emerged on the West Coast was the product of the old trading relationship profoundly modified by the influence of missionaries. What happened in Africa in the middle and later nineteenth century must be seen as the joint outcome of trade and of the religious revival in Britain which began with the Methodist movement and continued with the Evangelicals and the Tractarians.

Missions established schools; the schools were intrusions into African societies and they were designed to change those societies completely. They were meant to substitute for magic and divination a theory of causation based on Aristotle and Newton; for the close nexus of tribe and kinship, the self-sufficient individual; for the worship of ancestors, for a spirit world permeating inanimate objects, for a strong if sometimes arbitrary life force, the forms of Christianity which had developed in the Western world. These in Britain were usually highly individualist and frequently arid in appeal to a sense of beauty and to deep human needs. Thus there arose within African society a cleavage between the traditional and the Westernized. To the spiritual fruits of this cleavage we shall return in the last part of this book; here there remain two points to make.

First, the paternalism of the missionary—the attempt to make the pupil in the image of the master—continued as an element in West Coast societies right through till at least the Second World War; it was altruistic, benevolent, inspired by a strong sense of service, but nonetheless bound in the end to inspire in the pupil some degree of Oedipean resentment. This paternal attitude was not confined to missionaries but was shared by many administrators, indeed to some degree by most, although there was also in some an element of the jovial existentialism of the trader, a readiness to accept the African as he was and entertain no hopes of any rapid change. But it was axiomatic with all that change was desirable.

Secondly, the Cape conflict between town and Frontier was paralleled in the West by a stronger, though very different, cleavage between Coast and Interior. As the nineteenth century advanced, as explorers, traders, missionaries, pushed further inland, two opposed tendencies developed in European attitudes to Africans. The first of them was derogatory; it developed from a variety of linked sources, from the concepts of race for which de Gobineau may stand as the example and from the concepts of society grouped together under the term Social Darwinism. De Gobineau tried to explain differences in achievement, and particularly in technical development, in terms of hereditary ability, while the Social Darwinists suggested that social evolution, like biological, could only take place by the ruthless elimination of the unfit. British colonial administrators and missionaries in general would consciously have repudiated these ideas, but they were influenced by them nonetheless, and late in the nineteenth century administrative changes in the government services in the British West African colonies put barriers in the way of Africans rising to higher positions—a temporary reversal of an earlier trend.

At the same time, and at first sight somewhat paradoxically, there grew up a greater respect for African institutions which found expression in the idea of indirect rule. In fact, the opposition between the two sets of ideas was less than might at first sight appear; the assumption behind indirect rule was not that African institutions were in themselves good but that they were 'more suited for *them*' and could only be changed gradually. It was not so much a higher opinion of what was African as a lower estimate of the universal validity of what was European and a much less optimistic appraisal of African powers of absorption and adaptation. It is typified by Lugard's agreement with the Emirs of Northern Nigeria that their emirates should be preserved and that Christian missionaries should be prevented from converting or educating in Muslim areas; Lugard may have had some admiration for Islam but he also had some distrust for dogmatic Christianity and its effects. It is typical again of a general development that sixty years later many Nigerians from the North reproached the British with withholding the schools which their grandfathers had stipulated should not be introduced. The Northerners had in fact suffered through not learning what the missionaries brought; they had far fewer lawyers, doctors, higher civil servants than those nearer the coast.

West Africa, then, presented a picture very different from South Africa. Even at the height of colonial rule, each West Coast territory was a bundle of African societies, over which a loose network of European administration had been cast. It was rent by deep divisions between the traditional and the Western-oriented, between the Coast and the Interior, and these divisions often appeared to present themselves as tribal or ethnic. But they were divisions between African groups. There were divisions between Muslim, Christian, and pagan, even between Catholic and Protestant. But racial differences— differences of black and white—were not a serious part of the internal problems of any of these territories, because the Europeans, even when they ruled the country and dominated its economy, were not a true part of the structure of society. They were wedges thrust in, they split society, they changed it, but they were not part of it. They did not mean to stay and their numbers were small.

The different attitudes brought to Africa by the French, the Belgians, and the Portuguese will be touched on briefly in the last section of this chapter. Here it is necessary to contrast other British territories with the South and the West Coast. The factors involved are the same—the purpose with which Europeans came, flag, trade, or Bible; the climate and nature of the country and its economy; the kind of people who lived there and the nature of first contacts. The proportions in the mixture vary, as do the results. But on the whole, the three British territories in East Africa, with Northern Rhodesia and Nyasaland, can be spoken of in one breath. Trade with all these areas in the first three quarters of the nineteenth century was negligible; ivory was the only item of consequence. The flag was even more reluctant to become involved than in the West; the nominal suzerainty of the Sultan of Zanzibar could have been transferred to Britain on a number of occasions had the British Government wished. Pressure to assume sovereignty was less from traders and financiers—for whom the hope that minerals of value would one day be found could be no more than a hope—than from missionaries, from opponents of the Arab slave trade, and from those who, as the century wore on, came more and more to believe in the mission to civilize—what became known in 1903 as 'The White Man's Burden'. The flag did not move in until it became necessary to keep others out. When at last other claimants began to appear and the Protectorates to be proclaimed, the administrators who came to these territories were in general paternalists, bent on improving the African; the easy acceptance inherited from the old trading society of the Coast was much less frequent. African mistresses were not so common as on the West Coast; it was unknown to get drunk with the old chief.

These are broad generalizations. The first exception which has to be made is Kenya. This was early proclaimed 'white man's country', because the height of most of central Kenya makes it a pleasant place for Europeans all the year round. It is a fertile and beautiful country, and from about 1910 till 1950 there was a trickle to Kenya of the younger sons of the English landed gentry, of retired officers, of squires *manqués*, who here were able to re-create a vanished world of farming and country sports and cheap servants. There were also South Africans but the younger sons and the cavalry officers were more conspicuous. The trickle grew larger immediately after each of the two world wars, and after the second, included a number of Europeans whose mother tongue was not English. Many of the newcomers were serious farmers who had little capital and had to work hard to make a living. The settlers transformed the economy of the country; they created a farming industry. But the numbers were never large; figures quoted for population of African descent in 1962 were 8,366,000 or 96.9 per cent of the total; Europeans were only 56,000, of whom many were businessmen and officials, lightly anchored to the country. Some of the Europeans meant to live in Kenya till they died and hoped that their children would live there after them, but these were quite a small proportion of the total European community which again was only 0.65 per cent of the whole. Here too a very light top-dressing of Europeans had hardly become one with the surrounding land.

The other exception is Northern Rhodesia, which was always affected by its proximity to Southern Rhodesia and from the late 1920s onwards was changed by the beginnings of large-scale copper-mining. Southern Rhodesia was virtually an extension of South Africa, to which we shall return in the final section; Northern Rhodesia was in one sense an extension of Southern Rhodesia and had been intended by Cecil Rhodes as another stage in the route to Cairo. Some of its white inhabitants thought it should be conducted on the same principles as South Africa. 'We shall consistently oppose', wrote Leopold Moore, editor of the *Livingstone Mail*, on 9 July 1910, 'the employment of natives where they compete with . . . white men. . . . it is better to pay a white man three times as much as a native than to run the risk of evolving a native, as contrasted with a white man's state.' Two months later he had to report that the Administrator did not share his views. Northern Rhodesia was in another sense an extension of Nyasaland, that is to say, colonial office territory. Though frequently in peril, and always a border-line case, it always fell into the category of 'tropical dependency' which, as Sir Harry Johnston wrote to Lord Salisbury on 31 May 1897, 'must, in the interest of the native races, be ruled from Downing Street'. He was making a distinction between Africa North of the Zambezi, and the area to the South, where 'climatic conditions encourage true colonization' and where 'the direct rule of Downing Street may cease'. It was a distinction tacitly accepted by the British Government for the next half-century.

## 4 The Need for Labour

This chapter has so far endeavoured to sketch the development of the different patterns of race relations which arose in South Africa and in the colonial territories further North. Common to all has been the prolonged and gradually developing crisis arising from the arrival from Europe of men belonging to a kind of society quite different from any in Africa. Before their coming, there was exploitation and inequality in Africa, as we have seen, for example, in Ruanda. There were many groups who lived by raiding their neighbours. But the white men brought with them forces of a more deeply disruptive nature—ideas about causation and human society, about man's relationship to man, about man's place in nature—utterly opposed to traditional African concepts. These new ideas and the circumstances in which they were introduced had everywhere an effect that was profound. But it was more harsh and abrupt where the white men came to stay. This is not to suggest that British officials in most of Africa mixed more freely with Africans than Afrikaners; indeed, the reverse was often true. But the aloofness of birds of passage is far less important than that of those who are part of African society. One feels his whole existence is at stake; the other can go home. As adults, South Africans hardly communicated with indigenous Africans except as master and servant; yet as children they had been brought up by Africans and in the country had often played with African children. Their feelings towards Africans were consequently ambivalent and highly loaded with emotion.

We have seen the line of social definition hesitate on the two criteria of religion and slavery, settling finally on colour as the division. We have also seen that the motives which brought white men varied, the emphasis being—to summarize excessively—in the West on trade, in Nyasaland on conversion, in South Africa on land. But there is a further diversity in the historical dimension. The Dutch who came to the Cape in the seventeenth century came from a Europe still torn by wars of religion. It was still a generally accepted assumption that the religion of the state and of all its population should properly be that of the government; religious tolerance was an exception. Again, the stratification of society was generally taken for granted. This was the background from which Dutch officials and settlers both came. We have spoken of the Frontier spirit and suggested that the division was as much between Cape Town and the Frontier as between Dutch and English, but there is another element to be distinguished in this complex situation; the English were the product of the Age of Enlightenment. The assumptions of the seventeenth century were all in question; both in the religious and the social field, the response might take a variety of forms, but it was always alien to the outlook of van Riebeeck and his contemporaries. The British who came to the Cape might be agnostic, deist, or evangelical, but they were unlikely to be in sympathy with seventeenth-century Calvinism; they might regard the French Revolution as a threat to society or—less probably—as the birth of a new age, but they could not be unaffected by it. But Dutch society in South Africa was a fragment detached from an earlier Europe; an element in the difference between Cape Town and the Frontier was the continual infusion into the Cape of more recent ideas.

There was thus not only an interplay of European and African forms of thought but of European thought from two periods. And as the nineteenth century progressed—and increasingly in the twentieth century—to this conflict in the world of ideas was added the paradox that a few Africans were absorbing, direct from Europe, concepts of politics and society which were basically in conflict with those of white South African society, which in general were those of earlier generations. For a fragment transplanted from a parent society to a new environment seems usually to be tenacious of the ideas and manners of the parent and to preserve them long after they have disappeared in their native form.

But there was another factor in the relationship between white and black in Africa that was widespread South of the Zambezi and of which the effects are far more obvious than these cross-currents of chronology and thought. This was the question of labour. It was one of the essential premises of everyday life in modern Europe that men would respond to the offer of wages by offering their labour in exchange. As the nineteenth century advanced, it became increasingly a European belief that work was a positive duty, whether for oneself or for others. But both these ideas were strange to Africans in South and Central Africa, who saw no reason why they should go to work for someone else, nor why they should produce for the benefit of another a surplus beyond what was needed for their own maintenance. A conflict of interest developed over labour that was even more fundamental than that over land.

The solution found in Portuguese territory was to require any tribal African to work for six months in the year, though in fact the requirement was never anything like universally enforced. In British territory this would not, after 1834, have been acceptable to Parliament; it would have been forced labour and near to slavery. Once slavery had been abolished by Parliament, it became something of an obsession to prevent others from engaging in a practice which was believed to be profitable but morally wrong and which the British were inclined to take a full meed of moral credit for abandoning. But it was felt legitimate to impose a hut tax or poll-tax which must be paid in cash. As cash could seldom be earned except by service to Europeans, this was a form of coercion—but economic coercion was acceptable to legislators of the period of Mill and Bentham, though political was not.

Thus, throughout the Southern half of Africa during the nineteenth century, the pattern became increasingly general of young African men leaving their homes in order to earn enough to pay the tax; soon, they wished to earn more than that, enough to satisfy certain wants, which at first were simple—a blanket, a few cooking pots—but later became more ambitious—a bicycle, a gramophone, the cost of marrying. But when enough was earned for that purpose, the young man would go home until the need for cash again became strong. The system of 'migrant labour' thus developed; it was widespread in Africa but in South Africa it became an institution of a far more rigid kind. With the discovery of gold and diamonds and the beginnings of industry, labour was 'recruited' by organized agencies from distant areas of high population—such as Nyasaland and Mozambique—and the whole process, though physical conditions were stage by stage improved, became more and more impersonal.

From early days, African employees of all kinds, frequently even domestic servants, lived in a 'location' at a distance from European residences. 'Labour' for the mines was housed in special camps or hostels and fed by the employers; the system reached a depth of depersonalization that was utterly foreign to the young African. He came to the labour lines or the location from a world in which he had been firmly placed at the centre of a web of social links deeply felt—links with parents, grandparents, ancestors, and the unborn; with collateral kin; with relatives by marriage; with political and economic chiefs, often with a king who *was* the land in which his people lived. All this had gone and now he was a unit of labour, sleeping on an iron cot in a concrete dormitory, a place smelling of sweat and disinfectant, very like a zoo or a prison.

Perhaps if he had been more often encouraged to bring his wife and live permanently near his work, the labourer might have built up a new set of relationships. But in South Africa 'migrant labour', at first an expedient to which there was no alternative, became a policy. It did not encourage the labourer to develop into a skilled townsman but to remain a tribesman who periodically transformed himself for a year or eighteen months into an unskilled town labourer. That it operated against any increase in efficiency and industrial skill is only the beginning of the evils that followed. The labourer was tied to a wife who belonged to the old culture; it was she who brought up the children. He was at the same time retarded by his family and divided from them. In the villages, the women have suffered not only from loneliness but from responsibilities for which they were not trained, and severe neuroses have been reported; the men, on the other hand, have been put under different kinds of strain, resulting in prostitution, homosexuality, and drunkenness.[1]

Migrant labour was a widespread custom which began with the imposition of hut tax or poll-tax and the spread of a money economy. It was, I repeat, at first inevitable; as a general rule, it was only for a limited period that Africans would leave their homes. But as the economy developed, this difficulty diminished; Africans wanted more and more goods that only money would buy and they became more ready to leave their homes. In the different territories, very different

---

[1] This is the view which I accept. See Audrey Richards *et al.*, and S. van der Horst, in Guy Hunter (ed.), *Industrialisation and Race Relations*. A somewhat different view is expressed by W. Watson, *Tribal Cohesion in a Money Economy: A Study of the Mambwe People of Northern Rhodesia.*

attitudes towards migrant labour emerged. In the Katanga copper mines, Belgian policy was in general to urbanize; they encouraged Africans to live in a *centre extracoutumière*, to settle down as part of a permanent industrial labour force. On the Copper Belt of Northern Rhodesia, it was Government policy to make villages in tribal areas more attractive; this was inspired by the general attitude expressed in Indirect Rule, the wish to preserve as much as possible of the old culture. But the copper companies differed; they wanted men who would live near their work for long spells, if not permanently, and would become more efficient. A compromise between these views resulted. Only in South Africa was a rigid government policy enforced *against* the natural development of increasing urbanization. For example, at Welkom in the Orange Free State, early in the fifties, the mining company proposed to make 10 per cent of their accommodation suitable for married couples; the Government would not permit more than 3 per cent.

Successive governments have in fact moved in turn step by step further in the direction of separating the races in every sphere of life. This has entailed, as one consequence, the attempt to prevent a permanent African population from growing up in the towns. The reasons are not economic; indeed, the economic arguments are all in favour of a more permanent, better trained, more skilled labour force. As Sheila van der Horst has pointed out, it was industrialization and the move to the towns which led to the enunciation as a political doctrine of the policy of separate development.

Here is one more example of the cumulative spiralling effect of a rigid relationship of dominance and subordination between two groups sharply differentiated. There is a white anxiety about European culture, which is felt to be in danger of dilution and degradation; at the same time, there is sexual anxiety, guilt about the past, the jealousy of white women, desire, often, but not always, suppressed by white men. So the African must be kept at a distance; he must be encouraged to keep his true home far away, to come to the towns only on a temporary visit without his wife and children. He is as far as possible segregated from contact with the culture of the dominant group, which it is feared he might dilute or even submerge. He cannot of course be entirely segregated. The desire to keep him at a distance is at war with the desire to sell him newspapers and transistor radios, let alone a host of less dangerous goods. But the policy of segregation and the means of enforcing it result in a hostility to white people which too often means that the African labourer in a South African town has no acquaintance with the thought and art of Europe and America, though he welcomes their material products. He is thus denied the possibility of that 'improvement' which the missionaries had hoped to effect; there is little communication between the two groups except at work, and, as groups, each is confirmed in its bad opinion of the other. Exceptions are sometimes made for an individual; he, it will be said, is not like the others.

In South Africa there has also been a special, if subsidiary, effect. The young African must leave his home in the country, where there is no work, and go to the town in order to earn money with which to pay his tax, to get married, and to prove himself a smart and modern youth. While on that visit to the town, he must as far as possible be herded into all-male 'compounds' or kept out of sight in 'locations' where there is an excess of males. His behaviour in these circumstances is predictable. The white population know little of what goes on in the locations but all they hear confirms their previous opinions; the natives are promiscuous and lustful. The whites are therefore careful not to trust their women out alone at night. If an assault on a white woman takes place—or is imagined—emotion is extreme and legal penalties severe. And this situation again spirals; in the early stages, Africans are reported to have sometimes thought that this jealous preservation of white women meant that some magical advantage was to be obtained by sexual intercourse with them; there is repeated, and much stronger, evidence for their anger that white men should interfere with their women and prevent them so savagely from retaliation; finally, in the later part of the twentieth century, and both in educated Africans and American Negroes, there is a feeling—expressed in the novels and autobiographies of many intellectuals—that with the white woman at least the black man can show he is the better man and overcome—not to say revenge—the humiliation he has endured.

We have spoken of the Frontier mentality and the Cape outlook. After the Jameson Raid, this distinction looked more than ever as though it lay between English and Afrikaner. Then came the South African War, in which the Frontier mentality, after initial successes, suffered a military defeat. With an optimism which it is now easy to call pathetic, a British Government in Whitehall assumed that in the South Africa of four provinces set up by the Act of Union in 1910 the Frontier mentality would dwindle away; the Cape view, gradualness, the 'improvement of the native', would make steady progress. Instead, the Frontier grew stronger; the decisive point in this process again concerned labour.

South African farming is traditionally extensive and a stage was reached after the First World War when there was no more fertile land to be had for the asking. The younger sons of Afrikaner farmers began to come to the towns and seek jobs; the poor white problem was born. In such a society as South Africa's, with a sharp horizontal line between the top group and the rest, it is essential to the peace of mind and morals of the top group that they should believe their superiority to be due to inherent, and if possible, moral qualities; they must also impress this on the subordinate group. The myth of their superiority is destroyed if people of their own group fall to the level of the lower group. Poor whites are felt to be an outrage. We have seen how the problem of the poor Tutsi was dealt with in Ruanda.

But South Africa was a capitalist, individualist society. These new-comers to the towns were confronted by employers who were pre-dominantly immigrants of fairly recent origin. They were usually English-speaking or European, not Afrikaner, feeling little sympathy with the ideals of Afrikanerdom. They employed highly skilled and highly paid white artisans, many of whom were also imported from Europe, backed by a force of unskilled African labour. The ratio of skilled wages to unskilled was usually seven to one, but sometimes ten to one or more. The employers felt little emotional obligation to poor, uneducated, and unskilled Afrikaners and saw no justification for pay-ing them the high wages with which they had induced men with special qualifications to come from abroad. These wages for expatriates were competitive with American or Australian wages, countries whose average income per person was four times that of South Africa. The obvious policy for South African employers, from a purely business point of view, was to reduce stage by stage the number of highly paid expatriates, replacing them gradually by more highly trained Africans, and moving towards a flexible labour force with the top wages appro-priate to the national income, with a lower ratio of skilled to unskilled pay, and with skill as the only category to determine wages. It would surely follow that such a labour force would not migrate every year or eighteen months but would live on the spot with wife and children. But this they were not able to achieve.

What happened is a long and complicated story. Briefly, the Afrikaner, Nationalist, or Frontier conviction that whites must not be poor made common cause with the Trade Unionist axiom that skilled labour must not be diluted. In the early days of industrialization, it was the immigrant white skilled labour which had formed Trade Unions on the European model and in these Africans never obtained a substantial footing. This combination of the Trade Unions and the Frontier was helped by the voting system, which in their optimism the British Government had allowed to be tilted so as to over-represent the rural, that is the Afrikaner, vote. Faced by this strong political com-bination, the employers abandoned in the early twenties a position in which economic interest had coincided with long-term estimates of the country's best line of social development. No doubt the step was made easier by considerations of immediate peace with the most important part of their labour force and some sympathy with the Frontier point of view.

The South African employers never renewed the attempt to produce a rational wage structure; their interests became progressively less and less able to influence political decisions. Step by step it was made more difficult for Africans to express their views as organized labour. They were excluded from white unions and their own unions were forbidden to strike. A succession of Acts[1] limited the number of apprentices, kept up the demand for skilled labour with high wages, and set up a system of collective bargaining between employers' associations and specified Trade Unions. But Africans, who always found it extremely difficult to get into these unions, have since 1956 been altogether excluded by law from membership of Trade Unions which operate under the Industrial Conciliation Act. They are thus effectively shut out from a wide range of skilled employment; further, there is another group of jobs in government concerns in which unskilled white labour has priority over non-white for employment and is paid higher wages for the same work. This is known as the Civilised Labour Policy.

The horizontal line between white and non-white was thus prevented from tilting and the superiority of every white person re-asserted. Meanwhile, the 'reserves', originally set up to prevent Africans from losing all their land to white men, came to be regarded not as refuges to which Africans might go when they pleased but as a kind of limbo in which they must be confined as to permanent abode, although they were expected to send their young men to work in white territory. Separation, like migrant labour, began as an expedient and became a doctrine. It was enforced by the Group Areas Act of 1950,[2] by which areas were established outside which each racial group might not live permanently or own property. This was particularly hard on Indians, who often lived by trade with other groups. They had often been forced to pay a higher price than a white man for a shop or a house on one of the few sites[3] previously available to them; when forced by the Act to sell, it was seldom possible to get a fair price and some shopkeepers were put out of business.

It became more and more clear that Cape liberalism had been defeated. There was no hope for the empirical, step-by-step, approach to a solution in which colour was envisaged as becoming less important than acquirements of skill and education and all that the missionaries had meant by 'civilization'. Its place was taken by a doctrinaire determination to construct instead a society in which white 'civilization' could not be contaminated. But what was defended was the 'civilization' of the Frontier, a religion of the seventeenth century, a family life that was Victorian, and a social order that was a modern and industrialized form of Sparta's. Majority white opinion became by the

---

[1] The Mines and Works Act, 1911, amended 1926; Apprenticeship Act, 1922; Industrial Conciliation Act, 1924; Wage Act, 1925.

[2] Amended six times; consolidated 1957 and again amended 1961.

[3] Few because in large areas restrictive covenants forbade sale to non-whites.

middle of the twentieth century singularly out of sympathy with the climate of political opinion in the rest of the world. The hierarchical arrangement of society, nineteenth-century concepts of penology, of education, of the obligations of the state to individuals, were being questioned in the great cities of Europe and America, in universities all over the world, but by very few in South Africa.

# CHAPTER X

# South Africa and the World Scene

## 1 Dominance Proclaimed

Cape liberalism was defeated. The dominance of one group over another which had resulted from their different stages of development was first defined by custom and then elevated into a principle. There is no need to write in any detail of the system which now prevails in South Africa; it has been described often enough. But the essence of it is that six-sevenths of the country is reserved for one-fifth of the population, who are classed as white; one-seventh is reserved for 'the Bantu', that is, those of African descent, who are two-thirds of the total. In the white area, the blacks are not permitted to own property, to vote, to move without documents. They must use different means of transport and public facilities of all kinds; in the white towns, they may work but not sleep. They may not bear arms and are excluded from the armed forces. The higher forms of employment are legally for whites. Education is separate and the education of Africans is of a special kind, suited to what the white rulers judge to be their needs. The line between the races is regulated by law and it does not tilt; it operates in all departments of life.

The continued existence of a state which enshrines in law a system so repugnant to what most of the world regards as right has effects throughout the continent and the world. It can best be seen against the development of French and British imperial policy. There had always been divided opinion in Britain about the right policy to colonies, stemming from the dilemma inherent in an imperial democracy. As we have seen, the British had always repudiated the racist answer that 'the natives' are permanently inferior; they professed the paternalist view that they would one day grow up and be free. But they had been content to put off the day of freedom. There was pride in the Empire and reluctance to give it up, but little true conviction behind the postponement, because no sense of principle and no certainty of interest. Trade was what mattered and there were always those who believed that trade might be just as good without the cost of imperial rule.

After the Second World War it became clear that an immense effort would be necessary to continue the postponement in India and that a war-weary country was not prepared to face such an effort for a purpose in which few had much belief. India was followed by Ghana; the defeat of the French at Dien Bien Phu pointed the moral that the British were on the right road and that it was a mistake to try to keep control by force over a country whose leaders were determined to lead it to independence. This was in accord with the general trend of social thought and purpose, which lay in the direction of providing greater equality of opportunity by cheap education, of greater permissiveness in the up-bringing of children, and of redistributing wealth by taxation. The trend was enhanced by the necessity of competing in propaganda with Communist Russia.

To this kind of thought, the South African Nationalist was hostile. In the old Frontier spirit, he would rather go down fighting than make any concession; a gradualist solution was utterly abhorrent; he abhorred the idea of putting one foot on the 'slippery slope'. Africa was his home; he could go nowhere else; he could not emigrate like the British from India or Ghana. He would not be a suppliant where he had been a master and to a people he despised. The British attitude was spineless and hypocritical. This was the feeling of the rank and file but there were many variations.

The Dutch Reformed Churches have gone through much searching of soul in their endeavours to reconcile with their religion the social and economic separation of the races. There have been repeated crises when a few have protested that national policies are incompatible with the teachings of Christ, but again and again the majority have repudiated such doctrine. Again, the leaders of the National Party have on the whole expressed official views less embattled than those of most of their supporters; they, far more than their followers, are aware of the weight of world sentiment opposed to them and it is clearly their policy, on the one hand, to be strong enough to resist any military attack from any combination of African powers and, on the other, to avoid action that would bring them directly into conflict with their main trading partners and investors, Britain and the United States.

This policy would no longer be defended by an educated Nationalist on the lines that might have been put forward by his counterpart sixty years ago. Arguments from the Old Testament, about the curse of Ham or the tower of Babel, which were sometimes put forward even twenty years ago by Ministers of the Dutch Reformed Church, are no longer urged publicly. Nor are biological arguments about permanent inferiority regarded as intellectually respectable, though traces constantly recur in conversation. It will rather be argued that recent events in Africa have demonstrated the wisdom of the traditional South African view. Belgian withdrawal from the Congo resulted in chaos;

the argument that the British had prepared more carefully than the Belgians, and that Nigeria would prove a more lasting structure, has fallen to the ground. Tanzania was once regarded as an example of the peaceful devolution of power, but mutinies followed independence and certain businesses with foreign capital have been expropriated. Such ideals as free speech and freedom of the person unless convicted before a court have no hope—it will be said—of surviving under an African government. Further—it will be argued—no African country will have anything but a minority government; if there was an African government in, say, Rhodesia, it would, in practice though not in theory, represent only a fraction of the African population and would respect their wishes even less than the present government. The white group is far better qualified, technically and in every other respect, to maintain an efficient and prosperous economy, which is in the interests of all. There is no future for a European in an African country in which an overwhelming majority of the voters are African.

These are not arguments which can be brushed aside. There are few countries in the world in which a visibly different minority can feel that it receives justice from a majority, and this is clearly even less probable when the minority is rich and has not behaved with conspicuous justice when in power. 'There is no reason to suppose', wrote the South African Bureau of Racial Affairs in a pamphlet dated 1952, that 'the Bantu will act differently and more fairly towards the European population than the Europeans were or are prepared to be towards the Native population' [sic].[1] There are in fact white industrialists in Zambia to-day who regard their business prospects with optimism and Kenya has behaved with generosity to its whites, but few would look forward to a satisfactory future for their children. English-speaking people in Africa have in the past usually taken it for granted that they would live at least as well as their cousins in Europe, that they would have the same standards of education, and could really enjoy a double nationality with the ability to go to Britain if things took a turn for the worse. They are surely right in thinking that this will become increasingly difficult.

On the other hand, the argument that the new Africans do not represent their people is less than half the truth. It does indeed contradict the assumption in the previous argument that voters will always support their own race. In the state of feeling likely to prevail in Africa for some years to come it seems probable that an African government, even though demonstrably inefficient, will be preferred to a European because it will certainly be regarded as far more likely to have African interests at heart. Further, it is surely either hypocritical or obtuse to speak of 'freedom of speech' or 'freedom of the person' when arguing

[1] South African Bureau of Racial Affairs, *Integration or Separate Development.*

in favour of present South African policy. Neither is conspicuous in South Africa to-day, except for supporters of the Government.

The South African attitude is regarded with anger throughout Africa. To insist openly on separation of the races must at the best mean dislike; the entire social situation confirms the African view that it is more than dislike, a fear of contamination. The Afrikaans language uses different words for men and women of European and of African extraction and in conversation many white South Africans frequently reveal their belief that 'people' are white. That Africans often make the contrary assumption does not help them to regard this as any less insulting.[1] At the same time, every leader of a newly independent African state knows very well that African incomes, though low compared with European, are higher in South Africa than anywhere else in the continent. He knows, too, that no combination of African states can be a military threat to South Africa. Both points increase his resentment. Poverty and even hunger can be forgiven more easily than humiliation, and he feels South Africa's social policy, South Africa's strength, and his own impotence as a humiliation to himself and every African.

That is not to say that a Ghanaian or Nigerian leader will risk much to avenge the wrong; their internal problems are too pressing. Countries which are nearer geographically have strong economic links which they cannot afford to give up. The extreme example is Malawi; of a million-odd workers, half are employed in subsistence agriculture, less than 200,000 earn cash wages in their own country, and more than 300,000 spend their working lives abroad; of these, 200,000 are in Rhodesia and 80,000 in South Africa. Their return would be a disaster and some compromise with emotion is necessary. But hostility to South Africa is a constant in the external affairs of African states and provides an emotional appeal to the electorate, much like hostility to Israel among the Arabs.

The effect of this deep sense of injustice is perhaps sharper in relations with Britain and the United States than with South Africa. To most African leaders South Africa is the touchstone by which Britain and America are judged. The most sympathetic Englishman who is at all realistic must tell them that no British government is likely to sacrifice more than £200 million of exports or risk £1,000 million of investments in an attempt to persuade South Africa to change internal policies. The attempt could only succeed if backed by an immense national effort which would have no popular support. An American, though his country's stakes are less absolutely and much less proportionately, would make a similar reply. To the African, this confirms distrust and a conviction of white hypocrisy. It was the whites, he would say, who enslaved him and who took away his land wherever

[1] *Ntu* means 'person' and Bantu is the plural, Muntu the singular.

it suited them to live permanently; they continue to despise him and for all their professions will do nothing to help him. His view is fed by what he hears of race relations in the United States, and increasingly to-day in Britain.

The student of race relations thus sees in Africa, and indeed in the world, a picture which in 1969 is gloomy. Gone are many of the illusions which he might once have entertained. He had, no doubt, long ago foreseen that the trend against colonialism would mount. He had already discounted the argument, beloved of white men in Africa, that 'the real native in the bush' would not follow the educated young men, with whom he had nothing in common, but would vote as told by his traditional chief. This would have meant that change came slowly. On the contrary, he has seen everywhere the triumph of nationalist political parties over traditional leaders and change whose speed multiplies in geometrical progression. More reasonable hopes have gone the same way. It was once legitimate to see some prospect that, in the Cape Province at least, the line between white and non-white would tilt, as Coloureds and Africans acquired wealth and power, until eventually it blurred. That trend too, as we have seen, has been reversed and a system of dominance not only established but proclaimed.

## 2 A Variety of Cases

Something not wholly dissimilar from Cape liberalism went North from South Africa to Rhodesia, and it was the dream of some observers that in Southern Rhodesia a British readiness to go step by step, to make concessions and press no principle too far, would in the end produce a society in which black and white could mix without the white being always on top. The story of the Federation, of the reasons why it came into being and why it failed, have been told elsewhere.[1] But one aspect which concerns race relations must here be stressed. Whatever other motives they had, those in England who proposed the Federation—and in the early stages it had supporters from both sides of the House of Commons—believed that by increasing the proportion of Africans to whites, by including Southern Rhodesia in a Federation with Northern Rhodesia and Nyasaland, they were speeding up the development of Southern Rhodesia towards a day of 'partnership' between the races. This ideal was proclaimed—though not defined—in the preamble to the Constitution. But while some Africans in Southern Rhodesia shared this view, welcoming the reinforcement in numbers and the prospect of liberal pressure from Britain, Africans in

---

[1] See Philip Mason, *The Birth of a Dilemma; Year of Decision: Rhodesia and Nyasaland in 1960*; Richard Gray, *The Two Nations: Aspects of the Development of Race Relations in the Rhodesias and Nyasaland;* James Barber, *Rhodesia: The Road to Rebellion.*

Northern Rhodesia and Nyasaland saw only the reverse—a reinforcement of the whites and a brake on their progress towards independence.

In fact, racial feeling on both sides was too strong for gradualism. Southern Rhodesia had been very much the frontier in the 1890s; there had been the Matabele War and the Matabele and Mashona Rebellions. In the homes of white Southern Rhodesians, as in those of South Africans, there were pictures of white men desperately defending themselves against yelling hordes of attackers with tossing plumes and flashing spears. There was an element in the white population, even in the 1950s, in whom the Frontier was still strong; there was also an element of recent immigrants from Europe, artisans who found themselves with high wages and a higher standard of living than ever before, in a privileged position which was clearly threatened by African advance. Against these groups stood on the whole the professional and business classes, many of whom cherished the old Cape dream of gradual African education and eventually a mixed society.

African political leaders, inexperienced in politics, were confronted with a much more complex problem than in British colonies, where they had to deal only with the Governor and behind him a distant and half-hearted Whitehall, already half convinced of the justice of their cause. They were impatient for power at once, or at least on a time-table comparable with Ghana's and Kenya's. Their impatience reinforced Frontier attitudes; so did pressure from Britain which was sharp enough to be irritating but gentle enough to be ignored. As at the Cape, so in Southern Rhodesia the Frontier won. White voters put into power governments increasingly committed to keeping the line between white and black clear-cut and horizontal. Northern Rhodesia and Nyasaland split away and became independent African states.

We have been looking at race relations in Africa in modern times as basically a confrontation between European and African, with certain variable factors at work on either side to produce different results in different parts of the continent. This confrontation holds the centre of the stage, but there are two important secondary issues. First, the withdrawal of colonial powers has left naked a variety of situations previously cloaked in decent veils of custom and mythology. The dominance of the Tutsi in Ruanda, for example, was taken for granted, before the coming of Europeans, as was that of Arabs in Zanzibar and the Kenya coast. Of a slightly different order were the relations between the Fulani, the Hausa, and the Kanuri Muslims of Northern Nigeria with pagans and Christians further South, and of the Muslim Arabs of Khartoum, again with pagans and Christians to the South. Here, in both cases, religion and culture are as important as descent in defining the dominant and subordinate groups, but—again, in both cases—there is a territorial division and a history of slave-raids by the

Northern Muslims. In Zanzibar and Ruanda, the old static relationship between a dominant minority and a passive majority broke up when the colonial power withdrew; the myths on which it had depended were shattered. In Nigeria and the Sudan, actual physical power had been with the Northerners and they had less need for myth, but there was a difference between the two cases. The Southern Nigerians on the coast had made more progress with Western education than the Northerners; the Southern Sudanese were still isolated and backward. With independence, Khartoum resumed an ancient dominance, which the South now actively resented; in Nigeria, a more complicated situation arose, because the Northerners had felt themselves threatened by the progress of the Southerners. But in all four cases, the imperial dialectic had resulted in a similar process. In each case a relationship had been generally taken for granted before the arrival of the imperial power. Its natural evolution under the pressure of forces generated within its own system had been suspended under the empire, but the ideas on which the old relationship depended had been destroyed; on the withdrawal of the imperial power, dammed-up forces were released and conflict was inevitable.

The other secondary issue is the presence in some territories of a third group as well as Europeans and Africans. The typical cases are the Indians of East Africa and of Natal, the Syrians and Lebanese of West Africa, and the Cape Coloured. We have seen the processes by which South Africa came to draw a line between white and non-white instead of accepting a spectrum or gamut of colour and class. A rational calculation might have suggested that, even in default of a spectrum, the whites should make allies of the Coloured and the Indians, but this too was rejected. Indeed, a special anger and irritation is sometimes in evidence in white South African comments on Indians.[1] This is partly perhaps because commercially Indians are more often rivals, particularly in Natal, than the Zulus and perhaps also because the whites of Natal built up a picture of the Zulus as a strong, simple, military people whom they admired as well as feared. To have ousted such a people from their land induced a feeling of guilt which demanded a scapegoat. Similar feelings were expressed in Kenya by whites after the Mau-Mau rebellion. They would acknowledge that the Kikuyu had had real grievances and add that more should be done to help them. But towards the Asians in general the same people would, almost in the same breath, express extreme hostility, which may be interpreted as compensation for the unwilling concession made to Africans.

There can be no serious dispute that the Dow Commission in 1955

---

[1] MacCrone's tests reveal a much more negative attitude to Indians than to African natives among English-speaking students. Among Afrikaans-speaking students the unfavourable views are stronger in both cases but the difference is less marked.

was right in paying tribute to the Asian contribution to the economic development of East Africa. There was also a rather odd benefit to East Africa; it was consideration of the Indian question that led the Colonial Office to formulate in 1923 the Devonshire Declaration on the paramountcy of African interests. But to Africans, the Asian often appeared mainly as an obstacle; he was the skilled artisan who would not impart his skill or the shopkeeper who charged high prices. To the Europeans he seemed sometimes a potential rival—and it ministered to a sense of virtue to prevent his exploiting the African.

It was sometimes argued in the mid-fifties by Kenya Europeans that the presence of Asians took the sting out of the confrontation of white and black and eased the situation. This is true insofar as Asians took the place of European artisans and daily-paid workers. The Asians perceived that they were vulnerable far more quickly than European artisans would have done and, in fact, they *were* far more vulnerable, because far more easily abandoned by Whitehall. But to the outcome in Kenya the presence of Asians made no direct difference at all. There was a clash of interest between the British Government and the white settlers; the British Government did not want political responsibility for a country that would have to be held by force, while the settlers wished to keep as long as possible a privileged position by which they were socially dominant and had most of such political power as had been delegated. Kenya was a colony and the ultimate responsibility still rested with Parliament in Britain; the whites were only three-quarters of 1 per cent in proportion to the African population and could not have maintained themselves without imperial support, let alone against imperial force. They gave in at once to a show of firmness. What might have happened if there had been no Asians but British artisans in large numbers instead is hardly worth speculation.

The more intelligent Asians had long ago calculated that this outcome was inevitable and most of these had endeavoured to make their peace with the Africans in advance. Their presence did not affect the political solution; to the climate of independent Kenya it has contributed a useful variety instead of a stark opposition, but it has not reduced xenophobia as regards jobs. In the middle range of jobs, Indians formed a far higher proportion than in the population as a whole; to-day there is a natural African desire to make up the deficiency and the Indians suffer. They share the resentment and envy, but not as a rule the unwilling admiration, directed towards Europeans. Some have become citizens of the territory where they live and the best they can hope for is to be allowed to go their way unobtrusively without active discrimination against them. Others clung to the hope that they need not commit themselves to the dangers of the new country but could keep British citizenship and move to Britain if things became difficult. This—to the shame of Britain—has proved an illusion and their future is now obscure.

Nor has the presence of Syrians and Lebanese in West Africa much altered the situation; there too it was a contribution to the poly-chromatic nature of society but before Independence the important variables were three—early history, the trader relationship, and the impermanence of the European rulers; after Independence, the important cleavages have lain elsewhere—between tribes, between educated and uneducated, between expatriates and natives of the country.

It has been argued, with great authority, that the outstanding mis-take made by the British in Africa was to delegate power too soon, particularly in South Africa, where the decisive moment was the Act of Union in 1910, and in Rhodesia, where it was in 1923. These were countries in which the educated and propertied were of a different race and had different interests from the majority. There is a famous saying of Lord Acton: 'The men who pay wages ought not to be the political masters of those who earn them. . . .' This was exactly the situation we created in South Africa. Could we avoid it in East Africa, where there were many tribal groups as well as Asians and Europeans? It was argued during the fifties that only under a strong imperial power could such diverse interests live peacefully side by side; imperial rule should therefore continue until an indigenous civil service and political leaders had been trained. Independence would come when the majority was sufficiently secure and enlightened to treat the minorities with forbearance; they would be further protected by constitutional safeguards.

Two points in this type of argument are valid. There was a real difference between Kenya and Southern Rhodesia. In Kenya, a Governor responsible to Parliament in the United Kingdom worked with a Legislative Council with a settler majority: in Southern Rhodesia, the Government, within very wide limits, was responsible to a local white electorate. On the whole Parliament (like the Crown of Spain in respect of native policies in Mexico and Peru) acted as a check on legislation that was unfavourable to native interests. It is easier to be liberal from a distance. Undoubtedly also Crown Govern-ment made easier the transition to independence based on majority rule, which was accomplished in Nigeria and in the Trust Territory of Tanganyika without rioting or repressive measures. It is equally true that Britain has not been able to guide South Africa or Rhodesia to independence based on majority rule and those who supposed that these countries would follow that path by themselves were mistaken.

But surely the influence of a distant Parliament can only be effective up to a certain point. The smaller the colony, the further Parliament can push it. But a strong colony will not be pushed to abandon interests regarded as vital. The decisive point in every case has been the size of the white majority and their power to assert themselves, measured against the willingness of the imperial power to use force. Britain never quite forgot Ticonderoga and Crown Point; the lesson was repeated in Majuba and in the South African War. White colonists fighting in their own territory could be very difficult to coerce. It was all very well to re-establish Crown Government in Jamaica in 1865, and more recently to assert imperial power in British Guiana. These are small colonies accessible by sea. It would have been a very different matter to attempt to maintain effective control over native policy in South Africa and surely it could only have resulted in direct opposition much earlier than in fact occurred. It is surely idle to suppose that any arrangement reached between South Africa and Britain after 1910 could have had much influence on the development of domestic policy; the South African leader who was most friendly to Britain was not notably in disagreement with his fellow-countrymen over native policy. The entrenched clauses protecting the remnants of Cape liberalism were quickly overthrown.

The border cases are Kenya, Zambia, and Rhodesia. In Kenya and Zambia, it was possible to maintain Crown responsibility until independence and to impose the kind of constitution Britain wanted, because the settlers were comparatively few and had no armed forces at their disposal. They were also divided and some of them supported the constitution which was imposed. In Southern Rhodesia, a larger body of settlers had been given a considerable degree of self-government in 1923 and, in the late 1950s, when the difference with Britain began to develop, they already had a small but effective air force and well-armed white troops. They were determined on the course of action they wished to follow, while to most voters in Britain the dispute was remote and not of much importance. It seems to the present writer very doubtful whether a determination to make Southern Rhodesia a Crown Colony in 1923 could have been sustained; in fact, the choice given the electorate in a referendum was to join the South African Union or to become a self-governing colony. If the alternative had been to become a Crown Colony, the answer might well have been different. And would it have been possible to keep a Crown Colony of such a kind on a course acceptable to Britain? Rhodesia's goodwill to Britain lasted so long as there was no interference with domestic policy. Distant colonies—if they are large enough and not surrounded by sea—have a way of getting their will if they want it badly enough.

There was the same lack of political realism about the argument that it would have been better to have maintained imperial rule in Kenya until the majority were ready to behave with tolerance to the minorities. It contained three unrealistic assumptions: first, that the

imperial power would accept the expense and odium of such prolonged rule without any advantage; secondly, that a majority of the
colonial people would co-operate in the process of learning; third, that
tolerance would increase in such circumstances. None of these is
sustainable. Once the phase has ended when colonial rule is taken for
granted, the colonial power has only one sensible course: this is to
choose the most efficient group with a substantial following and put
power in their hands. In an earlier phase, while the colonial bluff still
works, the imperial power can usefully try to blur and tilt the lines
between one group and another. There is a period when fruitful direction is possible. But in the final phase, when it is clear that withdrawal
is imminent, suspicion and hostility grow between groups who believe
themselves different and the imperial power can only dam forces
which will be stronger when at last released.

To say that it was unrealistic to talk in the 1950s of continued
imperial rule is not to say that the course of events in Rhodesia was
inevitable. In the early fifties, white public opinion was more malle-
able, and African leaders expected far less, than by the end of the
decade. An imaginative leader who understood the currents of world
affairs and had a shrewd gift for managing men might have changed
the course events took; unfortunately, the Rhodesian leader with most
imagination lacked shrewdness, and the shrewd and experienced
manager was already old.

The emphasis of this discussion has been heavily on former British
territories. During the 1950s it was more profitable than it seems to-day
to speculate on the effect on race relations of the varied approaches of
the different colonial powers. Subsequent events suggest that the differences were superficial. The Portuguese claimed that their approach
was realistic and humane, and had stood the test of centuries. They
were not, they claimed, racist and had from the start recognized the
duty of converting Africans to the Catholic faith; if a convert was
educated in European thought and customary behaviour, possessed
some property or was qualified in a profession, and was certified by
parish priest and district officer to be of good behaviour, he could be
officially recognized as *assimilado* and receive all the privileges of a born
Portuguese citizen. But the political privileges of a Portuguese citizen
are not very impressive; economically, the status meant the same pay
as a European—but the likelihood that a European would get the job.

The most important dimension—parity of esteem—is the hardest to
measure, but there is a wealth of evidence that although the distinctions which they have made legal have not been framed on the basis
of race, many Portuguese have expressed opinions about Africans as
illiberal as any recorded of Afrikaners. The hollowness of claims about
assimilation is shown by the fact that, in 1950, after 400 years of
association with Portugal, there were only 30,089 *assimilados* in Angola

and only 4,353 in Mozambique. Taking the two together, this is less than half of 1 per cent of the population. On the other hand, the Portuguese did not regard it as realistic to treat Africans who were not *assimilados* as though they were the citizens of a modern state. Until 1963, they were subject to a special system of law, the *indigenato*, and were liable to six months' forced labour in every year.

The traditional Portuguese system thus assumed that African culture was in every way inferior to Portuguese; it was a view less humiliating than the South African only because the taint of Africanism was not indelible nor personal. The approach was paternalist, in the extreme sense of regarding education as completely successful if the child grows up in the exact image of the father. To-day, there is a new policy which professes far greater respect for African institutions, but by now the temper of the whole continent is such that it is unlikely to succeed. No educated African with any self-respect would now be prepared to acknowledge, in the company of other Africans, the basic Portuguese doctrine that Mozambique and Angola are part of Portugal. Endemic rebellion in both territories suggests that the attempt to immunize Portuguese territory against an unease affecting the whole continent has failed.

The French and the Belgians as colonists practised forms of paternalism that were distinguishable from the Portuguese but based on the same underlying premises: that France (or Belgium) had a *mission civilisatrice*, that French culture was in every respect superior to African, that Africans could acquire this culture and become civilized, but that until they had they were primitives—in effect children or wards—and should be ruled for their good by those who were civilized. There was a difference between them, the Belgians being more sceptical of African ability and more reluctant to assimilate. The first university in the Belgian Congo was founded only in 1953. With the same basic assumptions as the French, the Belgians pictured a slower development; they were more fearful than the French of the results to Africans of losing one culture without acquiring another. The real success of the French has arisen, not so much through a greater respect for the African, as through a greater respect for the intellectual.

## 3 From a Great Height

Let us stand back and look at this vast continent South of the Sahara with the widest possible lens, from a height so impressive that we can see the whole and consider at one moment the history of the last three centuries. The basic fact, near the centre of every problem of every African state, is the confrontation of African and European. Three centuries ago contacts had hardly begun; two centuries ago they were peripheral; everywhere, in the last century and a half, they have been disruptive. The Iron Age tribal culture of the Bantu-speakers has everywhere been modified and often has been destroyed; while a few have come to terms with Western culture, far more are suspended uneasily between a past they have come to scorn and a future that is beyond their reach. Politically the Zambezi is the dividing line between the predominantly African territories which are now all independent and the Southern group—South Africa, Rhodesia, Mozambique, and Angola. These are still ruled by whites: South Africa and Rhodesia because they are countries where white men came to stay; the other two because Portugal is too small and too poor to let go, whereas Britain, France, and Belgium calculated that it would be cheaper to let go and hope for a continuance of trade. South Africa has been described by van den Berghe as 'in effect a white government with an internal colonial empire';[1] the phrase is also true of Rhodesia.

The two halves of the continent are linked by the mood of Africans; a mood of anger which the prisoners and exiles from the South share with the Presidents, Prime Ministers, and dictators North of the Zambezi. The latter are everywhere products of the West, usually of the mission school and the Western university or military college; they are eager that their countries should move into the world of to-day and be accepted as equals; they want to forget the speed with which they have passed through centuries of development; they want to establish new relationships with developed countries. At the same time, they are resentful of a culture which has supplanted their own, in which they see many faults, and whose complete superiority they are determined not to acknowledge. Their attitude to white men has changed twice in little more than a generation: first, from one in which admiration and envy were predominant to one of profound ambivalence; and secondly, to one in which suspicion and frustration begin to take the lead. In the phase of ambivalence, they admired white men as hardworking and intelligent although cold, cruel, and inhospitable, even to each other. To-day, they are deeply conscious of a world scene in which African states are poor and the rich states are white, in which South Africa is avowedly a country of white supremacy, while the United States and Britain acquiesce—it appears to them—in South African policy and, whatever they profess, are in practice little better themselves.

It is esteem that is the decisive factor. Negro Americans and African intellectuals alike see South Africa as the symbol of a world order and a world attitude that is humiliating. Resentment at humiliation adds suspicion and distrust to a relationship with the richer countries that was in any case bound to be difficult. The United States and the industrialized countries of Western Europe have much to offer that

[1] *Race and Racism.*

Africa wants—capital, technical skill, markets; negotiations over all these are influenced by the consciousness of humiliation.

Some of the old ambivalence towards white people remains and much ambivalence towards what 'the West' has to offer. This does not mean only electric power, high dams, and airlines but many Western institutions and ideas—democracy, the liberty of the Press, the liberty of the subject, Christianity, Marxism, Existentialism. Towards all of these, the African intellectual of to-day looks with a mixture of envy, admiration, irritation, and anger, but above all with a determination not to borrow slavishly. The conscious will to forge a new identity based on an alien tradition is not new; Charlemagne and Peter the Great, the great Japanese reconstruction of the nineteenth century, provide variants on the theme. What is new to history is the vastness of the continental scale, the depth of the emotions roused, above all the mixture of attitudes expressed towards a tradition which is repudiated with envy and admiration but nonetheless resentfully followed.

The hostility felt for the West, the consequent opportunity for Chinese and Russian diplomacy, are thus largely the result of the course taken by race relations in South Africa. We have seen how this happened, how social definition crystallized on the line of colour, instead of on religion or freedom; how the line between the races showed signs that it might tilt or blur but instead hardened and became horizontal. Regarding the scene from this height, in so vast a perspective, the feeling of inevitability is strong; the forces which produce the result seem to follow an unalterable pattern. It is easy to see why developments in West Africa have followed a course so different from South Africa's—but could anything have changed South Africa? To a hypothetical question there can only be a hypothetical answer. But two conclusions are justified. First, there have been distinct phases in the development of South African history and in each phase there has been a cumulative increase of rigidity and a worsening of race relations. Secondly, there were periods, at the beginning of each phase, when the situation was much more fluid than it later became; a leader with a real understanding of what was happening might have altered the course of development profoundly when industrialization began and the first Trade Unions reached the country, again in 1910, immediately after the First World War, and possibly, though much more doubtfully, after the Second. There was also the possibility of a different development in Rhodesia.

# CHAPTER XI

# Spanish America

## 1 Aims and Limitations

Let us turn now to the parts of America which speak Spanish, and in particular to those where there were highly developed cultures before the Spaniards came. There were three high cultures, Aztec, Inca, and Maya. We have already looked at the Incas and Aztecs in Part I. The Mayan political structure had crumbled before the Spanish Conquest and parts of the area it had covered were under Aztec domination, but developments under Spanish rule were not the same here as in the Valley of Mexico and are instructive.

The main purpose of this chapter is to consider the social structure of these areas and the differences between them, the special interest of course lying in the extent to which this social structure has arisen from the Conquest of the Indian empires by Cortés and Pizarro and the dominance of Spanish over Indian. The Conquest was the starting-point for the present societies; there was then a clear-cut division in each area between the two races, the two cultures. Since then the cultures have fused but in an irregular pattern, leaving pockets of almost pure Spanish and of predominantly Indian custom and tradition. Biologically, too, there has been mixing of rather the same kind; there are very few whose genes do not contain some mixture both of Spanish and of Indian. But there are sections of society where clearly the Spanish element is biologically as well as culturally predominant, and others where the reverse is the case. There is also a Negro element, biologically stronger than is often supposed. There are wide differences between the regions, even within one political nation-state, differences not only in the physical features of the population—so far as they can be distinguished and measured—and in the demographic proportions—so far as they are known—but differences also in the way people look at physical facts, interpret them, and describe them. To disentangle the biological basis from the social interpretation of it is one of the main tasks. Clearly it is impossible, in any reasonable compass, to do more than indicate the broadest outlines of this diversity. But I shall try to suggest some reasons for the most outstanding differences.

In the first place, the social and political climates of Mexico and Peru are very different. In both countries, there is repugnance to the idea of any hard-and-fast social line between groups defined by purely racial characteristics. In both countries, on the other hand, the word '*indio*' is derogatory; it is used to mean stupid, backward, ignorant, and poor. In both countries, it is socially preferable to look Spanish rather than Indian. But there has been a far more complete fusion in Mexico, and since 1910 Mexico has been, in theory at least, a revolutionary and egalitarian society, while Peru is still essentially an aristocratic society trying to reform itself. For this difference, there are a variety of reasons; I shall try to throw some light on those which arise from the social structure, and to look in the same spirit at differences between Peru, Bolivia, and Ecuador.

But this does not exhaust the questions that need to be asked. The Spanish Crown put Indians under special protection and forbade their enslavement; no such scruples were felt about Negroes, of whom the terms used are in general more derogatory, and whose place in the scale of esteem is generally lower. This needs discussion. Finally, arising out of and affecting all that has gone before, there is the difference between the Spanish colonies and the Anglo-Saxon, particularly those in the Deep South. Not only did the Spanish and English colonists treat slaves differently but they approached the problem of social definition with widely different assumptions about society. Neither ignored biological characteristics; indeed, in both kinds of society, distinctions which were supposed to be based on race have at some stage formed the core of the social structure. But the initial distinctions, at once cultural, religious, and biological, at first so obvious and so simple, were gradually and unconsciously modified and re-defined by the customs and laws of the two kinds of society, one stressing biology, the other religion, language, and culture. And with this difference of stress went a different solution; the North Americans drew a line of definition, while the Spanish constructed a social spectrum which really was like a cross-section of a rainbow; there were gradations and blurred edges between the clear blues, reds, and yellows. Further, the definition of what made blue and red and yellow varied from one region to another. And the question of which segment a man belonged to became, on the whole and in most regions, as time passed, less dependent than before on his physical appearance, or even his known ancestry, and more a matter of speech, education, wealth, and power. Everyone who has looked even casually at the subject is aware of this difference between Spanish and Anglo-Saxon but there has been much controversy about the reasons; they have not always been examined in a broad enough context.

## 2  The Republic of the Indians

Let us begin by looking at what is common to the three areas—Maya, Inca, Aztec. In all three were people practising agriculture and accustomed to some kind of centralized control. There were other Indians, certain warlike tribes in difficult territory who long resisted conquest by Aztecs or Incas as well as by the Spanish; we are not at present thinking of them, nor of the jungle people, whether genuine primitives in small food-gathering groups or fugitives from the imperial power who adopted the same kind of life. The peoples with whom we are concerned are those already part of a society built in tiers, with a system of privileges and duties and specialized functions.

These more highly developed societies were the most easily subdued. They were attached to their land; they were used to obedience and to paying taxes or dues in labour; they transferred their habit of submission from an authority to which they had become accustomed to one that was new and alien. The speed and completeness of their submission has always been felt to require explanation; it can best be understood by looking at the nature of the two societies. The Peruvian system was much the more centralized and monolithic, and the capture and execution of Atahualpa, so soon after Pizarro's arrival, was for the Incas a catastrophe so complete, so shattering, that their conquest was accomplished almost before it began. The much more prolonged and arduous struggle with the Aztecs, as we have seen, could hardly have been successful without the help of the Tlascalans and other Indian allies. But this only carries the question a stage further back; the Tlascalans, who had long resisted the Aztecs, only became allies after they had been defeated by the Spaniards in war, and their defeat—in spite of overwhelming superiority in numbers—first requires explanation. It was mainly due to a completely different view of human life and its relation to the divine. This is summarized in a sentence by Pitt-Rivers: 'In every encounter in which they were defeated, the Indians saw the judgement of Providence and the fulfilment of an ill omen, whereas the Spaniards took their reverses as lessons from which to learn how to avoid defeat in the future.'[1]

Almost everyone who has written anything of the two conquests has stressed the number of omens and prophecies, particularly in Mexico, about the destruction of the empire and about the coming of pale, bearded strangers of divine origin from the East. But perhaps not enough emphasis has been laid on the Aztec concept of time and their anxiety that the miracle of the sun's daily renewal should be continued. Time is thought of in cycles; one age comes to an end, all is destroyed, and a new age begins.[2] Every fifty years all fire must be extinguished;

[1] Julian Pitt-Rivers, *After the Empire: Race and Society in Middle America and the Andes.*
[2] It is recorded of the Baluyia of Kavirondo that they pray every day to God 'to let the sun rise and shine as usual'. Gunter Wagner, in Daryll Forde (ed.), *African Worlds.*

a night of fasting and mourning ends with cries of joy, when torches lighted with new fire from a sacred spot are brought to every household so that the hearth and home may be renewed. To a people with such beliefs, the cataclysm of Spanish conquest was the end of an age, something against which it was useless to strive.

This is not to deny that a most important part was played in the rapidity of the conquest by the superior weapons, and in particular firearms, of the Spanish, still more by their horses, which in both Mexico and Peru at first filled the Indians with alarm. But the hard-fought fights in Tenochtitlan show that these first impressions wore off quickly; the Mexicans were ready to face these dangers and to fight—but they lost heart. And their loss of heart, which one of their living descendants, Octavio Paz,[1] has described as a wish for death, a racial suicide, was due to their view of the nature of human life and its relation to the divine.

Submission after defeat is due in part to the same cause—the concept of divine power as all-powerful, continually manifested in human affairs, but arbitrary in its operation, unaccountable, not always responsive to the appeasement it constantly demanded. But it is also due to the identification of religion with society and the embodiment of both in the monarch. This was particularly the case with the supreme Inca, but in Mexico too—as in so many African societies—the sovereign was one with his land and his people; he is priest as well as monarch; his sickness is a symbol of some sin, impurity, or misfortune in society; his fertility is the earth's and he must start the planting season, start the new year on its way, re-light the sacred fire. Hope therefore was at an end when strangers asserted their superiority over the sacred monarch.

Europeans have spoken of 'nobles' both in Mexico and Peru. But, in fact, although of noble descent, they had no power except that which was derived from the Emperor. They were thus more like the *mansabdars* or great officials at the court of Akbar or Shahjehan than like the Dukes and Counts of Europe, who succeeded their fathers by hereditary right in landed properties in which they had a call on the services of vassals. European nobles could thus combine with each other and wage war on the Crown; the Inca and Aztec 'nobility' were noble by birth but had no hereditary fiefs, only appointments. When the Crown ceased, they were left with no inheritance but their noble blood.[2] This surely is the reason why in so few generations the Indian nobility virtually disappeared. Some married into Spanish families but the nobility of

[1] See O. Paz, *The Labyrinth of Solitude*.

[2] There are two qualifications to this. The Incas in their early conquests allowed local chiefs to rule their people but later replaced them by officials, that is, by Incas of the royal clan. The Aztecs, on the other hand (as mentioned in Part II, Chapter V, Section 1, page 72), did in the last stage of their history create fiefs for Aztec nobles in conquered territory. But they had little time to acquire firm roots of local power.

their descendants survived because of wealth and success which was derived from Spanish sources; if the line of the lords of Tlascala survived as noble, it was because Doña Luisa married a Spaniard.[1]

Spanish American society can only be understood through an understanding of Spain and of Spanish history. Columbus reached the Caribbean in the year when the Moors were driven out of Spain; the conquest of Mexico followed a quarter of a century later and of Peru ten years after that. The thoughts and attitudes of the Conquistadors, and still more the actions of the Crown, were shaped by recent events in Spain and by the pressures that arose from them. It is convenient, if over-simplified, to think of a quadrilateral of forces, arising from four centres of power in Spain, and a triangle of three concepts. The interaction of these forces and concepts produced the ideal by which Spain sought to rule in America.

The quadrilateral was composed of the interests of the Crown, the Church, the Nobles, and the Commons. Spain, it cannot be said too often, had just emerged from the long struggle with the Moors, which had been waged by a number of feudal leaders. It was only in 1479 that the two greatest of the Spanish kingdoms, Castile and Aragon, were joined in a dual monarchy when Ferdinand, the husband of Isabella, Queen of Castile, succeeded to the throne of Aragon. The union remained personal in the subsequent wearers of the Crown; these two, and many smaller kingdoms, kept their separate identities and jealously preserved their *fueros* or special privileges. Even in the eighteenth century, a King of Spain was permitted to enter Barcelona only after knocking at the gate and announcing himself as the Count of Barcelona. In the sixteenth century, unity was the crying need and the question for the Crown was how to define and establish unity. The decision was to respect the identity of the separate kingdoms and the privileges of the cities but to unite by religion. At the same time, the attitude of the Crown to the great nobles must be one of watchfulness if not hostility; the Crown must always seek allies against the strength of the feudal grandees. The Church, like the Crown, was a unifying force and indeed the main instrument by which unity could be achieved; in particular it was a useful ally to the Crown in two respects. The Church could act as a counterbalance to the military power of great feudal leaders; in an embattled world, it might sometimes be preferable for the Crown that lands should be held by an Abbey rather than by a Count. Secondly, the Church provided in the parish priests the machinery for contact with the people and a focus for popular feeling.

To the Commons, on the other hand, the feudal nobility were usually the nearest and most direct oppressors. In England, the barons succeeded in representing themselves—somewhat implausibly it seems to-day—as the champions of equal rights before the law, as the

[1] See Part II, Chapter 6, Section 2, p. 100.

allies of people against the Crown; the nobility of Castile missed this opportunity. They obtained exemption from taxation and thus banished themselves from the Cortés; as those who claimed nobility were about one in ten of the population, this ensured the hostility of the Commons as well as the Crown. But the Commons had no direct means of asserting themselves as an order except by alliance with Church or Crown. It is not surprising therefore that the Crown tried to use Church and Commons as a means of strengthening its own central authority against the grandees. It was a complex relationship, because in the reigns both of the Emperor Charles V and of Philip II of Spain, the Crown often stood against the Pope on behalf of a *national* Church. And while the Church in Spain sometimes supported the Crown against the Pope, it also sometimes supported the people against the King.[1]

The quadrilateral, with three corners usually in shifting alliance against the fourth, is to be seen against a triangle of three concepts which affected conduct—the idea of a religious frontier and a war for Christ's Kingdom; the idea of honour and the need to support it by gold; and finally the overlordship of the Church and the relation of Christ's Kingdom on earth to certain Christian values.

The first of these concepts is perhaps the simplest. Spain had been engaged in warfare for five hundred years. At the death of Al Mansur, the Conqueror, in 1002, far the greater part of Spain was under Muslim rule; there followed two hundred years of uncertain and fluctuating strife till the turning-point of the battle of Las Navas de Tolosa in 1212, after which the Christian forces were in the ascendancy. But it was not till 1492 that the Kingdom of Granada in the South was conquered, the last Moorish power. Later in the same year came the decrees expelling the Jews. In 1525, Charles V obtained a dispensation from the Pope to disregard an oath that he would not convert by force the Mudejares, the Muslims who had stayed true to Islam; three-quarters of a century later his grandson decided to expel the Moriscoes, that is, those converted from Islam. The intention of the Crown, to unify by religion, thus runs entirely clear for more than a century.

But the social situation in which this intention operated was very confused. During the early part of the Moorish wars there had been in the broadest terms a division between Islamic powers and Christian, which was also usually a division between people of Gothic or Iberian stock and people whose origins were Arab or Berber. But it had been far from clear-cut; there had been Christian subjects of Muslim princes and the reverse; there had been alliances and even marriages between princes of the two faiths; el Cid, the champion and symbol of Spanish chivalry, served a Muslim prince for years. Morisco builders, using Moorish techniques of tiled work, were sometimes employed in

[1] Salvador de Madariaga, *Spain*.

parts of Spain that had been conquered three hundred years earlier.

Through all this diversity, social definition must have been of paramount importance; if a man moved away from his own country, where he was known, he would want to know how he stood with those he met, and they with him. And just as the Crown defined the nation's unity in terms of religion, so the individual defined a man by religion rather than by physical appearance, although his appearance no doubt created a presupposition as to what his religion would prove to be. Spaniards had, then, been accustomed, long before the conquest of Mexico and Peru, to moving in a social world in which they were conscious of a frontier, and of a frontier that was finally religious. But there was apt to be confusion between the religious, the cultural, and the physical signs by which a person was identified as belonging to this side of the frontier or that.

Some writers have put a rather different emphasis on Muslim rule in Spain; they have pictured the civilized brown Muslim in his castle, consulting exquisite manuscripts in the decorative Arab script, while the illiterate Spanish peasant toiled in the fields below. They have found in this a reason for the fluidity of the Spanish outlook on race; a Spaniard, they argue, could not identify either civilization or social superiority with a fair skin. This, however, should not be taken too far; Arab, Berber, Moor, and Spaniard do not differ so widely in skin colour and there were African slaves. The important point is that identification had for four centuries been by religion; latterly, it had been very often by the religion of one's ancestors.

For at least a century before the conquest of Mexico, the Christians had in fact been dominant in most of Spain and for some time a most important distinction had been between 'old Christians' and 'new'. Converts from Islam and still more from Judaism were suspected of having given way not through conviction, but from fear or in hope of gain, and of turning, behind closed doors and at night, to ceremonies which their neighbours believed were devilish and unhallowed. It became important—indeed, for many offices under the Crown and for entry to certain religious and knightly orders, essential—to prove what was called, most misleadingly to modern ears, '*limpieza de sangre*' or purity of blood. This meant that sixteen great-great-grandparents, and the generations between, had been good Catholics; to post-Mendelians, it is a thoroughly confused idea—for how can the stain of apostasy or heresy be transmitted genetically? But it was not, as in the laws of Virginia, a *biological* stain with which these provisions were concerned; it was the stain of erroneous belief, of wilful refusal to believe the truth.

It was not so much, then, that a fair man had been used to thinking of a dark man as more 'civilized' than himself—as his better in learning and technology. It was rather that men not very different in colour, nor latterly very different in learning or technology, had differed sharply in what they believed. They had come to identify friend or enemy by religion—and when open enemies became so few as to be unimportant, they began to look for hidden enemies—heretics and apostates. And this means of social identification they took with them to America; they thought of a religious distinction as at least as important as a biological.

The Spaniard of the time of Cortés then had moved always in a world ruled by a sharp religious frontier. With the defeat of Granada, there was a shift to America of the external frontier—the point where a man of honour could make his fortune, lance in hand, against the foes of Christ and his Church. The internal frontier was now the line between old Christians and new, between true Christians and false. The ferocity of a frontier affected the actual Conquest in both Mexico and Peru. It was one of the continual tasks of Cortés and of the friars who accompanied him to restrain his followers from immediate and wholesale onslaught on every ceremony and every sacred place of the indigenous religion. The rank and file chafed at a more politic approach. Their honour was involved; their expedition was a Crusade; it was an affront to themselves and to the cause they represented to stand by and see such things. They must overthrow the idols and set up the Cross; they must end human sacrifice and punish the worship of devils. It was this spirit which, in the absence of Cortés, drove them to break out and attack the Aztecs in the heart of Tenochtitlan on one of their most sacred days and very nearly brought the invasion to a disastrous end.

It was honour[1] then which brought the Conquistadors to America. Honour is both the honour paid me by other people and an internal standard from which I cannot depart without losing my self-respect. 'Honour is the patrimony of the soul and the soul belongs to God', says Calderon in *The Mayor of Zalamea*. Honour can take various forms —for a man or a woman, for a soldier, a priest, or a peasant. But we are concerned with the form of it that sent the Conquistadors to New Spain. As I have said, one man in ten was noble and many were as poor as Don Quixote or poorer. To a younger son from some tiny and impoverished holding in Castile, nobility and honour could be a burden;[2] in theory he could neither plough nor engage in commerce,

[1] Julian Pitt-Rivers has written extensively on honour not only in the book which forms part of this series but also in the *Encyclopaedia of Social Sciences* (Article: 'Honor'). If I have any understanding of the idea not derived mainly from him it is drawn from Northern India, where it seemed to me that Rajputs and Muslims shared a concern for honour that resembled the Spanish. But, as I have said in the foreword, Pitt-Rivers cannot in any way be held responsible for what I have written.

[2] When Parolles has been exposed as a braggart and a coward, he decides to live without the burden of honour and yet to sleep as soft and eat as well as any captain. 'Rust, sword! Cool, blushes! And Parolles live Safest in shame....' *All's Well that Ends Well*. See also J. Caro Baroza in Peristiany (ed.), *Honour and Shame: The Values of Mediterranean Society*.

and could expect no honour from others unless by fighting he could win glory—and gold, the sign of glory.

It was for glory and for gold, then, that the impoverished *hidalgo* went to America. He did not go for trade, like the first English to India. Nor was he seeking escape from a society he repudiated, like the New Englander, or a property on which to build a replica of an aristocratic society he admired, like the Virginian. He wanted gold he could take back to Spain, where he would buy land so that he would be honoured in his home country. Not all the Conquistadors could claim even an impoverished nobility;[1] they came from many levels of society. But on arrival in the New World, it was the *hidalgo's* ideal of honour that they adopted. In both Mexico and Peru, their greed for gold—not in the future, but now, in a portable form—was a factor in the brutality and completeness of the Conquest; their contempt for agriculture was important in what followed. The Conquistador—if for lack of gold he was forced to stay in the New World—must be a feudal overlord and draw his wealth from serfs and peasants. It was his concept of honour, of what was due to nobility, that put out of the question any class of pioneers or small-holders as in New England. He could not plough himself; he must have labour.

But honour meant also self-respect, which might be forfeited by infamous conduct. In Spain, the Church and the neighbours consti- tuted an external court of appeal by which self-respect could be vali- dated or impugned. These external courts were much weaker in America; the standards one expected of others and of oneself became step by step less exacting. The concept of honour had reconciled greed for gold with conscience and the teaching of the Church; in the New World, the relaxation of standards brought to life the conflict between these two.

The Pope's supremacy as the symbol of Christ's Kingdom on earth was very real to Spaniards of the sixteenth century; this, together with the teaching of the Gospel as the friars interpreted it, made the third side of the triangle of concepts which influenced the fate of the American Indian. It was due to this that the nature of the American Indian was solemnly debated in Spain;[2] no such debate took place in England regarding the Negro, and when Parliament discussed India, it was not the soul or the religion of Brahman or Rajput that was the subject of controversy, but the political principles that should govern British rule. The dispute between Las Casas and Sepulveda was however specifically as to whether the American Indian had a soul; once it was decided that

---

[1] Indeed, it has recently been argued that none could, but this seems improbable. See James Lockhart, *Spanish Peru, 1532–1560.*

[2] The history of this debate is told by Lewis Hanke in *Aristotle and the American Indians.* Apart from special occasions, there was an enquiry by the British Parliament into the affairs of the East India Company every twenty years, notably in 1813, 1833, and 1853.

he had a soul to be saved, certain consequences followed. He was a possible Christian and it was the duty of a Christian captain to convert him; it was not justifiable to make war on him unless he had first been offered a chance of salvation and had refused it; he must not be enslaved. If he accepted baptism, he became a ward of the Church and the direct vassal of the King of Spain.

Both Crown and Church distrusted the nobles and in Spain had turned for support to the Commons. In the New World, the Indians took the place of the Commons; a Spaniard who went to the New World fancied himself an *hidalgo* when he arrived, whatever he might have been before.[1] The Crown's distrust for the Conquistadors and their successors, a determination to prevent the growth of any rival to its power, runs through the history of the Spanish empire and its institutions. It is manifest in the treatment of Cortés and it became a feature of the system. A new Viceroy began his term of office by hearing complaints against his predecessor; this was known as the *residencia*. At any time he might be the subject of a *visita*, when an inspector would arrive from Spain with instructions to hear complaints against the Viceroy and to report on him direct to the Crown. Not only that, but he had power, if he thought it necessary, to suspend him from office directly.[2]

The Crown's suspicion of its own officers and dread of a powerful and independent aristocracy survived so long as there was an empire in Spain. The idea that the Indians were wards of the Church and the Crown, with souls to be saved, was not quite so lasting. But it was strong enough, in the sixteenth century, to produce a concept which affected later developments everywhere, that the Indians were a community, or a series of communities, to be protected and instructed, with rights and privileges and duties. It was a concept as shadowy, as ill defined if you like, as Augustine's vision of the City of God, but nonetheless powerful in its effects. It was the idea of the Republic of the Indians—a commonwealth in which under the guardianship of Church and Crown, they could grow and be instructed. The phrase is specifically applied to the Indian communities of the second half of the sixteenth century, but the concept for which it stands began to grow not long after the Conquest. It arose because the Pope had entrusted the King of Spain with the duty of converting the Indians and because certain Dominican Friars, and notably Bartolomé de las Casas, applied to them some quite simple ideas from the Gospel; it would perhaps not have gone very far if it had not been for the Crown's jealousy of the Conquistadors and its fear of great independent fiefs.

---

[1] Hanke quotes from Manila in the eighteenth century words which he applies to the Spanish empire throughout its history: 'Do Spaniards work the soil and plant crops in these islands? Certainly not! On reaching Manila all become caballeros.'

[2] C. H. Haring, *The Spanish Empire in America*.

It was to this idea that the Indians owed the protective elements in the *encomienda*, the earliest institution by which Spanish domination was asserted. The *encomienda* was not an estate in the European sense, vested in the holder and his heirs for ever; it was originally a trust, which might be transmitted to a son but after one generation reverted to the Crown. The *encomendero* was not entitled to live on his *encomienda* nor to claim labour from its inhabitants; he was entitled to tribute from the inhabitants but the amount was assessed by royal officials. If he wanted labour, he was supposed to apply to a royal labour exchange and he must pay labourers—even his 'own' Indians from his own villages—at the same rates as anyone else.[1] So at least ran the royal decree of 1549; one may suspect that in America things did not happen exactly as was intended in Madrid. But the slavery of Indians was increasingly limited from 1530 onwards; the last case of Indian slaves to be set free was heard by the *audiencia* of Mexico in 1561.

Under the *encomienda*, then, the Indians were wards to be protected. The *encomendero* was entrusted with the duty of seeing that they were baptized and instructed in the Catholic faith. In practice, perhaps, there was less difference than appears on paper between the *encomienda* and the later *hacienda*;[2] nonetheless, the law governing the one was devised by the Crown to protect the Indians, while the latter was developed by the colonists for their own purposes. There was a struggle in Spain to make the *encomiendas* perpetual, but this failed, and instead they died away, being gradually replaced by two institutions, the *hacienda* and the *republica de indios*, the Indian commune.

The *hacienda* became in fact the typical instrument of Spanish colonial domination. It was a self-contained estate, owned in full hereditary right; it could be sold or mortgaged. It sometimes had its own chapel and school, usually its own carpenters, wheelwrights, blacksmiths, shoemakers, and so on. Of its main labour force, some lived on the estate, often occupying a plot of their own and giving labour in return for the right to cultivate; others came from a nearby Indian commune and worked for wages, in kind or cash. Both usually borrowed from the estate-owner for weddings or funerals and found themselves caught in debt from which they could seldom escape; they thus became virtually serfs. The system varied widely from region to region in details, but everywhere it was ownership not trusteeship and the relationship of the estate-owner with his labour-force was one of exploitation. It became domination rather than paternalism in the special sense in which I have used that term.

[1] Eric Wolf, *Sons of the Shaking Earth*.

[2] Not only was the *encomienda* often treated without any regard for the aspect of trusteeship, but even when the ideals were remembered, they were often harshly administered. Hanke notes that it was common for an Indian to be punished with twenty-four lashes for not attending Mass.

The Indian communes, to which the term 'republic of the Indians' was frequently applied, were established in large numbers in both Mexico and Peru. These communities held land in common and were jointly assessed to a tribute, of which a part went to the imperial exchequer and part went to a community chest for local projects. Communal officials administered traditional law within certain limits and settled their own disputes. It was, in fact, a small-scale, localized form of what the British were later to call indirect rule—but with the difference that it was not in direct continuity with an older, traditional society. It would have borne some resemblance to the lowest tier of what modern India calls *panchayati raj* if it had not been that the communes were interspersed among the *haciendas* and so often economically dependent on them.

## 3 *The Social Rainbow*

The Spaniard then came to the Indies with a clear sense of a religious frontier. He came from a society in which the most important distinctions were between Christian and infidel, between old Christian and new. It was also a stratified society in which inequality was taken for granted, but it was not always easy to place a stranger in the social hierarchy without enquiry. He might have Jewish or Moorish blood[1] and if this were known, it would expose him to suspicion, distrust, and hostility. But by valour in war or by the honourable acquisition of land or gold, the stain could be excused and might be formally wiped away by royal recognition. It was a stain in the blood, but a stain of wrong thinking, of wilful refusal to see the light; it was not biological.

It had been established that Indians had souls to be saved. Throughout the sixteenth century, the consequences of this were being worked out with increasing detail and thoroughness, culminating in Philip II's basic decree of 1573 laying down the proper procedure for new conquests. But from as early as 1513, the principle had been that no subject of the King of Spain might declare war on Indians without formally offering them a chance of submission and salvation. Like the requirement that English magistrates should read the Riot Act before using force to disperse a crowd, the offer must often have presented difficulties in practice, but it existed.

The concept of Indians as wards, as vassals of the Crown, entrusted to the King of Spain by the Pope—all that led to the idea of the Republic of the Indians—meant that the Indians could not be ignored or excluded from the ranks of humanity. Such catholic ideas, imposed by Crown and Church, might sometimes increase the hostility felt towards the Indians by the Conquistadors and their descendants;

[1] The atmosphere of suspicion on this subject is well conveyed in Salvador de Madariaga's novel, *Heart of Jade*.

there were periods in certain regions when the Church refused absolution to *encomenderos* who would not make restitution of lands they had won by war not justly declared. But at no period could a Spaniard in the Americas exclude the Indians and say of himself and his fellow-countrymen, 'We, the people . . .'[1], in the sense in which these words were used in South Africa. This phrase—excluding the rest of the world and thus the reverse of catholic—was perhaps not used by the Afrikaners before the nineteenth century, but it was the result of a process which began soon after van Riebeeck reached the Cape, when, as we have seen, they decided to define themselves neither by religion, nor by status as slave or free, but by colour. The same thought is perfectly expressed[2] by a series of resolutions on the Indian question of an Assembly in New England in the 1640s:

1. The Earth is the Lord's and the fullness thereof.                    Voted.
2. The Lord may give the Earth or any part of it to his chosen
              people.                                                    Voted.
3. We are his chosen people.                                            Voted.

When Cortés reached Mexico, there was at first no difficulty about defining anyone's place in the scheme of things. There were Spanish and Indians, no one else. But from the start the Spaniards distinguished Indians from each other. There were Kings, nobles, and leaders; there were toilers in the fields. There were the minor states along the coast, of Campeche and Tabasco, all overshadowed by the great central power of the Aztecs at Tenochtitlan; there was the vigorous independent power of Tlascala;[3] soon there were faithful allies as well as enemies. After the Conquest, there were Indian nobles of high rank who had been baptized. The beginnings of a social rainbow became mistily apparent.

But at this stage it would really be more accurate to say that there was a rainbow of social gradation among Indians overlapping with another among the Spanish. The overlap became less and disappeared. Over a period of a century or more, the Indian noble lost his occupation. There was no place for him in the new dispensation as a leader of his people; he might become Spanish and lose his Indian identity or he might stay Indian and lose his nobility. One fate or the other must befall him. And something similar soon began to occur to the *mestizo*. Much depended on the rank of his father and the nature of the union between his parents. There was all the difference in the world between the relationship of Cortés and Malinche and the brutal encounter of

---

[1] 'Ons, die Volk. . . .'

[2] Garrard Mattingly, *Renaissance Diplomacy*, quoted in *Aristotle and the American Indian*.

[3] Prescott always refers to Tlascala as a Republic but I am not clear why. It sounds more like a confederation of chiefs, not constitutionally different from the Aztec state. But he has, I suspect, a feeling that a state which maintains its independence against an empire *ought* to be a republic.

Spanish soldier with Indian woman after the sack of a town. Malinche's son was Don Martin Cortés, the second Marquis of the Valley of Oaxaca, appointed by Charles V a Knight of the Order of Santiago—the impurity of his blood excused. There must on the other hand have been many *mestizo* children raised by mothers who never knew the father's name; these were socially Indians.

The situation however became increasingly complex. There were great differences between the regions, particularly in the proportions between Spanish and Indian. Where there were many Spaniards, there were soon many *mestizos*. Some were acknowledged and legitimized—and some were actually legitimate by birth—and these became virtually white. But before long there grew up in many places an intermediate population between Spanish and Indian. By the beginning of the seventeenth century it was common to find at the centre of each region a town, built in the Spanish style round church and *plaza*, where the *encomenderos* lived in fine houses; nearby would be a quarter of *mestizo* shopkeepers and artisans and other quarters of unskilled labourers, who in appearance were predominantly Indian but were beginning to be hispanicized. In the countryside, the *hacienda* was beginning to replace the *encomienda*; it was managed by *mestizo* bailiffs when the owner was in his town house, as he frequently was. Interspersed among the *haciendas* were Indian communes. Already '*mestizo*' was a word that began to describe a class rather than the biological origin of an individual.

The upper class were those with landed estates; they included the sons of Conquistadors, such as Don Martin, sometimes also daughters by Indian mothers, who might inherit all their fathers' rights.[1] Such an heiress would be likely to marry a Spanish man. There is a Brazilian proverb that money whitens; so, emphatically, does land. But although the landed upper class were socially Spanish or white, whatever their origin, there was a distinction made, after the first generation, between those born in Spain and those born in America. The latter were *criollos*, and were despised by the royal officials and officers of the army, whose patronizing airs were in turn resented by the *criollos*. *Gachupines* or *chapetones* are the names (says Pitt-Rivers) which the American-born applied to them. The name varied according to region, but nowhere was it any more complimentary than 'limey' or 'pommie'.

To belong to the 'white' class, it was necessary to be legitimate or legitimized; the distinction of importance among the whites was between *gachupín* and *criollo*. The *mestizos* were those who had not been

---

[1] There was an unusual case in Peru. Pizarro took as concubine an Inca princess, daughter of Huayna Capac, Emperor until 1525. Pizarro gave the *repartimiento* (feudal rights) over Huaylas (see pp. 255–7) to his daughter by this woman. But as the child was only six years old, the *repartimiento* was administered by her grandmother Contarguacho, who of course was of unmixed Indian descent.

admitted to their fathers' full status; their origins were clouded by the stain of illegitimacy. Among them, there was an always increasing variety of distinctions. There are several lists,[1] illustrated by paintings, of terms which are supposed to apply to the various genetic combinations and permutations between Spanish, Indian, and Negro, and their offspring down to several generations. They date mainly from the eighteenth century and seem to have been commissioned by wealthy patrons—usually, it seems, Spaniards from Spain—at a time of economic expansion, when the upper class would be disturbed at the prospect of upstarts joining their ranks and would be anxious to define and fix the classes as they stood, or as the upper class liked to think they stood. There was a system of referring to people by the proportion of Spanish blood they were assumed to have—a quarter, a half, an eighth.[2] There were words for persons of mixed Indian and Negro blood, in various proportions, which seem to have varied from region to region. There were names denoting shades of colour and names suggesting some genetic misfortune, such as 'throw-back' (*torna-atras*) or some expectation of achieving white status in one more generation, such as 'wait-and-see' or 'it hangs in the balance' (*tente-en-el-aire*). It would probably be a mistake to regard all these expressions as generally accepted. There are so many of them—more than fifty have been listed—and they show so much variation that they must be regarded as no more than popular classifications; they are not legal definitions such as those under which the South African Government now compels all its subjects to register. All these types were known in general as *'las castas'*—'the breeds' or 'the races'—but they were not in the least like the castes of India. There is a vivid illustration of the atmosphere of bourgeois society in the Spanish Empire in the eighteenth century in a footnote of Pitt-Rivers:

The blend of their antecedents supposedly determined their colour but legal status was a matter of descent rather than appearance. As late as 1788 we find (in the Archives of the National Historical Institute in Caracas) a case in which a citizen of Merida in the Andes is suing the town council for denying him, on the grounds of his non-white status, the right to carry an umbrella. He emerges victorious in the end after three years judication and an appeal to the high court in Caracas, vindicated as *blanco de segunda clase*, with the right to carry gloves and a sword as well. At no point does it appear that it was thought possible to tell whether he was 'white' by looking at him.

Those who could not establish such rights were *'las castas'*, and were disqualified from certain guilds and orders and from high posts in the administration. They formed one band in the social rainbow, but it was blurred at the edges and there were gradations within it. But this was a prism of Spanish-speaking persons, by the eighteenth century

[1] They are described by Julian Pitt-Rivers in 'Mestizo or Ladino?'

[2] The British in India sometimes spoke of a person of mixed descent as being, say, four annas, eight annas, or ten annas in the rupee, a rupee containing sixteen annas.

a far broader spectrum than in the first days of the Conquest. The Indian spectrum, on the other hand, had shrunk, because the road to social advancement for an Indian was to cease to be an Indian, to leave his community, to speak Spanish, to live in a town. To be an Indian meant usually to live in an Indian community or as a peon on a *hacienda*. In a generation or two, the descendants of an Indian who had come to town would no longer be classified as Indians, except in a derogatory sense by their superiors in the social scale.

The Catholic insistence that the Indian was a man with a soul had helped to make sure that his blood should not be regarded as an indelible stain and that the status of 'Indian', as of 'white', should be determined by religion, culture, and social standing rather than on purely biological grounds. It had also led to the idea of the Republic of the Indians; it had protected the Indians as direct vassals of the Crown and placed them in communities which for local purposes ruled themselves. Like 'indirect rule' in Africa, this was benevolent in intention but in practice isolated the community it sought to protect. It slowed down adaptation to Spanish ways and excluded Indian communities from the national life. They contributed to the economy, but little more. So long as they stayed in their Indian communes, they were spared the degradation and loss of self-respect which come with life in the slums of a great city, but only by exclusion from the individualist world in which—harsh though it may be—individual progress is possible.

Thus by the end of the eighteenth century, in the greater part of the Spanish Empire in America, the two overlapping social rainbows of the mid-sixteenth century had been replaced by a single spectrum. It consisted of broad bands of colour with blurred edges and many gradations within each band—for those who were not Indian. A man's place in the grading depended on a number of factors, appearance being of less importance than descent, and descent—so long as any deficiencies had been wiped out by the sovereign—counting less than the ownership of land. There were people within the spectrum descended from Amerindians on both sides, but most of such people were in the lowest category, messengers, servants, and casual labourers in the towns. In the countryside, however, there were Indians who still spoke an Indian language and lived in an Indian community; they were outside the spectrum.

From this social system, coupled with the Spanish idea of the *hidalgo* and the fact that every Spaniard became in his own opinion an *hidalgo* on setting foot in America, stemmed an attitude to manual work that was to be lasting. Work in the fields was something for an Indian; to abandon it was the first stage of a rise in the social scale. 'Work is God's punishment', say the people of Aritama to this day. By 'work' they mean manual work, and they acknowledge that they need and want more food and that if they worked more they would eat better. But they would still prefer not to work.[1]

This picture of a social spectrum with the Indians outside it is a broad generalization. Differences between the regions were to be found from the beginning and they increased after independence from Spain. To these developments and to some of the main differences we now turn.

## 4 *The Second Revolution*

In the first quarter of the nineteenth century, the Spanish colonies in the New World made themselves independent of Madrid. This was a part of what Pitt-Rivers calls the dialectic of empire; it was inevitable that it should happen and its essence was that conflict between Spain and the colonies became an internal conflict between rulers on the spot and the people they ruled. But whatever the forces that drive men to revolution, they will justify their acts by slogans and ideas. And however remote those ideas may be from the immediately operative forces, they are apt to influence subsequent events. The slogans of the Liberation arose from the philosophy of the Enlightenment; liberty and equality were for all. Legal distinctions and privileges were therefore abolished and there could no longer be litigation about who might carry swords and gloves.

But, in practice, the difference for the Indian was that the last remnants of his special status as a ward of Crown and Church were even further reduced. The Crown's protection had gone; the Church was in most regions weaker, and where its strength was most, it was usually because the Church had become an ally of the ruling landed class. Typical in the nineteenth century was a party of landowners and Church leaders opposed by another party that was anti-clerical and mercantile; the landowners often wanted a strong central government, the merchants a federal government and greater regional autonomy. In both parties, the dominant group was as a rule mainly *criollo*. In fact, the driving force behind the slogans had usually been *criollo* resentment at bureaucratic intervention from Madrid and the arrogance of Spaniards from the peninsula. Whichever party was in power, deference was paid to foreign financial, trading, engineering, and mining interests. Peruvian history—one Peruvian told me—has fallen into four periods: rule by native Peruvians, rule by the Spanish, concealed rule by the British, and now concealed rule by the Americans.

The social structure was therefore still basically a spectrum from which the Indian was excluded. Indeed, as the century proceeded, his lot generally grew harsher. The burden of debt peonage mounted;

[1] G. and A. Reichel-Dolmatoff, *The People of Aritama*.

the land owned by the Indian communities became less and less. The first revolution, the rebellion against Spain, proved in most of South America to be a prolongation of the feudal system, not, as Simon Bolivar had dreamed, the birth of a new nation, but the fragmentation of an empire into provinces which often ignored what was Catholic and protective in the old tradition as completely as it disregarded the egalitarian principles that the new constitutions asserted.[1]

But in Mexico, from the first, there were differences from the standard pattern. In the first stages, even of the First Revolution, there were elements of agrarian revolt, of peasants led by middle-class intellectuals; these elements had been virtually defeated and the royalist cause seemed triumphant when the situation was unforeseeably turned inside out. The liberals within the royalist camp managed to secure power, whereupon the conservative landowning *criollo* group went over to the insurgents and with their backing proclaimed independence and the first Mexican empire.[2]

There followed a confused period in which ideas of liberty and of a more even distribution of land never wholly died and from which emerged a creative stage, that of the Reforms. Ramon Juarez, a man of markedly Indian appearance and said to be a Zapotec Indian on both sides, was their architect; he was responsible for the liberal constitution of 1857 and for the series of reforms which followed. He would perhaps not have gained power if it had not been for Mexican resentment at the intervention of the United States, who in 1848 annexed California and New Mexico by what Mexicans regard as an act of simple and wholly unjust aggression. The reforms of Juarez, which revoked special privileges and greatly reduced the power of the Church, provoked another foreign intervention, this time by the France of Louis Napoleon. The French emperor was a victim of a delusion unfortunately frequent among those who are confronted by a régime they do not like; he believed that the whole Mexican people was groaning under the tyranny of Juarez and that a small French force would topple him over, whereupon the liberated Mexicans would acclaim with joy a Catholic monarchy. Mexican dislike of interference was not the only factor that proved him wrong; their own civil war over, the United States also played a part. Juarez returned to power and Napoleon's candidate, the Emperor Maximilian, ended his life before a firing-squad. This double outrage on her independence reinforced the trend in political and economic theory which was in fashion at the time; Mexico's feet turned decisively against the Church and the feudal tradition and towards a theoretical egalitarianism.

But it was still highly theoretical. There followed a second period in which the language of freedom was used in public but when in fact

---

[1] O. Paz, *The Labyrinth of Solitude*.
[2] Ibid.

more land came into the hands of large landowners, whose hold on their peasants increased. In the long Presidency of Porfirio Diaz, reason and progress were mentioned in the proclamations, but as in the period of extreme *laissez-faire* in England, freedom meant freedom to exploit. Communal holdings were believed to be backward and inefficient; common land was waste land. As in England at the time of the enclosures, the social advantages of independence and of life in a community were ignored. Mortgages on the land of Indian communities were foreclosed; common land was sold. The Church estates were broken up, but usually to fall into the hands of those with no motive but exploitation. By 1910, 54 per cent of the national territory was in large estates, 20 per cent in smaller private holdings, 10 per cent waste land, 10 per cent owned by the state, and only 6 per cent remained communal, that is, Indian.[1] Communal land belonging to villages and towns had been almost ended. The remnants of the Republic of the Indians showed only the last flickerings of life.

The Second Revolution, that of 1910, began with a series of popular explosions, mutually antagonistic and contradictory. It was not based on an intellectual movement; indeed, it did not need one. The proclaimed principles of the Government were enough; all that was necessary was to apply them. The Revolution sprang from leaders among the middle classes produced by industrial growth—men angry at the contrast between what was proclaimed and what happened— from industrial workers in the towns, ill-organized and incoherent, and from land-hungry peasants. The group which most clearly expressed the anger of the countryside at loss of land was that led by Zapata, but he was defeated; the faction which eventually emerged triumphant began by applying the principles of Juarez, but came increasingly to adopt those of Zapata. It was from this that there emerged the modern Mexican version of an ancient institution.

The typical units of government under the Aztecs had been the *calpulli*—groups of people with joint rights in land, for which they jointly paid tribute. The Indian communities of the sixteenth century were not direct successors of the *calpulli* but no doubt they operated more easily because the *calpulli* were remembered. The modern *ejido* stands in a similar relationship to the older communities; they had in most cases perished and the *ejidos* had to be created. There are various forms of *ejido;* in the most usual, the cultivated land is held in joint ownership by the community but is divided into plots for each *ejidatorio;* he can pass his plot on to his son but may not lease, sell, or mortgage. Pasture and forest are common and use of them is joint.[2]

[1] Moises Gonzales Navarro, in Claudio Veliz (ed.), *Obstacles to Change in Latin America.*

[2] This was almost exactly the traditional system of village communal holding in the Himalayan district of Garhwal.

There is a standard size for the *ejidatorio's* holding, which varies according to rainfall and the possibility of irrigation; but, in practice, holdings are sub-divided or combined. Progress in setting up these communities was slow after the Revolution; the leaders themselves were still landowners and the idea that joint tenures were backward still lingered—and indeed had some justification; preference went to individual small holdings, five times as big as an *ejidatorio's*. Not till the mid-thirties under President Cardenas did the process of creating *ejidos* begin to accelerate. But it then became rapid and, by 1962, almost a quarter of the country and almost a third of the cultivated land had been distributed to *ejidos*.

The *ejido* is far from being the most efficient means of production.[1] I have dwelt on it as a symbol of the attitude of Mexican society to the agricultural labourer, who as a rule was biologically more Indian than Spanish. The detail of Mexican politics in the nineteenth century is full of bloodshed, of violent reversals, of bitter faction. But social movement is much smoother and more consistent. Neither the First Revolution, which brought independence, nor the Reforms, nor the Second Revolution, in fact made dramatic changes in the life of the peasantry at the time. At each stage ideals were proclaimed only to be neglected in the rapid oscillations of political power; but throughout the whole process, the hope of a more equitable distribution of land never wholly died. And the Second Revolution did occur; even though Zapata was defeated and his ideas hardly acted on for twenty years, this Revolution is accepted by all Mexicans as one of the decisive events of their national history.

Social movement was consistent because it tended always in the direction of a less sharp social definition. This result was accomplished by a paradox; something was achieved for the benefit of those who were in the main biologically Indian but it was at the expense of those who were labelled 'Indian'. The nineteenth century was disastrous for the Indian communities that were in existence at Independence. Except in isolated pockets, they ceased to exist.[2] But when Zapata looked back to them and his ideas became embodied in law as the *ejido*, what was created was not specifically Indian; it was peasant. Mexico to-day is a country that is five-sixths homogeneous; 85 per cent of the people speak of themselves as *mestizo*. There are many contradictions in their attitude to race; almost all will speak of Indian ancestry and the national mythology—the great frescoes of the town halls and the statues in the *plazas*—laud the Indians and denigrate the Spaniards. But the physical traits that are admired are Spanish, not Indian, and few would care to be thought wholly Indian in descent, while no one will boast that he speaks only an Indian language. To

[1] See an unpublished paper by François Chevalier, *Ejido and Stability in Mexico*.
[2] Octavio Paz, *The Labyrinth of Solitude*.

look Indian carries the suggestion of humble origin, but the number actually outside the social spectrum is only one-sixth of the total and for five-sixths of the nation there is some feeling of homogeneity and a fluidity of social definition, a readiness to adjust ideas about who make up the group thought of as 'we'.

It is very different in Peru. Here, it is true, everyone denies that race in itself, that is, biologically, has any social significance, but everyone concedes that there are two cultures, and most will agree that this constitutes one of the main problems of the country. The two cultures are, in the simplest and crudest terms, Hispanic and Indian—though this requires much qualification. But about half the population in Peru and Ecuador belong to the Indian culture, while in Bolivia it is more like 70 per cent. Bolivia perhaps had its second revolution in 1952; Peru and Ecuador have not yet had a second revolution and seem to be at a stage like that of Juarez's Reforms in Mexico. Why do these countries define so large a proportion of their population in terms which in practice exclude them from the main stream of national life?

## 5 The Two Cultures in the Andes

In Peru, Ecuador, and Bolivia, there are two cultures which may be called Hispanic and Indian; they may also be thought of as the cultures of the coast and of the highlands, or as modern and traditional. They differ in all three respects, but in none of the three is there a clear-cut line between the cultures. There is no community in these three Andean countries wholly untouched by either Spanish or Indian influences; there are many local variations and it will often be difficult to assign an individual or a group to one or the other. But the broad distinction remains and can best be illustrated by describing extremes.

At one extreme is the great city of Lima on the coast, at the other are the Indian communities of the highlands. Lima is essentially a modern city; everyone speaks Spanish and no one calls himself an Indian. Even the latest arrival from the *sierras* will put on clothes of a European type, avoid Indian habits such as chewing coca, and try to talk Spanish. He will no longer drink *chicha* (maize beer) nor pour a libation of it ceremonially. There is poverty, unemployment, and under-employment; wages are low and, as in Victorian England or modern South Africa and Jamaica, quite humble middle-class people employ domestic servants. There are the office messengers who are always to be found where wages are low and who are dispensed with when they rise. There are, in short, many features common to the capitals of former colonial territories, but it is a city of one culture, to which all aspire to belong, and although there are extremes of wealth and poverty, they are expressed in terms of class rather than race. There is one social spectrum, in which racial characteristics are only one determining factor of several.

At the other extreme come the more remote of the Indian communities in the high Andes. In Peru, there are some four thousand of these communities, almost as many in Bolivia and half as many in Ecuador.[1] They are the successors of the Indian communities of the late sixteenth century, in most cases registered and to some extent reorganized by more modern legislation. Among themselves, the people speak Quechua—or Aymara in parts of Bolivia—though the men usually speak some Spanish. They are nominally Catholic but engage in a variety of magical and animistic practices; their land is owned by the community but the use of cultivated land is individual; holdings however are usually very small and the most they hope for is subsistence. It is usually only by emigration that cash can be earned. Interspersed among them are *haciendas*, which, except for those affected by the *Reforma Agraria*, have not changed much since colonial times. The peons on the *haciendas* also belong to the Indian culture; they too obtain from their holdings a bare subsistence, and in return for this must work for the owner.

In these communities, the diet is very low in animal protein and often low in calories. Intestinal parasites are common. The life is laborious and monotonous; there are few reserves and very little ability to save. On the *haciendas*, there is much regional variety; traditionally, the most oppressive were in Southern Ecuador, where the peon was often obliged to work for the *haciendas* till four in the afternoon every working day throughout the year, leaving only the evening for work on his own holding to produce the food for his family and himself. In Peru, it was general that he should work 180 days in the year. From this form of existence, there has seldom been any local opportunity to escape. Migration to the plains has been the one way out, and from some communities the number who have taken it has been very high; 40 per cent of the population born in Pacaraos, a native community in the valley of Chancay in Peru, now lives in Lima or in the mining centres. But this valley runs down to the central coast not far from Lima. The isolation of the remoter communities in the high *sierras* is still considerable.

In their inhospitable surroundings, these lonely groups often develop in a high degree the hostility and suspicion with which rural people so often meet outsiders. A team from Cornell University which was preparing a report[2] for I.E.R.A.C., the Ecuadorian Institute of Agrarian Reform and Colonization, found several rumours in circulation as to their own sinister intentions. They were going to kidnap the children, steal the land, or cheat the inhabitants in a variety of ways;

[1] See an unpublished paper by José Matos Mar.
[2] Ecuadorian Institute of Agrarian Reform and Colonization, *Indians in Misery*.

plots were made to kill them. In 1961, a team of doctor, nurse, and social worker in Ecuador *were* killed and burnt. The Cornell team in the Colta Lake zone found that: 'After years of exploitation, it is difficult for the Indians to believe that a group of strangers living in their midst does not have an ulterior motive. . . . Altruism is an idea outside their experience. . . .' In their findings, the Cornell team put high among obstacles to progress the degradation and humiliation of the Indian, resulting in suspicion of strangers and resistance to change.

This is not peculiar to the Andes. Wherever the agricultural expert, the missionary, or the anthropologist goes, he is likely to encounter some degree of distrust and resistance to advice. And for this there are sometimes better reasons than appear at first sight. The atmosphere of these communities, usually at an altitude of between 9,000 and 13,000 feet, can be illustrated by two anecdotes from Peru told me by a man who has lived among them thirty years and believes he has won a little of their confidence—though he hastened to add that an outsider can never win it all. He was present on one occasion when officials of the Peruvian Government were trying to persuade men from one of these communities to try a new breed of sheep. They were met by blank refusal, repeated again and again, with no reason given. At last the officials gave up in despair and left. My informant tried to discover why they refused, and after much patient probing found that they recognized that the new sheep produced more wool than their own, and of a longer staple that would sell better. It was bigger and would reach maturity more quickly. But it would eat more and they thought it was likely to be less hardy; if it died, the Government would expect them to pay for it, and in any case they wanted the wool not so much to sell as to make into *ponchos* for their own use. For this they believed the short-staple wool would keep out the rain better than the long, perhaps because it was greasier. They had thus quite rational arguments; the new sheep was a risky investment that would lock up capital they could not afford and it was meant for a cash economy in which they were not yet interested. But they would not reveal their reasons to strangers.

The same informant told me that in his view the deepest wish of these people was to be treated 'not like an Indian but like a person'. And what it means to be treated 'like an Indian' he revealed in the course of illustrating another point. Nearly all the children in these high communities were by Peruvian law illegitimate and the mother had no protection if she and her children were deserted. My informant, who was a Protestant missionary, had only slowly come to understand the reasons for this. But he had discovered that a couple would usually take each other by a ceremony which he thought was pre-Christian; after much discussion the parents would consent, gifts would be exchanged, much *chicha* would be drunk, libations would be poured and perhaps an animal killed, and the couple would then consider themselves married; the union would usually be permanent. At intervals, sometimes after four or five years, a priest would turn up at the community and persuade as many couples as he could to be married with the blessing of the Church; these rites too they would understand and again there would be much drinking and festivity. But the couple would still not be married by Peruvian law. For this they must go to the Registrar in the town fifteen or twenty miles away. He would be *mestizo*—that is, belong to the other culture—and would speak Spanish and they would find it hard to understand. They would be told, 'Wait! *Espera*!', and might be kept waiting days or even weeks. They would need birth certificates, and of course they had not such things, and two other certificates; all these—or exemptions in lieu of having them—they would have to obtain from officials who would treat them with contempt. 'Wait! *Espera*!'—this was the sharp command they would continually encounter. Even if they bought presents of eggs and guinea-pigs it was not much better. And when all the formalities had been satisfied, after days of waiting, there would be a gabble of legal Spanish which they could not understand—and they would stand puzzled. 'Are we married?' they would ask and often the official would be too impatient with the stupid Indians even to tell them that. This it is to be treated as an Indian.[1]

It is hardly necessary to emphasize further the sense of separation between the two groups. The poverty and isolation of the hill Indians has impressed itself on all foreign observers, and Peruvian officials themselves agree that there are two cultures, the traditional and the modern. And throughout the Andes the difference is generally expressed in terms of superior and subordinate. In the Ecuadorian report already referred to—to take only one example of many—much is made of the deference required of Indians. In this area there are a handful of 'white' or *mestizo* shopkeepers and bar-keepers; officials sometimes pay visits. The team found that since the *mestizos* consider the Indians 'no better than animals' they have no hesitation in exploiting them; the Indian is required to express his sense of white superiority by the form of address he uses and must kiss the hand of the 'White', but not touch it, laying a corner of his poncho over the 'White's' hand.

There are wide regional differences and we are describing a dynamic situation in which change is taking place. Some will argue that the 'two cultures' of the Andes are a thing of the past, that the agrarian reform laws are breaking the powers of the *hacendado*, that education to-day provides a way out. But in both Peru and Ecuador the operation of the laws of agrarian reform is extremely gradual. In Peru large areas are exempted and the procedure leaves open many avenues for

[1] This account was confirmed as substantially correct by a Peruvian of high standing in the University of Cuzco.

escape or delay. In Ecuador, the *hacendado* has been instructed by the law to allot holdings in their own right to his *huasipungeros*—that is, the peasants on the *hacienda* who work for the owner in return for their plots. But he has often been able to make these new holdings so small that they are more in his power than ever. Informants told me of contractors who bribed officials to force Indians to work for them for nothing. I heard of Indians branded with hot irons and of the five years of litigation required to get justice. 'White people and *mestizos* still think of Indians as virtually slaves', an informant told me.

Their attitudes have not changed at all. Even members of the *Instituto Indigena* who will write in favor of Indians will not recognize an Indian in the street or shake hands with him in public. There are a few Indians who want to get to school and college but they have not the money and there is opposition. It is a real struggle.

The remote communities in the high *sierras* form one extreme of a continuum of which the other end is Lima. To complete the picture it will be enough to refer to two small towns in the *sierra* which have been the subject of studies in the 1960s. They are intermediate between the extremes. In one of those, Paucartambo, Andrews[1] found that there were three 'socio-cultural classes', in numbers forming 10, 20, and 70 per cent of the population of the town, which in 1961 was about 1,700. In the surrounding district, the percentage of the lowest class would be higher. The terms he uses for these classes are '*mestizo*', '*cholo*', and 'Indian', all racial terms, but he recognizes that they are social rather than biological. Members of the lowest class are distinguished from the others by clothing, by standard of living and lack of education, by Quechua as the mother tongue and poor knowledge of Spanish, and by the use of coca. They do not refer to themselves as *indios* but as *los pobres*, the poor, or *los bajos*, the low ones; they too—they consider—are physically *mestizos* and the difference is only one of wealth and opportunity. The 10 per cent of the population classed as *mestizo* speak Spanish as their mother tongue and in every respect have better education and a higher standard of living; they regard the lowest class as different from themselves in a much more radical way; they call them *los indigenas*, the natives, *los indios*, or *los aborigines*. Andrews himself believed that most of the 'Indians' in Paucartambo were in fact of mixed ancestry, though physical characteristics that are typically Indian—straight black hair and mongolian eyes—were more common among them than among the *mestizos*. The *cholos* are an intermediate class; the term is used in the Andes of someone who is of Indian origin but begins to abandon Quechua and typical Indian behaviour. *Cholo* is an established intermediary status, indicating a position rather less ambivalent than the phrase used in

[1] David Henry Andrews, 'Paucartambo, Pasco, Peru: An Indigenous Community and a Change Program.'

Southern Mexico: '*Indio revestido*'—the Indian who has been dressed again in Spanish clothes. But the word is used with different shades of meaning in different areas and will have a different sense in one mouth from another; it is frequently used by people of higher social standing, that is, *mestizos*, of people below them who are trying to improve their status. But Indians use the term too and between equals it is used as a friendly form of address, like 'chum' in English. I heard '*chola*' used in Bolivia with approval by a person classing himself as '*blanco*'; he was speaking of the market-women of La Paz who were good, kindly folk. But he warned me not to use the term of a man, who, from me at least, would regard it as derogatory.

Paucartambo is a town. None of *los pobres* there were living in an Indian community and it seems possible that some observers would have classed them differently; class depends on the eye of the beholder. The term 'gentleman' in Victorian England illustrates the point; Dickens uses it of people who would certainly not have been regarded as deserving the title by Jane Austen, still less by George Meredith. Pitt-Rivers found whites of old family in Lima who regarded all but themselves as Indians while in the Peruvian Andes he found Indians who regarded everyone but themselves as white. In Paucartambo Andrews thought that within the limits of the town no one of the lower class could come to be regarded as a *mestizo* within the lifetime of one generation, because he would be remembered. *Mestizos* professed ignorance of Indian customs and snubbed any attempt at breaking the barriers, but it seems clear that the 'Indians' of Paucartambo were part of a spectrum, while Indians who formed part of a community would be outside the spectrum.

Huaylas[1] is also a small highland town, with an urban population in 1961 of over 1,000, the headquarters of a district of 5,000 to 6,000. But it is an essentially rural area, in which everyone depends indirectly on land and almost everyone raises some produce for his own consumption. But, say the inhabitants, 'there are no real Indians' in Huaylas; the census of 1940 recorded 2 per cent of the population as Indian, while in the two neighbouring districts the percentage was 61 and 62 per cent. The census records of the nineteenth century show Huaylas with around 30 per cent of Indians, and there are further anomalies in the recent records of births. In 1906, there were 88 *mestizo* births to 66 Indian; in 1927, there were 218 *mestizo* births but no Indian; in 1934 there were 36 *mestizo* and 234 Indian; from 1937 to 1941 there were no Indian births but a steady level of around 300 *mestizo*. These vagaries are directly related to changes of the district secretary and clearly display how subjective are the standards by which 'race' is judged, once the

[1] Paul Larrabee Doughty, 'Peruvian Highlanders in a Changing World: Social Integration and Culture Change in an Andean District'.

unmistakable criterion of living in an Indian community is abandoned.

Huaylas was chosen for his study by Paul Doughty because it was primarily *mestizo* and he wanted to test certain hypotheses. He had a clear picture of the two cultures, Indian and *mestizo*, based on what he had seen himself at Vicos and on the literature, particularly a study of Recuayhuanca near Vicos by Joan Snyder. The Indian was regarded by the *mestizo* as typically dirty, primitive, and ignorant, and was denied access to the means by which these characteristics could be altered; at Recuayhuanca, Indians who had been away to earn money and had adopted Spanish dress and customs and the Spanish language were not accepted by the *mestizos*; on the other hand they themselves —having presumably moved into the intermediate class of *cholo*— despised the Indians who had not moved or changed their ways. His hypotheses were based on the supposed rigidity and exclusiveness of these two cultures. It was generally assumed—he argued—that the problem of Peru was to be solved by 'improving' the Indian. But might it not be the case that this could not be done until *mestizo* attitudes changed; that the problem of Peru, like the dilemma of the United States, was essentially a white problem? Since there was a great lack of information about *mestizos* in the *sierra* it was worth testing his hypotheses in a *mestizo* community.

He found that in fact Huaylas was an exception to almost all he had expected; the social structure was much less rigid and there was unusual public spirit and a strong feeling of local pride. There was eagerness to initiate public works and a readiness to contribute labour to carry them out. There was rivalry between the *barrios* or wards but this was worked off annually at *fiestas* and forgotten afterwards. Suspicion and distrust of the central government were marked, however, and to this must be attributed the anti-clericalism which was strong among the men, even though they described themselves as '*muy catolicos*'.

Local pride and public spirit he attributed to a variety of reasons, notably the absence of *haciendas* and Indian communities, and the fact that everyone in Huaylas depends on the land, which is distributed comparatively evenly. This distribution seems to have taken place in the early days of the republic, when the liberal principles of Bolivar were acted on in this district, while elsewhere they were ignored or made an excuse for concentrating more land in the hands of a few. This became an area of small holdings, and the fact that the district is famous for its harvests no doubt contributed to the local conviction of being superior to neighbouring districts. Altogether, Huaylas is for Peru an unusually homogeneous society. Further, the people of Huaylas take an optimistic view of their economy; they think improvement can be achieved—something so rare in a peasant community that it has sometimes been supposed that to persuade them of this is the first step towards progress.

I do not believe that this unusually favourable picture is to be attributed to the optimism of a likeable and extrovert observer. The evidence is thorough and convincing. I have dwelt on Huaylas, although I believe it is an extreme exception, partly because the expectations that were falsified illustrate the general rule, partly because it exemplifies the great variety of local situations, but above all because it is an exception, not only to the general pattern of Peruvian society in the *sierras*, but also to the general rule that a problem cannot be solved by saying that it does not exist. That seems to be exactly what did happen in the early days of the Republic when, for some unexplained reason,[1] the land here really was distributed. The Indian community was replaced by a body of small and relatively prosperous farmers who became *mestizos*. Once the process had begun, it accelerated and the Indians of Huaylas disappeared, only to be occasionally resuscitated by a socially ambitious district clerk. The result in Huaylas is a class society in which physical appearance is of secondary importance, but in which racial mixture can be wryly remembered. For example, a popular song about a mining disaster ends:

> Such is life, Cholita,
> And such is life, Zambita,
> For two miserable *reales*
> The poor man loses his life.

'Cholita' of course is the affectionate diminutive of *chola*, and 'Zambita' is a girl who is the offspring of Negro and Indian.

## 6 Comparisons

In Huaylas, then, as in Mexico, everyone is *mestizo*. But for most of Peru, the two cultures are a pressing reality and a sharp obstacle to progress. Why has Peruvian society defined itself so differently from Mexican? The answers, I believe, are to be found in the nature of the pre-Columbian empire and in the Spanish reaction to the geography of the Andes.

As we have said, the empire of the Incas was far more monolithic than that of the Aztecs and the shock of its destruction must have been more intense. It had been on the whole a benevolent autocracy and had been felt as part of the divine order; it was replaced by a much *worse* government, in the sense that it did less for the people. A visitor to the Andes has only to use his eyes to see evidence everywhere of Inca terracing abandoned, of a decline in population, as well as a fall in the standard and in the extent of cultivation. The Incas

---

[1] The *encomendera* early in the sixteenth century was the granddaughter of the Inca emperor. But it does not seem likely that two hundred and fifty years later this tradition contributed to the special treatment of this area. (See p. 243.)

had wanted good harvests; the Spaniards wanted gold to take away. The *encomenderos* of Peru seem frequently to have treated their responsibilities with contempt and to have abused the right to levy forced labour; the Inca forced labour or *mita* had been for the good of the community, the *encomendero's* was for himself. All this contributed to the Andean peasant's sense of loss; he retired within his own defences and avoided, so far as he could, all contact with his conquerors.

Language made this easier for him than for the Mexican. Quechua was the language throughout the empire (except in the Aymara-speaking parts of Bolivia) and it formed a bond between Indians.[1] At the same time, the fact that Quechua was so widely spoken induced the Spaniards to learn it and speak it. It was of value to them to a greater extent than Nahuatl could be in Mexico, when many other Indian languages were still spoken. And because the Spaniards learned Quechua, the Indians did not need to learn Spanish, as they far more frequently did in Mexico. Thus, as speakers of Quechua only, they were distinguished from the Spanish who used Quechua as a second tongue. In Mexico, the bilingual man more often belonged to the subordinate culture and aspired to the superior; in Peru, the bilingual more often belonged to the dominant group and looked down on the unilingual. But the difference is one of degree and can be exaggerated.

Of greater importance is the geography of the Andes. The climate of the Valley of Mexico for a Southern Spaniard is reminiscent of home; on the other hand, Vera Cruz, the port of entry, was hot and malarial. No other course suggested itself than to rebuild Tenochtitlan as a Spanish city and make this the centre of government. But Cuzco, at nearly twice the height, the Spanish found uninviting, while the coast was dry desert, which by irrigation could be made fertile. It was free from malaria and surprisingly cool for a latitude so near the equator. On the Feast of the Epiphany Pizarro founded the City of the Three Kings, now known as Lima from the river Rimac on which it stands. It was a completely new site; he rejected Pachacamac, a ceremonial Indian centre only twenty miles away; Lima became the centre of government and the seat of the Viceroy. It has ever since drained population away from the *sierras*; in colonial times, the great landowners, even if they drew their wealth from the hills, looked on Lima as the centre of civilization; to-day, Lima sucks from the impoverished Indian communities and the little towns of the Andes all who hope to improve their chances in life. No one can apportion with accuracy the biological inheritance of any part of Peru but there can surely be no doubt that Lima has proved a cultural sponge, drawing off the Hispanicism of the mountain country and leaving the Indian behind.

[1] There are, however, parts of Ecuador where local languages survived the Incas but were replaced by Quechua under the guidance of the missionaries.

Quechua and Lima are perhaps enough by themselves to explain why Peru and Mexico are so different in the proportions of Hispanic to Indian. But there is a third factor, the sheer poverty of the *altiplano*, the high plateau country. The corridors of the Andes, the valleys of 9,000 feet or so, are attractive places to live, but not the country of 13,000 feet or over, the high moorland. The people of this territory stayed Indian because there was nothing there to exploit and it was worth no one's while to disturb them.

The Andean parts of Ecuador and Bolivia are a continuum of highland Peru and many of the same factors apply. In both there are two cultures, but relationships between them are different. In Ecuador, they are probably more sharply divided even than in Peru. Quito, the centre of government, stayed in the hills and there is no phenomenon exactly comparable with Lima, but the wealth of the country lies on the coast, where almost all the goods for export are grown. Foreign traders and banks have come to the coast and attract the modern elements. The distance between the two cultures in the hills must be due partly to this and partly perhaps to the fact that the empire of the Incas was recent and there was a less developed civilization for the Spanish to make use of. Whatever the cause, in the hills the division of society quickly became complete; there was Spanish landowner, Indian serf, and little between. A middle class grew slowly, and that principally on the coast. Certainly, it was in Ecuador that I heard the most strongly expressed views as to the incurable inferiority of Indians.

The Andean part of Bolivia is also geographically a continuation of Peru, but Bolivia has no coast. Since the coast in the other two countries is Hispanic, this in itself alters the balance. Peru and Ecuador, including their coastal element and depending on how one draws the line, may be about half 'Indian'; Bolivia is two-thirds or three-quarters Indian. In recent years this section of the community has attained a confidence in being Indian that is quite foreign to Peru. Bolivia had its Second Revolution in 1952, forty years after Mexico's; as in Mexico, the Revolution changed the emphasis rather than making startling changes that affected the peasant at once. As in Mexico, the Bolivian revolution has seemed to stand still or run backwards, but a change has all the same taken place. And it is one-third of the country, not five-sixths as in Mexico, which belongs to the Hispanic culture. For this one-third, a highly vulnerable minority, the question of how the two cultures can be integrated is vital; the one culture fills the ranks of civil service, schoolmasters, lawyers, university teachers, doctors. The other is still a peasant culture and has to be transformed if it is to play a part in the modern world. Bolivia's problem in this respect is different in kind because the numerical proportions are different.

The closer one looks, however, at the situations in any of the countries we have considered, the greater are the diversities and the qualifications that become necessary within any generalization. We have seen that about five-sixths of the people of Mexico are in a single culture, one social spectrum. The one-sixth who are outside this and are still counted as Indians present among themselves an immense diversity. In the highland parts of the Southern state, Chiapas, which marches with Guatemala, they are two-thirds of the population; but in the state as a whole they are only 10 or 11 per cent. Even in the highlands of Chiapas to-day, two Indian languages are spoken. The Indian groups differ from each other in many of their religious beliefs, in their attitudes to their neighbours, and to the *ladinos*, that is to say, those who are not Indians.[1] Pitt-Rivers has discussed at length the differences between the Indians, their relations with the *ladinos*, and their spiritual beliefs. Some of these communities are those from the sixteenth century which survived the nineteenth; others are new creations since the Second Revolution; there are thus constitutional differences between them as well as social.

The criterion of what makes an Indian is his integration into an Indian community. 'Integration' is, I suggest, a word to be used cautiously and seldom without qualification. Integration into what? And to what extent? And does it mean disintegration from something else? In the case of these small Indian communities, of not more than four or five thousand people each, it is clear as a rule that a man either belongs to the community or he does not. Birth or marriage are the only ways in, and even marriage does not qualify entirely. A man may leave for a time and come back, or he may leave and never come back; it may not be easy to say what his intentions are while absent, but if he does return he must accept the total situation, a network of duties, ties, and obligations. But when he is integrated in an Indian community, he is excluded from the mainstream of Mexican life. If an Indian leaves Chiapas for Mexico City, he ceases to be an Indian; he becomes simply a poor Mexican.

Back in Chiapas, he is faced by two cultures, at least as divergent as those in Peru. Even where *ladinos* and Indians appear to be engaged in some shared activity, they may have quite different ideas of what is happening. For example, both may engage during Holy Week in ceremonies which outwardly reveal no difference of intention; but to the Indians the Holy Cross may be a spiritual force in its own right with power to make rain, with a personality of its own, addressed as a saint. The Holy Sepulchre too has an autonomous power and represents to them the sowing of seed and the rebirth of life in the harvest. In one *pueblo*, the *ladinos* taking part in the processions are identified by the Indians with 'the Jews', the enemies of Christ.

But deeply divided though the two cultures are, they interact on

[1] Julian Pitt-Rivers, 'Words and Deeds: The Ladinos of Chiapas'; 'Mestizo or Ladino?'; 'Pseudo-kinship'.

each other and the *ladinos* of Chiapas have many beliefs which they repudiate when confronted with someone from Mexico City or the United States. Witchcraft, for instance, they will say is confined to Indians and no *ladino* believes in such things. This they say because they know that people from the Western or modern world generally scoff at such beliefs, but they will often add some revealing phrase, such as, 'I don't really believe in it of course but . . .'; and then there will follow (recounts Pitt-Rivers) 'a wealth of anecdote giving incontrovertible testimony of the effects of witchcraft'. The *ladinos* of this isolated state thus form a sub-culture within the main stream of Mexican life; but this is not a threat to the homogeneity of the whole. The fact that they define themselves as 'not Indian' forces them to accept, ostensibly and outwardly, the system of thought which is sceptical of witchcraft.

Thus we come back to the question of 'integration'. It is clear that the *ladinos* in Chiapas are part of the national life and are defined as distinct from the Indian population of the state. To-day therefore they are unlikely to insist on increased autonomy for Chiapas as against the federal government. But this was not always so; early in the period of the Second Revolution, the landowners of Chiapas led a rebellion against the revolutionary government. It was reactionary; its leader, General Pineda, rebelled because the government was anti-clerical and passed a law prohibiting debt peonage. The rebellion was largely successful, which is one reason why Chiapas is still so different from the rest of Mexico, and the memory of this rebellion therefore provides an example of the dilemma in which the landowning class of highland Chiapas continually find themselves. They still disapprove of the federal government's wish to break up estates but they are debarred from being Chiapanec rather than Mexican because they are a minority in Chiapas. So they must be good Mexicans—and this means approving of the revolution—yet continue to be proud of Pineda, and this they have contrived to do by turning their hero into a 'revolutionary' hero and forgetting that in fact *his* revolution was intended to overthrow the Mexican revolution which they now profess to admire.

In the long run their dilemma is more acute than most of them probably perceive. For some of them still have estates—here called *finca* not *hacienda*. They may conceal the extent of their lands by allotting parts of them to sons and cousins, or they may avoid alienation by keeping on the right side of the head of the department of land reform. But the danger remains. And *ladinos* of a much larger class, who have no estates, profit by keeping the Indians poor and ignorant so that they are available as cheap labour. It is hard to believe that any Indians would to-day follow a Pineda and they must rather be assumed to agree with Mexico City that *fincas* should be broken up and the status of Indians improved. The estate-owners as *ladinos* are 'not Indian' and must therefore be on the side of Mexico City in respect of education, modernity, and everything that is likely to encourage the Indians to rebel against their subordinate status. The only escape from this dilemma would have been to continue as reactionary regionalists —and they are no longer strong enough for this; political control of the state is no longer in their hands, but with the bourgeois *ladinos* of the plains.

There are two curiosities of terminology to which Pitt-Rivers draws attention and which throw some light on the question of how people define themselves and integrate—or do not integrate—into other groups. In the part of Mexico which was the Viceroyalty of New Spain, North of the Isthmus of Tehuantepec, we have to-day *mestizos* and Indians. In Guatemala and Chiapas (which were once the *audiencia* of Guatemala) there are *ladinos* and Indians. But in Yucatan the '*mestizos*' are the people who speak a Mayan language and wear Indian clothes, and this term is not used of those who speak Spanish and wear city clothes, who refer to themselves by some such periphrasis as '*gente decente*'—respectable people—a term which elsewhere is not opposed to *mestizo* but synonymous with it.

Pitt-Rivers suggests that it is not mere accident that *ladino* is used in Guatemala and Chiapas for just the person who in New Spain is *mestizo*. The term '*ladino*' was used in Spain before the conquest of Mexico for an African who had adopted Spanish speech.[1] Guatemala and Chiapas were controlled by the Church, mainly by monks of the Dominican Order. It was their business to convert and educate and they therefore used a cultural term to describe the acknowledged product of their energies—the educated Indian who spoke Spanish. No doubt racial crosses occurred but it was preferable to conceal them beneath a cultural white sheet. In New Spain on the other hand, the secular arm was predominant, and the Spanish laymen were proud of their paternity; here therefore a term was used which emphasized genetic origin.

This is not a matter on which certainty is possible; it can never be more than an interesting hypothesis, and the same is true of the even odder anomaly from Yucatan. This region was distinguished from Chiapas and Guatemala by language. Here a form of the ancient Mayan language was universally understood and, as in Peru with Quechua, the Spanish learnt it and spoke it. Here it was possible for an Indian chief to keep his own language and his identity as an Indian although he spoke Spanish. The offspring of the estate-owners were distinguished from such Indians not by language but by genetic factors and thus were known as *mestizos*. Thus *blancos*, *mestizos*, Spanish-

[1] In Brazil, assimilated Negro slaves were known as *ladinos* as late as 1800 (see D. Pierson, *Negroes in Brazil*).

speaking Indians, and monolingual Indians continued until the Indian rising of the mid-nineteenth century; this the whites regarded as a race war and therefore extended the term *mestizos* to cover all those who did not rebel. Only the 'rebels' were Indians and after the war the term came to apply mainly to the rebels who retired into the jungle and remained undefeated. Whether this account carries conviction or not, it draws attention to the variety of ways in which people define themselves and the society they belong to.

But in the highlands of Chiapas, Indians have survived, in isolated peasant communities, poor, uneducated, looked down on by the *ladinos* but not outlaws or jungle-dwellers. And Pitt-Rivers suggests that they find in their life considerable compensations; certainly there are Indians who having made good in a wider world come back to an Indian *pueblo*. Why is this? In the first place, there is the satisfaction, common to many small communities, of knowing and being known, of being linked by many strands into an intelligible community. Pitt-Rivers argues that the system of religious belief is consistent, although in a sense it is a falsification to speak as though 'religious' belief could be separated from secular, for it is an important mark of this kind of world that religious and secular are not distinguished. It is a world in which 'strength of spirit'[1] is all-important and this, though bestowed by divine gift, can be cultivated and improved by holding a series of offices known as '*cargos*' (a word which may mean a burden as well as an office or post) in the religious fraternities connected with saints and feast days. There is a regular hierarchy of such posts and they must be held in the proper order, rising from humbler posts to the more important. On taking office—which usually involves expense and always fasting and sexual abstinence before the relevant *fiesta*— the office-holder takes an oath and thereby becomes sacred and immune from witchcraft. When his office is complete, he is a *pasado*—like a Masonic Past Master—and although it is now possible to assail him by witchcraft, his power is considerably enhanced and he may escape. If he is a good man, the guardians of the *pueblo* will probably defend him against evil. To be good and deserving of protection means that he is willing 'to show respect where it is due, to serve his people, to spend his wealth in *cargos*, to help his needy neighbour, to give presents of food to others, to beware of provoking jealousy and to avoid quarrelling which incites witchcraft. . . .'[2]

These are achievements that would win respect in any rural community; if the system of thought is such—as it is here—that they not only win respect from men but protection by spiritual forces together

---

[1] It seems in this respect to have affinity with the 'Bantu philosophy'; see Placide Tempels, *Bantu Philosophy*.

[2] Julian Pitt-Rivers, 'Social, Cultural, and Linguistic Change in the Highlands of Chiapas'.

with personal strength of spirit—then he is indeed a happy man. And if he is healthy and successful and respected he can be confident that he has a strong spirit. There is here a spiral of good fortune which the modern world offers to few. It is a dangerous and exciting life, because the reverse of the spiral also holds good; if not crowned with success, the aspirant for spiritual power has lost the favour of the guardians and has deserved it. He must be a bad man and if a bad man is not killed by witchcraft he is liable to be killed as a witch. There is no doubt that in these communities many such murders do occur. It is play for high stakes.

But the game depends on the world of the *pueblo* being enclosed, shut off completely from that of the *ladinos*. The traditional Indian does not regard the *ladinos* as 'people'; witchcraft will not touch them, partly because their flesh and their smell are so unpleasant that they would repel the familiar[1] of any self-respecting witch. Yet there are many Indians, forced to leave the community and work in the town, whose aspiration is to become *ladinos*. Inconsistencies should never surprise any student of human affairs; nothing is more common than dual and inconsistent sets of beliefs and values, kept in separate compartments and used by the same person. But this need not here be the case; the Indian who wants to become a *ladino* is unlikely to have been the successful holder of *cargos* just pictured. The satisfaction of the latter arises from the fact that his world is enclosed; to him, if he can understand what is happening in it, the world of the *ladinos* must seem strangely cold, poor, and unsatisfying. It is built up of two-way relationships—employer and employed, buyer and seller, landlord and tenant. The motto of this world is '*no me toca*'—it doesn't touch me; I can pass by on the other side. No one in the Indian community can ever do that.

One more region must be brought into these comparisons; it is important because it illuminates the whole problem. Guatemala is in many ways like Chiapas, with which under the Spanish it formed one administrative whole. But it is a unified sovereign state, instead of a state in Federal Mexico; it has three times the population of Chiapas and 53 per cent of the population are classed as Indian, whereas in Chiapas as a whole the proportion is only about 11 per cent. It is thus in numerical proportions more like the highland parts of Chiapas. But in the Western region of Guatemala, the Indians are everywhere twice as strong as the *ladinos*, and in one department they are as high as 97 per cent. And here the social structure is quite different from Chiapas. Here the Church was strong enough in the seventeenth century to keep to a minimum the alienation of Indian land to Spanish overlords

---

[1] Julian Pitt-Rivers, 'Social, Cultural, and Linguistic Change in the Highlands of Chiapas'. But the *naqual* is not quite the 'familiar' of European witches.

and in the nineteenth century the even more dangerous alienation in the name of free enterprise. Indian society therefore developed organically and to be an Indian does not necessarily indicate a servile status, as in Southern Ecuador. There are towns predominantly Indian, and some Indians are comfortably off. They have kept many customs characteristically Indian but have modified or changed them where necessary; this is very different from the deliberate revival of forgotten custom associated with *indigenismo* as a cult. And because of this healthy and continuous modification it is not possible to draw a smooth curve of acculturation and place a person or a community in it. There are towns where many people classed as Indian speak Spanish in the home; this is mostly where they are in minority, but even where the population is overwhelmingly Indian there are some. There are some communities where most Indian women, even the well-to-do, dress in Indian style, even when they speak Spanish in the home. Dress and language, the two indications of being Indian, which in highland Chiapas usually correspond, here vary independently. Just as biological characteristics vary independently of social, so too do the cultural characteristics. And ethnic affiliation—whether a person is Indian or *ladino*—cannot be decided by any one of these criteria. The census authorities in Guatemala have therefore wisely decided that the sole ground for classification shall be public opinion in the community.

Let us turn to a broader conspectus. At the beginning of this chapter, two questions were asked on which I hoped to throw light. One of these has, I believe, been largely answered by implication already. The difference between racial attitudes in Spanish and English colonies was due to the nature of the societies they came from and to their view of man's place in nature and society. The Spaniards came from a society far from homogeneous, divided, until quite recently, between different kingdoms, different religions—Christian, Moslem, Jew—and different ethnic groups—Spanish, Berber, Arab. In this variety, religion became the unifying force and the cardinal factor in social definition. Thus a converted Indian became part of the Spanish polity. The Church was a strong centralized institution, with universal values and dogmatic views as to the salvation of all souls; in Spain, it shared with the Crown an interest in defending the people against the nobles and thus obtaining their support. In America, the Indians took the place of 'the people' and the *encomenderos* that of the nobles.

In contrast, the English came from a far more homogeneous society, less rigidly stratified, with a strong sense of its own identity against the rest of the world. There was no tradition of anyone becoming English except by birth or residence for several generations. The Anglican Church had no firm centralized direction and in Virginia, for example, so strong was the Vestry system that a parish priest was 'completely dependent on the goodwill of his leading parishioners'.[1] The power of the Crown was less; already, in the early seventeenth century, a beginning had been made of the system perfected in the eighteenth century, whereby nobles and squires professing to represent the people ruled in the name of a monarch with little personal power. The younger sons of this ruling class went to Maryland and Virginia and decided, with virtually no interference by Crown or Church, how they would define their own society and treat their subordinates; before the end of the seventeenth century, they framed stringent laws against racial mixture. They were colonists not conquerors; they drove the Indians away and made little attempt either to rule or to convert them. And here, as we saw in Part II, the nature of the indigenous society played a part.

But this is by no means the whole story. There are exceptions to all national differences; nevertheless, broad differences do exist. Below the surface of social and political organization there lay between Spanish and English profoundly different attitudes to sex, to religion, and to the self. The Spanish layman seemed eager to proclaim his male potency, the Englishman as a rule to conceal it. To say that this was due to a difference between Catholic and Protestant outlook is only to put the question a stage further back. No doubt, a view of the world that stressed the sacramental is of help in resolving the conflict between spirit and flesh that has disturbed Europeans since Plato, and Christians since St. Paul. No doubt the practice of confession helps to resolve the parallel conflict between a man's ideal of what he would like to be and what he knows he is. But why does one nation as a whole reject such aids to personal integration and another cherish them so eagerly? It is not easy to be dogmatic about the psychological components of the attitudes of men who died three centuries ago; but, to this observer at least, it seems that the Pauline dualism over sex as well as a strong sense of race difference is present in the order of the Governor and Council of Virginia in September 1630 that 'Hugh Davis be soundly whipped, before an assembly of Negroes and others, for abusing himself to the dishonour of God and shame of Christians, by defiling his body in lying with a Negro'.[2]

It was largely due to the influence of a Church with a strong central authority that, to take one example, it was reckoned a virtuous act in Spanish colonies to bequeath a slave his freedom when making a will. In Virginia, on the other hand, there was hostility to such manumission and even to the existence of freedmen within the territory, culminating in 1852 in the provision in the State constitution that the General Assembly might restrict the power of owners to free their slaves and pass laws for the removal of the free Negro population.[3] But the attitude to paternity seems, in my view, to stem from a deeper psychological cause.

[1] H. S. Klein, *Slavery in the Americas*.　　　[2] Ibid.　　　[3] Ibid.

This question is linked with the difference in Spanish attitudes to the Indian and to the Negro. Let it be said first that there was a similar, though far from identical, difference in the English colonies too. The English colonials never had to deal with Indians of a high culture. They and their successors drove the redskins westward, exterminating many during the journey, and eventually produced a situation in which the redskin might be a problem to himself but was no longer a danger to the white man. When the Iroquois were a military confederation of six nations, they were a military threat; when that power was broken, a Mohawk seeking employment was not felt to present a social or economic challenge. It became a matter of pride to own to an Indian great-grandmother, which in any case implied incidentally that one had family records and had been some generations in America. In the United States, almost as in Spanish America, the Indian came to be defined as much by affiliation to a community as by genetic origin; it became possible to be a part-time Indian, leaving the status of Indian in the Reserve and taking it up on return. But it is not possible to be a part-time Negro. The Negro came as an individual and as a slave and, since the only society to which he could belong was white society, it was necessary, if he was to be excluded, to exclude him completely, and as an individual.

For the Spanish colonies, too, there was the background of slavery and the association of African appearance with slave ancestors. The Indian was sometimes enslaved and was often little better than a slave, but he was protected by law as the Negro never was; marriage with an Indian was possible as it was not with an African. Why was this? Africans had never been respected as a military threat. There was too the fact that the Pope had made Indians, but not Africans, wards of the King of Spain. Perhaps this is enough to explain the fact that they were not protected by law from slavery as the Indian was; I do not think it is enough to account for the lower place they always held, except as labour, in the Spanish mind. Las Casas, for instance, for long excluded the Negro from the benefits he fought to secure for the Indian.

I suggest, as a hypothesis, that this has something to do with the great Chain of Being which, since Plato and Plotinus, through Augustine and Aquinas, had been a part of Western thought.[1] If God had created a universe of equal beings, the argument ran, it would have been an incomplete world; to make it complete, He had to create a full range of beings, from archangels and angels through men and animals to snails and slugs. This idea of a hierarchic scale was revived in the nineteenth century by the Social Darwinists in a different form, but

---

[1] It derives from what some theologians call the Principle of Plenitude, the idea that a perfect world must be full and must therefore include lower forms of being.

at the time of Cortés it was part of the stock-in-trade of theologians, and, in a simpler form, of all Spaniards. If Negroes were put lower in the hierarchy than Indians, as they were, it seems plausible that this was on grounds of colour, because of the strong associations of darkness with evil. This runs through the metaphor of Greek, Latin, and Hebrew and, therefore, of European languages; it is also to be found in Persian and Sanskrit.[1] It is not a matter in which proof is possible, but the Spanish were not immune from this confusion of biological fact with religious and poetic metaphor.

## 7 Conclusions

We are back again, whichever way we turn, at the same problem, varying from one region to another in the terms used, and presenting very different aspects because the proportions differ between the two cultures. To increase the number of examples would undoubtedly provide fresh nuances and emphases. But the point has been reached when it is necessary to try to sum up the essence of the situation which in varying forms presents itself in these areas of Spanish conquest and high Indian cultures, to consider the assumptions underlying the various approaches to it, and to see if we can detect any tendencies likely to develop.

The question is everywhere one of social definition and of integration into one or another of two societies. Definition and integration in this sense are like the opposite sides of a piece of thin metal embossed with a picture which shows in reverse on the other side. An individual may be defined by *mestizos* as Indian; by other Indians of his own community he is seen as an integrated part of their own familiar society. At the time of the Conquest, there were two quite separate cultures, Hispanic and Indian; the result of the Conquest was everywhere a stage where the Hispanic culture was dominant, being represented by *encomenderos*, priests, officials; there was usually an intermediate group of *mestizo* artisans and clerks, and at the other end of the scale the peons on the estates and the Indian communities. The relationship between estate-owner and Indian was many-stranded in the sense of covering all aspects of life, like that of a feudal serf to a European seigneur. Behind and beyond any legal obligations lay a vast hinterland of undefined rights and duties, the expectation of total protection on one side and total service on the other.

From this many-stranded dominance to the single-stranded relationship of factory-hand with his employer is a long journey, interspersed by many intermediate stages which to some extent reproduce the older link. The *patron* reappears in many forms; he may be a foreman or a political leader or the official of a local authority. He may

[1] I have argued this at more length elsewhere; see *Encounter* (April 1968).

extend his rule by *compadrazgo*; that is to say, he will let it be known that as a man of influence and authority he is a good man to have as *compadre*, the godfather of one's child. A *compadre* may be an equal or a relation but sometimes a superior is approached, and in this case, if the invitation is accepted, the relationship which arises may be one of patronage, not dissimilar from that of the Tutsi overlord and his client. The understanding behind it may be on one side, 'I am your man', and on the other, 'I will protect you'. But it will not be so binding as the relationship in Ruanda.[1]

But whatever are the intermediate stages, there has been an assumption running through legislation, Spanish and republican, common to Mexico and Peru, to the *Institutos para los Indigenas* and to the programmes of American aid. It is expressed in the motto of the *Instituto Nacional Indigenista* of Mexico: '*Redimir al Indio es integrar la patria*'— 'To redeem the Indian is to integrate the Fatherland.' This comes to mean, in effect, that the Indian must be persuaded to give up being an Indian; until recently this has almost everywhere been the sole condition on which he can improve his lot. To redeem the Indian is not so often to-day seen, as it was in the nineteenth century, as simply a matter of getting him to change his speech and dress; it is recognized that the first thing is to get him to conceive an economy which can be improved, an environment which can be controlled. He, of course, is not the only peasant in the world to think of this world's goods as a fixed amount and of anyone who gets more than himself as a cheat, to picture all strangers as cheats, and to limit his own moral responsibility to a close circle of kin and neighbours. F. G. Bailey, speaking specifically of peasants in Orissa, in the Indian Union, has suggested by implication that most peasants share this outlook.[2] Government officials usually wish to change it and most academic studies involve the assumption, explicit or implicit, that it must be changed. It is, for example, implicit in the title—*Indians in Misery*—of the Cornell-I.E.R.A.C. report already referred to and it is explicit in its conclusions.

If the extreme peasant outlook is to be changed, I agree with Professor Bailey that it will not be done by moral exhortation but—if one rules out the extremes of compulsion said to have been used in communist countries—only by demonstrating some course of action that produces visible results quickly and does not interfere with some other aspect of peasant life which the outsider does not understand.

---

[1] The relationship of *compadrazgo* varies from one region to another: as between Hispanic and Indian and as between one Hispanic and another; and according to the interpretation of individuals. But there is always a link of a special kind; ' . . . *matar a un compadre es ofender al Creador* . . .'—'to kill a *compadre* is an offence against the Creator' —runs a saying quoted by Pitt-Rivers, implying that it is no offence if you kill someone else. And I was told that this concept constantly recurs in confession; it is much more serious to cheat or abuse your *compadre* than anyone else.

[2] F. G. Bailey, 'The Peasant View of the Bad Life'.

But it is as well to recognize the extent of the changes that are likely to occur, of the resistance that is likely to be met, and of the ills that will follow and have to be set against the advantages. Indians in Ecuador have killed those who came to redeem them; others no doubt have been prevented only by fear from doing the same. 'Certain of the Indians frankly expressed their desire to continue living like their ancestors', write the authors of the Cornell-I.E.R.A.C. report—and it is reasonable to assume that others who were not so frank had similar desires. And, as we have said, there are cases of Indians who have made good coming back to their community to be reabsorbed.

There must, then, be compensations in the Indian life. It is not all misery, or at least not in Chiapas. There is, first of all, a choice of reaction to the world outside the Indian community. The established *ladinos* pour scorn on the *indio revestido*, the Indian who has just abandoned Indian clothes, and to this one answer is to become as nervously ultra-Spanish as one knows how to contrive. But, with greater confidence and sophistication, it is also possible to assert firmly that one *is* different and would prefer to be a first-class Indian rather than a second-class Spaniard. This, as we saw in Part I of this book, is the answer being given increasingly, all over the world, by the people who in the last century were colonial subjects. It remains, however, a somewhat negative answer unless being an Indian provides some positive compensation as well. And as we have seen there are clear suggestions that it does.

Is it possible for the Indian to keep some at least of the advantages of being an Indian and yet make some progress in health and well-being and control of his surroundings? It will certainly not be easy, because, as we have seen, one of the attributes of the good Indian is not to arouse jealousy. And this is surely an obstacle in most peasant societies. In the Himalayan district of Garhwal, I recall a situation that constantly recurred; I would meet a soldier discharged from the army after seven years' service or more, on his way back to his village. Army pay was high by Indian standards, rations were good, and a man acquired a strong spirit of confidence in self and pride in the regiment. He had been taught that he must look after the health of himself and his family, using a mosquito-net if he lived below a certain height, taking sanitary precautions, eating vegetables—and he had accepted a host of other admonitions which he believed were good for himself and for the people. Cheerfully and confidently he would tell me his plans; but a year later I would find him listless or dispirited; his fellow-villagers would not let him live better than themselves.

This kind of jealousy may perhaps be overcome by some evolutionary process within the system. But the world of spiritual conflict is another matter. It is hardly consistent with modern business and agriculture. The old conception of redeeming the Indian by integrating him into the mainstream of modern life, means the disintegration of his old world and very likely a serious disintegration of his personality. There is no need here to enlarge on what has so often happened to tribesman or countryman suddenly brought to the big cities and faced with destruction of his whole system of beliefs and therefore with the loss of his self-respect, his self-confidence, his moral standards. It has been said often enough. But it is not enough merely to keep him in his village. Human beings are seldom consistent; there are cases of school-children who will explain to their teacher how the movements of the earth and the heavenly bodies cause an eclipse but at home will agree with their parents on some magical or mythological cause. To teach a peasant to spray his crops against rust, mildew, and blight will not prevent his attempting to propitiate the spirit of the corn. He may all his life apply in different contexts two contradictory systems of causality. But new beliefs end a static system; they introduce movement and the need for adaptation. They make way for a spirit of questioning that is applied to social institutions as well as to crops.

It is surely a very large assumption that agricultural success will be enough to replace a complex spiritual world that has evolved through centuries. The first task for an Institute for the Natives is therefore psychological; unless it can introduce new beliefs which give life some meaning—and this is hard for bureaucracy—it must recognize that every step in providing new techniques opens the way for some invasion in the world of ideas. There are plenty ready to enter a house that is swept and garnished—Communism, Nationalism, Regionalism, various forms of emotional revivalism. One thing seems certain: expectations are growing. There will be more comparison with the life of others; the sense of deprivation and discontent will increase.

These are generalities which in varying degrees have application to most peasant communities. To return specifically to Spanish America, in parts of Ecuador and Guatemala there are Indian communities in which a middle class begins to emerge. A man who has made money as a trader is continuing to speak an Indian language and to dress in a way that marks him as Indian; 'in Quetzaltenango, the second city of Guatemala, the *ladinos* complain to-day that the Indians are getting all the commerce of the town into their hands and are running them out of business'.[1] Otevalo in Ecuador is a somewhat similar case. What has not, so far as I am aware, been studied is the system of beliefs and values of these new middle-class Indians. Is it only in their clothes and speech that they differ from the *ladino* middle classes? And how does this situation compare with Paraguay, where an Indian language is the official language of the state? On the assumption, however, that they are still Indian in a deeper sense than this, is there any prospect of

[1] Julian Pitt-Rivers, *After the Empire: Race and Society in Middle America and the Andes*.

something of this kind becoming more general, and what might be the consequence? Is it a reasonable hypothesis that with the emergence of a middle class from a subordinate ethnic group, there will arise also greater regional awareness and perhaps a demand for greater regional autonomy?

Consider for a moment the Welsh. In the nineteenth century, to speak Welsh only was an unmistakable sign of being not merely rural and backward but poor and uneducated. Even to have spoken Welsh in the home suggested such an origin and the path to advancement was not merely to learn English but to merge in English culture. But to-day there is a confident assertion that it should be possible to stay Welsh—not unilingual but bilingual and Welsh in culture and feeling—and yet make a career of distinction; there begins also to be a political movement for autonomy. This is surely linked with a different attitude, both in England and Wales, to the rigidity of class, and to more widespread opportunities for education, wealth, and power.

Surely something of this kind is likely to occur wherever there is a substantial element of the population still classed as Indian, and where an Indian middle class begins to emerge? Quetzaltenango in Guatemala, Yucatan, parts of Ecuador, the Zapotecs, come to mind. Can successful traders and lawyers hold the confidence of the rural classes from which they spring and will they have the public spirit to act as leaders to rural communities? If they do, there seems to be a possibility of regional revolutions, essentially Indian in character, in which Indians will keep their self-confidence and a pride in being Indian. There is here a possibility of something different from the bogus *indigenismo* of those who have first become *ladino* or *mestizo*, in other words Hispanic in outlook, and who then proceed to retrace their steps and deify aspects of an imaginary past.

Where this does not happen, it seems likely that the cities will continue to suck away from the Indian communities a high proportion of young men; to be 'Indian' in the sense of belonging to a community and speaking an Indian language will be increasingly to be backward and the term will apply to fewer and fewer. The distinction between 'Indian' and '*mestizo*' will thus become less important as a formal classification and there will be more and more people inside the social spectrum who were once classed as Indian and outside. Since there are fewer formal barriers, since few know their neighbours as members of a community in the anonymous jungle of a great city, people will feel more and more the need for marks of identification. Racial characteristics are thus likely to become more rather than less important.

There is another possible line of development, which arises more from the world situation than from changes in the local scene. The sense of anger and betrayal, so widespread among people who are not white and among the young, has produced a doctrine of absolute revolution, that is to say, a revolution that does not commit itself in any detail to the society it will build when it has overthrown the present. In South America, revolutionaries of this school proclaim that only the complete destruction of capitalism, and therefore of North American influence, can liberate the Indian. Revolutionaries of the Castroite school have introduced armed bands into Peru and Bolivia, but so far it appears that they have not operated in areas of massive Indian concentration, nor have they had so far much popular support, still less any support that proclaimed itself *indigenista*, or specifically Indian. It seems that so far the Indian communities have seen no more reason to trust these white strangers than the others who have exploited them in the past. But it would be rash to predict that this distrust will continue indefinitely; even in the Andes, the sense of a permanent social structure is breaking down, everyone has heard of *progreso*, and more and more people compare their way of life with that within wider and wider circles.

# CHAPTER XII

# The Caribbean

## *1  The Essence of Colonialism*

There is a sense in which the Caribbean displays the essence of colonialism. It is true that in one respect this region is different from most of the colonial world; there are only fragmentary remains of a native population subjugated by invaders. But it is the essence of colonialism, and indeed of most forms of rule of the many by the few, that the few impose on the many a spiritual yoke which comes to govern their day-to-day actions, more constantly and pervasively, if less obtrusively, than the physical force which lies in the background. Nowhere did this happen more completely than in the Caribbean. Whole societies were persuaded to imitate a way of life that was quite unfamiliar to them, one they had little hope of attaining and not in itself particularly estimable; what was more serious, they came to despise themselves and their own way of life.

The region is of wide extent and enormous variety. Every island is different from the others; they differ in resources and in the kind of agriculture for which they are best suited, still more in the proportions in which the human elements are mixed. To these differences between the islands we shall come back in Section 3 of this chapter. They are not to be underestimated. But it remains true that there is something that can be called a Caribbean *style*, something to be found in almost every island and every section of society, an approach to life and human society which is recognizably Caribbean. There is also a structure of society which, with many variations and differences of emphasis, recurs in island after island and which I shall call the standard Creole structure. I shall describe this standard structure in a generalized form and then touch briefly on some variations from it. In the fourth section I shall illustrate the obsession with colour which is part of the Caribbean style and some of the paradoxes which result from the confusion between physical skin colour, colour as a mark of identity, and colour as a moral symbol. Then we must look at the population groups who are not part of the standard Creole structure, of which much the most important are East Indian, and finally consider the very serious dilemmas which confront every section of the Caribbean populations.

The region is a natural laboratory, illustrating in immense variety the problems which men face in their social, political, and economic life; it is a microcosm, rather a constellation of microcosms, better adapted, perhaps, than any other part of the globe to the study of ideas about race and their consequences. But those who live there are creatures of flesh and blood, not merely objects of study. They do not stand still to be watched; as we look, we can see the growth of their hunger, their confusion, their resentment at the world that has made them and taught them to despise themselves. But it is a resentment that displays itself only in flashes against a background of resilience, humour, and adaptability to the predicaments with which they are faced.

## 2 The Standard Creole Structure

Everything in the Caribbean comes from somewhere else—not only the people and the luxury goods but even the staple foods, the crops, and the animals. It would not be quite true to say that only the crabs and the flying-fish are truly native. In the mainland territories of British Honduras and the Guianas, for example, there are Amerindian populations, but in the islands the exceptions are neither many nor important. The Spanish virtually exterminated the Arawak inhabitants, not of intent, but first by war and conquest, later by forced labour and disease. Some of the more warlike Caribs lasted longer but the small groups who are still referred to as Caribs are negligible in numbers, and both in ancestry and culture more Creole than indigenous. As it became clear that there was little hope of a native labour force, slaves were brought from Africa to work for the masters of the islands and it is with the slaves that Caribbean society begins.

The riches of the islands were greatly exaggerated, but it was true, until about the end of the eighteenth century, that they were a convenient source for much that could not be grown in Europe. At first for strategic reasons and later for their wealth, they were highly prized by European nations; they became the reward of victory and, either by conquest or treaty, changed hands frequently. The various European masters—English, Spanish, French, Danish, Dutch—their political and economic systems, their outlook on religion and sex—made one set of variable factors in the rich diversity of the Caribbean. But most of the territories in some degree share the Caribbean style and exhibit the Caribbean structure. I shall however describe the style as it developed in the British islands with only occasional references to French, Dutch, and Spanish.

The plantation with its slaves is the basis of the society which grew up. Comparisons have been drawn between the forms of slavery in the different islands and in Brazil and the Southern States. It is usually concluded that, except in one respect, the Caribbean was the most oppressive of these three and that within the Caribbean the Dutch and English systems were more rigid than the Spanish. This does not mean that individual masters of these nations were more cruel; perhaps there was more difference between individual masters and conditions on their estates, even in the same territory, than between one territory and another. But what is important for future development is that the system was harsh and that the slave reaction to it was less submissive than in the Southern States; slave insurrections were more frequent and perhaps even more severely repressed. The songs of slavery in the Caribbean are less often resigned and melancholy than in the South, more often defiant and resentful.

These effects may be related to two linked causes: the absenteeism of many estate-owners and the small number of whites. If a landlord never visited his estates, or came only once a year, there was hardly room for the growth of any personal knowledge of his slaves. He left his affairs to an agent, who reported to his employer in terms of goods produced, irrespective of the human cost. It was generally accepted in the Caribbean islands that it did not pay to treat slaves kindly or breed from them; the best policy was to 'work the slaves out and trust for more supplies from Africa'. One agent boasted that he had 'made my employers 20, 30, or 40 more hogsheads of sugar per year than any of my predecessors ever did; and though I have killed thirty or forty Negroes per year more, yet the produce had been more than adequate to that loss'.[1]

Increasingly the agent aimed to make a profit for himself as well as his employer so that he could set up an estate of his own. And in general it was the owners who could best afford to be magnanimous who were most likely to stay in Europe. Absenteeism contributed to the generally low proportion of whites, both directly and indirectly. The effect spiralled; there were few whites and therefore few amenities or opportunities. If the owner had lived on his estate, there would have been more opportunity for white professional men and artisans; life would have been more attractive. It need hardly be emphasized that the fewer the whites the less secure they could feel and the sharper the reprisals they would call for at any sign of rebellion.

In one respect only slavery was here less rigid than in Virginia. More slaves were freed and the existence of a free black and a free coloured population was not resented in the Caribbean as it was in the Southern States. This is vital to the development of the typical Caribbean structure and it must be attributed partly to the absenteeism of the great estate-owners and the small numbers of whites, partly to the

[1] Henry Coor, quoted in D. Lowenthal's forthcoming book, *West Indian Societies*.

different nature of American and Caribbean society. Because there were few whites, there was no corporate objection to the freeing of slaves; there was no class of skilled white artisans, clerks, or shop-keepers to object. Owners therefore followed their individual wishes and released their children by slave women if they felt inclined. Sometimes they released a man by will as a reward for good service. In Cuba, a slave was sometimes sent from the plantation to the town and established by his master as a wheelwright or a shoemaker, the tools and materials being supplied by his master, to whom half the takings were to be remitted.[1] But this system of leasing a man his freedom does not seem to have happened in British islands.

There was a greater readiness in the islands than in Virginia or in Maryland to acknowledge responsibility for children begotten on slave women. Even in the South, and even before independence, American society was to some extent in protest against its European origins. Its intellectual tenets were those of the Enlightenment and egalitarian ideas were strong. To such a society the Negro slave presented a dilemma from the start. If he was a man and a brother, he must be admitted to all that that implied; there could be no half-way house. He must be altogether in or altogether out. And it was decided—in the obscure and largely unconscious way in which a society decides on its own definition—that he should be altogether out, that any Negro ancestry should be a disqualification.

But resident estate-owners and agents in the Caribbean islands were in no sense in protest against the metropolitan powers and they were not conspicuous for their contribution to the philosophical theory of the state. There were no Washingtons or Jeffersons here. They were not in the least egalitarian; they accepted the premise of inequality as completely as the Tutsi or a Southern Brahman. It was natural that men should be graded in ranks or degrees and it seemed equally natural, from a very early stage, that the grading should take account of colour. There was perhaps never one island where all the estate-owners were wholly white, where all the slaves were black labourers, and where all of mixed blood were free and in middle-class occupations. But there was an expectation that affairs would be arranged in this kind of simple hierarchy. The reality of course became increasingly more complex; among the free middle classes the range from skilled artisan through small capitalist to estate-manager or lawyer, was generally expected to correspond to some extent with a range of shade in skin colour from black or almost black through various degrees of brown to the tint of parchment or ivory. In general, the lighter the shade the greater was the expectation of wealth and salary and power.

Nor were the other two main classes simply white and black; there were gradations among them. Some white fathers acknowledged their

[1] H. S. Klein, *Slavery in the Americas*.

coloured children, brought them up among white people, and married them to whites; there were soon gradations of whiteness in white society. That is to say, there was some mixture of genes within a social class generally described as white. There was also the distinction between those born in Europe and those born in the Caribbean. In some islands there were poor whites, the descendants sometimes of indentured servants, sometimes of convicts. Among the slaves, the greatest distinction was between house slaves and field hands; the lighter in colour had far the best chance of being picked for work in the house or as grooms and gardeners. But there was also a distinction between those caught in Africa and the Creole slaves[1] born in the Caribbean. Creole slaves were approved by their masters as more docile, but for just the same reason were often suspected by their fellow-slaves, who thought they were too much inclined to accept the system into which they were born and therefore liable to betray any plots into which the others entered.

Thus it was a feature of the characteristic Caribbean structure that there should be an escape route from slavery. It was easier for a woman than for a man and the easiest road lay through the master's bed. But for someone, for the children at least, there was a hope. This was perhaps one reason why the West Indian slave was less submissive than the Virginian; it is part of the main argument of this book that a belief that nothing can change has been an essential part of the structure of all stratified societies. Where this is absent, there is resentment and often revolt.

The process of constructing three graded classes began very early and was well established before the emancipation of the slaves. Let us recall that there was a quarter of a century of agitation and controversy before the slave trade was outlawed by the British Parliament in 1807 and another quarter of a century before Emancipation in 1834–8. During all this time there were frequent debates in Parliament, public meetings, lobbying, pamphleteering.

There was thus every opportunity for white estate-owners to see their danger. They kept up their defences till the last, but in the end, in most islands, their appreciation of this danger induced them to drop the more rigid forms of segregation between themselves and the coloured middle classes and to make, in part at least, common cause with them against the black masses. In the century between Emancipation and the Second World War, the process continued; the original three-tier system became more and more eroded at the top. The whites became fewer and more posts of a higher grade passed to the coloured middle

---

[1] The Spanish practice in Mexico and Peru was to apply *criollo* to whites born locally. But the word seems first to have been applied to slaves born in the New World. In this chapter I use it in the French form to mean 'born in the Caribbean' but of European or African descent, excluding East Indians, Amerindians, and Chinese.

class. It was not a change of structure but simply a movement away from the Caribbean of the top layer and some promotion for those who stayed. The movement away pervaded the whole of the upper class; those who could afford it educated their children in Europe, and of the educated only those came back who saw no opportunities in the metropolis; the ambition of the most successful in the islands was to escape.

The development can be seen as one continuous movement through three centuries. There was first the establishment of a social pyramid—not like the pyramid of Cheops but of the Central American type, built in three tiers or stages; then the crumbling of the top stage and a movement upward to rebuild it from below—and this process repeated, until the two upper stages became continuous. The essential structure, the outline of the pyramid seen from afar, remains much the same. But this continuity was not so apparent to those taking part.

The first break with the past was the great shock of emancipation; the owners had prophesied that the economy would be ruined and the former slaves would do no work, while the slaves had supposed a golden age would follow. Neither prophecy in fact came true; the economy was declining already, because the world markets were changing, but emancipation did not make so sudden a change as had been expected. Indeed, there was some increase in the production of sugar at first, due mainly to the injection of capital paid in compensation for the loss of the slaves. This however did not last long. Some of the more enterprising slaves left the estates but most were quite unprepared for any other life, and every means that could be devised was adopted to keep them where they were. It was not for their own good, argued their rulers, that they should be allowed to relapse into the idleness that was widely believed to be part of the genetic heritage of the African. The whip had been so long the means of making them work that few employers could envisage anything but other forms of coercion. To keep their former slaves as nearly as possible in the same condition as before was the object of most. Emancipation, it has been often said, was not complete a hundred years later.

Coercion in its new shape took different forms in different islands. But everywhere there was a determination to keep wages down and to stop any opportunity to earn money in other ways. So there was opposition to independent farms and small holdings; there was discrimination in employment against those whose colour suggested that they ought to be working in the fields. Above all, there was the search for another source of cheap labour, and particularly indentured labour from Asia. The importation of substitutes for slaves, where it took place on any scale, had other important consequences; for the moment we are concerned with its effect on the characteristic Creole structure. It not only gave the planters what they immediately wanted, hands in

the sugar-cane fields, but also kept wages down and reduced opportunities for the former slaves.

Emancipation is the first big landmark of the nineteenth century;
the importation of indentured labour was a consequence of emancipation which extended in space over many territories, British, French, and
Dutch, and in time over the second half of the century and into the
twentieth. There was another development in the last one-third of the
century which was confined to the British territories: the resumption
of political control by the metropolitan power. In Jamaica, the occasion
for this was the rising at Morant Bay in 1865 and the extreme severity
of the repressive measures that followed; the causes were everywhere
deeper and indeed in some islands the process had begun before this.
The instinct of the British in the seventeenth century had been to
establish, wherever they hoisted the flag, a local replica of their own
peculiar form of government—a Governor to represent the Crown and
two Houses to pass the laws. These legislatures were far from democratic, but they were generally referred to at the time as representative;
there was an element of election, on very strictly limited qualifications.
And in the Caribbean they were in fact representative but generally of
one class, the plantation-owners.

But the main purpose of the plantation-owners was to find new forms
of coercion to replace slavery. To Westminster their methods did not
always seem very enlightened. Newly arrived Governors and travellers
alike complained that these local bodies were filled with men of
depressingly low calibre. By the 1860s it seemed in Westminster to be
obvious not only that small colonies could be run much more efficiently
by the Governor and civil servants, under the general direction of the
Colonial Office, but that by this means the interests of the mass of the
people could be better protected, peace maintained, riots and scandals
avoided. There was little idea of preparing these small territories for
self-government; indeed, one of the arguments for making them Crown
Colonies was that otherwise it would be hard to avoid extending the
franchise, which would mean a step-by-step extension to the black
masses. Perhaps this weighed as much with the local Houses of Assembly
as the more obvious consideration that it would now be a direct imperial responsibility to maintain order and preserve them from any
revolt of the masses.

In Westminster, it must have seemed important to avoid such
another controversy as had followed Morant Bay. The enquiry
into Governor Eyre's repressive measures attracted eminent partisans;
Ruskin, Tennyson, and Carlyle were among his supporters and Carlyle's
advocacy expresses a doctrine of white racial supremacy, a conviction
that idleness was an inherent African characteristic, an utter lack of
comprehension of the effects of slavery, that were probably widespread
among his countrymen, still more of course among the planters. There

was thus little opposition to the change to Colonial Office paternalism; all classes felt it would make them safer. Barbados was the only exception.

This was a change in political control. It hardly affected the social structure, perhaps slightly accelerating that movement away from the top that was characteristic of the Caribbean. It was now perhaps a little less worth while for a man of ambition and intelligence to stay in his island home. There was a greater insistence than before that there must be no legal or formal distinction on grounds of colour and, as we have seen elsewhere, the response to the abolition of a formal distinction is frequently an increase in prejudice. When the legal barriers go down, the psychological defences go up. We should expect, and do in fact find, that when slavery came to an end there would be an increase in discrimination based on shades of colour.

Every society we have looked at has shown at some stage a certain hesitancy about how to define the dominant group. In the Caribbean, the main distinction at first was between slave and free, but this broad distinction was quickly modified by considerations of race and colour. The European indentured servants worked out their time and became free; some of the children of African women and some of the more skilled and trusted Creole slaves were released, and an intermediate class of free blacks and free coloured arose. It became a society of many grades and distinctions—but the distinction of slave and free continued to be of overriding importance until slavery showed signs of coming to an end. At this stage, the free part of society first closed its ranks against the slaves and then when emancipation became a fact, established strong barriers of discrimination against the former slaves, for whose identification colour became the principal badge. This was the general picture. Now let us look at variations on this general theme.

## 3 Variations on the Theme

Every island differs a little from the others. Let us compare two not at opposite extremes, but sufficiently dissimilar, Barbados and Jamaica. Barbados has been British since 1610, the only island of any size that has never changed hands. It is smaller than Jamaica and almost the whole island is cultivated. There are no inaccessible mountain retreats and hardly any waste land. Estates have not been so large nor absenteeism so frequent as in Jamaica; more whites have lived in the island to run their own estates and make it their real home. There were fewer breaches, before slavery came to an end, in the simple division into two categories, white and free, black and slave; the proportion of free coloured continued to be less and the 'coloured' even today are hardly more numerous than the whites. They do not, as coloured, constitute a separate class.

All this—both geography and the division of society—meant that emancipation made less change in Barbados than elsewhere. The field hand on the sugar estate could not run away into the mountains and laboriously hew himself a small holding, as he could in Jamaica. He had virtually no alternative but to work for wages and, since sugar was —and is still—overwhelmingly the main crop, and since work in the sugar-fields is seasonal, he had to learn quickly that as a 'free' man he must save when he had work if he was not to starve when he had none.[1] The black Barbadian became known throughout the Caribbean for a thrift, an industry, and a punctuality that the whites and the light coloured of other islands regarded as exceptions to their general picture of those of African descent.

The whites of Barbados too were not quite the same as the whites of other islands. Here the spiral of absenteeism was reversed; because there were more whites there were more amenities and opportunities. There were schools for the children and more respect for education; the men elected to the legislature represented more constituents and behaved more responsibly. And they established a different pattern of race relations, more rigid and more formal, more strictly defined, more paternal in the better sense of the word. They grumbled no doubt about their servants and employees, but they were better than those of other islands. They came to speak of them as fellow-Barbadians, in spite of the more rigid social distance at which they were kept. Because there were so few coloured, people of unmixed slave descent began to move into middle-class and professional posts—lawyers, doctors, civil servants, judges. The convention was eventually established that Barbadians of either colour—and in effect there were only two colours —but of the same sex could meet in outward amity, for cricket, for business, in church and office—but not in the home, the club, or the hotel, never, in short, where both sexes might meet on terms of equality. This was a fleeting relationship, since it became fully established only in the twentieth century, but while it did last it was unique in the Caribbean; it was nearer to Virginia than Jamaica in the two respects that it was more a two-colour structure than a graded continuity and that the pattern of behaviour expected between the two groups was understood on both sides. But if there were two colours there were three classes, for the black and coloured professionals were as far removed from the peasantry in Barbados as the coloured middle class elsewhere.

Barbados, alone of the British islands, kept its seventeenth-century 'representative' constitution, not only long after Jamaica became a Crown Colony, but until after the Second World War. The higher proportion of whites and the greater solidity of the planter class were among the reasons for this. In the 1880s and 1890s there were as many as 16,000 whites, about 10 per cent of the population; there are still

[1] G. E. Cumper (ed.), *The Economy of the West Indies.*

10,000, though now it is only 4 per cent of the population. The planters stayed in the island and looked after their land and their people. They felt more secure, partly because of numbers and partly because their former slaves had so little choice of action. The Barbados House of Assembly had indeed taken very positive steps to supplement the fact that their former slaves had no mountain or jungle in which to take refuge. Their Masters and Servants Act of 1840 made it virtually impossible for a former slave to break away from work on the sugar estate except by emigration; it was not repealed until the 1930s and it tied him almost as firmly as a Tudor apprentice in England.

But even among the whites and even in Barbados, there were distinctions. There were the descendants of the West of England peasants transported by Judge Jeffreys after Monmouth's rebellion, still almost unmixed biologically but living in a style indistinguishable from that of the surrounding black peasantry. These were the 'Redlegs', who to other Barbadian whites were, at least until the Second World War, socially as far removed as the former African slaves. And there was another, less extreme, distinction among the whites: estate-owners and high officials formed a class apart from 'Bridgetown whites', the business folk and lesser professionals.

Martinique is in some respects in contrast with Barbados, but in others nearer to Barbados than to other British islands. There is not so much an imperceptible gamut of colour as a series of in-marrying groups hierarchically ranked and linked into one political and economic system. No one in Martinique, say the Martiniquans, is wholly black, but those who are not white fall into three groups: these are the *grands mulâtres*, who own plantations, have large businesses, and live like white people; the *petits mulâtres*, that is, the lesser bourgeoisie; and the mass of the peasantry. The latter are in general darker and the two groups of *mulâtres*, like the coloured middle classes elsewhere in the Caribbean, are excessively concerned with colour as a sign of social status. But, writes Lowenthal, 'between both these (lighter-coloured) groups and the whites a firm line is drawn; fraternal relations in politics and economic affairs, friendship between men, but absolutely no family contacts, intermarriage completely barred, property ownership separated by colour'.

This is reminiscent of Barbados and so is the division among the whites, though it is much more rigid in Martinique. As in Barbados, there are *petits blancs* who are culturally non-white, in speech and way of life. These *békés goyaves* are, says Lowenthal, 'totally beyond the pale' to the *grands blancs*. They make half of Martinique's two thousand whites—but there are sharp divisions even among those who remain. There are perhaps a dozen families who constitute the true aristocracy, control the biggest properties, and marry among themselves. There is a second group of more recent arrivals and less prosperous branches of the ancient families, and a third, who are treated as whites but spoken of in their absence as '*pas tout à fait blancs*' because of some distant *mésalliance*: 'Only in recent years have these three groups begun to coalesce, but they all maintain themselves aloof from social contact, and above all from intermarriage, with poor whites, French whites from Europe and above all coloured Antilleans.'[1]

It is not necessary to multiply examples. We shall come back to three important territories, Guyana, Trinidad, and Surinam, when we deal with the East Indians. It is enough to say that almost every island can be shown as a variant on the kinds of society to which we have already referred. There is the classless white island of St. Barthélémy, a dependency of Guadeloupe; almost the entire population is white, the descendants of Breton immigrants in the seventeenth century; like the Redlegs of Barbados, they are poor and unlettered, and live much like the descendants of black slaves, except that they do not marry with black or coloured from other islands and their life is centred on marriage and the father. Carriacou and Barbuda are almost wholly black and have remained stable, virtually classless island communities through the centuries. On Saba, Bequia, the Saintes, and la Désirade, each with only a few thousand people, there are separate communities, segregated for marriage but similar in way of life and occupation. Sometimes the segregation is between coloured and black, sometimes between white and non-white. In the Caymans, there are white, coloured, and black, and the Cayman whites do not marry outside their own group, but they are not an aristocracy. They are working sailors, who sign on for long ocean voyages on liners while their neighbours work as off-shore fishermen.

In Haiti, since the days of Toussaint L'Ouverture, who successfully resisted both the Napoleonic armies and the British, there was traditionally a small group of light coloured who formed the aristocracy. To-day, many of these have been banished and those who remain share power and privilege with ambitious and successful black men; this successful class have been estimated at 1 per cent of the population of 5,000,000, while another 7 per cent are reckoned as middle class in the sense of artisans, retail shopkeepers, clerks; 'undifferentiated in colour from the black peasantry, this middle class, along with the black élite, is as remote from and as disdainful of the masses as are the mulattoes'.[2]

In the Windward Islands, Grenada, St. Lucia, and Dominica, there are no longer resident West Indian-born whites; there are a few expatriate birds of passage, but the islands are in effect ruled by the light coloured and well educated, the descendants of the old middle class of free coloured. They form an establishment into which it is

[1] David Lowenthal, *West Indian Societies*.
[2] Quoted ibid.

still not easy for an outsider to force his way. Montserrat also has lost the top group of a three-class system and is left with only the coloured and the black masses, but differs from the Windwards in that the coloured are too few to maintain their power; they have become a minority instead of an élite. Everywhere except in the very small classless islands, there is somewhere in the structure the segment of middle-class coloured, graded by wealth, by education, and by descent, of which colour is the outward sign.

## 4 Ambition and Fantasy

To describe the characteristic Caribbean structure is of course to over-simplify. It is easy to see that there is a social pyramid, corresponding to some extent with colour, from which the top tier is constantly removed and elements from the tier below promoted. But to understand what it feels like to be part of this structure and to venture on any predictions as to possible development it is necessary to go back to the thought with which this chapter began: that these societies display the essence of colonialism, the imposition on another people of a system of values not their own.

In the Caribbean this took a particularly unhappy form. It was not done deliberately; no one consciously set himself to mould the minds of the Caribbean populations in the forms they took. But the social structure, the realities of power in the nineteenth century, the self-confidence of the Victorian age, combined inevitably to drive home the lesson, already implicit in language and metaphor, that 'white' meant all that was desirable and 'black' meant everything that was to be despised and avoided.

This was the universal conviction, which translated itself into different ambitions at different levels of society. At the top, the most rich, the best educated, and the most talented, wanted to leave the islands altogether; in a much larger middle-class belt, the ambition was to behave as much as possible as white people were thought to behave. Of the black masses, it is more difficult to speak with certainty; few can seriously have supposed that they could escape permanently from the situation in which they found themselves. No doubt for most of the time they accepted the social order as inevitable. But it is unlikely that they were consistent. We know that they sought escape in a variety of ways and may be confident that in most men there would sometimes be sudden spurts of ambitious fantasy and sometimes flares of anger and resentment.

One thing, however, they learnt unequivocally: to despise themselves and all they stood for. Mothers would tell their children: 'Stop acting like a nigger'—but how was the child to behave? Like a white man? He must, then, adopt the white belief that blacks were idle, dirty, lustful, stupid, and improvident. He was forced to condemn himself by every step he took towards the only goal he could perceive. Further, the essence of being a white man was to have black men under his orders; how could he do that if there was any change in *society*, if black men ceased to obey orders? And so he was forced to a *personal* solution; he came, in a confused way, to picture himself, in his happier moments, as an exception, truly white in spite of a dark exterior. But this was not how others saw him, and so his illusion was liable to frequent and bitter betrayal.

Fantasy was thus a way of escape from a paradoxical dilemma. We have seen that the Caribbean slave was less submissive than the Virginian, and this was partly because there really was a way of escape from slavery; there were free blacks. When emancipation came, all escaped from slavery and the former slaves generally broke away from the plantations whenever they could. But they had not escaped from blackness nor from their own mental bondage. They usually accepted the idea of *degree*, in the sense used in the quotation at the beginning of this book, that is to say, that society is arranged in a hierarchy. They did in general accept the 'white' view that 'white is best'. From this their only escape was the fantasy of being personally an exception to the rule.

Everything in West Indian society conspired to heighten the contempt for all that was West Indian. Education, for those who achieved any, was relentlessly European; primary education was designed for children in Europe and the clever sons of more successful and usually light-coloured parents who went to secondary schools learnt cricket and Latin Grammar, just as their contemporaries did in England.[1] And while the source of this contempt was in the first place the social system, it was reflected back and affected the way the social system was perceived. Everyone who is white is rich and free—this is how the social scene had looked traditionally. Therefore—so complete was the conviction that white was good—anyone who is successful is spoken of as white. The point needs to be illustrated by anecdote—and there are many stories, but the lesson to be drawn is not at all that which is usually intended when they are told.

On my first visit to Jamaica I met a woman doctor whose father had sent her to England to an expensive boarding-school; she had qualified in England and done her hospital appointments. She was extremely dark. She told me how she had once driven in her car to a remote village where cars were seldom seen; it was inhabited by a group descended from German peasant immigrants who came in the nineteenth century; like the Barbadian Redlegs, they live just as their black neighbours do but they do not intermarry. She heard two or three of

[1] For an eloquent description of the completeness of this process, see C. L. R. James, *Beyond a Boundary*.

the village children—tow-headed, red-cheeked, barefooted urchins—running beside her car and calling out: 'Look at the pretty white lady!' This was not mockery; anyone who rode in a car was white.

More recently I stayed in Jamaica with the owner of an estate growing bananas. He had asked some of his neighbours, also estate-owners, to meet him to consider raising money to support the political party which they thought likely to promote their interests. When they had finished their business, they turned, not unexpectedly, to talking of their labour problems. One of them expressed a sentiment frequently heard in Victorian times among the landlords of Ireland, a sentiment I heard thirty years ago in India and ten years ago in Rhodesia. He said: 'What these people really want is leadership, and they expect it from white people, people with faces the colour of *ours*.' Of the seven or eight present, only one would have been regarded as white in the United States, and two were very dark indeed; the speaker was by no means light.

There are, as I have said, many anecdotes of this kind and they are usually told in order to prove that the sense of colour is negligible in this society, being lost in the strong awareness of class. There is a belief among English people of the upper middle classes that it is more respectable to make distinctions on the ground of class than of colour. But, in fact, the true meaning of this kind of language is surely almost the opposite; the sense of colour as a value is so strong that words about colour are used to denote success, riches, knowledge, power, while biological facts are concealed behind polite euphemisms. My host, who by American standards was the only white man in this group, used the phrase 'white men' of them all in their presence, but not when they had gone, and I suspect that each of the others would have distinguished himself from those who were darker when talking to those who were lighter. Lowenthal has an anecdote from Dominica which illustrates admirably the way in which each man draws the line in relation to himself. His informant agreed that a certain club was less exclusive than it used to be; 'in fact', he added, 'perhaps now they wouldn't mind having me—but I'm not sure I'd want to belong to a club where they'd have anyone as dark as I am'.

'Colour' does not in this world mean only complexion, but hair and features which suggest African origin. 'Bad hair', throughout the Caribbean, means crinkly hair. Distinctions which are not perceived by visiting white English or Americans are of importance to West Indians. 'My wife is black', I was told by an extremely distinguished and unusually frank West Indian, 'and when she goes into a store where she is not known, she gets the full treatment. They look the other way, they serve anyone else first, they may even address her contemptuously—until they find out who she is, when they are all obsequiousness.' It became evident as this conversation proceeded that my informant did not regard himself as black and expected me to be aware of a difference in origin and class background between himself and his wife. But this had not previously occurred to me. I was not sufficiently sensitive to West Indian nuances. Everyone, however, is aware of distinctions within his own society which would escape the notice of a foreigner.

It is not enough to recognize that some correspondence is to be expected between social position and colour, in the broad sense of indications of African origin. Perhaps the deepest wrong that has been done to the Caribbean people is that they have been brought up in a society in which traditionally everyone wishes he was someone else. But while once he had an ideal, though only in fantasy any hope of attaining it, to-day the typical West Indian does not even know who it is he wants to be. The search for an identity, which I prefer to call the search for a pedigree, is more acute in the West Indies than anywhere else.

The search produces many strange results. For the less sophisticated, these usually include in varying proportions elements of the Biblical and the 'Ethiopian'.[1] The Ras Tafaris of Jamaica are characteristic in including both. They took as their name the title held by the present Emperor of Ethiopia before he ascended the throne; they began with two fundamental beliefs: that the Emperor Haile Selassie was divine and that the only salvation for black men was a return to Africa. With these go repudiation of all that is white and a number of subsidiary beliefs, based as a rule on isolated passages of the Old Testament, often taken clearly out of context and depending on the wording of the King James translation. Thus Psalm 18: 8: 'There went up a smoke out of his nostrils', authorizes, and indeed enjoins, them to smoke hemp; Numbers 6:5: 'he shall be holy and shall let the locks of the hair of his head grow', means that the inner group must distinguish themselves by long braided locks; Jeremiah 8:21 which says: 'For the hurt of the daughter of my people am I hurt; I am black', means not only that white men have exploited black women—a point that hardly requires scriptural proof—but that God himself is black. (In modern translations, the meaning is usually taken to be: 'I mourn'.)

Behind all this are two real predicaments—that of the descendant of black slaves who sees no place for himself in a world of white values which teach him only self-contempt; that of the landless peasant lost in a city which for him has no moral standards and no goals that he can attain. At various times, Ras Tafaris have believed that a ship was coming to take them to Ethiopia—where of course all their troubles would miraculously end. The movement has inherited much from

---

[1] There is some repetition here, and elsewhere in this section, of points made in Part I, Chapter III, Section 2. But the argument demands that the point should be made in both places.

Marcus Garvey and also notably from the prophet Bedward, who tried to fly to Heaven about the end of the nineteenth century; it has provided a rallying-point not only for social and personal discontent but for some experienced criminals. But the fundamental disease of which this movement is one symptom is expressed in many others too.

It would be shallow to suppose that social and racial discontent was the sole cause of pentecostal movements, talking with tongues, spirit possession. But there are in the West Indies many emotional religious outlets which include these manifestations. Many are sects which have broken away from European churches, sometimes because they do not provide a service which meets the needs of an unlettered congregation, sometimes owing to the personal ambition of a man who is aware that he can lead but who is frustrated in every other channel. Everywhere, even in the islands nominally Catholic, there is some opposition between the religion of the people, as it is understood and as it influences their lives, and the formal organized religion of foreign missionaries. There is widespread belief in a spirit world, which can be influenced or even compelled by magical practices, and in a Deity who can be persuaded or cajoled into favourable intervention. Widespread also is the belief in 'salvation', the certain knowledge that a glorious future life is assured. There is much in common between the separatist sects, which have rejected the older churches, and the folk-beliefs which operate in parallel; and surely in all there is an attempt to break out from a social system which in its personal application is intolerable.

For the highly educated, the means of establishing a pedigree were different. The first step is negative: it is to protest that one is no longer going to accept white glorification of white achievements. This, the beginning of the doctrine of *négritude*, is expressed in Aimé Césaire's poem glorifying those who have never invented or discovered anything, which has already been quoted (in Part I, Chapter III, Section 2).

The next and more positive phase is best expressed by Frantz Fanon, a French Antillean who identified himself with the Algerian Independence movement and who wrote:

The unconditional affirmation of African culture has succeeded the unconditional affirmation of European culture. On the whole, the poets of Negro-ism oppose the idea of an old Europe to a young Africa, tiresome reasoning to lyricism, oppressive logic to high-stepping nature, and on one side, stiffness, ceremony, etiquette, and scepticism, while on the other frankness, liveliness, liberty and—why not?—luxuriance but also irresponsibility.[1]

If this quotation fairly expresses what the poets of *négritude* are saying, as I think it does, the educated West Indian can hardly find here a really comforting answer to his problems. In the first place, he is not African; he has been brought up to despise Africa and if he now consciously reverses his attitudes and sets himself deliberately to admire

[1] *The Wretched of the Earth.*

what he thought barbarous, he cannot be at ease unless he is dishonest. Nor indeed does this really give him what he seeks—a culture of his own in which he can take pride. It does not in fact describe a culture— with artistic achievements of which one can be proud—so much as a mood or a temperament. It is still saying: 'Hurrah for those who have never invented anything'; it is taking the white man's derogatory picture of the Negro and re-stating it in positive and acceptable terms. But this does not still the latent unease. It says: 'Yes, you are right. We can never be what you are. So it is better to give up trying and shout aloud that we are charming, gay, and spontaneous even if we are as idle, feckless, and irrational as you always said we were.' This is how it rings in many a West Indian ear. And from white men it invites questions which are not easy to answer. Is 'high-stepping nature' going to balance a budget, build aeroplanes and motor-cars and fertilizer plants? These things, surely, call for 'tiresome reasoning'. If there was patronage in the old 'white' assumption that black men were capable of reason and would learn to do these things in time, it is surely, as Fanon concedes, irresponsible to reject reason because it involves hard work and because there is so much which has to be learnt from some- one else. What, a critic is entitled to ask, distinguishes man from the animals? Not high-stepping nature, surely, but the use of tiresome reason; lyricism, yes, but also mastery of the environment, which depends on forgoing immediate advantage for future good. And it seems very doubtful whether artistic achievement of any considerable dimension can be achieved without such typically 'white' qualities as perseverance and self-discipline.

These objections to *négritude* as formulated by the poets are no doubt among the reasons why it is the creed only of a small minority. There is also the feeling that it is bogus: 'a tiger', wrote Wole Soyinka, 'does not go about proclaiming its tigritude. It just pounces.'[1] If it is still not clear what is the equivalent of a pounce for the West Indian intellectual, politicians and voters increasingly provide their own inter- pretation. For them, it means that a man who hopes to be elected must show his solidarity 'with the race'; it means a new confidence but also an aggressiveness towards the white, perhaps still more towards the West Indian coloured. It means that they are to-day aware of an outer world which discriminates against them and against which they have to assert themselves. It means that the personal search for a pedigree is fruitless; what they are looking for is an achievement by the group as a whole.

## 5 The Two Creole Cultures

Judgements about the values by which people govern their lives will

[1] Quoted by David Lowenthal, in *West Indian Societies*.

always be open to controversy. There will not however be much difference of opinion about the gulf which separates the two main groups in
the standard Creole structure—the coloured professional middle class
and the black peasantry. There is in the first place a great difference
in standard of living. The West Indian societies are not absolutely the
poorest of underdeveloped countries, but they rank high among those
in which wealth is most unevenly distributed. For example, 5 per cent
of Jamaican households enjoy 30 per cent of the national income,
while at the other end of the scale 20 per cent of the households have
only 2.2 per cent of the income. Those in the top group have sixty times
the income of those in the bottom. The contrasts are glaring, not only
extreme in themselves but openly exposed to view. The difference in
economic circumstances is reflected in different ideas and attitudes.

We have already mentioned the contrast between formal and folk
religion. There is a similar divergence in attitudes towards law, order,
police, and justice. Among the masses, the law is everywhere regarded
as alien and hostile, something devised in the interests of the light-
coloured upper class. No doubt this goes back to the days of slavery,
when all authority was something to be evaded whenever it could be
done with impunity, when theft from the masters was seen as a form
of revenge. But the result to-day is that a criminal often can neither be
arrested nor convicted; this is particularly true of offences such as
illicit distilling, with which everyone is in sympathy. The attitude is
reminiscent of the Irish peasantry in the last century; the execution of
criminal justice is repudiated because the whole society is felt to be
unjust. It is difficult to recruit for the police and it has sometimes been
necessary to draw on men from other islands. The ideas of the ruling
class are in marked contrast; it is true that political parties try to
suborn the police and accuse each other of succeeding, but members of
the upper and middle classes in general look on the police as their
natural protectors and expect preferential treatment; their attitude to
authority resembles that of the corresponding classes in Victorian
England.

This dualism is not confined to criminal law; there is, writes Lowenthal, a widespread system of land tenure and inheritance which
operates among the peasantry, uncodified, but understood by themselves and altogether at variance with the system administered in the
Courts set up by the State. It is a parallel, unofficial system, which
cannot be replaced by a legal system because of the formidable expense
of surveying the plots, registering them, and dealing with the disputes.
There is a similar division of ideas about marriage. Here too memories
of slave culture are strong; for the slaves, marriage was virtually
impossible. To-day, among their descendants, it is common for a young
man to form an attachment to a girl and visit her at her home, any
child being left with her parents and no disgrace accruing. Later the

couple—or one of them with another partner—may decide to settle
down in 'common law marriage' or 'faithful concubinage' and this may
continue until the children are grown up. Formal marriage is not to
be undertaken until the couple can afford it; it will then be a ceremonial affair with special clothes and a party in a rather old-fashioned
'white' style; the arrival of the first grandchild is often felt to be a
suitable moment. Both man and woman often see certain advantages
in this pattern of life; it may mean considerable independence for the
woman, and almost always more responsibility for the children lies on
her than on the man.

In contrast, upper-class patterns of marriage are European and the
family is centred on the father. In the British islands, attitudes are
generally Victorian; in the French, at least among the whites of
Martinique, they were until recently better described as pre-Revolu-
tionary. Marriages were often arranged by parents, and since no girl
must marry a man darker than herself and many light-skinned and
ambitious men go overseas, there are many light-skinned spinsters—
a problem that Rajput nobles of the higher clans used sometimes to
meet by killing their daughters at birth. Illegitimacy in the white or
light-coloured groups is a serious stain. And it is unmentionable—the
deepest possible disgrace to her family—that a woman of the upper
class should engage in a liaison with a dark-skinned man of the lower
class. But the reverse is a peccadillo. Men marry light for social prestige
but often sleep dark for excitement and pleasure. It has been suggested
that in the Roman Catholic areas, because motherhood is regarded as
holy, pleasure in sex is sought elsewhere. The Protestant ethic on the
other hand is more deeply infused with a feeling of shame about all
sex and therefore a freedom from restraint and greater release with a
casual partner before whom no pretences need be kept up. In varying
degrees, this remnant of slavery and the *droit du seigneur* is widespread
in the Caribbean. To its effect, we shall return.

Language too divides the classes. In almost every island, there is
a formal language—English, French, Spanish, or Dutch—but also a
patois that is very different. In some islands the official language is
English, the patois French; but even where there is no complication of
this kind, the difference is formidable. In Jamaica the speech of the
street is a dialect of English but it is not recognizable to an English ear;
it sounds to the newcomer like a foreign language. Almost everyone
born in the islands understands the patois to some extent; most also
understand the formal language. But the difference of language has
been a barrier to the lower-class child at school and a barrier between
the classes. From what has been said already it will be guessed
that the upper-class light-coloured frequently pretend they do
not understand the Creole patois, even if they talk it in the home,
and anyone who comes back to the West Indies from abroad is likely

to insist 'to all who listen that he has forgotten how to speak Creole'.[1]

The extreme example of how the lower class looks on the official language comes from Haiti. To the former slaves a patois of their own was useful as a means of concealing their intentions from their masters; the tradition continued in the nineteenth century and to-day Creole has become a symbol of sympathy with the people and an essential for anyone who seeks election. But that is not all: 'to most Haitians, even the well-educated, Creole is the language of truth and reality, French a tongue of bluff, mystification and duplicity; the very term for speaking French is also that for offering a bribe and for glossing over dishonest thoughts and actions with respectability. . . .'[2]

In the typical Caribbean society, now perhaps passing, the ghost of the slave-owner still walks, although from so many islands his descendants have gone. Both the two main classes believed, until lately, that it was good to be white and to behave as though white. But there was a difference in their pictures of white behaviour, and of how it could be adapted to their own circumstances. They were divided by language, religion, attitudes to law and marriage; each class saw the other as monolithic and sometimes could hardly perceive individual differences within the group. Coming home after a few years absence, a white lady told Lowenthal: 'It was sad to walk out in the street and not to recognize anyone. We never met the coloured people when we were children and I never did learn to distinguish between them.' Each group was apt to picture the other in stark and simple terms: the black masses are idle, irresponsible, dirty, and promiscuous; the rich whites are cold, greedy, cruel, and inhospitable. And yet it is misleading to emphasize this division without also stressing that the society is a continuum as well as a two-class structure, that there is understanding between the classes, that there are border-line cases, people thrusting up from the lower level to the higher, and above all continual instances of ambivalence. The belief that 'white' is good, implicit in so many Caribbean customs and explicit in so many Caribbean sayings, is combined with a deep suspicion of white intentions. It is perhaps not inconsistent to believe that it is good to be 'white' but that it is unlikely in general that 'white' people will behave disinterestedly. But a man rising in the social scale and employed by an international firm will accept in his work a standard of respect for authority and property quite foreign to his native village; he will move from one culture to the other and change his values as he switches from the metropolitan language to the patois.

In one matter the two cultures were until lately agreed: they were both convinced that firmly entrenched in the order of things was *degree*, in the sense used in the quotation from *Troilus and Cressida* set at the beginning of this book. And it was not felt unnatural that this *degree*

---

[1] Quoted by David Lowenthal, in *West Indian Societies*.
[2] Quoted ibid.

or hierarchy should be carried into sexual relations. As we have seen, men tried to marry light but traditionally exploited darker women outside marriage, as in the other hierarchical societies we have looked at. This traditional behaviour must have an effect on personalities in both groups. The man from the lower group sees himself humiliated in the most intimate fastness of his identity; the man from the upper is buttressed in the conviction that his superiority is not an accident or the result of convention but has a true validity in worth and manhood. More recently, the reverse is felt to revenge the humiliation; to sleep with a white woman smoothes away the memory of social slights and asserts the male identity and the male triumph of the black.[1]

The upper-class woman in the traditional system must be unusually generous if she does not become jealous and bitter, and if those in her power do not suffer in consequence. It is harder to know what the dark woman feels; as we have seen in slavery, the master's bed was the quickest, often the only, means of escape from cruel drudgery. After emancipation, the feeling persisted that to be taken up by a white man might lead to good fortune. But neither in such a case, nor when a woman had been tricked into compliance or virtually forced by her defencelessness, was she likely to bring up her children with much respect for the men of her own class and colour who had failed either to win her or protect her.

This deep-rooted tradition in Caribbean life must surely have affected profoundly all classes and both sexes. Because it arises from the dominance of one group in the social structure, because until recently there was no redress, it has reinforced one male in his sense of superiority and the other in his humiliation; it has embittered the women of both groups. And this is one reason why 'degree' in the sense of hierarchy begins to be repudiated in the Caribbean societies.

## 6  Outside the Structure : The East Indians

There are a number of minority groups who do not form part of the standard Caribbean structure. Three of these, as Lowenthal points out, are generally regarded, by those inside the structure, as outside it and below; four are outside, but parallel with the upper tiers of Creole society, usually able to obtain admission if they seek it—and this they have increasingly done. Of these seven minority groups, only one, that of the East Indians, needs much attention.

The four parallel groups—Jews, Portuguese, Chinese, and Syrians—

---

[1] There is a distinction to be made here. The fact that darker women have traditionally been exploited in this way will not be seriously disputed; the effect on social and personal life here suggested is a matter of interpretation which some will question. It is a hypothesis, deduced from novels and conversation, not from controlled research by psychologists.

have much in common. There are ancient communities of Sephardic Jews in Curaçao and Jamaica, some originally refugees from Brazil, some from Europe; they have been reinforced by individual emigrants. They have made their way in commerce, in government service, in the professions; they usually marry among themselves, and by the black masses will be thought of as belonging to the rich, white, or light-coloured group. The Portuguese in Guyana came from Madeira in the mid-nineteenth century as indentured labour, and were at first despised by black Creoles as 'white niggers' who had come to do slave work, while West Indian whites never regarded them as true Europeans. They were not a success in the sugar-fields and those who stayed on soon moved into retail trade. In Jamaica and Trinidad and other islands, the Chinese have a similar history of indentured labour followed by shopkeeping; both communities have become Creolized in their way of life and outlook but remain sufficiently distinct to be never wholly free from the danger of an outburst of popular jealousy at their success and clannishness. They have both been objects of such hostility.

The 'Syrians'—they come in fact from many parts of the Levant—the fourth of these groups, came as merchants and traders, never as labourers; they are widely distributed and universally successful; they often retain roots in the Levant but many marry Creole wives and become Creolized. They share with all these groups the dilemma that, until lately, every consideration urged them to approach as closely as they could to the light-coloured ruling class but that, as the masses learn the power democracy has given them, they may find such an identification increasingly dangerous, while complete isolation may be even more dangerous still. Many Chinese shops were looted and burned in 1966 in Jamaica when it was reported that a Chinese shopkeeper had mistreated a Negro employee.

American Indians are outside the Creole structure but generally regarded as below it. In Guyana, most of them are 'jungle Indians', food-gathering primitive groups in the inaccessible country of the interior; they present the same kind of problem as such groups do elsewhere. They are not one of the central problems of Guyana. Their future is unlikely to be happy; such peoples need a tolerant and imaginative approach which they have seldom received. They are looked on by the Creole Guyanans with mixed feelings; the urban Negro regards them as savage, primitive, uncivilized, and therefore to be despised; further, there is a positive hostility because these jungle Indians were used to hunt down runaway slaves. Lowenthal suggests that there might well be a deeper historical resentment; it might also be argued that if the Indians had been ready to work, and had not later been favoured by the Crown of Spain, there need have been no slaves in the West Indies. There are thus many historical grounds for resentment, which may have started a tradition. On the other hand, in the higher tiers of Creole society, Indians are preferred because lighter of skin than Negroes and it is possible to acknowledge and even boast of an Indian ancestor. In British Honduras the American Indians have quite another significance; as Spanish-speaking they form a link with Guatemala and are a factor in an international dispute; as Roman Catholics, they are further divided from the Creoles.

The Javanese in Surinam are a special case, partly because it was Dutch policy to recognize ethnic divisions and encourage territorial segregation. Surinam has both Indians and Javanese, who are divided by religion, the Javanese being Muslim and the Indians mainly Hindu; both came as indentured labour but the Javanese later, between about 1890 and 1930. The Javanese are really the extreme example of the case which the East Indians display in a less pronounced form. Like the East Indians, they were despised by the Creoles—white, coloured, and Negro alike—yet themselves despised the Negroes, and even the East Indians, on the grounds of their own lighter skin. Isolated from the rest of the population in Surinam, not only by religion, language, and culture, but by location, they have had less time to adapt themselves than the East Indians and have in fact made fewer adaptations.

The East Indians came as indentured labour in the second half of the nineteenth century. In three areas, their numbers made them an important element in the population; these are Guyana, Trinidad, and Surinam, where they are between 40 and 50 per cent of the total. They are present in other islands, notably Jamaica, Martinique, and Guadeloupe, but in much smaller proportions, and here they conform more closely to the Creole pattern of behaviour and their presence is of much less social significance and politically unimportant. Like the other groups who came as indentured labour, they were regarded in all areas with contempt by those whom they replaced; they had come to do slave work. But to the Negroes they returned the contempt; the Indians were lighter-skinned, which was important in their own system of values as well as to the Creoles; they had the European type of hair and feature; they had a culture and a language of their own. Pride in their own culture was something of which they were less conscious at first than later; after the Independence of India, its importance increased greatly.

But this was by no means all; each group despised much that the other valued. Indians regarded themselves as thrifty and hard-working, and thought the Negroes idle and improvident, thievish and aggressive. The picture was reversed by the Negroes, to whom the Indians were mean and tricky skinflints, grasping, suspicious, and secretive, while they themselves were generous and warm-hearted. These impressions of each other are widespread, but on the whole, the Indian of the Negro is more negative than the reverse; where Indians are in smaller minorities, as in Jamaica, it is not uncommon for a Negro man to say he would like an Indian wife, who would save money, spend wisely, and be obedient. Indians, on the other hand, are afraid of losing their daughters to people of whom they have this extremely unfavourable picture; it would be defilement, they say; Negroes have no true concept of marriage. They have a picture of Negro lust seeking Indian beauty.

Where the Indians are in smaller minorities, there is necessarily more communication and people know more about each other; fixed unfavourable stereotypes are less extreme than where the proportions are more equal and it is possible for one group to segregate itself. But their pictures of each other still take the same forms and they correspond to real differences, in behaviour, in values, in family and personality structure. The Indians on the whole have remained in the countryside; the Creoles, wherever possible, have moved to the towns. Where the Creoles have stayed in the country, they have usually lingered on as subsistence farmers, escaping periodically to earn wages elsewhere. But the Indians have farmed for cash, investing capital and employing high degrees of skill in specialized forms of agriculture such as growing rice. If successful, they would invest in rice-milling machinery or some business enterprise in the countryside. For long they neglected education as the road to success, mainly because they feared that the mission schools would convert their children to another faith and separate them from their families. But the Creole boys, already converted, saw the school as the way to white-collar jobs and positions of authority and so obtained a very considerable lead over the Indians in government service and employment in the large businesses of the towns.

The Creole home too is quite different from the Indian. The traditional 'Hindu Joint Family'[1] hardly exists in the Caribbean; emigration and the labour lines for the indentured sugar-cane cutters effectively ended it. The East Indians of the Caribbean break up into the nuclear family of husband, wife, and children far more quickly than their counterparts in India would do. But they keep close ties with the wider family and still regard it as the duty of a father to marry off his daughter young; in the family that results, the husband is firmly the centre of authority, though he will long continue to be submissive to his father. It is the deepest social disgrace for a woman to be involved in any affair before marriage or outside marriage.

It is not surprising, in view of these differences, that a recent study found the personality structures of low-income school-children in Trinidad quite different for Creoles and East Indians. Conformity, internalization, and self-control were important for the Indians,

---

[1] It is a basic concept of Hindu personal law that all the property of the family is owned jointly in equal shares by all the male members. This is only terminated when one sues for the right to break away; thus the presumption is that the family is joint unless it is legally determined that it is not.

and they related what they did to past traditions and future prospects; the Creoles were more concerned with independence and self-expression and with what could be realized in the present.[1] Despite these differences, some adaptation of each to each did take place in colonial days and the Indians were beginning to approach a little more closely to a Creole outlook. The East Indian groups in the Caribbean were less cohesive than those in Fiji and Mauritius; their culture had been more influenced by their surroundings and this seems due to the one factor of physical distance from India which made it more difficult for them to visit their old homes, to marry there, to receive, in short, continual cultural reinforcements. In the Caribbean the Indians had almost abandoned their caste-structure and many dietary restrictions; where they were in a small minority they often became Christians and where numbers were more equal, they forgot a little more of Hindu rites year by year.

But with the coming of Indian independence, this process began to slow down, and as the independence of Caribbean territories drew closer, it went into reverse in the areas where equality in numbers led to rivalry. With increasing understanding of the voter's power to influence events, the Indians have laid greater stress on cultural differences and have tried to revive the use of Hindi. But it has been an artificial revival; the stimulus has had to be sought from outside. In Trinidad and Guyana, the two areas of special rivalry, this has encouraged among the Creoles a tendency to wear African clothes and to glorify an African past that is largely imaginary.

Both Creoles and Indians have reason to fear the future. The present tendency is for East Indians to increase more rapidly, largely owing to their earlier marriages. In Guyana, Trinidad, and Surinam they will be in the majority over all other sections of the population within a few years and this is frightening for the Creoles if it is assumed that voting is to be by race. On the other hand, Indians in Guyana, where tension is most acute, have seen themselves as faced by the typically insensitive reaction to minority claims of a dominant group with a dominant culture. It has not been very different in Trinidad.

Dr. Eric Williams constantly affirms the ideal of a multi-racial nation, but he means by this that there shall be one unified nation with one culture in which all may play a part whatever their race; he does not mean that there should be any provision for a different culture and has indeed referred to Hindu leaders as a recalcitrant minority. In neither territory do Creoles contemplate any kind of integration or unification except that the East Indians should abandon their own culture and behave more as Creoles do. In both, the East Indians were insufficiently represented in the teaching profession and the civil service, and there was a far more marked discrepancy in the police. In Guyana, at the

[1] Quoted by David Lowenthal, in *West Indian Societies*.

time of Independence, the proportion in the police was only one East Indian to four Creoles, and in the higher ranks the East Indian share was even lower. In Trinidad, even as recently as 1964, there was only one Indian in twenty in the police force. East Indians argue that until the disproportion has been made even, they should have a higher percentage of recruits than their numbers warrant; as things are, they cannot hope for fair treatment. In short, the East Indians fear that rule by the other community means that they will be kept in a position of permanent inferiority from which they can never escape; the Creoles consider that unless they take steps to prevent it they will themselves be in just that position before many years.

In Guyana, in the years immediately after the Second World War, there was a brief period in which Creoles and East Indians combined in the P.P.P. (People's Political Party). Politics were still new and they were able to agree that they wanted independence; the party was at first an alliance of Indian and Creole peasants and Creole urban workers against the dominant light-coloured group and the British. The leaders of each group recognized the cleavage of interest and saw it as so great that they must make concessions and work together. This coalition—for it was hardly a single party—lasted from 1950 to 1955. When the split came, it was, overtly at least, on differences of personality and of ideology: Burnham, the Creole leader, regarded Jagan, the East Indian leader of the party, as an inefficient administrator as well as a Marxist; Jagan and his followers looked on Burnham with suspicion as a bourgeois capitalist. Jagan came back into power in 1957, with some Creole supporters as well as Chinese and Portuguese who followed him on ideological grounds, but a majority of the party, much the most solid single element, consisted of East Indians. He beat Burnham's P.N.C. (People's National Congress) mainly because he had a better established political machine. But he soon felt the pressure of interests from the main body of his supporters—and these interests were seen by both supporters and opponents as racial.

The Federation of the West Indies was one important issue; the British Government hoped to set it up because they thought it offered the best hope of political and economic stability. But to Guyana the issue was bound to appear racial. The East Indians were likely soon to outnumber all other groups; they hoped for an entirely independent Guyana. Creoles similarly saw in the Federation some hope of countering the East Indians' majority. This was only the first of many questions in which the interests of the East Indians, as predominantly rural and as a separate culture, diverged from those of other Guyanese and the slogan of voting 'for one's own kind' began to be heard. The phrase in Hindi is *'apne jat'*—literally 'own kind or caste'—but corrupted in the Caribbean to *'apanjhat'* as one word. Burnham's Creoles joined forces with a group of Portuguese and other minority interests, but these soon split away under Peter d'Aguiar to form a third party. By the elections of 1961, the solidarity of the Creoles was almost as strong as that of the East Indians and voting was almost entirely on racial lines. Back in office, Jagan could hardly avoid going further on the path already begun of supporting Indian interests; with the civil service and police hostile in the extreme to his measures, it is not surprising that there were race riots in 1963 and 1964.

During the three years after the elections of 1961, the British Government were under pressure from the United States—who looked on Jagan as a potential Castro on the American mainland—and were receiving strong representations from the Creole group in the same sense. They were persuaded to apply to Guyana electoral arrangements which were calculated to give Jagan a minority of seats; this they achieved, although his party had more votes than any other. By establishing in Guyana a particular form of Proportional Representation, instead of the methods usual in other parts of the Commonwealth, the British Government extricated itself from an immediate difficulty. A coalition of Burnham and d'Aguiar has kept Jagan out of power since 1964. There has been less bloodshed and plenty of American aid, but such manoeuvres will not have reduced the Indian sense of frustration, fear, and injustice. Attempts to attract Creoles from other territories have not so far changed the situation materially; giving the vote to Guyanese abroad can only postpone the reckoning. Only three courses appear to be open to the Creoles if they are to avoid a reversal of their present ascendancy. One is to encourage massive Creole immigration from other parts of the Caribbean; the second is to abandon the pretence of democracy; the third is to make real concessions to Indian interests now.

In Trinidad, the course of events has been somewhat similar, but they are at an earlier stage of development. Eric Williams professes that his policy is multi-racialism but it might also be described as the exclusion of Hindus; he has recruited Muslim East Indians to his Cabinet and has exploited the jealousy of Brahmans still felt by the groups formerly outside the caste system, such as Chamars. But this does not endear him to the main body of East Indians. Muslims are about one-fifth of the East Indians in Trinidad and their occupations and interests are in most ways similar to those of the Hindus.

In Surinam, the East Indians are about two-fifths of the population to two-fifths Creole and one-fifth Javanese. As we have said already, the policy of the Dutch Government was one of physical segregation and the East Indians of Surinam have mixed less with Creoles and absorbed fewer of their ideas than their compatriots in Trinidad and Guyana. Political parties are avowedly racial but there is less political tension, a frank recognition of difference, and some readiness to divide the spoils of office. But two factors appear outstanding: political awareness seems to be at an earlier stage of development than in Guyana or Trinidad and there are sharp divisions within each ethnic group. Colour divides the Creoles and religion the East Indians; even the Javanese, all nominally Muslim, are divided as to whether to face Mecca to the West, as they did in Java, or to the East, as the longitude of Surinam would suggest. It seems probable that as the possibilities open to political parties become more widely understood, the internal differences will recede and the main ethnic groups will harden into parties sharply opposed. As between Trinidad and Guyana, it can be said positively that tension is sharper in Guyana and it is incontestable that the East Indians here are more numerous and more of a threat. It is also said that the East Indians of Trinidad are more dispersed, more Creolized, in short a less rigidly defined block, than in Guyana, but the demographic factor seems the more potent of the two.

There is one further point, often made by Trinidadians who are in comfortable positions and usually by those of lighter colour. They will first express the official view that Trinidad is free from racial prejudice and discrimination and that people of all colours and kinds mix happily together. When pressed, however, the more discerning will admit that there is social advantage in light skin, a political advantage in a dark, and that hostility is growing between East Indian and Creole. The establishment's talk of racelessness is largely myth, they will concede; nonetheless, they will add, Trinidadians act out their mythology. They do mix on many social occasions and the great national festival of Carnival serves not only as a mixing-bowl but as a safety-valve for high spirits and competitive instincts. But this is surely a Creole point of view and the East Indians who share it are exceptions.

## 7 Summary and Conclusions

Let us summarize what we have found in the Caribbean. In spite of the unique qualities of the society in every Caribbean territory, there is a standard style or structure in relation to which each actual example can be shown as a variant. This standard Caribbean society began as a basic two-class structure of masters and slaves; legal status was the most important distinguishing mark and there were European in-dentured servants as well as Negro slaves. But race was also recognized as a distinction and the original two classes almost from the beginning were graded internally, while very soon a third class grew up, of free persons who were neither masters nor slaves. The members of this middle class were frequently of mixed race and there came to be a general expectation—never exactly realized—that 'white' persons should belong to the upper class, 'coloured' to the middle, and 'black' to the lowest class of slaves.

The middle class was even more graded than the others; it covered a wide range and there was a general expectation that wealth and social position would increase with lighter colour. 'Colour' became an elastic term, including hair formation and features, but capable of being to some extent modified by success and social position; this was within the middle class. But as the agitation developed against the slave trade, and later against slavery, the 'white' upper class, which in most islands had included some who were not of pure European descent, began to lower its barriers against the coloured and, in the typical structure, the three classes of the middle period were collapsed into two, based on 'colour' in its specialized Caribbean sense as an indication of former legal status. The lower of the two classes was predominantly African in descent and consisted mainly of former slaves and their descendants; the upper of the two classes was white or coloured, or both, in different islands. But although a two-class society, the typical structure might also be seen as a continuum, with some movement from one group to the other and border-line cases who would be placed in one category or the other according to the position of the observer.

This was one of the most colonial of all societies, in the sense that the dominant group imposed on all sections of society their own belief that to be 'white' was best in every respect. What this meant was variously interpreted. To the coloured middle class, it generally meant an attitude to marriage, to law, and to constituted authority similar to that of the Victorian middle class. But although, at some social levels and at some levels of consciousness, beliefs of this kind were sometimes expressed by the lower class also, they were usually held, ambivalently and simultaneously, with a very different set of folk-beliefs, often survivals from a slave society. The folk-beliefs included a folk religion, with pre-Christian and magical elements, not all African but sometimes mediaeval European; an attitude to marriage and the family clearly attributable to slavery; and similarly a readiness to condone, if not approve, petty larceny, a hostility to authority and the police, which must be seen as growing from the life of the slave on the plantation. But it is interesting that in Britain, West Indian immigrants have generally shown themselves more law-abiding than the average of the population. They are a self-selected sample from the Caribbean population and must be taken to be those who mean to get on in life and therefore to be consciously adopting what they believe to be 'white' standards.

In the typical structure, there has been a drain away from the top of the social pyramid of the wealthiest and ablest and therefore a social movement upward in the middle class. This was accompanied, until the last twenty years, by an increased consciousness of shades of colour among the middle class and growing discrimination. This has begun to change and the phenomenon of token dark faces begins to appear in board rooms. But there has been little change in the very uneven distribution of wealth between classes, even in those territories where the ruling party purports to stand for the interests of the black lower class. Here there is a division of power—political and economic—between racial groups; this seems unlikely to last.

Of the groups outside the standard Creole structure, those minorities who have been most successful in business and the professions and government service—Jews, Portuguese, Chinese, Syrians—have until lately seen it as their interest to conform increasingly to the coloured ruling group—but to-day this may become dangerous, though it is more dangerous to be isolated. Their dilemma is that of the whites and lighter coloured, which will increase in intensity as the power of the vote is more and more understood. The most important group outside the Creole structure consists of the East Indians, who in three territories are as strong, or almost as strong, as the Creoles in numbers, and who if present trends continue will soon be stronger. In these areas, rivalry and tension increase as numbers increase, except in Surinam where the awareness of political possibilities seems to be less. The one prediction in which it is possible to have confidence is that devices for excluding the East Indians from power are unlikely to be effective for long and on the other hand will probably increase their resentment. All the indications suggest an increasing divergence of the leadership of the two cultures.

The Caribbean region as a whole faces dilemmas from which there seem no escape. These are small territories, separated often by considerable distance and it is not easy for them to combine; the attempt to include them in a Federation they have decisively rejected. But they are over-populated and generally suited by climate and resources to producing goods of which the supply is greater than the world's demands. Openings for emigration have been closed one by one; their awareness of what happens in the rest of the world is growing, their sense of deprivation and of injustice. Awakened expectations are not linked with any goals that it is reasonable to expect. Here is as explosive a situation as can well be imagined and the more so because the search for a pedigree described in Part I of this book is more acute in the Caribbean than anywhere else.

# CHAPTER XIII

# Brazil

## 1  The Colonial Background

Brazil was provisionally described earlier in this book as a society of
fluid racial definition. That is to say, race is not in Brazil the sole and
overriding factor in determining a man's position in society, but one
of several. The point is expressed in the well-known Brazilian proverb:
'A rich black man is a white and a poor white man is a black.'
What this means has already been illustrated in the chapter on the
Caribbean.

But this is only the beginning of a complex set of attitudes to colour
and race, about which widely differing views have been expressed.
Anyone who attempts a comparative study of race relations in different
parts of the world should make some attempt to include Brazil because
of resemblances with Spanish-speaking America, the Caribbean, and
the Deep South—and yet there are sharp differences from all these.
It will be as well to begin with points about which there is general
agreement.

Brazil became part of the Portuguese Empire comparatively late,
when the small Atlantic kingdom was already extended to the limits
of its strength by the task of holding vast possessions in Africa and Asia.
A government was established in 1532, the year before Pizarro strangled
Atahualpa and effectively ended Inca rule in Peru. But the new territories in America were regarded as of less value than the older. They
were sparsely inhabited and offered little opportunity for trade; the
inhabitants were food-gathering jungle tribes with a primitive social
structure and had little to offer that the Portuguese valued. Nor did
they successfully provide the labour which was the first need if the
country was to be developed; they were few enough when the Portuguese came, and their numbers were rapidly reduced by European
diseases, but even if there had been enough of them, as slaves they
were a failure. They were used to the life of the forest, and they could
not be forced to make so immense a readjustment of their outlook on
life as to work long hours at incomprehensible tasks for another's
benefit. As in the Spanish colonies, the Church tried to protect them

and in 1613 their enslavement was made illegal. But it was a practical failure long before that and already the business of bringing slaves from Africa had begun.

Between four and five million African slaves, it is estimated, were brought to Brazil before the trade ended in the mid-nineteenth century. Many came from West Africa—Yoruba, Hausa, and Ewe, and some of these were Muslims, some being literate in the Arabic script; the other chief source was Angola and the Congo, and these were Bantu-speakers. They were not usually dispersed, as was the custom in the West Indies and the Deep South; a shipload from one area would go to the same part of Brazil and it was therefore much easier for the slaves to retain something of their own culture, and a number of African languages were spoken in Brazil within recent memory. It was most usual for the Muslims and other West Africans to go to Bahia and North Brazil, for Bantu-speakers to go further South.

Two institutions came into existence which were typical of this early stage of Brazil's history: on the coast, the *fazenda* or estate, often referred to as the *engenho* from the mill for crushing sugar cane that was the focal point; in the interior, the *aldea* or mission village. The *fazenda* was the typical patriarchal slave estate, with a white owner and his family at the head, with *mulatto* or black house-slaves and Negro field hands; it was operated for the profit of the owner, though the subsistence of the owner's family and labour force usually made a heavy demand on its productivity, and though profit was not always pursued with business-like vigour. But the *aldea*, also a self-contained community whose first economic task was its own subsistence, had as its ultimate purpose not profit, but conversion to Christianity. Here Indians were brought together from the forest, put into villages, and subjected to a strict paternal rule by the religious orders. Their previous culture was destroyed; they ceased to be Indians and became *caboclos*, a word with many variations of meaning, but usually implying a person of mainly Amerindian descent, but nominally a Christian, outwardly Western-ized, in fact the peasant or landless labourer in a rural society. The Jesuits in particular protected their Indians, in the early days, against raids by slaving parties, and later from demands for labour by neighbouring estate-owners; their policy of protection resulted eventually in their expulsion from Brazil at the end of the eighteenth century.

All observers of colonial Brazil agree on one point. The first Portu-guese were male, and manpower was a chronic shortage throughout the Portuguese Empire; economic and social necessity joined forces with inclination and Indian women submitted readily to Portuguese embraces. '*Ils aiment le sexe à la folie*', said a French visitor of the Brazilians.[1] There was regular concubinage and some unions were

[1] Gilberto Freyre, *The Masters and the Slaves*.

blessed by the Church, although in marriage a preference seems to have been established very early for women of mixed blood rather than pure Indians. When Africans began to arrive, the Portuguese masters bred children on their female slaves and soon a mulatto population also began to appear. But marriage with Negroes was at first unknown and always rare, and we have already referred to the case of an Indian chief in the eighteenth century disgraced by the Portuguese authorities for having married a Negro woman.

The history of colonial Brazil may be summarized with great brevity. Over a vast area, sparsely peopled by primitive tribes, the Crown of Portugal claimed sovereignty. But its effective control was weak and the reality was the establishment of a series of feudal estates; in each region, power was in the hands of their owners, a small estate-owning aristocracy. The Crown of Portugal regarded Brazil as a personal appanage and, although control was exercised through the *Conselho Ultramarino*, this body took little interest in anything which did not bring revenue to the Crown. There was less sense of religious mission than in the early days of the Spanish colonies and suspicion of the Crown's officers on the spot was even more deeply ingrained; it was paralysing to efficient government. The pettiest matters had to be referred to Portugal and delays were consequently excessive. The economy was essentially colonial and extractive, any surplus over what was needed for subsistence being destined for Portugal; slavery was the basis of the economic and social structure and observers usually commented that there was no middle class—only masters and slaves.[1] It is the structure erected on this foundation that is of such interest.

## 2 *The Two Views of Brazilian Society*

The most distinguished exponent of the established point of view about Brazilian society is Gilberto Freyre, whose books are vividly written and sensitive, while his knowledge of Brazilian history, memoirs, habits, and folklore is immense. His thesis, consistently and eloquently argued throughout his life, is that three genetic stocks—Portuguese, African, and Amerindian—and three corresponding cultures are in the process of fusing to form one new Luso-Brazilian culture, nation, and race. He argues that Portuguese enthusiasm for copulation made impossible the rigid race prejudice and impersonal relationships of Anglo-Saxon countries and led to an exchange of cultural features and vocabulary, which he illustrates with a wealth of detail. It is hard to resist him, as he describes dances, cookery, religious festivals, superstitions, music, dress, games, in which Portuguese, African, and Indian features have been woven together. But there is an accumulation of recent evidence to suggest that some of his points can be differently interpreted and

[1] Caio Prado, Jr., *The Colonial Background of Modern Brazil.*

that, however much one admires his pioneer work, his emphasis needs
to be corrected by a different perspective.

It must not be suggested that his picture uniformly idealizes a
vanishing past. Indeed, summarizing Freyre in a somewhat rococo
passage, van den Berghe writes:

> The classical analysis of this (the *fazenda*) system in Freyre's *The Masters and
> the Slaves* depicts the Portuguese planters as a slothful, sadistic, decadent,
> vicious, syphilitic, sensuous aristocracy linked in an ambivalently affectionate
> symbiosis with a masochistic class of Negro slaves whom they dragged through
> forced miscegenation in the indolent cesspool of their refined perversions.[1]

This heightens even Freyre's bright colours. But though individual
vices—indolence, self-indulgence, and cruelty—are certainly not left
out of Freyre's picture, it does seem possible that to some extent he
idealizes relationships. He writes from an essentially Portuguese point
of view, congratulating his forebears on the warm, human qualities with
which they welcomed African and Indian women to their beds—or
rather hammocks, for the hammock was a cultural feature native to
America and adopted into the Luso-Brazilian complex. But a later
generation is bound to ask whether in fact the fusion was quite so
generous as he suggests.

For three centuries, Africans were enslaved and transported to
Brazil; can it really be argued that this did not involve a contempt for
their status as human beings? Or that the contempt was free from
any belief that they were hereditarily inferior? It is inherently improbable, and the evidence collected by Professor Boxer proves that
it was not so. And how can the different attitude to American Indians
be explained except on the grounds of prejudice about colour? It was
manifest before Africans could be regarded as either a threat or as
rivals. From the point of view of sex, on which Freyre lays so much
stress, there was no equality; the white master did not allow his male
slaves the freedom with women of his colour that he took for granted
with theirs. And to borrow hammocks and sandals, dance-steps, drums,
and *xaque-xaques*[2] is hardly an equal exchange for taking away
social structure, religion, and language and substituting a degraded
version of one's own. The exchange also involved a trifling matter of
freedom of the person and the subtler colonial theft of inherited
values.

It is nonetheless now the established and official doctrine of Brazil
that Brazilians have little race consciousness and do not discriminate
against a man on grounds of colour or race. This doctrine receives
support from the popular Press, which reacts with immediate hostility to
any report of racial discrimination; indeed, discrimination is banned by
law and punished by the courts. The doctrine is backed in general

[1] P. L. van den Berghe, *Race and Racism*.
[2] A musical instrument filled with pebbles which are shaken in rhythm.

by Freyre's thesis, from which it partly derives. It is further supported by Donald Pierson's valuable *Negroes in Brazil*. This, as Pierson himself emphasizes, is a study of Bahia rather than of Brazil; he acknowledges that conditions in Bahia are different from Southern Brazil or the Amazon Basin, and he perceives signs of change even in Bahia. But his general conclusion is that class rather than race is the determining factor in Bahian, and indeed Brazilian, society. He found that an overwhelming majority of black people (*pretos*) were in lower-paid and poorly esteemed jobs, and of whites in the best-paid and most esteemed jobs. But a few *pretos* were in highly paid and highly esteemed jobs and were generally accepted as leaders of the community; the same was true of a larger number of 'browns' (*pardos*) and although in general African appearance was often an indication of low social position, it was possible to overcome these social disadvantages.

Pierson's original work was done in 1935-7, but for the most recent edition of his book a survey was carried out among university students in five cities. By a majority of five to one, the students said they would prefer to belong to a mulatto family of high prestige rather than a white family of low prestige; by the same majority they would rather be a mulatto with a good education than a white with a poor education. There was a three to one preference for being black with a good education rather than white with a bad education.

No one can suppose, however, that university students are typical of the whole population; they are generally less concerned about race and by definition interested in education. Nor is the answer to a hypothetical question necessarily a guide to conduct when faced with a decision in real life. But such answers would be unlikely in South African universities and perhaps in British or American; they express the strong distaste for rigid racial discrimination which is widespread as an explicit ideal in Brazil. The question is how far reality corresponds with the ideal and whether there is a Brazilian dilemma comparable with the American. It is worth quoting Pierson's concluding paragraph:

This is not to say that there are no social distinctions in Brazil. . . . Neither does it mean that there is no discrimination or that blacks and mixed bloods are entirely satisfied with their lot. But it does mean (a) that a man of colour may, by reason of individual merit or favourable circumstance, improve his status and even achieve position in the upper levels of society and (b) that this position will then be with reference not merely to the darker group . . . but to the total community.

This is true so far as it goes and it records a marked difference from the United States, but it is open to the same criticism as Freyre's thesis. Society is arranged in tiers; promotion from the lowest tier is possible provided the candidate conforms to the ways of the upper. The whites in fact say: 'Provided you behave as we do, we will overlook the colour of your skin.' Now in a society organized purely on a class basis, this may or may not be a fair attitude; to discuss this would be a digression we must resist.[1] But if there are ethnic differences, it is surely open to objection. And Pierson spends some pages on demonstrating that in Bahia the *pobres*—the poor—who are predominantly of African descent, are of quite a different culture from the *ricos*—the rich—while his final hypothesis is that 'the race problem in Brazil, insofar as there is a race problem, tends to be identified with the resistance which an ethnic group offers, or is thought to offer, to absorption and assimilation'. He is right in thinking that this assumption is implicit in the official Brazilian view that 'we are all becoming one people'. But this, surely, is a white, or at least, European view, and it involves the belief that the Brazilian Negro is disappearing, both genetically and culturally, into a world of which the culture is predominantly European. This is just the kind of assumption which Negroes in the United States are beginning passionately to repudiate; translated into purely cultural terms, the same repudiation is the backbone of French separatism in Canada.

But, apart from this objection, which would have occurred to hardly any white investigator in the 1930s, there has been more recently a good deal of evidence which suggests that, whatever is proclaimed as the ideal, strong unfavourable generalizations are made about Negroes and in practice something very like discrimination does take place. Overt discrimination, which would be punishable by the courts, is hardly needed in a country in which there are great differences between rich and poor and the poor are mostly illiterate. Most of this evidence comes from Rio de Janeiro or São Paulo, a point to which we shall return. But studies by Wagley, Costa Pinto, Bastide and van den Berghe, and Florestan Fernandes suggest something very different from the official view. For example, while 92 per cent of students in São Paulo thought whites and Negroes should have equal opportunities, only 60 per cent regarded casual relations, and only 38 per cent any closer ties, as something they would themselves accept with Negroes; this again is an enquiry among students, who are likely to be more favourably disposed than most of the public. Segregation, not by law, but by custom, is reported in public parks, barber's shops, private clubs and associations, in some cinemas, at some sporting events. In a study of 245 newspaper advertisements for domestic servants, *all* employers asked for white servants. As to marriage, even in the 1930s and in Bahia, Pierson found only forty-two cases of inter-racial marriage out

---

[1] In fact, in a class society, if a man from the bottom tier reaches the top tier, people at the top usually criticize him if he does not behave as they do and make fun of him if he does. The conservative Press in Britain displayed both attitudes to the first Labour Party government. J. H. Thomas, for example, was usually depicted by cartoonists in a white tie and ill-fitting tail-coat.

of 1,269 marriages—though he argues that these figures concealed some cases in which one party classed as white had coloured ancestry. More recently, 93 per cent of white students in Bahia objected to marrying a Negro; in São Paulo, 95 per cent of white students said they would not marry a Negro and 87 per cent that they would not marry a light-skinned mulatto.[1] Florestan Fernandes in 1967, writing of São Paulo, says that: 'Mixed marriages meet with an almost insurmountable resistance as things now stand.'[2]

It is the general thesis of Fernandes that the Negroes in São Paulo have been bypassed by the economic and industrial expansion of the last century and a half; at the time of emancipation, the former slaves were quite unprepared for 'freedom', having no understanding of the nature of a commercial contract and believing 'freedom' to mean they need now work only when they felt inclined. They proved therefore most unsatisfactory employees and as, at this period, the government was encouraging immigration from Europe, they soon found that their way into the expanding economy had been blocked by European immigrants who were better educated, more skilled, and accustomed to working for wages. If Negroes were employed, unfavourable expectations were quickly confirmed and the familiar downward spiral had begun. The whole account sounds reminiscent of the Northern cities of the United States a generation earlier.

### 3 Comparisons

The discrepancy between these two views of race relations in Brazil is a matter of emphasis. Everyone is agreed that race plays a less important part in social definition than in South Africa or the United States, that it is only one determinant among many, and that attitudes about race are flexible. Pierson, for instance, points out that the racial terms in which a man is described will vary with personal feelings and in the same person's mouth on different occasions; the term used when he is out of favour will suggest that he is darker.

There is nonetheless a real difference between the two views, due in the main to three factors. First, Bahia and the North-East, the centre of the old plantation area, was the region where there were most Negroes, where the plantation system was strongest, where there has been the least social change, and where the spectrum of colour was most complete; it is primarily of this area that Freyre and Pierson are thinking, while more recent writers are writing of the industrial South. Secondly, a change is taking place; the economy is becoming less rural, people are moving to the towns; a feudal, rural society is being gradually superseded by a competitive industrial society. Thirdly, there is a change

[1] Roger Bastide, 'Dusky Venus, Black Apollo'.
[2] Florestan Fernandes, 'The Weight of the Past'.

in the world situation which heightens expectations and which throws doubt on the white assumption that those who are not white will wait for the material benefits of a richer world until they have learnt how to behave like white people.

But there are still many questions to be asked. The nature of Brazilian slavery has been much discussed, claims being made that it was much 'milder' than the West Indian or Virginian forms of slavery. There is sometimes confusion here, and of two kinds. First, in all three systems there was a distinction between house-slaves and field hands; in the controversies that raged before abolition, one party emphasized the hardships of the field hands, the other the affectionate relations that often existed between house-slaves and masters. It is therefore important first to be sure one is comparing like with like. But there is also a distinction between the nature of the institution and the conditions on a given plantation. The latter must have varied greatly from one district to another, between one owner and another and at different periods. It is hard to make any just comparison. Bahia, for example, was notorious for slave risings, which occurred in 1807, 1809, 1813, 1816, 1826, 1827, 1828, 1830, and 1835. They were usually betrayed in advance by a fellow-slave and therefore easily suppressed and cruelly punished. The series does not suggest that slavery was exactly enjoyed, but the persistence in revolt is probably due not so much to specially bad conditions as to the predominance in Bahia of Muslims who were better educated than those previously pagan. But irrespective of individual cruelties and kindnesses, the systems can be compared as institutions, and here there seems to me no doubt of the general thesis that the Brazilian institution was milder, and this in two ways that affected the social structure that eventually arose.

Manumission was frequent and since a slave could own property and earn money, he could buy his freedom. An owner who refused to release a slave on payment of his purchase price was the object of general disapproval, and eventually to refuse was made illegal. It was a pious act and indeed common practice to release slaves by will. The offspring of slave women and white fathers in particular were often freed and sometimes fully acknowledged and brought up as part of the family. Even those who remained legally slaves, if they had a skill which could earn money and were superfluous to the needs of the estate, were sent into the towns to work as carpenters, wheelwrights, shoemakers, and the like, remitting to their owner a fixed monthly sum and becoming as it were tenants of their own bodies. They were known as *negros de ganha*; since they kept their surplus earnings they were often able to buy their freedom.[1]

The institution of slavery, apart from local vagaries, was thus less impersonal than in Virginia or Jamaica, and this for two reasons,

[1] This also happened in Cuba, see page 277.

perhaps three. For the Portuguese, as for the Spanish, slavery was a legally recognized status in the Old World and the law embodied some aspects of the Roman personal law of slavery. Secondly, the Church was centralized and powerful and the Church insisted that a slave was a person with a soul. It is also argued, not with equal cogency, that the Portuguese had been familiar with Muslim slave-owners and had borrowed from them a picture of the slave as a junior member of the family rather than an article of farm equipment.

Be this as it may, the effect of frequent manumissions and of purchases of their freedom by *negros de ganha* was to diversify the simple two-tier system of masters and slaves. Three processes can be distinguished; there was a steady increase in the proportion of free persons to slaves; at the same time, those freed were at first far more often mulatto than black; finally throughout the last two hundred years, there has been an increase in the number of persons classed as white.[1]

The proportion of free to slave was about one to two in 1789, when the total population was estimated at 2.3 million and the slaves at 1.5 million, but by 1872, the slaves were only 15.2 per cent of the total; the proportion now was reversed and six to one. Those freed were at first predominantly mulatto; in 1828, Walsh (quoted by Pierson) estimated that there were 160,000 free blacks to 400,000 free mulattoes, while in Minas Gerais, in 1835, it was recorded that only one in four of the mulattoes were slaves, while only one in six of the blacks were free. The increasing proportion of whites can be illustrated from three dates: 1835, when 24.4 per cent of the population were white; 1872, when the percentage was 38.1 per cent; 1941, when it was 44.4 per cent.[2] But what is not clear is how much of this was due to white immigration and how much to less rigid standards of classification; about four million white immigrants are believed to have come into the country between 1830 and 1930.

The figures indicate a surprisingly rapid shift from the colonial two-tier system of masters and slaves to a three-tier system formed by the addition of an intermediate group of free persons of colour, largely of mixed blood. Yet there is the constantly recurring comment: 'Brazil has no middle class.' Foreign travellers in Brazil in the nineteenth century were usually far removed in wealth from the mass of the people and may have failed to distinguish gradations among them, but even observers from North America in this century repeat the

[1] Much has been written about the effect of numerical proportions, white to non-white, on the development of racial systems in Brazil and the United States. From the point of view of my comparisons, Brazil and the Southern States are not very dissimilar; in both, there is a higher proportion of whites than in South Africa, much higher than in, say, Jamaica. I have put a note on this at the end of the chapter so as not to interrupt the sequence of my own argument by controversy.

[2] P. L. van den Berghe, *Race and Racism*. But Rodrigues says that by 1940 the whites were 63·47 per cent of the population (José Honorio Rodrigues, *Brazil and Africa*).

point. It may be partly a matter of words; one may think of artisans
operating on their own account like the *negros de ganha* either as lower
middle class or as a higher tier of the lowest class. Such men were
certainly not rich and were far removed in their way of life from the
owners of *fazendas*. The comment may also reflect the continual influx
to the seaports of Portuguese born in the Iberian kingdom who
monopolized the commerce of the country and were bitterly disliked
by the Brazilian-born landowners. This was a middle class that was
not truly Brazilian.

But perhaps the deepest reason for this comment is that Brazilian
society was more a series of regional segments than a class society, each
regional segment being sub-divided into smaller self-supporting
*fazendas*. An artisan in a small town was very differently placed from a
field hand on a neighbouring *fazenda* but he was much more intimately
linked with the *fazenda* than with a man following his own occupation
in another small town. Colonial Brazil may be called a two-tier class
system showing signs of becoming a three-tier race system, but the
vertical divisions (between regions and *fazendas*) were probably stronger
than horizontal ties (between people of any but the upper class in
different regions). And it must be emphasized that the tiers were
everywhere blurred at the edges.

What we see, then, is the beginning, in colonial times, of a process
that continued in the period of the Empire—that is from 1822 to 1889.
It was not the emergence of a complete social spectrum, because of the
gap in wealth between the upper group, the owners of *fazendas*, and
their opponents, the Portuguese-born merchants, on the one hand, and
the class of free people of colour, on the other; but it sketched the
outlines of such a spectrum. There seemed every likelihood that there
would develop a basically three-tier social organization, based on a
mixture of colour and class. Discrimination in colonial times was still
sharp; at the end of the eighteenth century, 'persons received into the
Carmelite Order had to affirm that they would "throw out any
postulant who was proved to be of Moorish, mulatto or Jewish stock
or of any other abhorrent race" ';[1] there were regiments of the militia
that would accept only whites or nominal whites; there were others
that were for *pardos* (browns) and some for free blacks.[2] But instead of
becoming more rigid, barriers blurred and lines tilted; the spectrum
began to fill in, to make a continuum of colour and of class, with a
good deal of correspondence between the two criteria, but far from
total agreement.

In the British West Indies, we suggested that there was little opposition to the freeing of slaves and the growth of an intermediate class
of people of colour because there were few whites and in particular

[1] Caio Prado, Jr., *The Colonial Background of Modern Brazil.*
[2] Ibid.

few white artisans or small shopkeepers to object. But the proportion of resident whites in colonial Brazil was nearer Virginia's than Jamaica's; why were the lines of development so much more Caribbean than North American? We have already explained that there was a different attitude to slavery, but there was also a different attitude to work. 'Work is only for dogs and Negroes' (*Trabalho é para cachorro e negro*), quotes Pierson; and Prado writes: 'the depreciation of all forms of manual labour associated with slavery and the stimulus slavery provided for the masters to remain idle . . . created a contempt or aversion for any form of activity. . . .' The point is emphasized by most observers and, at the crucial stage of the early nineteenth century, slavery in Brazil thus provided its own antidote; there was little objection to free Negroes taking up any form of activity that meant physical work. 'Few are the mulattoes and rare the whites', wrote Vilhena,[1] 'who wish to work or practice any handicraft, not even those same paupers who in Portugal were nothing but servants and waited at table or wielded the hoe. . . .'

There was thus a stage at which there was no rivalry between freed Negro and lower-class white and this must have contributed to the development of a social spectrum. So far, though for somewhat different reasons, the movement closely resembles that of the West Indies. But there are important differences. In the West Indies the number of whites was always very small, the largest estate-owners were frequently absent, and, as we have seen, there was a continual loss from the upper tier of society of its ablest and most ambitious members to Europe. Thus a continuous movement upward from tier to tier was possible so long as the principle of a stratified society was accepted. And to-day, when this principle begins to be questioned, the number of whites remaining is so small that they are forced to accept the roles allotted them by the political majority.

But in Brazil the flow of whites was inward; the white immigrants of the last century are about as many as the black of the two previous centuries. And Brazil—not a string of tiny islands but a vast federation the size of a continent—is moving towards a competitive industrial age. The traditional structure was heavily stratified, but until lately the stratification was concealed, partly by the self-sufficiency of the regions and the strength of vertical regional allegiances, and partly by its stability. The basic assumptions were taken for granted; the system seemed likely to last. Those assumptions are now shaken and as society becomes more and more competitive the masses in the industrial South seem likely to be more and more divided on racial lines.

If numbers were the overriding factor in race relations, one might expect to find Brazil more like the Deep South than like the Caribbean.

[1] Quoted by Caio Prado, Jr., *The Colonial Background of Modern Brazil.*

The numerical proportions between the races at the end of the colonial period were not widely dissimilar; both were based on plantation slavery with one predominant cash crop.[1] But there were basic differences in the attitudes to work, to sex, and to religion. To these we have already referred, but there is one aspect of the religious difference which Pierson notes which has perhaps not been sufficiently emphasized. The Catholic Church stresses ritual, the community as a whole, the observance of certain minimal disciplines; it provides by confession and absolution release for internal stress and (it is intended) disinterested guidance for the individual. It thus aims at externalizing conflict for the majority of its members. The Protestant churches lay stress on individual conversion, the gathered community as opposed to the parish; they discourage any mediation between God and man and thus they internalize conflict. One emphasizes unity, the other diversity. It is far more likely, then, that Protestants will seek to identify themselves closely with an ethnic group smaller than the whole of mankind and that internal tension will seek release by identification with a group. I believe that this basic difference in outlook has been one important element in the different lines of development.

But there are other reasons as well. The South was threatened by the North and forced to abandon slavery; the whole structure of Southern society was shattered by the Civil War. In Brazil, slavery, as we have seen, dwindled long before abolition and was eventually ended by a consensus of opinion in which the Church was united with the liberals, intellectuals with merchants. There was therefore no need to make Negroes the scapegoats for hostility to abolitionists.[2]

To this I would add a hypothesis not, so far as I know, tested by historical research. The difference in the systems of power was considerable; in the Southern States, white men elected leaders who had to keep their votes. It is often said that the Southern whites disfranchised themselves in order to disfranchise the Negroes, but this is only true on the Federal level, and to be a political leader within the State meant flattering voters, who after 1789 included all males who were free. This was virtually synonymous with all who were white. The system of local political power in Brazil seems to have been to a greater extent a matter of building up a system of feudal power, patronage, reciprocal ties of obligation, and control of the local militia and other forces nominally central. All this is partly true of the South, but to a much lesser extent. In Brazil there was much less need to appeal to the interests or opinions of anyone other than the estate-owners, who could afford to be indifferent to the growth of a class of free coloured artisans. The narrowness of the Brazilian oligarchy, I suggest, contributed to the fluidity of the society.

[1] 'Latifundiary monoculture' is the term that some like to use.
[2] See C. Vann Woodward, *The Strange Career of Jim Crow.*

This, perhaps, is another way of saying that in nineteenth-century Brazil the premise of inequality was strong, in spite of some lip-service to the ideas of the enlightenment, while in the United States (as we have already said) the assumption that all men were brothers was so far accepted that there was no place in society for the Negro except on the understanding that he was not really a man. Brazil was a European society, hierarchically organized, and few seriously supposed that it would ever be different. Thus the growth of a social spectrum, in which everyone knew his place and showed respect to his superior, was natural and acceptable. On the other hand, in Brazil, as in the West Indies, the assumption of white superiority ran right through the whole structure.

There are a number of sayings and verses collected by Pierson in the 1930s of which he says that they are cultural survivals, now always uttered with a smile. One song begins:

> Whites sleep in beds
> Mulattoes in the kitchen
> Caboclos on the terrace
> Negroes under the hen-roost.

But if still quoted, even with a smile, such sayings—and there are many of them—indicate a prejudice not far below the surface and one that might easily be revived if circumstances were such as to encourage it. And there are many indications that they are.

Brazil's fluidity in racial definition was, as we have seen, very largely due to the stability of social ideas and a deep acceptance of the principle of inequality. It was taken for granted that men were unequal; there was no need to assert it. It follows that to-day, as the old patriarchal social system breaks up, as people move from traditional rural areas to the industrial centres, as the premise of inequality is challenged over so wide an area, two dangers arise. First, those who feel themselves threatened will begin to assert their superiority; secondly, whites will see they have common interests with whites, and blacks with blacks. Reversing the North American geographical direction, Negroes from the plantations of the North move towards the industrial South. But socially there is an ominous resemblance about the flow. Ill-trained for industrial life, Negroes whose fathers or grandfathers were field hands are trying to make their way into industries already manned by white immigrants from Europe. White peasants from rural districts in Brazil are also making for the factories. In this anonymous competitive world, a man's ancestors, his character, his skills are not known; he is identified by the one thing everyone can see—his racial uniform. And it suggests that he is unskilled, poorly educated, an irresponsible employee. As Florestan Fernandes says, 'in order to change this situation, the human groups directly concerned must become conscious of the situation and make an organized effort to change it. . . .' This means that not only the white groups, who are economically, culturally, and politically in power, but the Negroes, who are out, must see the situation as it is and by a process of reasoned conflict try to reach a new relationship which recognizes the identity of both. In this task, Brazil has one great asset, the conviction that racial discrimination is wrong; one disadvantage, the refusal to recognize that it occurs.

### Note to Chapter XIII

Marvin Harris has written vehemently in criticism of Gilberto Freyre's general thesis and has also assailed Frank Tannenbaum, whom he brackets with Freyre. But Tannenbaum's emphasis is different from Freyre's and is rather on the effect of Catholicism on the institution of slavery in Brazil as well as in the Spanish territories. This Harris entirely discounts and indeed he is contemptuous of all ideological factors in the situation. The need for manpower, he claims, is the main reason for what he calls the Descent Rule, that is, the exclusion from the white category in the United States of anyone with an element of Negro blood. There were not enough Portuguese for all the tasks which 'must be performed by free men', so the Portuguese had to beget mulattoes and free them. The same tasks in the Southern States were performed by the 'white yeomanry', because the numerical proportions in 1715 were 'reversed'. (They were not exactly reversed, because one in three is not the same as one to three, which is one in four, an arithmetical mistake he makes twice in his discussion.)

Nonetheless, there is something in this. Everyone who has written about the Portuguese colonies has emphasized this need for manpower and the numerical proportions were important—but they do not explain everything. Harris does also recognize the influence of the threat from the North to the whole Southern system of slavery. I agree with him in thinking it is unnecessary to look for anything in 'the Portuguese soul' to explain the difference, but to lay such overwhelming stress on the numerical proportions is to ignore slavery in other parts of the world. There was a similar system of slavery in Jamaica, where the numerical proportions were completely different from either Brazil or the Southern States but where the descent rule was much more like Brazil; there developed in South Africa a descent rule very like that of the Southern States—but in South Africa numerical proportions were more like those in Brazil than in the South.

The point will perhaps be clearer if we revert to the methods of Part II and list the factors which have been suggested as relevant, with some indication against each of the different attitudes to them in Brazil and the Southern States.

Table 5

Factors relevant to the rigidity of the Descent Rule in the United States as compared with fluidity of definition in Brazil (from colonial times in both cases)

|  |  | Brazil | Southern States |
|---|---|---|---|
| 1 | Religion | Catholic | Protestant |
| 2 | Legal position of slaves | Defined in Europe | Defined locally |
| 3 | Attitude to manual work | Despised | Admired |
| 4 | Premise of Inequality | Accepted | Rejected |
| 5 | Attitude to Paternity | Pride | Shame |
| 6 | External threat to system | Negligible | Strong |
| 7 | Dependence of ruling class on votes | Slight | More important |
| 8 | Proportions of white to non-white | 1715: 1 to 2 | 1715: 3 to 1 |
|  |  | 1835: 1 to 3 | 1840: 3 to 2 |
|  |  | 1872: 2 to 3 | 1940: 3 to 1 |

(Figures mainly from Marvin Harris, but others could be quoted, and since definition in Brazil is very uncertain they cannot be exact. Approximate reversal is true.)

Each of these eight factors, crudely summarized in the table, seems to me to have contributed to the result. Harris regards the last as of overwhelming importance. But interesting points—as usual—emerge as soon as the comparison is widened. Jamaica is a society of fluid definition, like Brazil, and resembles Brazil more than the Deep South in items 3, 4, 5, 6, and 7 of the table. It is more like the Deep South on the first two items (supporting Harris's view that they are unimportant) but utterly different in respect of numerical proportions. South Africa, on the other hand, resembles the Deep South more than Brazil in every respect except numerical proportion. The ratio to-day is approximately one white to four non-white; the immense labours of the Tomlinson Report in 1954 were based on the assumption that unless active steps were taken the whites would be even more heavily outnumbered. To what extent they were outnumbered in the past depends on where one draws the frontier of an expanding society. But there was always a mixed society within the frontier, an immense preponderance of black people beyond. White South Africans have always been outnumbered, and more so than white Brazilians, but they have developed on quite different lines. Afrikaners profess to be classless among themselves; 'we are an entire nation of aristocrats', one of them told me.

If men thought out where their material advantage lay and ordered their society on rational grounds, the South Africans would surely have tried to make of the mixed population allies against the Africans. But, we have seen, this did not happen. Why did they instead adopt a system excluding all non-whites from their society? Calculations of material advantage are only one factor among many; the sense of a threat was even stronger in South Africa than in the Southern States. And to me it seems quite unrealistic to rule out the emotions with which early settlers regarded the children of their liaisons with slave women. Such emotions were both the product of a past social system and factors in the system that followed; they are the subject we are investigating but also its cause. Later generations may be conditioned by what they conceive as social necessity to behave to their children in accordance with established patterns—but in the early formative stages, it is surely of some importance whether a man is pleased and proud to see his child or ashamed? Does he acknowledge his son or treat him as a slave? It will surely make a difference if he felt some affection for the mother. But to Marvin Harris this is a 'hoary sex myth' and we must picture the young father calculating the military needs of the colony in twenty years' time before he decides how to treat his child.

This is not entirely fair because of course the attitude of the government and of society do affect the individual's choice, and they will include these calculations. But Harris is a polemicist who invites reprisals. He thinks the necessity for artisans made it essential to free slaves. But in fact the *negros de ganha* performed exactly the tasks which he says only free men can do and continued to be slaves. It was a result of Roman and Portuguese law (which he discounts) that they could in many cases eventually buy their freedom. One could continue the argument indefinitely; I remain convinced that there are many complex causes for phenomena which he thinks can be explained by a few simple causes, all material. If he was right, for the same reason that the Deep South is more rigid than Brazil, Brazil should be more rigid than South Africa. But he is refreshing to read, clear, vigorous, widely read, and perceptive when not on this hobby-horse.

# PART IV

# CHAPTER XIV

# Conclusions

## 1 Main Impressions

We have looked at a wide variety of situations and many different human groups, at many stages of progress. Sometimes we have seen one group establishing over another a dominance that they have sought to maintain rigidly and have believed could be permanent, while another has been content with a far more fluid overlordship of which the whole nature has changed rapidly. But in every case we have looked at there *has* been change and it has never been possible to understand any situation as a cross-section in time without an excursion into the past and some attempt at perceiving the direction of change. Diversity between situations and movement within each situation have been the outstanding characteristics. Let us now stand back and try to summarize in the broadest terms what has emerged from the discussion.

In the first part of the book, I suggested that social stratification, by which one group or class in a society was assumed to be permanently superior to another, had been a condition of human progress. In a sense, it had been *the* social and political problem for the earliest empire-builders, who by some means had to persuade their subjects that it was their duty, indeed their inevitable lot, to work hard for long hours for the benefit of others and receive little reward. The immediate sanction of force could be applied to the occasional deviant; but the whole society had to be convinced that the system was necessary or inevitable, and this was usually achieved by persuading the masses that it had divine backing.

It was the next step that such empires should seek to increase their native labour force, and lighten its burden, by recruiting from con-quered neighbours a force of foreign and socially inferior workers. Stratification—the division of society by horizontal barriers—thus began to cut across the vertical divisions of mankind by speech, ancestry, custom, and geography. Thus there arose within a single political system distinctions of status which were sometimes emphasized by genetic physical differences. Genesis gives some hints of the position of foreign labourers in Egypt, for example, and limestone carvings show that the Egyptians identified Eastern peoples and Africans by facial characteristics and hair.

Empires on this ancient model rose, crumbled, fell, and were succeeded by others. Patterns not dissimilar were followed in the Mediterranean basin, in India and China, in America; they were beginning in Africa South of the Sahara. The inequality of man—the necessity for a social structure in which some toiled incessantly while others ruled them—was taken for granted in every political structure of any consequence. But the societies that succeeded Rome were shot through by a contrary set of ideas: that men were equal before God, that they ought to be equal before the law, that they ought to have some equality of opportunity. A process began of which technical advance was certainly one result, but perhaps neither the first nor the most significant. The individual became increasingly important; the nuclear family of husband, wife, and children began to replace the clan and the extended family, ruled by the grandfather. The process of learning was immensely accelerated by the invention of printing and this brought a new attitude to stored knowledge. Pre-literate societies rely on memory, which is so brittle that they are bound to pay high respect to old people and to tradition; the attitude survives in societies where books are few and handwritten, where few can read them. Printing opened knowledge to far more minds and also encouraged a far more free and enquiring spirit.

The individual became more important, and at the same time a new political and social structure began to develop in Europe, as regions under feudal overlords began to coalesce into nation-states. But the nation-states held a contradiction at the heart; the Habsburgs, the Valois, the Tudors, sought to build a structure with a centralized political authority and a stratified society of Crown, nobles, burghers, craftsmen, and peasants. But the Church, though itself highly stratified, taught—if it did not always believe—a revolutionary doctrine of the unique importance of the individual and of man's potential equality. These contradictory doctrines were held simultaneously: one of them provided the assumptions on which European societies were organized; the other, their professed faith, read daily in cathedrals and churches, acted on only occasionally but never wholly banished from popular consciousness. From this contradiction grew the tough inner strength of these new national societies which enabled them to overrun the rest of the world. Their political unity and their technical advantages— which in Asia, Mexico, and Peru were slight at the time of first contact —were the tools used to establish their dominance, but the secret of their success lay in the combination of individualism with political unity and discipline. At the same time, this contradiction made it inevitable that their colonies should eventually rebel.

Improved navigation was one tool which brought these new,

disciplined, but individualist, societies into contact with an immense variety of peoples in varied stages of development—empires like those of Babylon and Egypt in Asia and America, primitive states in Ashanti and Zululand, Iron-Age agriculturists, nomadic tribes, food-gathering groups. In Part II, I have tried to explore the interaction of a variety of factors which have contributed to the resulting relationships. The beliefs, conscious and unconscious, of the dominant group; their assumptions about their own society; the stage of development of the subordinate group; the nature of the country and the motives which attracted the conquerors; the degree of selection exercised by the sending society; the proportions of men to women among the conquerors and the attitudes to sex of both parties to the relationship— all these have helped to shape the result. No single factor has been overriding. But that is not to say that human volition—conscious or unconscious—has not played its part.

Indeed, the outstanding impressions made on my mind by the events in recorded history of which I have knowledge are the diversity of the situations arising from conquest and contact, the many-stranded nature of the causes, and the part played by the human will. Of these, only the last needs further emphasis. Everywhere decisions have been taken which have profoundly modified the relationship of the two groups, even when this was not the direct purpose. The ruling group has the power, if it will use it, to define its own limits and its own structure; the result will never entirely conform to the intention but it will be affected by it. One of the clearest examples is the decision of the Crown of Spain to unify its dominions on the basis of Catholicism, not of ethnic origin. There were two minor corollaries to this: the Crown tended to avoid direct confrontation with regional diversity; to support the people against the nobles, the Indians against the *encomenderos*. It was a deliberate policy, sustained for more than a century, and its influence on the relationship of Hispanic to Indian is felt to-day. No Spanish American country has openly repudiated the premises on which the policy was based and indeed all publicly subscribe to them, however great the gap between principles and practice. There have been second stages of decision, at the time of independence and again, in Mexico, at the Revolution of 1910. The original impulse may be sustained or reversed, though it may be very difficult to reverse, but room for an act of will is always present.

In India, the 'decision' to strengthen caste barriers was taken at a period when history is hard to disentangle from myth; I do not suppose that it was ever formulated in words. But the reversal of that ancient choice was a decision consciously taken and embodied in the constitution of 1952; it grew logically from the principles, themselves Western, which Indian nationalists had invoked against Western rule; whether it will succeed cannot yet be foretold with any confidence. In South

Africa, the decision was to divide society rigidly, and the criterion eventually chosen was neither religion, nor the status of slave or free, nor culture, but, instead of these, colour. The choice was made gradually, step by step, over four centuries; the barriers grew stiffer and higher with each step. But the policy is explicit; it is proclaimed by successive governments and the only opposition party of any size does not contest its basic assumptions. Southern Rhodesia too was presented with a clear choice and debated it, not only in the Press and in the legislature but in meeting-halls, in private conversations, wherever white people met. The majority of white people chose the course which would preserve their dominance as long and as rigidly as possible.

It is in the Caribbean societies that the conscious choice of those concerned has played the least part. Their development has been the result of decisions taken elsewhere, or by absentees, or by people whose descendants are no longer in the islands, by a class which no longer exists, and usually for reasons which had little to do with the human population that might result. This is true of most of the great landmarks of Caribbean history until the twenty years after the Second World War. The extermination of Caribs and Arawaks was not planned; the importation of Negroes was the result of initiatives in Europe and of absentee landlords or of planters whose main purpose was to make money quickly and go to Europe. The abolition of the slave trade, the emancipation of the slaves, the fall in the price of sugar, were the result of external forces; the same is true of the return to Crown Colony government in the British islands. The importation of indentured labour from Asia was, it is true, the result of pressure by the planters, but they as a class have ceased to exist. Even the independence of the British islands is the result of what had happened in India and Ghana at least as much as any activities in the Caribbean. It is only since independence that people who live in the Caribbean begin to have any chance of influencing the structure of their own societies.

In Brazil, as in Spanish territories, there were some attempts by Crown and Church to proclaim the individual value of human souls and the equal rights of Portuguese subjects. But they were intermittent and ineffective; in colonial times, the premises of human inequality and social stratification were so strong that there was little need to insist on them formally. Shortage of manpower encouraged a sexual enthusiasm that had nothing to do with mutual respect, either between man and woman or between master and slave, white and coloured. But with independence came the beginning, the first faint shadow, of a Brazilian dilemma, the gap between profession and ideals. The premise of inequality is no longer accepted; as men move to the cities, they are likely to be identified increasingly by appearance and the traditional attitudes of Brazil are likely to be tested. Brazil approaches a period of crucial decisions.

There is a second impression that emerges from this wide survey of patterns of dominance. Through long periods, men have accepted the premise of inequality as inherent in the world order. The bluff of the rulers has worked; soldiers and workers alike have done as they were told. Political stability over wide areas and for long periods has not been a normal condition, but *social* stability has been far more general; in tribes and villages men have gone about their business, concerned with birth, marriage, death, food; frequently also with the necessity of paying rent, tribute, blackmail, or forced labour to some exterior force. They have usually taken the social order for granted. But this is no longer the case. Revolt against the social order and the principle of stratification is not universal, but it is widespread. It is openly manifest everywhere, except in some isolated pockets of unawakened stagnation and where it is still rigorously suppressed, as in South Africa.

This revolt against the social fact of stratification is a secondary, but far more deep-rooted, phase of the political revolt against imperial control of colonies. It is inevitable—part of the dialectic of imperialism —that the colony should seek independence and doubly so in the case of the European expansion, because of the infection of individualism which Europeans brought with them. They could not keep to themselves the ideas or the social structure—at once individualist and disciplined—which had enabled them to establish their rule. And the colonial revolt—usually conceived, in the first place and on both sides, as of one racial group against another—has reinfected the imperial homeland, where it is translated into social terms. But here too a continual cross-infection or pollination is in progress between the racial and social aspects of revolt and counter-revolt.

This is a complex process with various interwoven strands, of which two may be simplified and exposed. In the 1950s, it became a commonplace among African nationalists that, until they showed they were in earnest by violence, fair words and promises were all they were likely to get from the British Colonial Office. They therefore showed that they were in earnest. There would then be a phase during which the Governor, backed by the Colonial Secretary, repeated that there could be no negotiations with those responsible for violence. But in the end the nationalist leaders would be released from prison, or brought back from exile in some remote island, and talks leading to independence would begin. Cyprus, Nyasaland, Kenya, repeated the lesson that Britain had not learnt from India and Ireland.

But Afro-Americans saw the point and applied the lesson. To-day it is a commonplace with them that whites do not listen till violence starts. Both from America and Africa, this doctrine came to Britain and was loudly proclaimed by some intellectuals of the West Indian and African population. The three sets of circumstances were quite different; in Nyasaland, for example—the extreme case—the proportion of black to white was 300 to 1 and there was a perpetual likelihood of a deficit in the tiny budget, which never rose so high as £7,000,000 of either revenue or expenditure. It was not hard to persuade the British that to hold such a territory against opposition would be not only expensive but uncomfortable to the conscience and altogether unwise. In America, a largely segregated tenth of the population could make itself felt, could in fact hurt the majority. But in Britain the numbers suggest that a certain caution is advisable.

The minority may push the majority till it hurts, till attention is attracted and the conscience of the well-meaning is aroused. But if they push too hard, to the point that the majority feels seriously threatened, frightened, and angry, they may produce a reaction that will hurt the minority. Their proportion to the majority is not very different from that of the Jews in pre-Hitler Germany and perhaps they are even more vulnerable. In so dangerous a situation it is arguable that it is unwise to provoke retaliation. It is a condition for the success of the tactics of violent protest that the majority should be open to reason and not goaded beyond endurance. In Britain, with proportions of one non-white to fifty white it is very much easier to be hurt than to hurt, and it is easy for the indigenous population to ask, 'Why then did you come?' The answer to this question is too complicated to appeal quickly to a large audience.

Both in Britain and in America, the application of the African lesson has led to a hardening of attitudes on the right wing of the majority. And here the second strand of the process of cross-infection comes into play. It is argued, on the left, that the forces of the right will inevitably appeal more and more openly to the worst prejudices of the majority and that they will therefore grow stronger. It becomes necessary, therefore, to mobilize the left, to force moderates to take sides, to outrage conscience by outrageous behaviour.

Such a line of argument will seem unreasonable to many because the policy proposed is likely to alienate more people than it attracts. Where the oppressed are in a majority and where their main hope is intervention from outside—as is the case in South Africa—it is reasonable to argue that the success of a moderate party would conceal the true nature of the situation and postpone a solution acceptable to the majority. But where a small minority is dependent on the goodwill of a large majority, it is irrational in the extreme to alienate moderate opinion. But here is likely to be launched an explicit attack upon reason. I have already quoted Frantz Fanon, '. . . the poets of Negro-ism oppose the idea of . . . tiresome reasoning to lyricism, oppressive logic to highstepping nature . . .'; and need only add that this attitude too has spilt over from the colonial and the coloured revolt to the wider revolt of youth against age and of the underprivileged against their rulers. It is right, perhaps, to rebel against the arid intellectualism of some academic teaching. It is right to rebel against rationalizations which defend established interests without recognizing the assumptions on which our society is based. But this is to criticize not reason but the misuse of reason. It is the plea of this book that the use of reason is one of the specific marks of man and that reason should be used to take account of as wide a range of facts as it can span. And facts include emotion.

This second outstanding impression needs to be summarized. Revolt against white dominance is part of a wider revolt, of poor against rich, of youth against age. No single aspect can be isolated because the whole complex arises from the rejection of the premise of inequality which for so long was the cement that held societies together and a condition of their progress. No alternative to inequality has yet been found that is consistent with freedom, and indeed the proclaimed principle of equality seems to be one of the factors in the exclusion of the Negro from North American society. If all men were brothers, it was decided that he should not be a man. And this seems to be of wider application. If men are no longer to be lords, burghers, and peasants, they will be the more eager to proclaim that they are English or French, and at the next stage, Bretons or Welsh. When a man leaves the village or the clan, where he knew everyone else—and knew moreover his occupation and income and his grandmother's maiden name—he will be more than ever before inclined to identify people by *appearance*. Thus stress on equality, if combined with any degree of freedom, is likely to produce a soil favourable to both regionalism and racialism.

There is a rider to this point about the essential unity of the different forms of revolt. The revolt against racial dominance has a special bitterness which puts it in a category by itself. This is not only because the uniform of colour is permanent, nor only because of the deeply insulting nature of the views held by racist writers in the last century and still present in the minds of many half-educated white people. The deeper cause for this special bitterness is seen most clearly (of the areas I have described) in the Caribbean, where slavery and colonialism stole the black man's soul and persuaded him that the only ambition worth striving for was something he could never achieve—to be white.

It is another outstanding impression left by these studies that the categories into which men classify each other are continually changing and that the boundaries of one category do not usually coincide with those of another for so long as is commonly supposed. This is so even in South Africa. At first the Dutch officials and peasants were clearly divided from the Hottentots by religion, language, culture, and colour. But a time came when the Cape Coloured were no longer distinguished by religion, by culture, or by language. Colour alone became the criterion for separation. Against the Bantu-speakers, some comparatively liberal white South Africans will even now argue that culture and language rather than colour are still the barriers to-day. But is this true? It does not seem so to me. Was not Professor Jabavu of Fort Hare as Christian by conviction, as European in culture and language, as the younger sons from Afrikaner farms who crowded into the cities after the First World War and whose presence gave rise to the 'civilized labour policy'? The categories may coincide with each other when the relationship begins but within a very few generations they begin to criss-cross and intersect, even where, as in South Africa, every effort is made to prevent it.

In Guatemala, we have seen an extreme example of the separation of social structure from ethnic affiliation and of an ethnic distinction from culture and language. There are in Quetzaltenango men of means who speak Spanish in the home and wear European clothes who are classed as Indians; others, clearly of the middle and professional classes, who speak an Indian language. These are in contrast with poorer men who are classed as Hispanic.

The simple classification with which modern South Africa began is no longer in accordance with the facts; the boundaries of culture, colour, language, and religion do not coincide Where this intersection of categories is recognized, it can be a social strength; where it is denied and an attempt made to enforce the coincidence of boundary lines, tension is bound to become acute.

There are two riders of considerable importance to the proposition that categories rapidly cease to coincide. A dominant or majority group will usually try to persuade both its own members and those of the subordinate or minority group that in fact the categories are permanent, that their superiority is due to inherent qualities, divinely ordained, supported by magic or a magical pseudo-science. The Tutsi would not admit to the Hutu that they ate solid food; the Incas were descended from the Sun; the British in India at one time believed they would die if exposed to the sun without a special kind of hat—but shortly before Independence, and in the face of American example, discovered that this was untrue. There is a vast network of racial mythology arising from this desire to keep dividing categories rigid and permanent.

The second rider follows from this. When such categories are once established and one group believes it is dominant and another is subordinate, they will both act in accordance with the roles allotted and in time their pictures of each other will become to some extent true. This is the familiar case of the self-fulfilling prophecy, and there is no need to enlarge on it further.

This last point, with its two riders, may be put in a different way to emphasize its importance. When Cortés met Moteczuma, when Livingstone entered what is now Malawi, the biological difference of which colour is the most obvious manifestation coincided with differences of language, religion and philosophy, political allegiance, methods of social cohesion, daily custom. The term 'race' came to be used as a shorthand expression for the sum of these differences, but in a few generations became misleading. Biological race was no longer an accurate pointer to cultural difference. Where the word race is still used as a means of social definition, it would be less confusing to put it in inverted commas or label it 'notional race'.

## 2 Underlying Assumptions

Certain underlying assumptions about the nature of man have been made in this book. To discuss them in detail would have made its length intolerable; it would be misleading not to state them briefly. It is assumed in the first place that man is a creature of passions, many of them hostile to society. He is the product of a long evolutionary process, in which it seems probable that among the qualities that have helped him to survive have been loyalty to the group to which he belongs and hostility, or at least suspicion, towards other groups and their members. And it surely cannot be doubted that in every human culture a child must learn some degree of restraint and self-discipline if it is to live with other human beings; the most elementary lessons are concerned with excretion and food, the last learnt and most difficult, with sex.

Thus every man is a battle-ground; his life in society involves coming to terms with both repressions and aspirations in himself. He represses elements disapproved of by society; he aspires towards heights he can never permanently inhabit. Thus he is always seeking for a balance, a resting-place, some certainty as to his identity, a place where he is at home. In more primitive conditions he found such a home in tribe, clan, kinship group, or village. In an impersonal, industrialized society, this is more difficult and one of the easier forms of escape from the search is to identify himself closely with a powerful group and project on to some other group the hostility he feels for elements in himself and for the society which expects of him standards he cannot attain.

Prophets have from time to time proclaimed solutions to political and social problems which have ignored this ancient conflict between self and society, this deep dualism in the nature of man, godlike in apprehension but beastly in appetite. If the tyranny of kings and priests were removed, how happy and virtuous man would be! When class and capitalism are destroyed, the state will wither away! But such Pelagian optimism about the perfectibility of man is hardly sustainable since Freud reinforced the teaching of St. Augustine about man's innate tendency to hatred and violence.

We must, in short, recognize that fear, greed, jealousy, and lust give birth to hatred, and in some degree these dangers are present in every man and every society. On the other hand, there are also in most societies elements of kindliness, sympathy, and a neighbourly readiness to help. But these are cultivated plants. The metaphor—an ancient one—may be usefully pursued. They were wild plants once, growing in limited kinds of terrain where soil and climate were favourable; the art of the gardener has widened the area where they can flourish. The process of civilization has in general extended the concept of who is the neighbour to whom kindly behaviour is owed. Once it was confined to the close group of kin and friends, later to village acquaintances, perhaps to the nation. But in modern life, horizons widen and there are many who recognize some obligation to be of help to all mankind—but on the whole ties are still weaker to those further away. The task for builders of society is to recognize both the dangers and the possibilities for good and to encourage a society in which it is easier for the latter to display themselves and in which jealousy, fear, and greed are checked and to some extent controlled.

The ancient imperialists—Pharaohs and Incas, rulers of Babylon and Persia—seem generally to have formulated their problem on lines very different from this, though with remarkable similarity as between themselves; they had three tasks: to keep rulers distinct from subjects; to keep the subjects in groups distinct enough to be used against each other and small enough to provide a sense of common identity; and finally they had to induce in their subjects a sufficient sense of wider identity to make them work—and some of them if necessary fight— for the empire as a whole. This was usually achieved by a mythology of the divine origin of rulers and divine sanction for their system of rule, myths which in modified forms have survived in various parts of the world until the recent past. But to-day myths are discredited and we have to seek new means of holding society together. We have to find means by which it becomes easier for men of different origins to live together. What we have said about the nature of man confirms the provisional view taken earlier, that it is more sensible to try to find political and social arrangements conducive to harmony than to hope for a change in man's nature or a series of individual conversions.

## 3 The Post-Imperial Dilemma

The problem of finding a new kind of social cement applies both in the former colonial territories and within the former imperial powers. In the colonial territories, the presence of a superior external force had arrested natural processes of evolution. In the crudest form, it had sometimes prevented one powerful group from eliminating a weaker; constantly it had prevented disputes from going to the arbitrament of war; it had sheltered alien groups who had come as traders or labourers. Imperial withdrawal released forces that had long been dammed and revealed tensions that had been buried. A period of disturbance is inevitable while the different elements—tribes, regions, classes, religions—rediscover a balance, an ecology, of their own. Meanwhile, in the metropolitan countries, a less obvious crisis arises. Energy that had flowed abroad is pent up at home and imperial pride, now sadly humiliated, seeks for a scapegoat.

In both France and Britain people from former colonial territories are present in considerable numbers. The old imperial dilemma takes a new form; the problem had been how to reconcile the denial of democracy to colonial peoples. A nation-state with a strong sense of identity and some degree of internal democracy had ruled very diverse peoples autocratically. Now the question is how to transform what was once an essentially homogeneous nation-state into a society in which a variety of different groups can live side by side. The old nation had been united by a common culture, a language, a pride in past achievement, a sense of imperial power; also by the operation of a disciplined hierarchical system widely accepted, to which the opposite pole was a sturdy individualism, an admiration for individual initiative and individual craftsmanship. Regional and ethnic differences had been forgotten in the aura of the successful nation-state but to-day they revive; if the colonies are independent—ask the regions—why are not we? At the same time, authority is questioned, discipline decried, and individual initiative often resented.

The metropolitan subjects of the former imperial power are doubly at a loss; their grandfathers had accepted the inequality of their society because inequality was part of the order of nature and because, though they were low on the ladder at home, they ruled over countless millions abroad. But the ladder is kicked away; the whole principle of a stratified society is denied. They find themselves leaderless and bereft of a faith and at the same time not only are they deprived of rule over the colonials but they are told to abandon their belief in their own superiority.

In such circumstances, the hunt for votes will encourage would-be leaders to bid against each other in exciting prejudice and hostility. The appeal is to deep-rooted human instincts which are easier to arouse than to allay. A written constitution cannot long withstand the strongly held wish of a majority to ignore or change it; indeed, no constitutional device is ultimately effective except by the will of a body powerful enough to give it support. What at present protects minorities in Britain is some degree of consensus of opinion about certain ideals, among which equality before the law and fair play probably rank first. There is also a considerable discomfort when the wretchedness of others is vividly presented.

Britain is at a decisive stage in history, not only in her own but in world history. We are in the process of taking a decision as to the kind of society we are to be; it is open to us now to re-define ourselves and our social structure or to close our ranks and fall back on the concept of the homogeneous nation-state, but now with an excluded minority in our midst. A movement in the latter direction is already being made and it shows signs of a readiness to assimilate foreigners who are white but reject to a lower category immigrants who are not.

For those who regard this as a danger, the question then becomes one of strengthening the consensus of opinion about fair play and equality before the law and if possible reversing the tendency of would-be leaders to outflank each other in illiberal proposals. In thinking of this we have to recognize that the electorate consists of individuals, each of whom is a battle-ground of repressions and aspirations and each of whom plays a number of social roles. But the parts a man plays on the stage of social life are not (as the famous speech in *As You Like It* suggests) played one after another in successive stages but in rapid alternation—as businessman or schoolteacher, father, husband, lover, friend, and chairman, perhaps, of the village cricket club. His behaviour in these different capacities will not always be consistent and it is certainly not going to be simple to influence the consensus of opinion to which so many people in so many moods and playing so many parts, will contribute and by which they in turn will be influenced. And a society has, surely, a legitimate right to define itself in terms acceptable to itself. The consensus cannot be ignored; it must be led, moulded, analysed, persuaded.

## 4 The White Democracies and a Just Society

> Lear: Thou hast seen a farmer's dog bark at a beggar?
> Gloster: Aye, Sir.
> Lear: And the creature run from the cur? There is the image of authority for you.

It was the recipe of the empire-builders, ancient and modern, to rely on authority of just the kind Lear describes. So long as the myth of empire, the illusion of permanence, held good, quite a small dog, endowed with authority, could control quite a number of beggars. But once the myth has failed, the beggar has only to stand still and the cur runs home, tail between legs. The 'authority' that was so potent derived from a mixture of coercion and a rudimentary consensus which produced acquiescence; it has been part of my argument that the proportions of this mixture vary enormously in different societies at different times. And even a rudimentary consensus sufficient to produce acquiescence will hardly exist unless a good many people in the state recognize some degree of justice in the society of which they form part.

The distinction between consensus and acquiescence is important;

one is active and conscious, the other passive and often largely un-conscious. In acquiescence, the society is thought of as permanent and change as out of the question—but this, as I have said, seems to demand *some* degree of consensus and a belief that *some* element of justice is present. An attitude of sullen resignation is not acquiescence. Mere acquiescence was the attitude of the Indian peasant in the Victorian period, accepting poverty as inevitable, usually regarding British rule as aloof, somewhat incomprehensible, but just in intention and pro-viding shelter against anarchy. There is a sense in which the British Empire in India was the last of the ancient empires; its objects were not too dissimilar from those of Akbar, the Pharaohs, and the Incas. Acquiescence of this kind is however a quite insufficient basis for a democracy; with increasing political awareness, it is bound to give way to the demand for a government based on consensus, that is, a common set of values shared between the subjects.

A consensus of values is essential to a true democracy. The special problem of race relations in Britain at the moment is one which every democracy is liable to face: how to maintain a consensus with a wide basis of support and some degree of generosity and tolerance to others. It is easy to debase the currency of the consensus, appeal to the worst in the electors, and on the basis of a moment when the worst is uppermost encourage them in an intolerance which is liable to spiral downwards, as in Hitler's Germany. The problem is to keep high the moral quality of the consensus and preserve a humane and kindly spirit in the society.

There is at present a wide variety of opinion in Britain on the subject of race and immigration; this arises because of two ideals of society, seldom explicitly stated by either party, and a very mixed idea of what is meant by justice. The two ideals of society are clear and quite distinct: one pictures a nation-state, homogeneous in language and custom; the other a new kind of society, more like the United States, in which there is believed to be equal opportunity for all, but in which there is a diversity of language and culture, various groups of varied origin keeping their distinctive nature and enriching the whole by their contribution. The two views differ in other ways: those who picture a homogeneous nation-state are usually much more reconciled to class differences, while those who value cultural diversity are generally hostile to class; the latter see the world as an industrial city to which the countryside is a playground, while the former often romanticize a rural scene that is disappearing. But the important difference is between homogeneity and diversity.

There are indications that at present the considerable majority of Englishmen still think of the homogeneous nation-state as their ideal. Many of those who on grounds of general benevolence or 'fair play' are favourably disposed to Asian or West Indian immigrants use expressions about 'rising to our standards' and 'learning our ways' which suggest that their ideal is the immigrant who becomes more and more English. If this is so, a minority of opinion-formers have every right to try to persuade them to a different opinion. But if they are unsuccessful and fail to persuade them that their society ought to be changed, it seems doubtful whether a government that professes to be democratic can do other than lead cautiously, step by step, a little ahead of the consensus. But we are approaching a question much larger than the machinery of opinion-forming, that of its ethics: who has a right to form someone else's opinion if he can? Everybody, provided he uses means that are open and tolerant and gives up the attempt when these fail. But the ethics of opinion-forming are outside the scope of this book.

As to conceptions of justice, we have spoken already of the Platonic ideal of justice, which resembles the Hindu. In Plato's just state, every man performs his allotted function and receives his due reward—in esteem, not in material things, because the ruling class, the Guardians, who in Plato's myth are composed of gold, live frugal and abstemious lives, dwelling in tents, not houses, and possessing nothing of their own, because 'otherwise they are sure to become wolves not watchdogs'. To the Hindu, also, the performance of allotted function—*varna-shramadharma*—is the essence of social life. The Platonic ideal is firmly centred in the state—a small state, by implication not much larger than Athens; the Hindu ideal includes little concept of the state, only of society. Both implicitly recognize that inequality on earth demands some justification—that is to say, that 'justice' on earth is not complete; both complement justice on earth by reincarnation, with the significant difference that in Plato's myth the soul chooses a plan of life from vast numbers of such plans drawn up by Necessity; thus responsibility lies with the individual and his soul is moulded by the choice he has made.

Both the Platonic and Hindu concepts of justice make for stability and a smooth-running community. But one is limited to the small city-state, the other to Hindu society, conceived as the *only* society, all-embracing, except for outer barbarians; both depend for their stability on the illusion of permanence and in both the imbalance of inequality is restored after death. To-day this is obviously insufficient, and justice is thought of as the distribution to each individual of his deserts not in the hereafter but on earth.

But what are 'deserts'? 'My lord, I will use them according to their desert', says Polonius of the players; and Hamlet replies: 'God's bodikins, man, much better; use every man according to his desert and who should 'scape whipping?' He is thinking of what a man deserves in his own eyes, or, in other words, in psychological and religious terms. In this sense, no man hopes for justice, rather he fears justice and hopes for forgiveness. But the kind of justice we are thinking of is different. We think of judicial justice—the settlement of disputes on known principles and the checking of crime; we think also of social justice, what a man gets from society in return for what he gives. Both these are firmly linked with rights and duties, which only have meaning in a human group with some degree of organization, a family, a tribe, or a state. But there is also another conception of justice, sometimes thought of as natural justice, but misleadingly, for it is highly artificial. This is ideal justice, something not enforceable in law nor to be obtained in any actual state. But as we become more civilized, the concept of ideal justice becomes a little less vague and unformulated; some aspects of it are now embodied in an international declaration of rights, with very imperfect means of enforcement, it is true, and rather a body of aspirations than a legal code. Embryonic though this is, it does embody a wider concept of justice. There are more and more people to-day who no longer think of justice as applying only to those who belong to our own community; indeed, this might be no bad starting-point for a definition of civilization. Most of us to-day have widened our concept of the community to which we belong and some begin to include in it the entire human race.

It is worth dwelling on this point for a moment. There are primitive societies whose concept of right behaviour applies only as between people within the group. In the Middle Ages there was a concept of behaviour proper among Christians but it did not operate for Saracens or heretics; in Victorian England there were still many who openly applied standards of conduct to their own behaviour towards people of other races quite different from any they would have contemplated towards Englishmen. There are still many such, and of course this insularity is not confined to the English. But there is a growing realization of a wider human community. The concept of a just national society embedded in an unjust world society is not sustainable as a permanent ideal and it seems unlikely that we shall move very far towards a *more* just national society unless we also take active steps to encourage a *more* just international society.

If the Platonic justice seems insufficient in a modern democracy, so does the extreme individualist concept of the early nineteenth century; this was a time when state initiative was reduced to a minimum and justice was conceived as preventing any action harmful to others; the ideal state was one which interfered to a minimum in personal life. It is not the purpose of this book to embark on a discussion of what constitutes a just society, which would mean another volume as long again as this. But it must surely embody the enforcement of certain minimum standards in various dimensions. If a man has neither work nor food, it is not enough to provide that he shall not be punished except after trial by his peers and in accordance with law; it is not enough that he should have the vote if he can be refused a seat in a bus because someone does not like the colour of his skin. In each of these four dimensions—judicial and economic, political and social, which includes esteem—steps have to be taken in a just society to ensure that there is some balance between rights and duties, obligation and reward. It is in the fourth category of social esteem that we are most backward, and legislation to enforce minimum standards, which is clearly essential, is only just beginning.

The kind of society we are thinking of is obviously more complicated than anything envisaged by Plato or the nineteenth-century individualists. Democratic societies are likely to become more complex still, unless they turn into some form of tyranny or dictatorship in which freedom of speech and movement is suppressed. This cannot be ruled out; pessimistic visions of the future such as *Brave New World* or *1984* envisage a stratification more hideous than anything devised by Tsar, Pharaoh, or Inca. But if democracy is preserved, certain consequences are almost inevitable. In a complex society, which was once stratified on fairly rigid lines but is becoming less rigid, discontent is likely to increase. If power is widely distributed, if speech is free and if a man can rise or fall in the eyes of his fellows, he is likely to compare his lot with others and be dissatisfied if he is not successful. And the more closely rewards are proportionate to intelligence, energy, and ability, the more intolerable failure is likely to be. It is less galling to say, 'He was born with a silver spoon in his mouth', than to acknowledge, 'He is abler than I am'. Relative deprivation, in Runciman's phrase, is likely to increase as people compare their achievement with others' in wider and wider circles.

There are however certain alleviations to this gloomy conclusion. As society grows more complex, the individual comes into contact with a wider range of people in relation to whom he plays various parts. It has often been said that in a simple society the villager or peasant was in a many-stranded relationship with the squire or seigneur who was employer, landlord, magistrate, and often much more; if he comes to town and works in a factory, he is in a single-stranded relationship with his employer. But he is also now in a great many other relationships—with a landlord who is not his employer, with a district health officer and a municipal refuse collector, with milkman, postman, shopkeeper, policeman, and so on. He may join a wide variety of clubs, associations, or informal circles who meet most evenings at the pub. He may go into local politics and become elected to the parish council; he may become a chargehand or a shop steward. He may win local esteem by some quite different means—as a winner at the flower and vegetable show, as a cricketer, or as merely a man who can tell a good story or is a good hand at darts. We saw that in India fifty years ago the same people were at the top in the four dimensions of ritual purity, economic prosperity, political power, and modern education; to-day, this is changed. In South India, the Brahman, by the very fact of his high position in the caste hierarchy, is hampered in politics if not positively debarred from success. He has lost his virtual monopoly in education. This is surely healthy and in a modern complex society it is surely a factor making for content if there are many diverse ways of winning esteem or achieving success.

It follows that in the society we are picturing we hope for as much intersection as possible of the categories by which people are classed. If there is a minority who speak in the home a different language from the majority, it will be a happier society if they do not all belong to the same class, either by wealth or education. Fortunately for Britain— and this is one of the signs of hope for the future—'colour' had early associations with Maharajas and cricketers as well as with lascars at seaports. The root of South Africa's disease is surely the attempt to preserve a rigid coincidence between categories which have ceased to represent the facts; it is no longer true that all Africans are culturally and educationally in one category and all Europeans in another. The United States will be an unhappy and divided society so long as the category 'Negro' overrides professional or educational qualifications.

There is one other cause for encouragement on the white side in Britain and the United States; the young are more tolerant in this matter than their grandparents. This is partly due to the spread of education and to the growing numbers of young people who are pre- pared to look at other cultures with a readiness to see a value in them and to rate them as different from their own but not necessarily inferior. Against this however must be set the rivalry that is likely to grow as the coloured minority in both countries becomes better qualified for jobs.

For those democracies in which white people are in a majority, there is no easy solution. They can solve the problem of their coloured minorities only by solving their own, that is to say by creating a more just society. Their task is to build up enforceable minimum standards of well-being in the four dimensions, political, judicial, economic, and social; and at the same time to sustain and stimulate a tolerant and kindly consensus of opinion, an operation in which every vocal indivi- dual of the society can take part, in which Press, radio, schools, and government are included. But in a free society the government can do only so much; it can stimulate and encourage something of which the germs exist—but the response it can elicit is limited by the consensus, the nature of the people to whom it appeals. The process is usually spiral or cumulative; once it has begun it is hard to reverse the direc- tion. It is the task of the opinion-formers to carry the consensus with them and in this there is a danger; why should the tyranny of opinion- formers be preferable to the tyranny of the mob? The answer to this is that in a democracy the opinion-forming function rests in every part of society and there is no separate licensed caste of opinion-formers. One thing is clear: that the democracies have to-day a better chance of understanding the nature of the decision they are in the process of taking than was available to the older societies at which we have looked.

The white democracies are only a part of the world. But they are a very important part, and so long as there is in their own societies a high degree of injustice, it will be emphasized and exposed by their visible minorities. And for so long, their relations with the rest of the world will be poisoned, and the help they can give limited.

## 5 Conclusion

We have looked at societies of a wide diversity in which men have attempted to impose their will on other groups and yet live together in a common organization. It is clear that dominance by one group of people over another is something of which no race or period has a monopoly; it is as old as the Pharaohs and springs from passions that are common to all men. We have seen that inequality was long accepted as a condition of life in a political society, but that to-day it is very widely rejected and a new social cement sought. We have seen that in all this diversity no single factor can be isolated as the sole cause of fluidity or rigidity in the system. Every society has been complex in the extreme and many factors have contributed to the result. But there has always been an element of choice open to the human will.

There is therefore no royal road, no broad and easy path, leading to harmonious relations between men of different race or ethnic stock. Indeed, there are several reasons suggesting that relations will deteriorate. These apply in different degrees to every free society, that is to say, to every society based on consensus and not on rigid repression. In the first place, whatever injustice or imperfection exists within a society will be brought to the light by the presence of a group thought of as different, and particularly so if they are visibly different. Resentment at injustice, at shortage of some good, or at unequal distribution, might have lain hidden, but will be exposed by the presence of a minority; it is likely to take the form of hostility between the two groups.

Secondly, feelings of resentment and deprivation are likely to grow throughout the world and that for two reasons. In general, people have far more opportunities than they did of comparing their lot with that of others, and—even more important—they no longer believe that the social order is permanent. An increasing number of people believe their wrongs can be cured.

The third cause for alarm is that relationships in city and factory are likely to become more and more anonymous and bureaucratic instead of personal and many-stranded, as they were in tribe or village; identification will therefore more and more depend on what is seen, the uniform of colour and race, instead of what is known, birth or craftsmanship, wisdom in counsel or neighbourly helpfulness.

Fourthly—and this point is closely linked with the world-wide rejection of the premise of inequality—men look for new ties to define their position in society. National identity will be one cause to which men will attach themselves, particularly if the nation is small or new and can think of itself as oppressed or threatened by enemies; regional autonomy is another; racism is a third, and by this is here meant hostility and the attempt to exclude from jobs and housing and the normal rights of a citizen. We have seen that the end of formal or legal differences has often meant that psychological barriers go up; the end of colonial empires is likely to produce increasingly the same results.

The fifth reason for taking the situation seriously is the rejection of traditional roads to success by Negro intellectuals and by the leaders of non-whites in many parts of the world. They begin to argue that they will be 'traitors to the race' if they make good in the white world; the whole group, they claim, must move up together. This is a reaction to a past, particularly in the United States, in which the most able and successful were lost to the minority yet not accepted by the majority. But it produces a fresh, and still more hostile, white reaction; the white majority *feel* that a safety-valve has been deliberately jammed; they *say* that just as they were beginning to overcome their racialism the blacks have stepped up theirs.

Yet with all these grounds for anxiety, one thing is clear. This book began by considering a dominance by one group over another so long established, and so much taken for granted, that the dominated are no longer regarded as human. That kind of situation survives in Southern Africa but seems hardly likely to recur in the same form elsewhere. Hostility, discrimination, and exclusion may exist without the denial of humanity, without the establishment of a rigid, institutional supremacy. The young are less prejudiced than the old, the educated than those who left school early. Every year more and more of the population in the white democracies go on from school to some form of higher education. Is there not hope here? Perhaps, but the possibility begins to shape itself of an upper tier of the successful and educated to whom race is of little importance compared with ability, and a lower tier of the unsuccessful, who are frustrated and conscious of deprivation and increasingly hostile to people of a different colour. In such a situation, incidents would inevitably occur and would affect international relations; the need for an international society would increase.

But this is to argue on premises which many of the young and many African and Afro-American leaders reject. Society, they argue, is corrupt, both national and international, and must be destroyed. They are, of course, right that it is corrupt, but this arises from the nature of man, who is mortal and corruptible:

> Shivering and fluttering between them choosing and chosen,
> Valiant, ignoble, dark, and full of light
> Swinging between hell gate and heaven gate. . . .

It is sensible to try to make society less corrupt or more just, childish to destroy the achievement of centuries because it is not perfect. There is nothing easy about making society more just; it is not to be achieved by any form of magic, but by hard thinking and patient effort.

We reject the Platonic recipe for justice—stability in a contented but unequal society in which there is an illusion of permanence. It is unjust and we do not want to buy harmony at the expense of justice. We know that separation cannot be equal but must always mean subjection of one group by another; that too is unjust. We are faced, then, by the appallingly difficult task of trying to create a society in which there is a good chance of different groups living together side by side and in which they will recognize that there is some degree of justice. A wholly just society is surely as unattainable as a society of any size in which everyone is equal. Small communities in special circumstances have sometimes for a short time attained equality, but have almost always broken down eventually. What is needed is a society in which the inequality is minimized, seen to be necessary, and seen to be compatible with justice. This can perhaps only occur in a society with a clear common purpose.

There is no easy way of building a society of the kind we seek, but it is possible to discern certain necessary ingredients. There is the task of emphasizing in the consensus of opinion the elements that make for tolerance, and discouraging, by legislation and every other possible means, those that do not. This will demand a concerted effort by the government, the Press, radio and television, and all those who form opinion—school-teachers, professors, writers, speakers. But it will not be enough unless there is also a determined attempt to create a more just society, in which minimum standards are enforced in the three dimensions of wealth, power, and esteem as well as equality before the law.

We are far more likely to achieve a society in which resentment is kept within bounds if society is thought of not as a homogeneous mass but as a system of overlapping circles. This has really two components; in a society which is to be reasonably harmonious, there will have to be full opportunity for the expression of a diversity for which the Welsh language, the Sikh turban, may serve as symbols. But there must also be overlapping of groups, so that no one category has overriding priority and people can win esteem in a variety of ways. It will be no bad thing if the aristocracy are powerless, if professionals who enjoy their work are not so well paid as those in occupations which are less esteemed and less intellectually rewarding, and if none of these categories coincide with each other.

And immense and concerted effort is necessary if some such society is to be achieved. It needs a sweeter, a fresher, a more universal, emblem than the flag of national sovereignty. But let us be under no illusions about the difficulty of the task. Man has the techniques, if he will use them, which would enable him to grow more food than he does and to limit his numbers to what he can feed, to live in peace and justice. What prevents him is himself, his own fear, greed, and jealousy. It is unlikely that there will ever be human creatures on earth free from these passions; personal life is centred on the ego, social life on the group. But the art of living in society is to devise means of harnessing and taming this unruly selfhood, of making it easier to live in amity with our neighbours. There are good reasons for supposing it will become more difficult rather than less. Our one asset is a generation passionately concerned to produce a more just society. Our young men dream dreams and see visions; when they can translate them into reality, a new faith may be born.

Here we must take into account a difficulty peculiar to the modern temper. Man is an earth-bound creature whose spirit demands a symbol to which hopes may be anchored, but to-day those who most eagerly repudiate injustice also question the validity of traditional symbols. It is the young who demand a just society but often it is also the young who reject the formulas and symbols which in the past served as a focus for the intermittent idealism of the majority. It is easier to fight for Cross or Crescent than for world peace or a just society; these ideals still cry for a prophet, sacraments, a faith. It is a personal belief—one that will no doubt be sharply contested—that no faith will endure unless it endows the universe with meaning, unless it relates timeless infinity to the human personality, unless, in short, it carries a personal and distinctly religious message as well as a generalized idealism.

# Notes

## Parts I and II

It is really not possible to quote authorities for most of the contents of Parts I and II. They are an attempt to assess the relationships between racial groups in the world to-day; they are reflections on the causes for the different situations which have arisen in different regions. The results are largely suggestions and hypotheses for which in the nature of things there can be no references. But there are debts on almost every page. It was probably from Vann Woodward's *The Strange Career of Jim Crow* that I first came to understand how psychological defences go up when legal barriers come down; from Gunnar Myrdal that I first perceived the force of the downward spiral of prejudice and self-fulfilling prophecy. Charles Wagley taught me what is meant by social race; Gary Runciman, by relative deprivation—and the list could go on almost indefinitely. Marie Jahoda in her contribution to *Man, Race and Darwin* put in a short space psycho-analytical views to which I have turned again and again to refresh my memory. Such concepts become basic elements in one's thought; one cannot be continually acknowledging them. This book is the result of sixteen years of reading, discussion, and travel; it is a mosaic of pieces gathered from many sources. I believe that novels often convey the atmosphere of a society better even than travel; this is particularly true of the Caribbean and of the Deep South, for which Faulkner's novels are invaluable. I decided from the start to interrupt the argument by footnotes as little as possible, but it was extremely difficult to achieve any kind of consistency. In the end, it seemed best to cut ruthlessly and to make acknowledgement by means of a Reading List which includes all the main sources.

## Part III

For Part III, I at first intended to provide separate reading lists for India, Africa, Spanish-speaking America, the Caribbean, and Brazil. These, and in particular the contributory volumes by Pitt-Rivers, Lowenthal, Maybury-Lewis, Hunter, and the contributors to the symposium *India and Ceylon: Unity and Diversity*, are also sources for these earlier sections. But there proved to be so much overlapping that in the end we decided to make our Reading List for the whole book.

## Chapters VII and VIII

In writing about caste in India, I have not referred only to books but have drawn freely on my own experience, which was almost entirely in the North-Western part of Uttar Pradesh, and mainly in the two districts of Bareilly in Rohilkhand and Garhwal in Kumaon. I have refreshed my memory of a number of standard old works, such as the Abbé Dubois's *A Description of the People of India*, as well as modern anthropological works to which specific reference is made.

Anantpur, the village described in Section 3 of Chapter VII, is about twelve miles from Bareilly. I have written about it in a novel, *Call the Next Witness*, which is based on a death, probably a murder, which happened there in 1930. I visited the village again in 1957. The Rajputs of the village, no longer landlords, still remember the case and vehemently assert that it was suicide.

## Chapters IX and X

For Africa, there is no contributory volume special to this series. I have drawn on the reading and travel—mainly in South Africa, the Rhodesias, Kenya, and Nigeria—undertaken in connection with the studies of Rhodesia published by the Institute in 1958–60 and with the Report of the Minorities Commission in Nigeria in 1957–8, and on subsequent general reading.

## Chapter XI

My instructor and chief source of information on Spanish-speaking America has been Julian Pitt-Rivers. I have drawn on early drafts of the book he is contributing to this group of studies, *After the Empire: Race and Society in Middle America and the Andes*; also on a number of articles: 'The Image of the Witch'; 'Pseudo-kinship'; 'Honor'; 'Words and Deeds: the Ladinos of Chiapas'; 'La loi de l'hospitalité'; 'Mestizo or Ladino?'; also 'Social, Cultural and Linguistic Change in the Highlands of Chiapas', a study conducted by the Department of Anthropology, University of Chicago, in July 1964 (unpublished). He has also helped me generously by many comments on this chapter.

For the pre-Columbian period and the Conquest, Prescott's *The History of the Conquest of Mexico* and *The History of the Conquest of Peru* are still the best starting-points. Prescott was a contemporary of Macaulay, whom he resembles not only in style but in point of view—Whiggish, Protestant, Anglo-Saxon, a firm believer in 'Progress'. Much archaeological knowledge has come to light since his time and I have mainly used Eric Wolf, *Sons of the Shaking Earth* (Mexico); Jacques Soustelle, *Daily Life of the Aztecs*; G. C. Vaillant, *The Aztecs of Mexico*; Miguel Leon-Portilla, *The Broken Spears*; G. H. S. Bushnell, *Peru*; J. Alden Mason, *The Ancient Civilizations of Peru*; Louis Baudin, *Daily Life in Peru under the Last Incas*. There is an enormous literature; Vaillant and Alden Mason both give excellent bibliographies.

I have also a considerable debt to Professor José Matos Mar, who arranged a special seminar to instruct me in the problem of the 'two cultures' of the Andes.

## Chapter XII

My first-hand knowledge of the Caribbean is limited to Jamaica, Trinidad, and Barbados. But no one attempting to study race relations can neglect this natural laboratory, with its many societies in which the races are present in such various proportions. I have had the good fortune to be guided through the labyrinth by David Lowenthal, whose book, *West Indian Societies*, comparing the Caribbean territories, will be the most comprehensive that has yet appeared. I have read two drafts but the final form is not yet ready as this goes to print. He has been most helpful over my own manuscript but of course bears no responsibility for anything I have written. I have leaned on him most heavily in the sections dealing with variations on the main theme and on the East Indians. In Jamaica I gave a series of six lectures at the University of the West Indies with a good deal of reference to social structure and these produced discussion that was very valuable.

As elsewhere, I have used personal information and novels, in which the Caribbean is particularly rich, to help me to form an impression. These are cited in the Reading List.

## Chapter XIII

Most unfortunately I cannot quote directly from Dr. Maybury-Lewis's work, *Race Relations in Brazil*, as the text in its final form reached me too late for my own book. But I am indebted to him for much advice and for a summary of his argument and conclusions, the more so as Brazil is the only area in Part III of which I have no first-hand knowledge. This is the main reason why my essay on Brazil is so much shorter than the others. The literature I have drawn on is cited in the Reading List, but I have relied on some books more than others. For Section 1 of this chapter, I have made much use of Caio Prado, Junior, *The Colonial Background of Modern Brazil*. In Section 2, Gilberto Freyre's great work, *Casa Grande e Senzala*, which appeared in English as *The Masters and the Slaves*, is the classical statement of the official doctrine; it is supported by Donald Pierson's *Negroes in Brazil*. Caio Prado provides an antidote, as does C. R. Boxer's *Race Relations in the Portuguese Colonial Empire*, and Charles Wagley's *Race and Class in Rural Brazil*; there are useful summaries of recent literature in P. L. van den Berghe's *Race and Racism* and Michael Banton's *Race Relations*. José Honório Rodrigues in his *Brazil and Africa* argues that Portuguese miscegenation failed, in both Africa and Asia, to provide the mixed population that had been hoped for. It was only in Brazil that miscegenation achieved its purpose; the Portuguese, he argues, were far more race-conscious than the Brazilians and it was only after Independence that Brazil freed itself from racialism. But the freedom was not complete; he gives interesting summaries of attempts in the twentieth century to prevent the immigration of Asians and Africans. Florestan Fernandes' study

*A Integracão do Negro na Sociedade de Classes* was not available to me in 1969 because I have no Portuguese. It has since appeared in an English version as *The Negro in Brazilian Society*. But I was aware of his views and found his article in *Daedalus* most useful.

Two conferences were held at the expense of the Ford Foundation at which the subject of this book and the supporting volumes was discussed.

The first was at Ditchley Park in November 1962 when the following were present:

| | |
|---|---|
| Sir Kenneth Grubb, Chairman | Dr. Roland Oliver |
| Mr. Peter Calvocoressi | Miss Margery Perham |
| Sir Alexander Carr-Saunders | Dr. Julian Pitt-Rivers |
| Professor Daryll Forde | Professor Margaret Read |
| Mr. Stanley Gordon | Mr. F. Seebohm |
| Dr. Juan Maiguashca Guevara | Mr. J. F. Sinclair |
| Mr. Christopher Hill | Mr. J. H. A. Watson |
| Mr. Guy Hunter | Mr. Guy Wint |
| Dr. David Lowenthal | Dr. Donald Wood |
| Mr. Philip Mason | The Rt. Hon. Kenneth Younger |
| Dr. David Maybury-Lewis | Dr. M. Zuberi |

The second was at Burley Manor in June 1966 with the following present:

| | |
|---|---|
| Mr. Peter Calvocoressi | Dr. Julian Pitt-Rivers |
| Mr. Richard Harris | Professor Margaret Read |
| Mr. Guy Hunter | Mr. E. J. B. Rose |
| Dr. David Lowenthal | Mr. J. F. Sinclair |
| Dr. Juan Maiguashca Guevara | Professor Hugh Tinker |
| Mr. Philip Mason | Mr. Guy Wint |
| Dr. Roland Oliver | Mr. Maurice Zinkin |

My thanks are due to all who took part.—*P.M.*

# Reading List

ABRAHAMS, PETER. *Jamaica, an island mosaic*. London, H.M.S.O., 1957.
*Tell freedom*. London, Faber, 1954.

ACKROYD, W. R. *Sweet malefactor: sugar, slavery and human society*. London, Heinemann, 1967.

ADINARAYAN, S. P. *The case for colour*. London, Asia Publishing House, 1964.

AFOLABI OJO, G. J. *Yoruba culture: a geographical analysis*. London, University of London Press, 1966.

AHMED, ZAHIR. *Dusk and dawn in village India: twenty fateful years*. London, Pall Mall Press, 1965.

ANDREWS, DAVID HENRY. 'Paucartambo, Pasco, Peru: an indigenous community and a change program.' Unpublished Ph.D. thesis, Cornell University, 1963.

ANSTEY, ROGER. *King Leopold's legacy: the Congo under Belgian rule 1908–1960*. London, Oxford University Press for Institute of Race Relations, 1966.

ANTHONY, MICHAEL. *Green days by the river* (a novel). London, André Deutsch, 1967.

APTHEKER, HERBERT. *Nat Turner's slave rebellion: together with the full text of the so-called 'confessions' of Nat Turner made in prison in 1831*. New York, Humanities Press, 1966.

ARDREY, ROBERT. *The territorial imperative*. London, Collins, 1967.

ARRIGHI, G. *Political economy of Rhodesia*. The Hague, Mouton, 1967.

AUSUBEL, DAVID P. *The fern and the tiki; an American view of New Zealand: national character, social attitudes and race relations*. London, Angus and Robertson, 1960.
*Maori youth: a psycho-ethnological study of cultural deprivation*. New York, Holt, Rinehart and Winston, 1965.

AXELSON, ERIC. *Portugal and the scramble for Africa, 1875–1891*. Johannesburg, Witwatersrand University Press, 1967.
*Portuguese in South-East Africa, 1600–1700*. Johannesburg, Witwatersrand University Press, 1960.

BAILEY, F. G. *Caste and the economic frontier*. Manchester, Manchester University Press, 1957.
'The peasant view of the bad life.' In *The Advancement of Science*, Vol. XXIII, no. 114, December 1966.
*Politics and social change*. Berkeley, University of California Press, 1963.
*Tribe, caste and nation*. Manchester, Manchester University Press, 1960.

BALANDIER, GEORGES. *Ambiguous Africa: cultures in collision*. London, Chatto and Windus, 1966.

BALDWIN, JAMES. *The fire next time*. London, Michael Joseph, 1963.
*Notes of a native son* (belles-lettres). London, Michael Joseph, 1964.

BANTON, MICHAEL. *Race relations*. London, Tavistock, 1967.
*The coloured quarter*. London, Cape, 1955.

BARBER, JAMES. *Rhodesia: the road to rebellion*. London, Oxford University Press for Institute of Race Relations, 1967.

BARNES, J. A. *Politics in a changing society*. . . . Cape Town, Oxford University Press, 1954.

BARZUN, JACQUES. *Race: a study in superstition* (rev. ed.). New York, Harper and Row, 1965.

BASCOM, WILLIAM R. and HERSKOVITS, MELVILLE J. (eds.). *Continuity and change in African cultures.* Chicago, University of Chicago Press, 1959.

BASTIDE, ROGER. *Les Amériques noires: les civilisations Africaines dans le nouveau monde.* Paris, Payot, 1967.

'Color, racism and Christianity.' In *Daedalus*, Spring, 1967.

'Dusky Venus, black Apollo.' In *Race*, Vol. III, no. 1, November 1961.

*Les réligions Africaines au Brésil: vers une sociologie des interpénétrations de civilisations.* Paris, Presses Universitaires de France, 1960.

BASTIDE, ROGER and VAN DEN BERGHE, PIERRE L. 'Estereotipos, normas e comportamento inter-racial em São Paulo'. In Roger Bastide and Florestan Fernandes (eds.), *Brancos e negros em São Paulo.* São Paulo, Companhia Editora Nacional, 1959.

BAUDIN, LOUIS. *Daily life in Peru under the last Incas.* London, Allen and Unwin, 1961.

BEALS, ALAN R. *Gopalpur: a south Indian village.* New York, Holt, Rinehart and Winston, 1966.

BEARCE, GEORGE D. *British attitudes towards India, 1784–1858.* Oxford, Oxford University Press, 1961.

BENEDICT, RUTH. *Race, science and politics* (rev. ed.). New York, Viking Press, 1959.

BENSON, MARY. *South Africa: the struggle for a birthright.* Harmondsworth, Penguin Books, 1966.

BERNARD, JESSIE. *Marriage and family among Negroes.* New Jersey, Prentice-Hall, 1966.

BERRY, BREWTON. *Race and ethnic relations.* Boston, Houghton Mifflin Co., 1958.

BERWANGER, EUGENE H. *The frontier against slavery: western anti-Negro prejudice and the slavery extension controversy.* Chicago, London, University of Illinois Press, 1967.

BEST, ELSDON. *The Maori.* 2 vols. Wellington, Polynesian Society, 1924.

BÉTEILLE, ANDRÉ. *Caste, class and power.* Cambridge, Cambridge University Press, 1966.

'Race and descent as social categories in India.' In *Daedalus*, Spring, 1962.

BIBBY, CYRIL. *Race, prejudice and education.* London, Heinemann, 1959.

BIESHEUVEL, S. *African intelligence.* Johannesburg, South African Institute of Race Relations, 1943.

BIRMINGHAM, DAVID. *The Portuguese conquest of Angola.* London, Oxford University Press for Institute of Race Relations, 1965.

*Trade and conflict in Angola: the Mbundu and their neighbours under the influence of the Portuguese, 1483–1790.* Oxford, Clarendon Press, 1966.

BLAKE, JUDITH. *Family structure in Jamaica.* New York, Free Press of Glencoe, 1961.

BOHANNAN, PAUL. *Justice and judgment among the Tiv.* London, Oxford University Press, 1957.

BONTEMPS, ARNA. *Black thunder* (a novel). Berlin, Seven Seas Publishers, 1964.

BOVILL, E. W. *The golden trade of the Moors.* London, Oxford University Press, 1958.

BOXER, C. R. *Race relations in the Portuguese colonial empire, 1415–1825.* Oxford, Clarendon Press, 1963.

'Negro slavery in Brazil: translation and annotation of a Portuguese pamphlet.' In *Race*, Vol. V, no. 3, January 1964.

BOXER, C. R. and DE AZEVEDO, C. *Fort Jesus and the Portuguese in Mombasa, 1593–1729.* London, Hollis and Carter, 1960.

BRAITHWAITE, LLOYD. 'Social stratification in Trinidad.' In *Social and Economic Studies*, Vol. II.

BRASS, PAUL R. *Factional politics in an Indian state: the Congress party in Uttar Pradesh.* Berkeley, University of California Press, 1965.

BRELSFORD, W. V. *The tribes of Northern Rhodesia.* Lusaka, Government Printers, 1956.

BRITISH COUNCIL OF CHURCHES. *The future of South Africa: a study by British Christians.* London, S.C.M. Press, 1965.

BROOMFIELD, J. H. *Elite conflict in a plural society: twentieth century Bengal.* Berkeley, University of California Press, 1968.

BROTZ, HOWARD. *The Black Jews of Harlem.* New York, Free Press of Glencoe, 1964.

BRYANT, A. T. *The Zulu peoples: as they were before the white man came* (2nd ed.). Pietermaritzburg, Shuter and Shooter, 1967.

BULL, THEODORE (ed.). *Rhodesian perspective.* London, Michael Joseph, 1967.

BUNTING, BRIAN. *The rise of the South African Reich.* Harmondsworth, Penguin Books, 1964.

BURNS, SIR ALAN. *Colour prejudice: with particular reference to the relationship between whites and Negroes.* London, Allen and Unwin, 1948.

*History of the British West Indies.* London, Allen and Unwin, 1954.

BURNS, E. BRADFORD. *Nationalism in Brazil: a historical survey.* London, Frederick A. Praeger, 1968.

BURNS, HAYWOOD. *Voices of Negro protest.* London, Oxford University Press for Institute of Race Relations, 1963.

BURY, M. *History of Greece* (3rd ed.). London, Macmillan, 1951.

BUSHNELL, G. H. S. *Peru* (new ed.). London, Thames and Hudson, 1963.

CAIRNS, ALAN C. *Prelude to imperialism: British reactions to central African society, 1840–1890.* London, Routledge and Kegan Paul, 1965.

CAMPBELL, J. K. *Honour, family and patronage.* London, Oxford University Press, 1964.

CARSTAIRS, G. MORRIS. *The twice born: a study of a community of high-caste Hindus.* London, Hogarth Press, 1957.

CARSTENS, PETER. *The social structure of a Cape coloured reserve: a study of racial integration and segregation in South Africa.* London, Oxford University Press, 1966.

CARTER, GWENDOLEN M. (ed.). *Five African states: responses to diversity.* London, Pall Mall Press, 1964.

*The politics of inequality: South Africa since 1948* (rev. ed.). London, Thames and Hudson, 1959.

CARTER, GWENDOLEN M. and others. *South Africa's Transkei: the politics of domestic colonialism.* Evanston, Northwestern University Press, 1967.

CARTHY, J. D. and EBLING, F. J. (eds.). *The natural history of aggression.* London, Academic Press, 1964.

CASH, W. J. *The mind of the South.* New York, Knopf, 1941.

CASSIDY, F. G. *Jamaica talk: three hundred years of the English language in Jamaica.* London, Macmillan, 1961.

CASTELLANOS, ROSARIO. *The nine guardians.* London, Faber, 1959.

CAWOOD, LESLEY. *The churches and race relations in South Africa.* Johannesburg, South African Institute of Race Relations, 1964.

CÉSAIRE, AIMÉ. *Cahier d'un retour au pays natal:* poème (2nd ed.). Paris, Présence Africaine, 1956.

CHAUDHURI, NIRAD C. *The continent of Circe: being an essay on the peoples of India.* London, Chatto and Windus, 1965.
*Autobiography of an unknown Indian.* London, Macmillan, 1951.

CHHIBBAR, Y. P. *From caste to class: a study of the Indian middle classes.* New Delhi, Associate Publishing House, 1968.

CHILCOTE, R. H. *Portuguese Africa.* Englewood-Cliffs (N.J.), Prentice-Hall, 1967.

CLARKE, EDITH. *My mother who fathered me.* London, Allen and Unwin, 1957.

CODERE, HELEN. 'Power in Ruanda.' In *Anthropologica*, Vol. IV, no. 1, 1962.

COLE, ERNEST. *House of bondage.* London, Allen Lane, 1968.

COLSON, ELIZABETH. *Marriage and the family among the plateau Tonga of Northern Rhodesia.* Manchester, Manchester University Press, 1958.

COLSON, ELIZABETH and GLUCKMAN, MAX (eds.). *Seven tribes of British Central Africa.* London, Oxford University Press, 1951.

CONTRIBUTIONS TO INDIAN SOCIOLOGY. Caste. Issue of April 1958.

COOKEY, S. J. S. *Britain and the Congo question 1885-1913.* London, Longmans, 1968.

COON, CARLETON S. *The living races of man.* London, Jonathan Cape, 1966.

CORWIN, A. F. *Spain and the abolition of slavery in Cuba, 1817-1886.* London, University of Texas Press, 1967.

COULTHARD, G. R. *Race and colour in Caribbean literature.* London, Oxford University Press, 1962.

COUPLAND, SIR REGINALD. *The exploitation of East Africa, 1856-1890: the slave trade and the scramble.* London, Faber, 1968.
*Kirk on the Zambesi: a chapter of African history.* Oxford, Clarendon Press, 1928.
*Wilberforce* (2nd ed.). London, Collins, 1945.

COWEN, D. V. *The foundations of freedom: with special reference to Southern Africa.* London, Oxford University Press, 1961.

COX, OLIVER CROMWELL. *Caste, class and race.* New York, Monthly Review Press, 1959.

CUMINOS, PETER T. 'Late Victorian sexual respectability and the social system.' In *The International Review of Social History*, Vol. VIII, parts 1 and 2, 1963.

CUMPER, G. E. (ed.). *The economy of the West Indies.* Kingston, Institute of Social and Economic Research, University College of the West Indies, 1960.

CURTIN, PHILIP D. (ed.). *Africa remembered: narratives by West Africans from the era of the slave trade.* Madison, University of Wisconsin Press, 1967.
*The image of Africa: British ideas and action, 1780-1850.* Madison, University of Wisconsin Press, 1964.
*Two Jamaicas: the role of ideas in a tropical colony, 1830-1865.* Cambridge (Mass.), Harvard University Press, 1955.

DAVENPORT, T. R. H. *The Afrikaner bond: the history of a South African political party, 1880-1911.* London, Oxford University Press, 1966.

DAVIDSON, BASIL. *Africa, history of a continent.* London, Weidenfeld and Nicolson, 1966.

*Black mother Africa: the years of trial.* London, Gollancz, 1961.

DAVIS, DAVID BRION. *The problem of slavery in Western culture.* New York, Cornell University Press, 1966.

DE BLANK, JOOST. *Out of Africa.* London, Hodder & Stoughton, 1964.

DEN BOER, W. *Laconian studies.* Amsterdam, North Holland Publishing Company, 1954.

DESPRES, LEO A. *Cultural pluralism and nationalist politics in British Guiana.* Chicago, Rand McNally, 1967.

DICKIE-CLARK, H. F. *The marginal situation: a sociological study of a coloured group.* Durban, University of Natal, 1964.

DICKINSON, G. LOWES. *The Greek view of life* (new ed.). London, Methuen, 1896.

DOBZHANSKY, T. *Genetics and the origin of species* (rev. ed.). New York, Columbia University Press, 1951.

*Heredity and the nature of man.* London, Allen and Unwin, 1965.

DOLLARD, JOHN. *Caste and class in a Southern town* (2nd ed.). New York, Harper, 1949.

DOUGHTY, PAUL LARRABEE. 'Peruvian highlanders in a changing world: social integration and culture change in an Andean district.' Unpublished Ph.D. thesis, Cornell University, 1963.

DOVER, C. *Know this of race.* London, Secker and Warburg, 1939.

DUBOIS, J. A. *Hindu manners, customs and ceremonies* (3rd ed.). London, Oxford University Press, 1906.

DUBOIS, W. E. B. *Black reconstruction in America . . . 1860–1880.* Cleveland, World, 1965.

*The souls of black folk: essays and sketches.* New York, Fawcett World Library, 1961.

*The world and Africa.* New York, International Publishers, 1965.

DUFFY, JAMES. *Portuguese in Africa.* Cambridge (Mass.), Harvard University Press, 1959.

*Portugal in Africa.* Harmondsworth, Penguin Books, 1962.

*A question of slavery: labour policies in Portuguese Africa and the British protest, 1850–1920.* Oxford, Clarendon Press, 1967.

DUTTON, GEOFFREY. *The hero as murderer: the life of Edward John Eyre. . . .* London, Collins, 1967.

DUMONT, LOUIS. *Homo hierarchichus: essai sur le système des castes.* Paris, Gallimard, 1966.

DUNN, L. C. and DOBZHANSKY, T. *Heredity, race and society* (rev. ed.). New York, Mentor Books, 1963.

ECUADORIAN INSTITUTE OF AGRARIAN REFORM AND COLONIZATION (I.E.R.A.C.). *Indians in misery: a preliminary report. . . .* Ithaca, Department of Anthropology, Cornell University, 1966.

EDUARDO, OCTAVIO DA COSTA. *The Negro in Northern Brazil: a study in acculturation.* London, University of Washington Press, 1966.

ELKINS, STANLEY M. *Slavery* (2nd ed.). London, University of Chicago Press, 1968.

EPSTEIN, A. L. *Politics in an urban African community.* Manchester, Manchester University Press, 1958.

EPSTEIN, T. SCARLETT. *Economic development and social change in South India.* Manchester, Manchester University Press, 1962.

ESCALANTE, AQUILES. *El Negro en Colombia*. Bogota, Universidad Nacional de Colombia, Facultad de Sociologia, 1964.

ESSIEN-UDOM, E. U. *Black nationalism: a search for identity in America*. Chicago, University of Chicago Press, 1962.

EVANS, MAURICE S. *Black and white in South East Africa: a study in sociology*. London, Longmans, 1911.

EVANS-PRITCHARD, E. E. *Nuer religion*. Oxford, Clarendon Press, 1956.

*Social anthropology*. London, Cohen and West, 1951.

*Witchcraft, oracles and magic among the Azande*. Oxford, Clarendon Press, 1937.


FALLERS, LLOYD A. *Bantu bureaucracy: a study of integration and conflict in the political institutions of an East African people*. Cambridge, W. Heffer, no date.

FALS BORDA, ORLANDO. *Peasant society in the Colombian Andes*. Gainesville, University of Florida Press, 1955.

FANON, FRANTZ. *Black skin, white masks*. London, MacGibbon and Kee, 1968.

*Studies in a dying colonialism*. New York, Monthly Review Press, 1965.

*The wretched of the earth*. London, MacGibbon and Kee, 1965.

FAULKNER, WILLIAM. *Intruder in the dust*. Harmondsworth, Penguin, 1966.

*Light in August.* Harmondsworth, Penguin, 1968.

FERGUSON, J. HALCRO. *Latin America: the balance of race redressed*. London, Oxford University Press for Institute of Race Relations, 1961.

FERMOR, PATRICK LEIGH. *The traveller's tree: a journey through the Caribbean islands*. London, Murray, 1965.

FERNANDES, FLORESTAN. 'The weight of the past.' In *Daedalus*, Spring, 1967.

FIRST, RUTH. *One hundred and seventeen days: an account of confinement and interrogation under the South African ninety-day detention law*. Harmondsworth, Penguin Books, 1965.

FIRTH, RAYMOND. *Economics of the New Zealand Maori* (2nd ed.). Wellington, New Zealand, R. E. Owen, 1959.

'The theory of cargo cults.' In *Man*, September 1955.

FORDE, DARYLL (ed.). *African worlds*. London, Oxford University Press, 1963.

FORDE, DARYLL and KABERRY, P. M. (eds.). *West African kingdoms in the nineteenth century*. London, Oxford University Press, 1967.

FORSTER, E. M. *A passage to India*. Harmondsworth, Penguin Books, 1966.

FORTES, M. and EVANS-PRITCHARD, E. E. (eds.). *African political systems*. London, Oxford University Press, 1940.

FRAENKEL, PETER. *Wayaleshi*. London, Weidenfeld and Nicolson, 1959.

FRANKLIN, JOHN HOPE. *From slavery to freedom: a history of the American Negro*. New York, Knopf, 1952.

FRAZER, SIR J. G. *The golden bough* (abr. ed.). London, Macmillan, 1959.

FRAZIER, FRANKLIN. *Race and culture contacts in the modern world*. New York, Knopf, 1957.

FREYRE, GILBERTO. *The mansions and the shanties: the making of modern Brazil*. London, Weidenfeld and Nicolson, 1963.

*The masters and the slaves: a study in the development of Brazilian civilization*. New York, Knopf, 1946.


GAIKWAD, V. R. *The Anglo-Indians: a study in the problems and processes involved in emotional and cultural integration*. London, Asia Publishing House, 1967.

GALBRAITH, JOHN S. *Reluctant empire: British policy on the South African frontier, 1834–1854.* Los Angeles, University of California Press, 1963.

GANN, L. H. *The birth of a plural society: the development of Northern Rhodesia under the British South Africa Co., 1894–1914.* Manchester, Manchester University Press, 1958.

*A history of Southern Rhodesia: early days to 1934.* London, Chatto and Windus, 1965.

GANN, L. H. and DUIGNAN, P. *Burden of empire: an appraisal of western colonialism in Africa south of the Sahara.* London, Pall Mall Press, 1968.

GELFAND, MICHAEL. *Medicine and magic of the Mashona.* Cape Town, Juta, 1956.

*Witch doctor: traditional medicine man of Rhodesia.* London, Harvill Press, 1964.

GENOVESE, EUGENE D. *The political economy of slavery: studies in the economy and society of the slave South.* New York, Pantheon Books, 1966.

GHURYE, G. S. *Social tensions in India.* Bombay, Popular Prakashan, 1968.

GIBBS, HENRY. *Background to bitterness: the story of South Africa, 1652–1954.* New York, Philosophical Library, 1954.

GIBSON, CHARLES. *The Aztecs under Spanish rule: a history of the Indians of the valley of Mexico, 1519–1810.* London, Oxford University Press, 1964.

GIFFORD, P. and LOUIS, W. R. *Britain and Germany in Africa: imperial rivalry and colonial rule.* London, Yale University Press, 1967.

GLUCKMAN, MAX (ed.). *Ideas and procedures in African customary law.* London, Oxford University Press, 1969.

*The judicial process among the Barotse of Northern Rhodesia.* Manchester, Manchester University Press, 1955.

*Analysis of a social situation in modern Zululand.* Manchester, Manchester University Press for Rhodes-Livingstone Institute, 1958.

GOODFELLOW, CLEMENT FRANCIS. *Great Britain and South African confederation, 1870–1881.* London, Oxford University Press, 1966.

GOPAL, RAM. *Linguistic affairs of India.* London, Asia Publishing House, 1966.

GORDIMER, NADINE. *Occasion for loving.* London, Gollancz, 1963.

GOSSETT, THOMAS F. *Race: the history of an idea in America.* Dallas, Southern Methodist University Press, 1963.

GOVEIA, ELSA V. *Slave society in the British Leeward Islands at the end of the eighteenth century.* London, Yale University Press, 1965.

GOVERNMENT OF INDIA. Commission on untouchability. *Report.* New Delhi, India Government Printer, 1968.

GRANT, DOUGLAS. *The fortunate slave: an illustration of African slavery in the early eighteenth century.* London, Oxford University Press, 1968.

GRAY, RICHARD. *The two nations: aspects of the development of race relations in the Rhodesias and Nyasaland.* London, Oxford University Press, 1960.

GREENFIELD, SIDNEY M. *English rustics in black skin: a study of modern family forms in a pre-industrialized society.* New Haven, College and University Press, 1966.

HAMMOND, R. J. *Portugal and Africa, 1815–1910.* Stanford, Stanford University Press, 1966.

HANCOCK, W. K. *Smuts.* 2 vols. Cambridge, Cambridge University Press, 1962–8.

HANDLIN, OSCAR. *The American people: a new history.* London, Hutchinson, 1963.

HANKE, LEWIS. *Aristotle and the American Indians : a study in race prejudice.* London, Hollis and Carter, 1959.

*Modern Latin America.* 2 vols. Princeton (N.J.), Van Nostrand, 1959.

*The Spanish struggle for justice.* Philadelphia, University of Pennsylvania Press, 1949.

HANNA, A. J. *The beginnings of Nyasaland and North-eastern Rhodesia, 1859–1895.* Oxford, Clarendon Press, 1956.

*The story of the Rhodesias and Nyasaland.* London, Faber, 1960.

HARING, C. H. *Empire in Brazil.* London, Oxford University Press, 1958.

*The Spanish empire in America.* New York, Oxford University Press, 1947.

HARLOW, VINCENT T. *A history of Barbados, 1625–1685.* Oxford, Clarendon Press, 1926.

HARRÉ, JOHN. *Maori and Pakeha: a study of mixed marriages in New Zealand.* London, Pall Mall Press for Institute of Race Relations, 1966.

HARRIS, MARVIN. *Patterns of race in the Americas.* New York, Walker and Co., 1964.

HARRISON, G. A. and others. *Human biology: an introduction to human evolution, variation and growth.* London, Oxford University Press, 1964.

HARRISON, SELIG S. *India: the most dangerous decades.* London, Oxford University Press, 1960.

HARTZ, LOUIS. *The founding of new societies.* New York, Harcourt, Brace and World, 1964.

HEARNE, JOHN. *The autumn equinox* (a novel). London, Faber, 1959.

*The faces of love* (a novel). London, Faber, 1957.

HEBER, REGINALD. *Indian journal.* London, 1923.

HENRIQUES, FERNANDO. *Family and colour in Jamaica.* London, Eyre and Spottiswoode, 1953.

HERSKOVITS, MELVILLE J. *The human factor in changing Africa.* New York, Knopf, 1962.

*The myth of the Negro past.* Boston, Beacon Press, 1958.

*Trinidad village.* An anthropological study of Toco. New York, Knopf, 1947.

HEUSSLER, ROBERT. *The British in Northern Nigeria.* London, Oxford University Press, 1968.

HILL, CHRISTOPHER R. *Bantustans: the fragmentation of South Africa.* London, Oxford University Press for Institute of Race Relations, 1964.

HOETINK, H. *The two variants in Caribbean race relations.* London, Oxford University Press for Institute of Race Relations, 1967.

HOLLEMAN, J. F. *Shona customary law.* Cape Town, Oxford University Press, 1952.

HORWITZ, RALPH. *The political economy of South Africa.* London, Weidenfeld and Nicolson, 1967.

HSU, F. L. K. *Clan, caste and club.* Princeton (N.J.), Van Nostrand, 1963.

HUDDLESTON, TREVOR. *Naught for your comfort.* London, Collins, 1956.

HUNTER, GUY (ed.). *Industrialisation and race relations.* London, Oxford University Press, 1965.

*The new societies of tropical Africa.* London, Oxford University Press for Institute of Race Relations, 1962.

*South-East Asia: race, culture and nation.* London, Oxford University Press for Institute of Race Relations, 1966.

HUNTER, G. K. 'Othello and colour prejudice.' In *The Proceedings of the British Academy*, Vol. LIII, 1967.

HUSAIN, S. ABID. *The destiny of Indian Muslims*. London, Asia Publishing House, 1965.

HUXLEY, ELSPETH. *Red strangers*. London, Chatto and Windus, 1964.

HUXLEY, ELSPETH and PERHAM, MARGERY. *Race and politics in Kenya: a correspondence between Elspeth Huxley and Margery Perham* (rev. ed.). London, Faber, 1956.

HUXLEY, FRANCIS. *Affable savages: an anthropologist among Urubu Indians of Brazil*. London, Hart Davis, 1957.

HUXLEY, J. S. *We Europeans: a survey of 'racial' problems*. London, Jonathan Cape, 1935.

HUXLEY, T. H. *Evolution and ethics 1893–1943*. The Romanes Lectures of 1893 and 1943 with additional papers. London, Pilot Press, 1947.

IKRAM, S. M. *Muslim civilization in India*. London, Columbia University Press, 1964.

INSTITUTE FOR CROSS-CULTURAL STUDIES. *Indians of Brazil in the twentieth century*. Washington, Institute for Cross-Cultural Studies, 1967.

INTERNATIONAL AFRICAN SEMINAR, Makerere College, Kampala, January 1959. *Social change in modern Africa*. London, Oxford University Press for International African Institute, 1961.

ISAACS, HAROLD R. 'Color in world affairs.' In *Foreign Affairs*, Vol. XLIV, no. 2, January 1969.

*India's ex-untouchables*. New York, John Day, 1964.

*The new world of Negro Americans*. New York, John Day, 1963.

*Scratches on our minds: American images of China and India*. New York, John Day, 1958.

ISHWARAN, K. *Tradition and economy in village India*. London, Routledge and Kegan Paul, 1966.

JABAVU, NONI. *Drawn in colour: African contrasts*. London, Murray, 1960.

*Ochre people: scenes from a South African life*. London, Murray, 1956.

JAHODA, G. *White man*. London, Oxford University Press for Institute of Race Relations, 1961.

JAMES, C. L. R. *Beyond a boundary*. London, Hutchinson, 1966..

*The black Jacobins*. New York, Random House, 1963.

JHABVALA, R. PRAWER. *A backward place* (a novel). London, Murray, 1965.

JOHNSTON, H. A. S. *The Fulani empire of Sokoto*. London, Oxford University Press, 1967.

JOHNSTON, SIR HARRY. *British Central Africa*. London, Methuen, 1897.

*A history of the colonialization of Africa by alien races*. Cambridge, Cambridge University Press, 1905.

JONES, ELDRED. *Othello's countrymen: the African in English Renaissance drama*. London, Oxford University Press, 1965.

JONES, PHILIP N. *The segregation of immigrant communities in the city of Birmingham, 1961*. Hull, University of Hull Publications, 1967.

JORDAN, WINTHROP D. *White over black: American attitudes towards the Negro, 1550–1812*. Chapel Hill, University of North Carolina Press, 1968.

JOSEPH, HELEN. *If this be treason.* London, André Deutsch, 1963.
JULY, ROBERT W. *The origins of modern African thought.* London, Faber, 1968.

KAUL, JOLLY MOHAN. *Problems of national integration.* New Delhi, People's Publishing House, 1963.
KAY, F. GEORGE. *The shameful trade.* London, Muller, 1967.
KAYE, SIR JOHN WILLIAM. *The administration of the East India Company.* London, 1853.
KERR, MADELINE. *Personality and conflict in Jamaica.* London, Collins, 1963.
KIERNAN, V. G. *The lords of human kind: European attitudes towards the outside world in the imperial age.* London, Weidenfeld and Nicolson, 1969.
KIEWIET, C. W. DE. *A history of South Africa, social and economic.* London, Oxford University Press, 1941.
*The imperial factor in South Africa: a study in politics and economics.* London, F. Cass, 1965.
KLASS, MORTON. *East Indians in Trinidad: a study of cultural persistence.* London, Columbia University Press, 1961.
KLEIN, HERBERT S. *Slavery in the Americas: a comparative study of Virginia and Cuba.* London, Oxford University Press, 1967.
KORTH, EUGENE H. *Spanish policy in colonial Chile: the struggle for social justice, 1535–1700.* Stanford, Stanford University Press, 1968.
KUNDSTADTER, PETER (ed.). *Southeast Asian tribes, minorities and nations.* 2 vols. Princeton (N.J.), Princeton University Press, 1967.
KUPER, HILDA. *Indian people in Natal.* Durban, Natal University Press, 1960.
*The uniform of colour: a study of white:black relationships in Swaziland.* Johannesburg, Witwatersrand University Press, 1947.
KUPER, LEO. *An African bourgeoisie: race, class and politics in South Africa.* London, Yale University Press, 1965.
*Passive resistance in South Africa.* London, Cape, 1956.

LA GUMA, ALEX. *The stone country* (a novel). Berlin, Seven Seas Publishers, 1967.
LAMMING, GEORGE. *In the castle of my skin* (a novel). London, Michael Joseph, 1953.
*Of age and innocence* (a novel). London, Michael Joseph, 1958.
LE MAY, G. H. L. *British supremacy in South Africa, 1899–1907.* Oxford, Clarendon Press, 1965.
LEON-PORTILLA, MIGUEL (ed.). *The broken spears: the Aztec account of the conquest of Mexico.* London, Constable, 1962.
LESSING, DORIS. *Going home.* London, Michael Joseph, 1957.
*The singing grass.* London, Michael Joseph, 1953.
*This was the old chief's country.* London, Michael Joseph, 1953.
LEVI-STRAUSS, CLAUDE. *The savage mind.* London, Weidenfeld and Nicolson, 1966.
*Structural anthropology.* London, Allen Lane, the Penguin Press, 1968.
LEWIN, JULIUS. *Politics and law in South Africa: essays on race relations.* London, Merlin Press, 1963.
LEWIS, GORDON K. *The growth of the modern West Indies.* London, MacGibbon and Kee, 1968.

LEWIS, OSCAR. *Pedro Martinez: a Mexican peasant and his family*. London, Secker and Warburg, 1964.

*Children of Sanchez*. London, Secker and Warburg, 1962.

*La vida: a Puerto Rican family in the culture of poverty*. London, Secker and Warburg, 1967.

*Village life in Northern India*. Chicago, University of Illinois Press, 1958.

LEYBURN, JAMES G. *The Haitian people* (rev. ed.). London, Yale University Press, 1966.

LEYS, COLIN. *European politics in Southern Rhodesia*. Oxford, Clarendon Press, 1959.

LIENHARDT, G. *Divinity and experience: the religion of the Dinka*. Oxford, Clarendon Press, 1961.

*Social anthropology*. London, Oxford University Press, 1966.

LINCOLN, ERIC. *The Black Muslims in America*. Boston, Beacon Press, 1961.

LINKE, LILO. *Ecuador* (3rd ed.). London, Oxford University Press, 1960.

LITWACK, LEON F. *North of slavery: the Negro in the free states, 1790–1860*. Chicago, University of Chicago Press, 1965.

LIVINGSTONE, DAVID. *African journal, 1853–1856*, edited by I. Schapera. 2 vols. London, Chatto and Windus, 1963.

*Missionary travels and researches in South Africa*. London, Murray, 1957.

LLOYD, CHRISTOPHER. *The navy and the slave trade*. London, Cass, 1968.

LLOYD, P. C. *Africa in social change*. Harmondsworth, Penguin, 1967.

LOCKHART, JAMES. *Spanish Peru 1532–1560: a colonial society*. Madison, University of Wisconsin Press, 1968.

LORENZ, KONRAD. *On aggression*. London, Methuen, 1966.

LOWENTHAL, DAVID. *West Indian societies*. London, Oxford University Press for Institute of Race Relations, forthcoming.

'Race and color in the West Indies.' In *Daedalus*, Spring, 1967.

(ed.). *The West Indies Federation: perspectives on a new nation*. New York, Columbia University Press, 1961.

LUTHULI, ALBERT. *Let my people go: an autobiography*. London, Collins, 1962.

LYTTON, DAVID. *The grass won't grow till spring* (a novel). London, Bodley Head, 1965.

McCLOY, SELBY T. *The Negro in the French West Indies*. Lexington, University of Kentucky Press, 1966.

MACCRONE, I. D. *Race attitudes in South Africa: historical, experimental and psychological studies*. Johannesburg, Witwatersrand University Press, 1937.

MACKENZIE-GRIEVE, AVERIL. *The last years of the English slave trade: Liverpool 1750–1807*. London, F. Cass, 1968.

MACMILLAN, WILLIAM MILLER. *Bantu, Boer and Briton: the making of the South African native problem* (rev. ed.). Oxford, Clarendon Press, 1963.

*The Cape colour question: a historical survey*. London, Hurst, 1927.

McPHERSON, JAMES M. *The struggle for equality: abolitionists and the Negro in the civil war and reconstruction*. Princeton, Princeton University Press, 1964.

MADARIAGA, SALVADOR DE. *The fall of the Spanish American Empire*. London, Hollis and Carter, 1947.

*Heart of jade* (a novel). London, Panther, 1964.

*The rise of the Spanish American Empire*. London, Hollis and Carter, 1947.

*Spain* (rev. ed.). London, Jonathan Cape, 1961.

MAINE, SIR HENRY. *Ancient law: notes on the history of ancient institutions.* London, J. M. Dent and Sons, 1954.

MAJUMDAR, D. N. *Caste and communication in an Indian village.* London, Asia Publishing House, 1958.
*Races and cultures of India* (rev. ed.). London, Asia Publishing House, 1961.

MALINOWSKI, BRONISLAW. *The dynamics of culture change: an inquiry into race relations in Africa.* New Haven, Yale University Press, 1945.

MANDELA, NELSON. *No easy walk to freedom: articles, speeches and trial addresses.* London, Heinemann, 1965.

MANNIX, DANIEL P. and COWLEY, MALCOLM. *Black cargoes: a history of the Atlantic slave trade, 1518–1865.* London, Longmans Green, 1962.

MANNONI, O. *Prospero and Caliban: the psychology of colonialization.* London, Methuen, 1956.

MANSERGH, NICHOLAS. *South Africa 1906–1961: the price of magnanimity.* London, Allen and Unwin, 1962.

MAQUET, JACQUES J. *The premise of inequality in Ruanda: a study of political relations in a central African kingdom.* London, Oxford University Press, 1961.

MARAIS, J. S. *The Cape coloured people 1652–1937.* Johannesburg, Witwatersrand University Press, 1957.

MARQUARD, LEO. *The peoples and policies of South Africa* (2nd ed.). London, Oxford University Press, 1960.

MARRIOTT, McKIM (ed.). *Village India.* Chicago, University of Chicago Press, 1955.

MASON, J. ALDEN. *The ancient civilizations of Peru.* Harmondsworth, Penguin Books, 1937.

MASON, PHILIP. *The birth of a dilemma: the conquest and settlement of Rhodesia.* London, Oxford University Press for Institute of Race Relations, 1958.
' "... but O! My soul is white": on the confusion of biological accident and symbolic metaphor.' In *Encounter*, Vol. XXX, no. 4, April 1968.
Philip Woodruff (pseud.). *Call the next witness* (a novel). London, Jonathan Cape, 1945.
*Common sense about race.* London, Gollancz, 1961.
'Gradualism in Peru: some impressions on the future of ethnic group relations.' In *Race*, Vol. VIII, no. 1, July 1966.
(ed.). *India and Ceylon: unity and diversity.* London, Oxford University Press for Institute of Race Relations, 1967.
Philip Woodruff (pseud.). *The men who ruled India.* 2 vols. London, Jonathan Cape, 1953–4.
*Prospero's magic: some thoughts on class and race.* London, Oxford University Press, 1962.
'Race relations and human rights.' In *Race*, Vol. X, no. 1, July 1968.
'The revolt against Western values.' In *Daedalus*, Vol. XCVI, no. 2, Spring, 1967.
*Year of decision: Rhodesia and Nyasaland in 1960.* London, Oxford University Press for Institute of Race Relations, 1960.

MASUOKA, J. and VALIEN, P. (eds.). *Race relations: problems and theory.* Chapel Hill, University of North Carolina Press, 1961.

MATTINGLY, G. *Renaissance diplomacy.* London, Jonathan Cape, 1955.

MAUNIER, RENÉ. *The sociology of colonies: an introduction to the study of race contact.* 2 vols. London, Routledge and Kegan Paul, 1949.

MAYBURY-LEWIS, DAVID. *Akwé Shavante society.* London, Oxford University Press, 1967.
*Race relations in Brazil.* London, Oxford University Press for Institute of Race Relations, forthcoming.

MBEKI, GOVAN. *South Africa: the peasants' revolt.* Harmondsworth, Penguin Books, 1964.

MEAD, MARGARET. *Continuities in cultural evolution.* London, Yale University Press, 1964.

MEAD, MARGARET and others. *Science and the concept of race.* London, Columbia University Press, 1968.

MEADE, J. E. and PARKES, A. S. (eds.). *Biological aspects of social problems.* London, Oliver and Boyd, 1965.

MEMMI, ALBERT. *The colonizer and the colonized.* New York, Orion Press, 1965.

METGE, JOAN. *The Maoris of New Zealand.* London, Routledge and Kegan Paul, 1967.
*A new Maori migration: rural and urban relations in Northern New Zealand.* London, Athlone Press, 1964.

MEZERIK, A. G. (ed.). *Apartheid in the Republic of South Africa: Rhodesia, South West Africa, sanctions, U.N. action.* New York, International Review Service, 1967.

MILLER, HAROLD. *Race conflict in New Zealand, 1814–1865.* Auckland, Blackwood and Janet Paul, 1966.

MITTELHOLZER, EDGAR. *The life and death of Sylvia* (a novel). London, Secker and Warburg, 1953.
*A morning at the office* (a novel). London, Hogarth Press, 1950.

MOFFAT, R. *Missionary labours and scenes in Southern Africa.* London, J. Snow, 1842.

MONTAGU, ASHLEY (ed.). *Man and aggression.* London, Oxford University Press, 1968.
*Man's most dangerous myth: the fallacy of race* (4th ed.). Cleveland, World Publishing Co., 1965.
*Race, science and humanity.* London, Van Nostrand, 1963.

MONTEJO, ESTEBAN. *The autobiography of a runaway slave.* London, Bodley Head, 1968.

MORRIS, DONALD R. *The washing of the spears: a history of the rise of the Zulu nation under Shaka and its fall in the Zulu war of 1879.* London, Jonathan Cape, 1966.

MTSHALI, B. VULINDLELA. *Rhodesia: background to conflict.* New York, Hawthorn Books, 1967.

MUJEEB, M. *The Indian Muslims.* London, Allen and Unwin, 1967.

MURRAY, E. G. *The basis of ascendancy.* London, Longmans Green, 1910.

MWASE, GEORGE SIMEON. *Strike a blow and die: a narrative of race relations in colonial Africa.* Cambridge (Mass.), Harvard University Press for Center for International Affairs, 1967.

MYRDAL, GUNNAR. *An American dilemma: the Negro problem and modern democracy.* New York, Harper and Row, 1944.

NAIPAUL, V. S. *An area of darkness*. London, André Deutsch, 1965.
*A house for Mr Biswas* (a novel). London, André Deutsch, 1961.
*The middle passage*. London, André Deutsch, 1962.
*Miguel street* (a novel). London, André Deutsch, 1957.
*The mystic masseur* (a novel). London, André Deutsch, 1957.
*The suffrage of Elvira* (a novel). London, André Deutsch, 1958.
NATH, DWARKA. *A history of Indians in British Guiana*. London, Nelson, 1950.
NAYAR, BALDER RAJ. *Minority politics in the Punjab*. Princeton, Princeton University Press, 1966.
NEAME, L. E. *The history of apartheid: the story of the colour war in South Africa*. London, Pall Mall Press, 1962.
NEWBURY, C. W. *The western slave coast and its rulers: European trade and administration among the Yoruba and Adja-speaking peoples of South-Western Nigeria, Southern Dahomey, and Togo*. Oxford, Clarendon Press, 1961.
NEWMAN, PETER. *British Guiana: problems of cohesion in an immigrant society*. London, Oxford University Press for Institute of Race Relations, 1964.
NEW YORK ACADEMY OF SCIENCES AND RESEARCH INSTITUTE FOR THE STUDY OF MAN. 'Social and cultural pluralism in the Caribbean: papers ... of a conference . . . held 27 and 28 May 1959.' From *Annals of the New York Academy of Sciences*, Vol. LXXXIII, Art. 5, 20 January 1960.
NGUBANE, JORDAN K. *An African explains apartheid*. London, Pall Mall Press, 1963.
NIEHOFF, ARTHUR and JUANITA. *East Indians in the West Indies*. Milwaukee, Milwaukee Public Museum, 1960.

OLIVER, ROLAND. *The missionary factor in East Africa*. London, Longmans Green, 1952.
*Sir Harry Johnston and the scramble for Africa*. London, Chatto and Windus, 1957.
OLIVER, ROLAND and FAGE, J. D. *A short history of Africa*. Harmondsworth, Penguin Books, 1962.
OLIVER, ROLAND and others (eds.). *History of East Africa*. 2 vols. Oxford, Clarendon Press, 1963–5.
OLIVIER, SYDNEY. *Jamaica, the blessed island*. London, Faber, 1936.
*The myth of Governor Eyre*. London, Hogarth Press, 1933.
O'MALLEY, L. S. S. (ed.). *Modern India and the West: a study of the interaction of their civilizations*. London, Oxford University Press for Royal Institute of International Affairs, 1968.
OMER-COOPER, J. D. *The Zulu aftermath: a nineteenth-century revolution in Bantu Africa*. London, Longmans Green, 1966.
OSOFSKY, GILBERT. *The burden of race: a documentary history of Negro–white relations in America*. London, Harper and Row, 1966.
OXAAL, IVAR. *Black intellectuals come to power: the rise of Creole nationalism in Trinidad and Tobago*. Cambridge (Mass.), Schenkman Publishing Co., 1968.

PADMORE, GEORGE. *Africa: Britain's third empire*. London, Dobson, 1949.
PAKENHAM, ELIZABETH. *Jameson's raid*. London, Weidenfeld and Nicolson, 1960.

PAN-AMERICAN INSTITUTE OF GEOGRAPHY AND HISTORY. Commission on history. *El mestizaje en la historia de Ibero-America*. Mexico, Editorial Cultura, 1961.

PANIKKAR, K. M. *Hindu society at crossroads* (3rd ed.). London, Asia Publishing House, 1961.
*Asia and Western dominance: a survey of the Vasco da Gama epoch of Asian history, 1498–1945*. London, Allen and Unwin, 1953.
*The serpent and the crescent: a history of the Negro empires of Western Africa*. London, Asia Publishing House, 1963.

PARAF, PIERRE. *Le racisme dans le monde*. Paris, Payot, 1964.

PARK, ROBERT EZRA. *Race and culture: essays in the sociology of contemporary man*. New York, Free Press of Glencoe, 1964.

PARRY, JOHN H. *The Spanish theory of empire in the nineteenth century*. Cambridge, Cambridge University Press, 1960.

PARRY, JOHN H. and SHERLOCK, P. M. *A short history of the West Indies*. London, Macmillan, 1956.

PATON, ALAN. *Hofmeyr*. London, Oxford University Press, 1964.
*The long view* (essays). London, Pall Mall Press, 1968.

PATTERSON, ORLANDO. *The sociology of slavery*. London, MacGibbon and Kee, 1967.

PATTERSON, SHEILA. *Colour and culture in South Africa*. London, Routledge and Kegan Paul, 1953.
*The last trek: a study of the Boer people and the Afrikaner nation*. London, Routledge and Kegan Paul, 1957.

PAZ, OCTAVIO. *The labyrinth of solitude: life and thought in Mexico*. London, Allen Lane, 1967.

PEARCE, G. L. *The story of the Maori people*. London, Collins, 1968.

PERHAM, MARGERY. *Native administration in Nigeria*. London, Oxford University Press, 1937.
*The colonial reckoning: the Reith lectures for 1961*. London, Collins, 1961.
*Lugard*. London, Collins, 1956–60.

PERISTIANY, J. G. (ed.). *Honour and shame: the values of Mediterranean society*. London, Weidenfeld and Nicolson, 1966.

PICON-SALAS, M. *A cultural history of Spanish America from conquest to independence*. Berkeley, University of California Press, 1962.

PIENAAR, S. and SAMPSON, ANTHONY. *South Africa: two views of separate development*. London, Oxford University Press for Institute of Race Relations, 1960.

PIERSON, DONALD. *Negroes in Brazil: a study of race contact at Bahia*. London, Feffer and Simons, 1967.

PIKE, FREDERICK B. *The modern history of Peru*. London, Weidenfeld and Nicolson, 1967.

PITT-RIVERS, JULIAN A. *After the empire: race and society in Middle America and the Andes*. London, Oxford University Press for Institute of Race Relations, forthcoming.
'Honor.' In *Encyclopaedia of Social Sciences*, Vol. VI, 1968.
'The image of the witch: the naqual.' Working paper for Association of Social Anthropologists, Cambridge, April 1968.
'La loi de l'hospitalité.' In *Les Temps Modernes*, no. 253, June 1967.
(ed.). *Mediterranean countrymen, essays in the social anthropology of the Mediterranean*. The Hague, Mouton and Co., 1963.

PITT-RIVERS—*cont.* 'Mestizo or Ladino?' In *Race*, Vol. X, no. 4, April 1969.
*The people of the sierra.* London, Weidenfeld and Nicolson, 1954.
'Pseudo-kinship.' In *Encyclopaedia of Social Sciences*, Vol. VIII, 1968.
'Race, color and class in Central America and the Andes.' In *Daedalus*, Spring, 1967.
'Words and deeds: the Ladinos of Chiapas.' In *Man*, Vol. II, no. 1, March 1967.
'Who are the Indians?' In *Encounter*, September 1965.

PLOMER, WILLIAM. *Turbott Wolfe* (a novel). London, Hogarth Press, 1965.

POEL, JEAN VAN DER. *The Jameson raid.* Cape Town, Oxford University Press, 1951.

POLANYI, KARL and ROTSTEIN, ABRAHAM. *Dahomey and the slave trade: an analysis of an archaic economy.* Seattle, University of Washington Press, 1966.

POPE-HENNESSY, JAMES. *Sins of the fathers: a study of the Atlantic slave traders, 1441–1807.* London, Weidenfeld and Nicolson, 1967.

POPPER, K. R. *The open society and its enemies.* 2 vols. London, Routledge and Kegan Paul, 1962.

PRADO, CAIO, Jr. *The colonial background of modern Brazil.* Berkeley, University of California Press, 1967.

PRESCOTT, WILLIAM H. *The history of the conquest of Mexico.* Chicago, University of Chicago Press, 1949.
*The history of the conquest of Peru* (2nd ed.). London, Allen and Unwin, 1959.

PRICE, A. GRENFELL. *White settlers and native peoples.* Cambridge, Cambridge University Press, 1950.

PYRAH, G. B. *Imperial policy and South Africa, 1902–10.* Oxford, Clarendon Press, 1955.


RADCLIFFE-BROWN, A. R. and FORDE, DARYLL (eds.). *African systems of kinship and marriage.* London, Oxford University Press, 1950.

RANGER, T. O. (ed.). *Aspects of Central African history.* London, Heinemann, 1968.
*Revolt in Southern Rhodesia, 1896–7: a study in African resistance.* London, Heinemann, 1967.
'The rewriting of African history during the scramble: the Matabele dominance in Mashonaland.' In *African Social Research*, no. 4, December 1967.

RANSFORD, OLIVER. *The rulers of Rhodesia: from earliest times to the referendum.* London, Murray, 1968.

RAVEAU, FRANÇOIS. 'An outline of the role of color in adaptation phenomena.' In *Daedalus*, Spring, 1967.

RAYNER, WILLIAM. *The tribe and its successors: an account of African traditional life and European settlement in Southern Rhodesia.* London, Faber, 1962.

READER, D. H. *The black man's portion: history, demography and living conditions in the native locations of East London, Cape Province.* London, Oxford University Press, 1962.
*Zulu tribe in transition: the Makhanya of Southern Natal.* Manchester, Manchester University Press, 1966.

REEVES, AMBROSE. *Shooting at Sharpeville: the agony of South Africa.* London, Gollancz, 1960.

REICHEL-DOLMATOFF, G. *Colombia.* London, Thames and Hudson, 1965.

REICHEL-DOLMATOFF, G. and REICHEL-DOLMATOFF, A. *The people of Aritama: the cultural personality of a Colombian mestizo village.* London, Routledge and Kegan Paul, 1961.

RHODESIA. Constitutional Commission 1968 Report. Salisbury, Government Printer, April 1968.

RHOODIE, N. J. and VENTER, H. J. *Apartheid: a socio-historical exposition of the origin and development of the apartheid idea.* Cape Town, Haum, 1960.

RICHARDS, AUDREY I. *Land, labour and diet in Northern Rhodesia: an economic study of the Bemba tribe.* London, Oxford University Press, 1939.

RICHMOND, ANTHONY. *The colour problem.* Harmondsworth, Penguin, 1955.

RISLEY, SIR HERBERT. *The people of India* (2nd ed.). London, Thacker, 1915.

RITCHIE, JAMES E. *The making of a Maori: a case study of changing community.* Wellington, A. H. and A. W. Reed, 1963.

(ed.). *Race relations: six New Zealand studies.* Wellington, Victoria University, 1964.

RITTER, E. A. *Shaka Zulu: the rise of the Zulu empire.* London, Longmans, 1955.

ROBERTS, STEPHEN H. *The history of French colonial policy 1870–1925.* London, Cass, 1963.

ROBINSON, RONALD, GALLAGHER, JOHN and DENNY, ALICE. *Africa and the Victorians: the official mind of imperialism.* London, Macmillan, 1961.

RODRIGUES, JOSÉ HONÓRIO. *Brazil and Africa* (2nd ed.). Berkeley, University of California Press, 1965.

ROGERS, CYRIL A. and FRANTZ, C. *Racial themes in Southern Rhodesia: the attitudes and behaviour of the white population.* London, Yale University Press, 1962.

ROSE, E. J. B. and associates. *Colour and citizenship.* London, Oxford University Press for Institute of Race Relations, 1969.

ROTBERG, ROBERT I. *The rise of nationalism in Central Africa: the making of Malawi and Zambia 1873–1964.* London, Oxford University Press, 1966.

ROUX, EDWARD. *Time longer than rope: a history of the black man's struggle for freedom in South Africa* (2nd ed.). Madison, University of Wisconsin Press, 1964.

ROYAL ANTHROPOLOGICAL INSTITUTE and INSTITUTE OF RACE RELATIONS. *Man, Race and Darwin.* London, Oxford University Press, 1960.

RUBIN, VERA (ed.). *Caribbean studies: a symposium* (2nd ed.). Seattle, Washington University Press, 1960.

RUNCIMAN, W. G. *Relative deprivation and social justice.* London, Routledge and Kegan Paul, 1966.

RUDOLPH, LLOYD I. 'The modernity of tradition: the democratic incarnation of caste in India.' In *American Political Science Review*, Vol. LIX, no. 4, December 1965.


SACHS, ALBIE. *The jail diary of Albie Sachs.* London, Harvill Press, 1966.

SACHS, E. S. *The anatomy of apartheid.* London, Collet's (Publishers) Ltd., 1965.

SALKEY, ANDREW. *The late emancipation of Jerry Stover* (a novel). London, Hutchinson, 1968.

*A quality of violence* (a novel). London, Hutchinson, 1959.

(ed.). *West Indian short stories.* London, Faber, 1960.

SAMPSON, ANTHONY. *Drum: a venture into the new Africa.* London, Collins, 1956.

SARTRE, JEAN-PAUL. *Black Orpheus*. Paris, Présence Africaine, 1963.

SCHAPERA, I. (ed.). *Western civilization and the natives of South Africa: studies in culture contact*. London, Routledge and Kegan Paul, 1967.

SCHREINER, OLIVE. *The story of an African farm* (a novel). New York, Fawcett World Library, 1960.

*Trooper Peter Halket of Mashonaland* (a novel). London, T. Fisher Unwin, 1897.

SCHWARZ, FREDERICK A. O., Jr. *Nigeria: the tribes, the nation, or the race—the politics of independence*. Cambridge (Massachusetts) and London, Massachusetts Institute of Technology Press, 1965.

SCHWIMMER, ERIK (ed.). *The Maori people in the nineteen-sixties: a symposium*. London, Hurst, 1968.

SEAL, ANIL. *The emergence of Indian nationalism: competition and collaboration in the later nineteenth century*. Cambridge, Cambridge University Press, 1968.

SEGAL, RONALD. *The crisis of India*. Harmondsworth, Penguin Books, 1965.

*Race war*. London, Jonathan Cape, 1966.

SELOUS, F. C. *Sunshine and storm in Rhodesia: . . . a narrative of events in Matabeleland*. London, Rowland Ward, 1896.

SELVON, SAMUEL. *A brighter sun* (a novel). London, Allan Wingate, 1952.

*An island is a world* (a novel). London, Allan Wingate, 1955.

*Turn again, Tiger* (a novel). London, MacGibbon and Kee, 1958.

SEMMEL, BERNARD. *Imperialism and social reform: English social imperial thought, 1895–1914*. London, Allen and Unwin, 1960.

SHAMUYARIRA, NATHAN M. *Crisis in Rhodesia*. London, André Deutsch, 1965.

SHEPHERD, R. H. W. and PAVER, B. G. *African contrast, the story of a South African people*. London, Oxford University Press, 1947.

SHEPPERSON, GEORGE and PRICE, THOMAS. *Independent African: John Chilembwe and the origins, setting and significance of the Nyasaland native rising of 1915*. Edinburgh, Edinburgh University Press, 1958.

SHIBUTANI, T. and KWAN, K. M. *Ethnic stratification*. New York, The Macmillan Co., 1965.

SIK, ENDRE. *The history of black Africa*. Budapest, Akademiai Kiado, 1966.

SIMPSON, G. E. and YINGER, J. M. *Racial and cultural minorities*. New York, Harper and Row, 1965.

SINCLAIR, K. *A history of New Zealand*. London, Oxford University Press, 1961.

SINGER, MILTON and COHN, BERNARD S. (eds.). *Structure and change in Indian society*. Chicago, Aldine Publishing Co., 1968.

SINGH, K. K. *Patterns of caste tension: a study of intercaste tension and conflict*. London, Asia Publishing House, 1964.

SINGH, KHUSHWANT. *The Sikhs*. London, Allen and Unwin, 1953.

*A history of the Sikhs*. 2 vols. Princeton, Princeton University Press, 1963–6.

SINGHAM, A. W. *The hero and the crowd in a colonial polity*. London, Yale University Press, 1968.

SIVERTSEN, DAGFIN. *When caste barriers fall: a study of social and economic change in a South Indian village*. New York, Humanities Press, 1963.

SLADE, RUTH. *King Leopold's Congo: aspects of the development of race relations in the Congo independent state*. London, Oxford University Press for Institute of Race Relations, 1962.

SMITH, E. W. *The life and times of Daniel Lindley (1801–80)*. London, Epworth Press, 1949.

SMITH, M. G. *Kinship and community in Carriacou.* London, Yale University Press, 1962.

*The plural society in the British West Indies.* Berkeley and Los Angeles, University of California Press, 1965.

*Stratification in Grenada.* London, University of California Press, 1965.

SMITH, MARIAN W. 'Towards a classification of cult movements.' In *Man*, January 1959.

(ed.). *The artist in tribal society: proceedings of a symposium held at the Royal Anthropological Institute.* London, Routledge and Kegan Paul, 1961.

SMITH, RAYMOND T. *British Guiana.* London, Oxford University Press for Royal Institute of International Affairs, 1962.

*The Negro family in British Guiana: family structure and social status in the villages.* London, Routledge and Kegan Paul, 1956.

SMITH, T. LYNN. *Brazil: people and institutions* (rev. ed.). Baton Rouge, Louisiana State University Press, 1963.

SOUSTELLE, JACQUES. *Daily life of the Aztecs.* London, Weidenfeld and Nicolson, 1961.

SOUTH AFRICAN BUREAU OF RACIAL AFFAIRS. *Integration or separate development.* Stellenbosch, S.A.B.R.A., 1952.

SPEAR, PERCIVAL (ed.). *The Oxford history of India* (3rd ed.). (*Part 1*, revised by Sir Mortimer Wheeler and A. L. Basham.) London, Oxford University Press, 1967.

SPICER, EDWARD H. (ed.). *Perspectives in American Indian culture change.* Chicago, University of Chicago Press, 1960.

SRINIVAS, M. N. *Caste in modern India and other essays.* London, Asia Publishing House, 1963.

*Social change in modern India.* Cambridge, Cambridge University Press, 1966.

STAMPP, KENNETH M. *The peculiar institution: Negro slavery in the American South.* London, Eyre and Spottiswoode, 1964.

STANTON, WILLIAM. *The leopard's spots: scientific attitudes towards race in America, 1815–1859.* Chicago, University of Chicago Press, 1960.

STEPHENSON, J. E. *Chirapula's tale.* London, Geoffrey Bles, 1937.

STEWARD, JULIAN H. (ed.). *Contemporary change in traditional societies.* 3 vols. Chicago, University of Illinois Press, 1967.

(ed.). *Handbook of the South American Indians.* 6 vols. Washington, Smithsonian Institution, 1946–50.

STODDARD, L. *The rising tide of colour: against white world-supremacy.* London, Chapman and Hall, 1920.

STOW, GEORGE W. *The native races of South Africa: a history of the intrusion of the Hottentots and Bantu into the hunting grounds of the Bushmen, the aborigines of the country.* London, Swan Sonnenschein and Co., 1905.

STOKES, ERIC and BROWN, RICHARD (eds.). *The Zambesian past.* Manchester, Manchester University Press, 1966.

STYRON, WILLIAM. *The confessions of Nat Turner* (a novel). New York, Random House, 1967.

SUNDKLER, B. G. M. *Bantu prophets in South Africa* (2nd ed.). London, Oxford University Press for the International African Institute, 1961.

SWAN, MICHAEL. *British Guiana: the land of six peoples.* London, H.M.S.O., 1957.

TABATA, I. B. *Education for barbarism in South Africa: Bantu (apartheid) education.* London, Pall Mall, 1960.

TANDON, PRAKASH. *Punjabi century, 1857–1947.* London, Chatto and Windus, 1961.

TANNENBAUM, FRANK. *Slave and citizen: the Negro in the Americas.* New York, Knopf, 1947.
*Mexico: the struggle for peace and bread.* London, Jonathan Cape, 1965.

TAYLOR, GRIFFITH. *Environment, race and migration.* Toronto, University of Toronto Press, 1949.

TEMPELS, PLACIDE. *Bantu philosophy.* Paris, Présence Africaine, 1959.

TEMPLE, C. L. *Native races and their rulers: sketches and studies of official life and administrative problems in Nigeria.* London, Cass, 1968.

THOMPSON, EDGAR T. (ed.). *Race relations and the race problem: a definition and an analysis.* Durham, Duke University Press, 1939.

THOMPSON, E. T. and HUGHES, E. C. (eds.). *Race: individual and collective behavior.* Illinois, The Free Press, 1958.

THOMPSON, LEONARD M. *The unification of South Africa 1902–1910.* Oxford, Clarendon Press, 1960.

THOMPSON, RICHARD. *Racial discrimination in New Zealand, South African sports tours: a bibliography.* Christchurch (N.Z.), University of Canterbury, 1966.

THORNTON, A. P. *Doctrines of imperialism.* New York, Wiley and Sons, 1965.
*The imperial idea and its enemies: a study in British power.* London, Macmillan, 1959.

TOYNBEE, ARNOLD J. *A study of history* (abr. ed.). 2 vols. London, Oxford University Press, 1957.

TREDGOLD, SIR ROBERT. *The Rhodesia that was my life.* London, Allen and Unwin, 1968.

TREVELYAN, G. O. *The competition wallah.* London and Cambridge, Macmillan and Co., 1864.

TUMIN, MELVIN M. *Caste in a peasant society.* Princeton, Princeton University Press, 1952.

TUMIN, MELVIN M. and FELDMAN, ARNOLD S. *Social class and social change in Puerto Rico.* Princeton, Princeton University Press, 1961.

TURNBULL, COLIN M. *Wayward servants: the two worlds of the African pygmies.* London, Eyre and Spottiswoode, 1965.

UNESCO. *The race question in modern science.* Paris, Unesco, 1956.

VAILLANT, G. C. *The Aztecs of Mexico.* Harmondsworth, Penguin Books, 1950.

VAN DEN BERGHE, P. L. *Caneville: the social structure of a South African town.* Middletown, Conn., Wesleyan University Press, 1964.
*Race and racism: comparative perspectives.* New York, Wiley and Sons, 1967.
*South Africa, a study in conflict.* Middletown, Conn., Wesleyan University Press, 1965.

VANDERCOEK, J. W. *Black majesty: the life of Christophe, King of Haiti.* New York, Harper, 1928.

VAN DER HORST, SHEILA. *African workers in town.* Cape Town, Oxford University Press, 1964.

VAN JAARSVELD, F. A. *The Afrikaner's interpretation of South African history.* Cape Town, Simondium Publishers (Pty) Ltd., 1964.

VAN RENSBURG, PATRICK. *Guilty land.* Harmondsworth, Penguin Books, 1962.

VATCHER, WILLIAM HENRY. *White Laager: the rise of Afrikaner nationalism.* London, Pall Mall Press, 1965.

VAUGHAN, GRAHAM M. *Ethnic awareness and attitudes in New Zealand.* Wellington, Victoria University, 1964.

VERNON, PHILIP E. *Intelligence and cultural environment.* London, Methuen, 1968.

VELIZ, CLAUDIO. *Obstacles to change in Latin America.* London, Oxford University Press, 1965.

VILAKAZI, ABSOLOM. *Zulu transformations:. a study of the dynamics of social change.* Pietermaritzburg, University of Natal Press, 1962.

VON FÜRER-HAIMENDORF, CHRISTOPH. *The Apa Tanis and their neighbours: a primitive civilization of the Eastern Himalayas.* London, Routledge and Kegan Paul, 1962.

WAGLEY, CHARLES (ed.). *Race and class in rural Brazil.* Paris, Unesco, 1952.

WARD, W. E. F. *The Royal Navy and the slavers.* London, Allen and Unwin, 1969.

WASHINGTON, BOOKER T. *Up from slavery: an autobiography.* London, Oxford University Press, 1965.

WATSON, WILLIAM. *Tribal cohesion in a money economy: a study of the Mambwe people of Northern Rhodesia.* Manchester, Manchester University Press, 1958.

WEBSTER, JOHN B. *The political development of Ruanda and Burundi.* Syracuse, New York, Syracuse University, Maxwell Graduate School of Citizenship and Public Affairs, 1966.

WESTERMANN, DIEDRICH. *The African today and tomorrow* (3rd ed.). London, Oxford University Press, 1949.

WHITAKER, IAN. *Social relations in a nomadic Lappish community.* Samiske Samlinger 2, Oslo, Norsk Folkmuseum.

WHITTEN, NORMAN E., Jr. *Class, kinship and power in an Ecuadorian town: the Negroes of San Lorenzo.* Stanford (California), Stanford University Press, 1965.

WILLIAMS, CHARLES. *Witchcraft.* London, Faber, 1941.

WILLIAMS, ERIC. *British historians and the West Indies.* London, André Deutsch, 1966.
*History of the people of Trinidad and Tobago.* London, André Deutsch, 1964.
*Inward hunger.* London, André Deutsch, 1969.

WILLINK, HENRY (chairman), Great Britain Colonial Office. *Nigeria: report of the commission appointed to enquire into the fears of minorities.* London, H.M.S.O., 1958.

WILLOUGHBY, W. C. *The soul of the Bantu.* London, S.C.M. Press, 1928.

WILSON, MONICA (HUNTER). *Reaction to conquest: effects of contact with Europeans on the Pondo of South Africa* (2nd ed.). London, Oxford University Press for International African Institute, 1961.

WILSON, MONICA and MATEJE, ARCHIE. *Langa: a study of social groups in an African township.* Cape Town, Oxford University Press, 1963.

WINIATA, MAHARAIA. *The changing role of the leader in Maori society: a study in social change and race relations.* Auckland, Blackwood and Janet Paul, 1967.

WOLF, ERIC R. *Sons of the shaking earth.* Chicago, University of Chicago Press, 1959.

WOOD, DONALD. *Trinidad in transition: the years after slavery.* London, Oxford University Press for Institute of Race Relations, 1968.

WOODWARD, C. VANN. *Origins of the new South, 1877–1913* (Vol. IX of *A History of the South*). Baton Rouge, Louisiana State University Press, 1951.
*The strange career of Jim Crow*. London, Oxford University Press, 1966.

WOOLF, LEONARD. *Empire and commerce in Africa: a study of economic imperialism.* London, Allen and Unwin, 1920.

WRENCH, JOHN EVELYN. *Alfred, Lord Milner: the man of no illusions, 1854–1925.* London, Eyre and Spottiswoode, 1958.

WORSLEY, PETER. *The trumpet shall sound: a study of 'cargo' cults in Melanesia* (2nd ed.). London, MacGibbon and Kee, 1968.
'Millenarian cults in Melanesia.' In *Human Problems in Central Africa*, March 1967.

WYNDHAM, H. A. *The Atlantic and slavery*. London, Oxford University Press, 1935.

YOUNG, KENNETH. *Rhodesia and independence: a study in British colonial policy.* London, Eyre and Spottiswoode, 1967.

# Index

SET BY
THE EASTERN PRESS LTD
AND REPRINTED LITHOGRAPHICALLY BY
EBENEZER BAYLIS AND SON LIMITED
THE TRINITY PRESS, WORCESTER AND LONDON

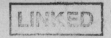
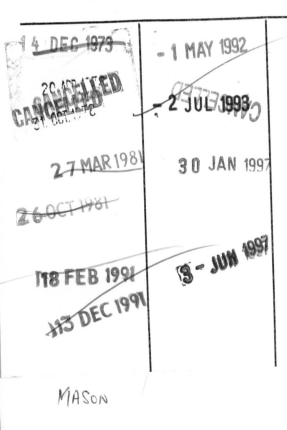